Art and Anti-Racism in Latin America

In this collection, artists and researchers collaborate to explore the anti-racist effects of diverse artistic practices, specifically theatre, dance, visual art and music. By integrating the experiences of Black, Indigenous and mestizo ('mixed-race') artists from Argentina, Brazil and Colombia, the text interrogates how art with anti-racist intent works in the world and brings special attention to its affective dimensions. Latin America's particular racial formations encourage us to move beyond the pigeon-holes of identity politics and embrace inclusive models of anti-racism, spurred by the creative potential of artistic innovation. The collection features overview chapters on art and anti-racism, co-authored chapters focusing on specific art practices, and five 'curated conversations' giving voice to additional artists who participated in the project. This title is also available as Open Access on Cambridge Core.

Peter Wade is Professor of Social Anthropology at the University of Manchester. He has led several large multi-country projects that support anti-racist activism in Latin America. He is the co-editor, most recently, of *Against Racism* (with Mónica Moreno Figueroa).

Lúcia Sá is Professor of Brazilian Studies at the University of Manchester. She has worked extensively on Indigenous literature and culture from Brazil. She is the author of *Rain Forest Literatures: Amazonian Texts and Latin American Cultures*.

Ignacio Aguiló is Senior Lecturer in Latin American Cultural Studies and Co-Director of the Centre for Latin American and Caribbean Studies at the University of Manchester. He is the author of *The Darkening Nation: Race, Neoliberalism and Crisis in Argentina*.

Afro-Latin America

Series editors
George Reid Andrews, *University of Pittsburgh*
Alejandro de la Fuente, *Harvard University*

This series reflects the coming of age of the new, multidisciplinary field of Afro-Latin American Studies, which centers on the histories, cultures, and experiences of people of African descent in Latin America. The series aims to showcase scholarship produced by different disciplines, including history, political science, sociology, ethnomusicology, anthropology, religious studies, art, law, and cultural studies. It covers the full temporal span of the African Diaspora in Latin America, from the early colonial period to the present and includes continental Latin America, the Caribbean, and other key areas in the region where Africans and their descendants have made a significant impact.

A full list of titles published in the series can be found at:
www.cambridge.org/afro-latin-america

Art and Anti-Racism in Latin America

Edited by

PETER WADE
University of Manchester

LÚCIA SÁ
University of Manchester

IGNACIO AGUILÓ
University of Manchester

Shaftesbury Road, Cambridge CB2 8EA, United Kingdom

One Liberty Plaza, 20th Floor, New York, NY 10006, USA

477 Williamstown Road, Port Melbourne, VIC 3207, Australia

314–321, 3rd Floor, Plot 3, Splendor Forum, Jasola District Centre, New Delhi – 110025, India

103 Penang Road, #05–06/07, Visioncrest Commercial, Singapore 238467

Cambridge University Press is part of Cambridge University Press & Assessment, a department of the University of Cambridge.

We share the University's mission to contribute to society through the pursuit of education, learning and research at the highest international levels of excellence.

www.cambridge.org
Information on this title: www.cambridge.org/9781009680530
DOI: 10.1017/9781009680547

© Peter Wade, Lúcia Sá and Ignacio Aguiló 2026

This publication is in copyright. Subject to statutory exception and to the provisions of relevant collective licensing agreements, with the exception of the Creative Commons version the link for which is provided below, no reproduction of any part may take place without the written permission of Cambridge University Press & Assessment.

An online version of this work is published at doi.org/10.1017/9781009680547 under a Creative Commons Open Access license CC-BY-NC 4.0 which permits re-use, distribution and reproduction in any medium for non-commercial purposes providing appropriate credit to the original work is given and any changes made are indicated. To view a copy of this license visit https://creativecommons.org/licenses/by-nc/4.0

When citing this work, please include a reference to the
DOI 10.1017/9781009680547

First published 2026

Cover image: Detail from the series *Chere*, © Wilson Borja Marroquín, by permission. https://wilsonborja.com/chere

A catalogue record for this publication is available from the British Library

A Cataloging-in-Publication data record for this book is available from the Library of Congress

ISBN 978-1-009-68051-6 Hardback
ISBN 978-1-009-68053-0 Paperback

Cambridge University Press & Assessment has no responsibility for the persistence or accuracy of URLs for external or third-party internet websites referred to in this publication and does not guarantee that any content on such websites is, or will remain, accurate or appropriate.

For EU product safety concerns, contact us at Calle de José Abascal, 56, 1°, 28003 Madrid, Spain, or email eugpsr@cambridge.org

Contents

List of Figures	page vii
List of Contributors	ix
Foreword	xvii
Mónica G. Moreno Figueroa	
Preface	xix
Acknowledgements	xxv

Introduction   1
Peter Wade, Ignacio Aguiló, Lúcia Sá, Carlos Correa Angulo, Jamille Pinheiro Dias and Ana Vivaldi

Curated Conversation 1: Anti-Racist Art in the UK and Latin America   29
Curated by Peter Wade

PART I ART AND ANTI-RACISM IN THE NATION

1 Unveiling Racialised Difference in Colombia: Insights from Artists and Artistic Practices   37
Peter Wade, Mara Viveros Vigoya, Carlos Correa Angulo, Rossana Alarcón and Liliana Angulo Cortés

2 The Cosmopolitics of Indigenous Anti-Racist Art and Literature in Brazil   72
Lúcia Sá, Pedro Mandagará and Felipe Milanez Pereira

3 Challenging Whiteness and Europeanness in Argentine Cultural Production   97
Ezequiel Adamovsky, Ignacio Aguiló, Alejandro Frigerio and Ana Vivaldi

Curated Conversation 2: Decolonising the Arts in Latin America – Anti-Racist Irruptions in the Art World 127
Curated by Ignacio Aguiló; translated by Peter Wade

PART II ARTISTIC PRACTICES, RACISM AND ANTI-RACISM

4 Resistance in Motion: Dance and Anti-Racism in the Afro-Contemporary Dance of Sankofa Danzafro 137
Carlos Correa Angulo and Rafael Palacios

Curated Conversation 3: On Curatorship 164
Curated by Ana Vivaldi and Peter Wade; translated by Peter Wade

5 Indigenous Arts and Anti-Racism in Brazil: Perspectives from the *Véxoa: We Know* Exhibition 172
Naine Terena and Jamille Pinheiro Dias

Curated Conversation 4: The Power of Guarani Rap 198
Curated by Lúcia Sá

6 Poetics and Theatre Research in the Reconstruction of Afro-Latin American and Mapuche Lives in Argentina 205
Ana Vivaldi, Lorena Cañuqueo, Miriam Álvarez and Alejandra Egido

Curated Conversation 5: *Casa Adentro* (Inside the House) – Anti-Racist Art Practices 234
Curated by Carlos Correa Angulo

7 Art and Anti-Racism in Latin American Racial Formations 240
Peter Wade

Final Reflections 265
Arissana Pataxó; Miriam Álvarez, Lorena Cañuqueo and Alejandra Egido; Wilson Borja

Bibliography 277
Index 305

Figures

1.1 *Lavanderas de Nóvita, Chocó, Cauca*, painting by José María Gutiérrez de Alba, 1875. page 42
1.2 *La república*, mural by Pedro Nel Gómez, 1937. 45
1.3 One of nine images from the series *Negro utópico* by Liliana Angulo Cortés, 2001. 55
1.4 Drawing from *Blanco porcelana* by Margarita Ariza Aguilar, 2010. 62
1.5 Photo from the series *Descendimientos* by Yeison Riascos, 2014. 63
1.6 *Muchacha de las aguas, Gimaní*: digital image created by Hanna Ramírez, 2021, to accompany the eponymous poem by Pedro Blas Julio Romero. 66
2.1 *Moema*, painting by Victor Meirelles, 1866. 75
2.2 Intervention into Andrea del Castagno's *Crucifixion and Saints* by Jaider Esbell, from his *Carta ao Velho Mundo*, 2018–2019. 84
2.3 *Camarão – Tapuya* by Denilson Baniwa, 2021. 88
2.4 *Indigente, indi(o)gente, indigen(a)-te* by Arissana Pataxó, 2020. 92
2.5 *Manto tupinambá* by Glicéria Tupinambá, 2020, for the project Um Outro Céu. 95
3.1 *El lancero colorado/El poncho rojo* by Cesáreo B. de Quirós, 1923, from the cover of *Nativa*, a nationalist magazine. 108
3.2 *Manifestación*, painting by Antonio Berni, 1934. 109

3.3	A mestizo 'Juan Pueblo' in a promotional poster for the Five Year Plan, 1947.	112
3.4	Juan Perón with an Afro-Argentine child, illustration from *Mundo Peronista*, 1955.	113
3.5	*¡¡Basta!!* poster by Ricardo Carpani, 1963.	115
4.1	Sankofa Danzafro dancers in their rehearsal retreat in Tumaco, March 2021.	140
4.2	Scene from 'Unction' in *Detrás del sur* by Sankofa Danzafro, Joyce Theatre, New York, 2024.	154
4.3	Scene from 'The Birth of a Warrior' in *Detrás del sur* by Sankofa Danzafro, Joyce Theatre, New York, 2024.	155
5.1	Gustavo Caboco and his mother, Lucilene Wapichana, 2020, in front of their collaborative works with Camila dos Santos da Silva, Divalda Silva and Juliana Kerexu, from the series *Where Is Indigenous Art in Paraná?*	185
5.2	Denilson Baniwa and his intervention in the car park of the Pinacoteca de São Paolo, 2020.	189
5.3	Tamikuã Txihi's jaguars, 2020.	191
6.1	Scene from *Tayiñ kuify kvpan* with Lorena Cañuqueo and Sofía Curapil, Escuela de Arte Municipal La Llave, Bariloche, Argentina, 2004.	218
6.2	Poster advertising *Afrolatinoamericanas: De voces, susurros, gritos y silencios* for a performance run in 2013.	219
6.3	Scene from 'Como dos gotas de agua' with Alejandra Egido and Miriam Álvarez, Contact Theatre, Manchester, UK, 2022.	231
7.1	*Cunhatain, antropofagia musical* (Cunhatain, Musical Anthropophagy) by Denilson Baniwa, 2018.	248
7.2	An early scene from Sankofa Danzafro's *La ciudad de los otros*, Battery Dance Festival, New York, 2015.	254
7.3	A later scene from Sankofa Danzafro's *La ciudad de los otros*, Battery Dance Festival, New York, 2015.	255
7.4	Scene from *Muestra final: Laboratorios de creación en casa*, video, 2020.	260
C.1	Photo of Mapuche women and children by Cristián Enrique Valck; probable date 1870; probable location Valdivia, Chile.	270

Contributors

NOTES

1. This list is alphabetised according to first names (given the fact that the relevant surname – the patronym – is the first surname for Spanish-language names and the second for Portuguese-language names).
2. The participants in the Curated Conversations are listed separately.

Alejandra Egido is the director of the Teatro en Sepia theatre company (TES) in Buenos Aires, whose members are Afro-descendant women, including Afro-migrant and Afro-Argentine women. TES has performed numerous plays, including the canonical work *Calunga Andumba*, written by Afro-Porteño actresses and playwrights Carmen and Susana Platero; *Afrolatinoamericanas*, by Egido and Lea Geler, which portrays the experience of Afro women in different periods of history; and *No es país para negras II*, written by Egido.

Alejandro Frigerio is a researcher at the Argentine National Council of Scientific and Technological Research (Consejo Nacional de Investigaciones Científicas y Técnicas, CONICET) and a professor in the Sociology Department of the Catholic University of Argentina and in the Social Anthropology Department of FLACSO (Latin American Faculty of Social Sciences) in Buenos Aires. His books include *Cultura negra en el Cono Sur: representaciones en conflicto* (2000), *Imigrantes brasileiros na Argentina* (with Carlos Hasenbalg, 1999) and *Argentinos e brasileiros: encontros, imagens e estereótipos* (edited, with Gustavo Lins Ribeiro, 2002).

Ana Vivaldi was a post-doctoral research associate at the University of Manchester, working on the project Cultures of Anti-Racism in Latin America. She is currently an honorary research associate in the School of Social Sciences at Manchester, and a sessional instructor in Anthropology and Sociology at the University of British Columbia. She is the author of *Urban Indigenous Assemblages: Qom Mobilities and the Remaking of White Buenos Aires* (forthcoming, 2026) and co-editor, with Laura Kropff and Valeria Iñigo Carrera, of *Movilidades obligadas: el desplazamiento a las ciudades como efecto del genocidio indígena* (2025). She has written several articles on the Toba/Qom people of Argentina, focusing on Indigenous mobilities and the politics of space.

Arissana Pataxó lives in the Coroa Vermelha Indigenous community in the Bahia region, one of the largest urban villages in Brazil, where she works as an art teacher and *patxôhã* language teacher. She is a visual artist and has created several exhibitions and artistic projects in Brazil. She has a degree in Fine Arts and a Master's in Ethnic and African Studies from the Federal University of Bahia and she is currently pursuing a PhD in Visual Arts at the same university.

Carlos Correa Angulo was a post-doctoral research associate at the School of Social Sciences of the University of Manchester, working on the project Cultures of Anti-Racism in Latin America. He is currently an honorary research associate at Manchester and a Consortium on Afro-Latin American Studies Fellow at Harvard University. He is the author of articles on Creoles and ethnic identities in Belize and Blackness in Mexico. His recent research and publications explore anti-racism and art practices and their impact on both artists and audiences in Colombia.

Ezequiel Adamovsky is a professor of history at the National University of San Martín and at the University of Buenos Aires; he is also a researcher at CONICET. He is the author of numerous books, including *Historia de las clases populares en Argentina, de 1880 a 2003* (2012), *El gaucho indómito: de Martín Fierro a Perón, el emblema imposible de una nación desgarrada* (2019) and *La fiesta de los negros: una historia del antiguo carnaval de Buenos Aires y su legado en la cultura popular* (2024).

Felipe Milanez Pereira is a lecturer in the Milton Santos Institute of Humanities, Arts and Sciences, Federal University of Bahia. He is the author of *Lutar com a floresta: uma ecologia política do martírio em defesa da Amazônia* (2024), *Guerras da conquista* (2021) and *Memórias sertanistas: cem anos de indigenismo no Brasil* (2015). He is a co-editor of the *Routledge Handbook of Latin America and the Environment* (2023) and of *Descolonizar la naturaleza. Por una ecología política latinoamericana: textos reunidos de Héctor Alimonda* (2025). He has also published numerous articles on political ecology and Indigenous thought.

Ignacio Aguiló is a senior lecturer (associate professor) in Latin American Cultural Studies and co-director of the Centre for Latin American and Caribbean Studies at the University of Manchester. His research examines the intersections of racial capitalism and cultural production in contemporary Latin America, with a focus on the Southern Cone and the Andean region. His publications include *The Darkening Nation: Race, Neoliberalism and Crisis in Argentina* (2018) and he has recently directed the project Indigenous Youth Cultures and New Media in Latin America.

Jamille Pinheiro Dias was a post-doctoral research associate working on the project Cultures of Anti-Racism in Latin America at the School of Social Sciences of the University of Manchester, where she continues as an honorary research associate. She is currently the director of the Centre for Latin American and Caribbean Studies and the co-director of the Environmental Humanities Research Hub at the Institute of Languages, Cultures and Societies (ILCS) at the School of Advanced Study, University of London, where she is also a lecturer in Latin American and Caribbean Studies. Her research focuses on environmental issues, Amazonian cultural production, and Indigenous arts in Latin America, with an emphasis on Brazil. She is the editor, with Marília Librandi and Tom Winterbottom, of *Transpoetic Exchange: Haroldo de Campos, Octavio Paz and Other Multiversal Dialogues* (2018), and has published in the *Journal of Latin American Cultural Studies*, *Environmental Humanities*, and the *Handbook of Latin American Environmental Aesthetics*, among others.

Liliana Angulo Cortés is an Afro-Colombian artist and curator who explores the body in relation to issues of racial and political identity, gender, language, power relations and Afro-Colombian culture. She has exhibited widely in Colombia and been a guest artist in Paris and Boston and an invited speaker at various universities in the United States. For a period she was deputy director of arts in Bogotá's Instituto Distrital de las Artes and later became the director of the National Museum of Colombia.

Lorena Cañuqueo was a research assistant in the project Cultures of Anti-Racism in Latin America, working in the Argentinian team. She has a PhD in Anthropology from the University of Buenos Aires and teaches at the National University of Río Negro. She is a member of the Mariano Epulef *lof* (Mapuche community) in the Anecón Chico area in Río Negro and a member of the Mapuche Theatre Group El Katango.

Lúcia Sá is a professor of Brazilian Studies at the University of Manchester. She has worked extensively on Indigenous literature and culture from Brazil. She is the author of *Rain Forest Literatures: Amazonian Texts and Latin American Cultures* (2004) and of various articles on the topic of native narratives. She recently directed the project Racism and Anti-Racism in Brazil: The Case of Indigenous Peoples.

Mara Viveros Vigoya is a professor in the School of Gender Studies and in the Department of Anthropology at the National University of Colombia. She is co-founder of the of the School of Gender Studies and has been its director three times. She is the author of *De quebradores y cumplidores: sobre hombres, masculinidades y relaciones de género en Colombia* (2002), *Les couleurs de la masculinité. Expériences intesectionneles et pratiques de pouvoir en Amerique Latine* (2018), *El oxímoron de las clases medias negras: movilidad social e interseccionalidad en Colombia* (2021) and *Breaking the Boundaries of the Colombian Socio-Racial Order: Black Middle Classes through an Intersectional Lens* (2024). She is the editor of *Black Feminism: teoría crítica, violencias y racismo. Conversaciones entre Angela Davis y Gina Dent* (2019) and *Una sociología sin fronteras: exploraciones sobre género y trabajo. Textos reunidos de Luz Gabriel Arango (1991–2018)* (2025).

Miriam Álvarez is the director of the Mapuche Theatre Group El Katango, based in Bariloche, Argentina. She also teaches and researches at the Instituto de Investigaciones en Diversidad Cultural y Procesos de Cambio, based at CONICET, Universidad de Río Negro. El Katango has staged the works *Kay kay egu Xeg xeg* (2002), a rereading of an old Mapuche story, *Tayiñ kuify kvpan* (Our Ancestral Ascendency, 2004), and *Pewma* (Dreams, 2006), all based on collective playwriting oriented by Miriam Álvarez.

Mónica G. Moreno Figueroa is a Black-mestiza, Mexican-British woman, a professor of Sociology at the University of Cambridge and Fellow in Social Sciences at Downing College, Cambridge. Her research focuses on the intersectional lived experience of 'race' and racism in Mexico and Latin America; anti-racism and academic-based impact; feminist theory, intersectionality and racism. She is an expert in qualitative research methods, visual methodologies and thrives on interdisciplinary collaborations. Mónica is currently leading the development of a new research institute on Global Racisms Institute for Social Transformation at the University of Cambridge with funding from the W. K. Kellog Foundation.

Naine Terena, a woman of the Terena people, is a researcher, university professor, curator, and artist-educator. In 2012, she founded Oráculo – Comunicação, Educação e Cultura, a cultural enterprise that fosters socio-cultural market initiatives. She served as Director of Education and Artistic Training in the Ministry of Culture (2023–2024) and led the Voropi Platform/2023 in North American universities. She is also the founder of Casa Vítuka, an artistic training space in Mato Grosso, Brazil, focused on Indigenous cultures. Currently, she coordinates the Museu-Lab of Art, Science, and Technology research project at the Federal University of Mato Grosso and the Indigenous Health Disinformation project. She curated the exhibition of Brazilian Indigenous art *Véxoa: We Know*, which opened at the Pinacoteca de São Paulo in October 2020.

Pedro Mandagará is an associate professor of Brazilian Literature at the University of Brasília. He is assistant editor of *Revista Cerrados*. His publications include a special issue of *Estudos de Literatura Brasileira Contemporânea*, on 'Contemporaneidades ameríndias: diante da voz e da letra' (edited with Devair Fiorotti, 2018) and *Sustentabilidade: O Que Pode a Literatura?* (edited with Rita Terezinha Schmidt, 2015).

Peter Wade is a professor of Social Anthropology at the University of Manchester. His recent publications include *Degrees of Mixture, Degrees of Freedom: Genomics, Multiculturalism and Race in Latin America* (2017) and *Against Racism: Organizing for Social Change in Latin America* (edited with Mónica Moreno Figueroa, 2022). He has co-directed the project Latin American Antiracism in a 'Post-Racial' Age (2017–2019), directed the project Cultures of Anti-Racism in Latin America (2020–2023) and was co-investigator on the project Comics and Race in Latin America (2021–2024).

Rafael Palacios is a dancer and choreographer and director of the Sankofa Contemporary Afro-Colombian Dance Corporation, which he founded in 1997 and which has performed in a dozen countries worldwide. He has a degree in Dance Education from the University of Antioquia; an MA in Education and Human Rights from the Universidad Autónoma Latinoamericana; and a diploma in Afro-Latin American Studies from ICESI University and Harvard University. In 2008, he obtained the

National Dance Award granted by the Ministry of Culture of Colombia and was National Dance Councillor during the period 2009–2011.

Rossana Alarcón was a research assistant working on the Colombian arm of the project Cultures of Anti-Racism in Latin America. She is a visual artist, with a degree specialising in pedagogy and an MA in Cultural Studies at the National University of Colombia. As an artist, she works in graphic design, illustration and ceramics.

Wilson Borja is an illustrator, visual artist, animator, graphic designer and teacher based in Bogotá. He is a former Fulbright scholar. Wilson has illustrated books, magazines and audiovisual materials for over fifteen years. Through drawing, painting, printmaking and animation, his investigative work explores different aspects of migration and the African diaspora. As well as a practising artist he is also a lecturer in the Facultad de Artes of the Universidad Nacional de Colombia. Wilson is part of the Afro artist collective Aguaturbia and the Consejo Audiovisual Afrodescendiente de Colombia WI DA MONIKONGO, as well as acting as the co-director of the graphic laboratory LaCimbra.

***

The following is a list of participants in the Curated Conversations (except for those whose names appear as chapter authors).

Abril Caríssimo (a.k.a. Bbywacha) is a visual artist and member of Identidad Marrón.

América López (a.k.a. América Canela) is educational director of Identidad Marrón. She practises and teaches visual arts

Andrea Bonilla is a dancer in Sankofa Danzafro.

Ashanti Dinah is an Afro-Colombian activist, poet and teacher.

Bruno Veron is one half (along with Kelvin Peixoto) of the rap duo Brô MC's from Dourados, Mato Grosso do Sul.

Daiara Tukano is an Indigenous Tukano artist and activist from Brazil.

Denilson Baniwa is an Indigenous Baniwa artist from Brazil.

Ekua Bayunu is a Black artist and activist from the UK.

Florencia Alvarado (a.k.a. Flora Nómada) is a visual artist, illustrator and member of Identidad Marrón.

Kelvin Peixoto is one half (along with Bruno Veron) of the rap duo Brô MC's from Dourados, Mato Grosso do Sul.

Kunumi MC (a.k.a. Owerá) is an Indigenous rap artist from the Krukutu *tekoá* (community) in Parelheiros, São Paulo.

Laura Asprilla Carrillo is a filmmaker and member of the Aguaturbia Collective in Colombia.

Loretta Meneses teaches and practises dance and performing arts; she is a member of Aguaturbia Collective in Colombia.

SuAndi is a Black poet, artist and activist from the UK.

Yndira Perea is a dancer and choreographer in Sankofa Danzafro.

Foreword

Several years ago, when Peter Wade and I were discussing the best approach to anti-racist discourses and practices in Latin America, we mapped out many different possibilities. We talked about what would make the most sense, what would be the most accessible fields, and what would be most feasible and fundable. We considered researching the media, social movements and activism, the legal field, governmental initiatives, and culture, art and artistic representations. We could have included social media and the psychological, wellness and beauty industries, alongside the emotional dimensions of racism. I would nowadays also be thinking about the anti-racist opportunities within health constraints and outcomes – not to mention AI.

At that time, we decided to begin with what squarely sat within the social sciences: social movements, activism and some aspects of the efforts to legalise racial discrimination, with a focus on the struggles and initiatives in Colombia, Brazil, Ecuador and Mexico. We developed a research project, Latin American Antiracism in a 'Post-Racial' Age, published several pieces documenting the turn to anti-racism in the region – such as the edited volume *Against Racism* (Pittsburgh University Press, 2022) – and put forward our arguments on what we called the alternative grammars of anti-racism and on the profound intersectional analytical needs of the field – particularly given the logics of *mestizaje* – while not claiming any sort of exceptionalism.

Having taken that journey, I am so excited to see in this book the results of the project Cultures of Anti-Racism in Latin America (CARLA), for which I was invited to act as the international adviser – and of which I became an extreme fan, following with great interest the project's aims to explore the 'anti-racist effects of different artistic media – theatre, dance, visual art – with a focus on the emotional affordances and affective intensities that these media generate'.

The CARLA project was profoundly shaped by the COVID-19 pandemic. Throughout nearly all the process, we could not meet, travel to see the contexts of production and meaning-making or get a glimpse of the audiences. The lockdowns we were all thrown into put a severe strain on the project, and the team, like many others around the world, had to resort to online alternatives.

Another major challenge – one that perhaps would have emerged regardless of whether the team had been able to meet in Argentina, Colombia or Brazil – was how to work between the artist's intention and worldview and the social implications of art and representation. This was a difficult question that pushed the team to grapple with an elusive and empirically challenging issue: the emotional life of art. The book offers insights around how to think about artistic intent: the creative forces, fuelled by love and rage, that drive artists to denounce, propose, sing out loud, bare their souls in theatrical plays and performances, vibrate with the visual renditions of animations and paintings, and dance with kind, strong, wilful steps.

When the whole project team finally met in person in April 2022, after many months of only online meetings, the energy was amazing – everyone was ready. I was so grateful to have been invited to witness, remember and experience what art can do, be it for a single person or a collective. Art can make a piece of legislation resonate more deeply, it can bind together a social movement, it can stick us to each other and remind us why we struggle – to completely eradicate the idea that some people are worth more than others, and to assert that dignity should belong to all, not as a limited good but as an unquestionable principle.

Mónica G. Moreno Figueroa

Preface

The origins of this book stretch back to a workshop on Cultures of Anti-Racism, held on 3 February 2017 in Manchester. It was organised by Peter Wade and James Scorer, colleagues in the University of Manchester's Centre for Latin American and Caribbean Studies (CLACS), and it brought together fourteen UK-based academics to present their work on diverse facets of anti-racist and decolonial art practices. The collaboration was partly intended to foster the existing links between the School of Arts, Languages and Cultures and the School of Social Sciences that CLACS had made possible, but it also drew on common interests in artistic production and identity – Wade's work on race, nation and music in Colombia; Scorer's work on comics in Latin America. The workshop led to the volume *Cultures of Anti-Racism in Latin America and the Caribbean* (2019), edited by Wade and Scorer, with the participation of a third editor, Ignacio Aguiló, another CLACS colleague, who had just published a book, *The Darkening Nation: Race, Neoliberalism and Crisis in Argentina* (2018), on race and nation in Argentina, seen through the optic of various artistic creations.

The workshop also acted as seed-bed for discussions between Wade, Aguiló and Lúcia Sá – also a CLACS colleague – about the possibility of seeking funding for a project that would pursue the same theme, this time in depth and making use of hands-on research work with artists. Sá had been directing a project, Racism and Anti-Racism in Brazil: The Case of Indigenous Peoples (with Felipe Milanez as co-investigator), that established a research network bringing together Indigenous leaders, artists and intellectuals with academics to 'discuss the rise in racism and violence against Indigenous peoples in Brazil, as well as strategies to resist it and contain it'.[1]

The stars were aligned, then, and over the next year, Wade, Aguiló and Sá met regularly to design the CARLA project.[2] Given our individual experiences and networks, the three of us opted to focus the project on Colombia, Argentina and Brazil, respectively, and we each invited colleagues from those countries to participate as co-investigators: Mara Viveros Vigoya (Universidad Nacional de Colombia), Felipe Milanez (Universidade Federal da Bahia, Brazil) and Ezequiel Adamovsky (CONICET, Universidad Nacional de San Martín, Argentina). Our choice of co-investigators was guided by our personal networks and the specific experiences of each colleague: Mara Viveros's well-known work with Afro-Colombians, plus her previous collaboration with Wade on the project Latin American Anti-Racism in a 'Post-Racial' Age (LAPORA);[3] Felipe Milanez's established record of working with Brazilian Indigenous artists – for example, in the project 'Sustainable' Development and Atmospheres of Violence: Experiences of Environmental Defenders;[4] and Ezequiel Adamovsky's pioneering historical research on race, class and nation in Argentina.

We invited other colleagues to act as advisors, due to their recognised expertise and experience: Liliana Angulo Cortés (independent Colombian artist and curator), Pedro Mandagará (Universidade de Brasília) and Alejandro Frigerio (CONICET, Universidad Católica Argentina). We also asked Mónica Moreno Figueroa (University of Cambridge) – director of the LAPORA project – to be our overall project advisor. The bid was submitted to the Arts and Humanities Research Council (AHRC) in July 2018 and in June 2019 we received the – by that stage, rather unexpected – news that the project would be funded.

Wade, Aguiló and Sá then set about hiring three post-doctoral researchers to work in the three countries and, from a very strong field of applicants, emerged three, each of whom happened to be a citizen of the country in which they would work: for Colombia, Carlos Correa Angulo; for Brazil, Jamille Pinheiro Dias; and for Argentina, Ana Vivaldi Pasqua. They all arrived in Manchester at the start of 2020 and the core Manchester team expanded from three to six. With the post-docs taking the lead, we collectively began to scope out possible artists with whom

---

[1] See https://gtr.ukri.org/projects?ref=AH%2FR004374%2F1.
[2] For more details of CARLA, see https://sites.manchester.ac.uk/carla/.
[3] On LAPORA, see www.lapora.sociology.cam.ac.uk/.
[4] Financed by the British Academy and based at the University of Sussex.

Preface   xxi

to work in each country, while also embarking together on a process of reading and discussion that would be the beginning of a longer collaborative endeavour, involving all the project's participants, to map out a conceptual basis for understanding anti-racism and art practice.

Around mid-March 2020, the COVID-19 pandemic caused the UK government to begin a series of lock-downs that massively disrupted our plans. Dias managed to escape home to Belém in Brazil and Vivaldi to Vancouver in Canada before all commercial flights were suspended. Correa was trapped alone in Manchester, which for him added to the existential pain of being locked down, but, in terms of the project, it made little difference, as everyone was working from home using virtual means of communication. As pandemic restrictions relaxed, Dias began to carry out some in-person research in Brazil from autumn 2020, which continued until spring 2022. In the autumn of 2020, too, Correa was able to travel to Colombia and, as restrictions allowed, gradually began in-person research that lasted until spring 2022. Vivaldi was finally able to go to Argentina for a few months in the autumn of 2021 and carry out in-person research. Meanwhile, the project hired several research assistants in each country, who worked closely with the respective post-doc and often also with the co-investigator: in Colombia, Rossana Alarcón (an independent visual artist and graphic designer); in Brazil, Arissana Pataxó and Yacunã Tuxá (both Indigenous artists and activist-academics); and in Argentina, Lorena Cañuqueo (a Mapuche academic, activist and actor) and Pablo Cossio (an independent researcher and activist).[5]

As with pandemic-limited research everywhere, online conversations and discussions became a key activity and the project team organised many of these, involving academics and artists together. These can all be viewed on CARLA's YouTube channel.[6] Coincidentally, the murder of George Floyd in Minneapolis in May 2020 and the subsequent global Black Lives Matter movement provided a backdrop for these discussions and indeed the project as a whole, as the effects of racism as a system gained centre stage across the world. We also held three online workshops with project researchers and artists, which were spaces to review progress and share ideas about art and anti-racism. At last, in April 2022, pandemic restrictions allowed us to hold a final in-person workshop, with

---

[5] In Brazil, Felipe Milanez worked hard to use CARLA money to fund an array of Indigenous artists to work as visiting researchers in UFBA: Graciela Guarani, Glicéria Tupinambá, Gustavo Caboco, Juliana Xukuru, Olinda Tupinambá and Ziel Karapotó.
[6] See www.youtube.com/channel/UCf2aulENOdu3-oKIvIj-R7w.

nearly all the project research team, including the research assistants – only Yacunã Tuxá and Alejandro Frigerio were not able to attend – and some twenty artists from Latin America. This was followed by a public Festival of Anti-Racist and Decolonial Art, held in Manchester's Contact Theatre, which featured the launch of the project's virtual exhibition and performances by eight of the artists or groups of artists with whom we had been collaborating.[7] The Festival was a vivid demonstration of the multiple partnerships and collaborations CARLA had achieved, bringing together academics, artists, activists and art-world institutions, and bridging distances between Black, Indigenous and mestizo people. The festival was followed by two workshops: in the first, the artists met with UK-based cultural industry people who had been invited to the Festival; in the second, the artists met together to discuss their own priorities and possible ways to continue collaborations with each other, across national boundaries.

After all the frustrations of the pandemic, these events were intense and affectively charged encounters, as well as being intellectually highly rewarding – and providing many elements that have fed into the current book. The events were an expression of something that we all – and our Latin American team members – feel strongly about, which is the need in arts and social science research to foster horizontal relationships, even in contexts in which research projects are funded by and based in institutions located in the Global North. Ironically, the COVID-19 pandemic helped us to achieve this: the budget that was destined to support in-person workshops in the three Latin American countries was repurposed so we could invite to the final events the research assistants and more artists than originally planned; and, along with additional funds from the University of Manchester, the money helped to support activities designed by the artists themselves.

A NOTE ON ORTHOGRAPHY AND TERMINOLOGY

We have chosen to capitalise the English words 'Black' and 'Indigenous', following current trends that seek to recognise the hard-won status of these political identifications of racialised subaltern people, but we do

---

[7] For details of the festival, see https://sites.manchester.ac.uk/carla/2022/04/26/festival-of-latin-american-anti-racist-and-decolonial-art/. For a documentary film about the festival, see www.youtube.com/watch?v=WB1fKmYkP9M&t=3s. For the virtual exhibition, see www.digitalexhibitions.manchester.ac.uk/s/carla-en/page/home.

not capitalise 'mestizo' and 'white'. The Spanish and Portuguese words *negro* and *indígena* are, however, not capitalised, following current usage in Latin America. On terminology: although we recognise there is a complex politics behind choosing to use 'Black' (or *negro*) versus, for example, 'Afro-descendant' or 'Afro-Colombian' (Restrepo 2021), in this book the terms are used more or less interchangeably.

Acknowledgements

We would like to acknowledge with thanks the financial support we received from various sources: from the grant for the initial one-day workshop that spurred the whole process (funded by the Institute for Latin American Studies at the University of London), to the main grant from the AHRC (AH/S004823/1) and the additional funding from the University of Manchester (drawing on their UKRI ODA funds).

We are very grateful for the contributions made by the members of the wider project team – the co-investigators, advisors and research assistants: their unstinting support was central to the success of the project. Our heartfelt thanks go out to all the artists who worked with us. They are too numerous to mention them all here, but most of them feature in our virtual exhibition and are referred to in these pages – and some of them are co-authors of chapters in this book, while others feature in the book's Curated Conversations. Their generosity is greatly valued and, from the comments they have made – informally and in the book's Final Reflections – we believe that they also found the experience a valuable one.

Thanks to the Research Office of the School of Social Science, University of Manchester, which provided excellent logistical support, and to John McCrory (John Rylands Research Institute and Library, University of Manchester), who designed and built the website for the virtual exhibition. And thanks, finally, to George Reid Andrews and Alejandro de la Fuente, general editors of the Afro-Latin America book series, who initially supported our book proposal; and to Cecilia

Cancellaro, the commissioning editor at Cambridge University Press, her assistant Victoria Phillips and the production team at the Press (led by Lisa Carter), who have seen the whole process through.

Peter Wade, Ignacio Aguiló, Lúcia Sá, Carlos Correa Angulo,
Jamille Pinheiro Dias and Ana Vivaldi

Introduction

Peter Wade, Ignacio Aguiló, Lúcia Sá, Carlos Correa Angulo, Jamille Pinheiro Dias and Ana Vivaldi

INTRODUCTION

This book emerges from a conviction shared among the contributors that art can play a key role in challenging racism. In Latin America and the Caribbean, the arts have long served as important tools of protest, solidarity and education to challenge racism. Nineteenth-century abolitionist poetry and early-twentieth-century Brazilian capoeira are two examples.[1] In Brazil, Abdias do Nascimento's Teatro Experimental do Negro (1940s–1960s) was a powerful voice against anti-Black racism, while Augusto Boal's Theatre of the Oppressed also addressed racism. In Chile, Víctor Jara used theatre and, more famously, music to challenge oppressions, including racism against Indigenous people. Performance and music combine in the 1970s' phenomenon known as Black Rio (Steinitz 2025; Treece 2022) and in the expressions of Brazilian carnival groups such as Filhos de Gandhy (founded 1949) and Ilê Aiyê (founded 1974), all of which challenged anti-Black racism, albeit in different ways. More recently, hip-hop has provided a fertile field for anti-racist sentiment, from the Southern Cone to Mexico and into Latin American spaces in the US (Dennis 2014; Fernandes 2011; Reiter and Mitchell 2008). Artists working with diverse visual media have used their practices to challenge racism, as this book shows for Argentina, Brazil and Colombia, and as other scholars have documented for countries such as Mexico (Ortega Domínguez and Abel 2023) and Cuba (de la Fuente 2008).

---

[1] Capoeira is an Afro-Brazilian martial art with elements of dance, acrobatics, play, music and spirituality.

Employing narrative and non-narrative techniques, the arts have the ability to engage people, mobilising concepts and meanings with an emotional and affective intensity, which makes art practices well suited to deal with racism's visceral dimensions and emotive logics. This is important because there is a mismatch between, on the one hand, the affective traction of racism and ideas about racialised difference and, on the other, the reasoned argument of much anti-racist policy and discourse. The logical statement that 'race is a social construction with no biological reality' has proven a weak anti-racist strategy. The formulation only hints at the power of social constructions as structuring forces in society; hence it only hints at the size and complexity of the task of changing structural inequalities. A related problem is that the formulation provides little leverage with which to address the fact that social constructions get deep into the psyche (Moore 2007), as well as the material human body (Hartigan 2013; Wade 2002), where they tap into emotions and affective intensities.

One productive way into the realm where concepts and meanings are powerfully charged with embodied sentiments and sensibilities is via literary, artistic and performative practices, whether textual or 'beyond text' (Cox, Irving and Wright 2016). These practices, while working through representational narrative and discourse, also engage – and potentially transform – the receiver affectively. Due to their dual capacity for generating representational and affective traction, artistic interventions are often identified as having particular creative potential in the political and civic domains (Beasley-Murray 2010; Flynn and Tinius 2015; Moya 2016; Sommer 2014, 2018, 2006b; Thompson 2014). The arts narrate stories and convey symbolic meanings through images, actions and words, and, in the process, mobilise emotions and affective responses that have effects that also go below the radar of discursive meaning. This makes them able to engage with racism's emotional logic and affective power – although art is always open to interpretation and its affective traction can also be deployed to other ends (see Chapter 7). While social policies addressing socio-economic conditions are vital to correcting racial inequalities, they may fail to address the powerful emotions – positive and negative – associated with racial differences in a highly racialised and unequal society.

Today there is a widespread climate characterised by the coexistence of, on the one hand, persistent denials of racism, or claims that it has been superseded by post-raciality, alongside, on the other hand, equally persistent and even increasing racial inequality, plus the resurgence of right-wing and populist movements, some of which have become more overtly racist over time (Gilroy 2000; Goldberg 2008; Hooker 2020; Lentin 2011, 2014). In this context, analyzing how artistic interventions can work against racism in its multiple dimensions becomes particularly relevant.

Our book contributes to this field by exploring in detail how artistic practices work in anti-racist ways in Latin American societies – more precisely, Argentina, Brazil and Colombia. We hope this will support anti-racist agendas in important ways, as well as contributing to scholarship on racism and anti-racism. Latin America is a particularly interesting region to explore these questions and perhaps learn some lessons that go beyond its borders. The region has a long history in which marked racial inequality has taken a particular form, shaped by low levels of racial segregation, the coincidence of class and racial hierarchies, and above all the hegemony of ideas about national projects of inclusion based on biocultural processes of racial mixture – *mestizaje* in Spanish, *mestiçagem* in Portuguese (Moreno Figueroa and Wade 2022; Telles 2004; Telles and Project on Ethnicity and Race in Latin America 2014; Wade 2010b). In varied ways across the region, the social and institutional recognition in colonial times of mixture and mixed people as constituting a social field different from Black, Indigenous and white people became, in the nineteenth century, a powerful ideology of nationhood (albeit more so in some countries, such as Brazil, Colombia and Mexico, than in others such as Argentina and Chile). The idea of *mestizaje* could be deployed against European scientific racist theories about mixture as degeneration, serving to make an authentic national virtue out of the unavoidable reality of racially mixed populations. Despite this, mixture as a process and mestizos as a category continued to be structured by racialised hierarchies with colonial roots and global reach, which gave high value to whiteness as a physical and moral status; hegemonic ideologies of mixture construed it as a process that would whiten and *mejorar la raza* (improve the race) of the nation's people (Appelbaum, Macpherson and Rosemblatt 2003; Stepan 1991).

The ideology of *mestizaje* has facilitated the denial or minimisation of racism and racial inequality – based on the claim that a society in which everyone is mixed cannot be racist – while powerful racist attitudes that privilege whiteness over darkness can hide in plain sight. The coexistence of a discourse of post-raciality (characterised by the use of denial, minimisation, delegitimation and gaslighting in relation to race and racism) with persistent and even increasing racism is a combination that has recently been identified for many parts of the world (Goldberg 2015;

Lentin 2016). But in Latin America, it has a very long history that goes back to at least the late nineteenth century and continues today, alongside a widespread turn to multiculturalism from the 1990s and, from about 2000, a more tentative and uneven turn towards an explicit and official anti-racism (Hooker 2020; Martínez Novo and Shlossberg 2018; Moreno Figueroa and Wade 2022). This forms the complex context for the artists with whom we worked in the project Cultures of Anti-Racism in Latin America (CARLA).[2] (This context will be discussed in relation to Argentina, Brazil and Colombia later on.)

We think that, for scholars and especially for activists and others promoting anti-racist agendas, there are important ideas about anti-racism to be derived from working closely with Latin American artists and observing how, through their artistic practices, they choose to address race and challenge racial inequality and racism in ways attuned to the particularities of Latin American racial formations. In this respect, a key theme that emerged during CARLA was the limitations of a narrow view of the impact of racism, as affecting only people seen as Black and Indigenous, albeit they are the most obvious concern given the violence of the racism they experience. In Latin American societies, the tendency for class and racial hierarchies to coincide and be mutually constitutive facilitates open agendas of social justice (Lehmann 2022) that can forge alliances between Black and Indigenous movements and, crucially, can open up the question of the role in anti-racism of mestizo (mixed-race) people, who also suffer the effects of racism – although they may perpetrate it too. A related aspect of a more open approach to racism is that the familiar focus on Black and Indigenous activist movements is broadened to include mestizo and 'brown' anti-racism, which incidentally may help to contend with the difficulties around the reification that often accompany identity-based movements – and which have been fomented by official multiculturalism. The art practices that feature in this book include examples of this kind of inclusive anti-racism, which goes beyond identity politics and addresses social injustice more widely (see Chapters 3, 6 and 7, and Curated Conversation 3).

Also important is the way in which the artists with whom we collaborated questioned and broadened definitions of anti-racism (see the section on this later in the chapter). For example, when commissioned to produce an anti-racist piece, Brazilian Indigenous artist Denilson Baniwa created a film about the monoculture of maize in the state of Mato Grosso

---

[2] For details of CARLA, see https://sites.manchester.ac.uk/carla/.

do Sul. Monoculture (literal and symbolic), land invasion and Christian proselytism are among the most insidious racist practices identified by our Brazilian Indigenous collaborators, showing that anti-racism for them goes beyond the recognition of Indigenous identity as being the key goal: at play are wider agendas of social justice linked to multiple differences.[3]

As noted, the way *mestizaje* has shaped Latin American racial orders raises the question of the role of mestizo people in anti-racist struggle (Carlos Fregoso 2024; Correa Angulo 2024). There is a significant difference between mestizo allyship and white allyship. If we consider Margarita Ariza, a Colombian artist with whom we worked (see Chapter 3), it is clear that she does not claim to be Black or Indigenous nor is she identified by others as such. Yet an important part of her anti-racist art work – specifically the work *Blanco porcelana* (Porcelain White) – focuses on the fact that, although she might be seen by many Colombians as white, she was considered by some of her own family members to be not quite white enough.[4] With respect to anti-racist work, her persistent labelling as *morena* (brown, brunette) by family members gives her a positionality different from that of someone who is identified and who identifies as white. She has a specific personal stake in anti-racism because, like many other mestizos and *morenos*, she has felt, in the intimate circulations of emotion and affect, the effects of Latin-American-style racism (Hordge-Freeman 2015; Moreno Figueroa 2010) – while she could in principle also form part of the non-Black and non-Indigenous majority of Latin American people who reproduce, intentionally or otherwise, racialised inequalities, even if they are not explicitly and directly racist.

This positionality directs our attention again to a key theme of this book, which is the operations of racism beyond the processes that impact on Black and Indigenous peoples: the figure of the mestizo or brown person highlights racism as a pervasive force that needs to be tackled by people who occupy a wide array of positionalities affected by it in different ways. Of course, the often lethal impact of racism on Black and Indigenous people is of a different scale from that experienced by a middle-class mestizo woman such as Ariza. But the wider point is that to focus only on anti-Black and anti-Indigenous racism risks obscuring

---

[3] This argument relates to the idea of 'alternative grammars of anti-racism', elaborated in Moreno Figueroa and Wade (2022) and Wade and Moreno Figueroa (2021).

[4] On *Blanco porcelana*, see https://issuu.com/margaritaarizaaguilar/docs/bp-jun29 and https://blancoporcelana.wordpress.com/. On intrafamilial racism and ideas of whitening, see Hordge-Freeman (2015), Moreno Figueroa (2008), Roberts (2012).

how racism operates as a structurally pervasive presence – which may also target working-class brown people in very violent ways (Aguiló and Vivaldi 2023: 561; Ferrari 2023), as highlighted by members of the Argentine art collective Identidad Marrón (literally, Brown Identity), with whom we worked.[5]

Another key area that emerged from our work with Latin American artists centred on issues of visibility and visibilisation. National projects in the region have traditionally been based on ideals of racial mixture and whitening, resulting in racial formations characterised by the ambivalent recognition and denial of Blackness, Indigeneity and non-whiteness (Appelbaum, Macpherson and Rosemblatt 2003; Wade 2010b). These elements – peoples, histories, cultures – were made invisible in some ways, but hypervisible in others. On the one hand, Blackness was, and often still is, denied and cast as 'foreign' in countries such as Mexico and Argentina; Black historical figures have been erased or whitened in many countries.[6] In the three countries where we worked and elsewhere, Indigeneity was, and often still is, cast as belonging to the past and in a process of decline or at best assimilation into a modernising nation. Blackness and Indigeneity have long been associated with low status and have functioned as a negative benchmark against which to judge 'progress', both national and individual, towards modernity and whiteness (Alberto 2022; Wade 2023).

On the other hand, widespread and institutionalised *indigenismo* or *indianismo* carved out a special place for Indigeneity, albeit with a discourse that mainly used the past tense and the passive, primitivist voice; the same can be said for *indigenismo/indianismo*'s smaller and less widespread cousin, *negrismo* (see Chapters 1, 2 and 3).[7] In both cases,

---

[5] On violence against brown Argentines, see the scene 'Marrón', written and performed by David Gudiño (a member of Identidad Marrón), in the video *Traspasar las Puertas de Cristal del Museo* (available at www.digitalexhibitions.manchester.ac.uk/s/carla-en/item/939, from 6'50". On the politics of the word *marrón*, see Chapter 3.

[6] See for example the exhibition *Black Enough?* curated by Margarita Ariza. It explores the systematic whitening of the portrait of the only Afro-descendant president of Colombia, Juan José Nieto Gil: www.digitalexhibitions.manchester.ac.uk/s/carla-en/page/margarita-ariza.

[7] The term *indigenismo* (Spanish) was coined in the 1930s by scholars to designate intellectual, artistic and political currents in Latin America, with roots in the nineteenth century and popular into the 1970s, but still present today, that valorise and romanticise a nation's Indigenous heritage and (sometimes) aim to protect its Indigenous populations, but ultimately guide them towards assimilation (Giraudo and Lewis 2012). The Brazilian equivalent, *indianismo*, has longer roots: the term appears in the 1880s, often as an object of criticism (Romero 1882: 179). *Negrismo* is a term coined post hoc by scholars

national projects included and valued a domesticated – and, importantly for our purposes, often aestheticised – form of non-whiteness for the aura of authenticity it lent to national identities that sought to distance themselves from Eurocentrism, but were nevertheless steeped in a modernist temporality of progress. The multicultural turn in Latin America simply added a new layer to this inclusion-plus-exclusion dynamic, rather than seriously changing the mould of the *mestizaje* project.

In a context in which erasure and invisibilisation are keenly felt, many Latin American artists seek to make Blackness and Indigeneity visible in ways that go beyond the confines of *indigenismo* and *negrismo* and their pigeon-holes of acceptable non-whiteness. But as national imaginaries based on *mestizaje* also involve processes of partial and conditional inclusion, in which a certain kind of visibility has long been present, strategies of visibilisation can risk being sidelined into pre-existing stereotyped pigeon-holes (see Chapter 7). Precisely because nationalist inclusion of non-whiteness has often taken an aestheticised form (Pinheiro Dias 2023), strategies of visibilisation that depend on aesthetic media have to work extra hard to break out of the confines of that inclusion; the aesthetic elements have to be carefully developed with close attention to their political implications.

Such dilemmas are present in many parts of the world but are perhaps particularly evident in Latin America, given the importance of the inclusion-plus-exclusion dynamic in the region. In the US and Europe, for example, Blackness (and other forms of non-whiteness) are more visible – as a clearly segregated element or as a 'problem' linked to the immigration of 'foreigners' – and less subject to incorporation as part of a putatively national culture of racial inclusion (Marx 1998; Wade 2015), notwithstanding their inclusion as culturally distinct components of a recently minted multicultural society. It is interesting, then, that the Afro-Colombian dancers with whom we worked (see Chapter 4) say that they 'dance to be heard', rather than dance to be seen. They are trying to find a pathway between the Charybdis of exclusion and invisibilisation and the Scylla of co-optative, conditional inclusion. The form taken by the Scylla in Latin America is particularly insidious and is an object lesson in the power of an inclusiveness that is real in part – as opposed

---

to describe a mainly literary movement promoted from the 1920s first by white Spanish Caribbean writers who valorised (and arguably appropriated) Afro themes and later by Black writers from the region (Badiane 2010).

to being mere rhetoric or illusion – but still functions to sustain racial inequality and make racism difficult to pinpoint.

In sum, then, we think that the material in this book makes some important contributions to what anti-racist activism and scholarship can learn from Latin American racial formations in terms of i) broadening definitions of anti-racism to include wider agendas of social justice; ii) addressing racism as a pervasive presence that implicates people who do not identify as Black or Indigenous, but also not as white, and who may be both victims and victimisers; and iii) managing the dilemmas created by the processes of inclusion-plus-exclusion, which are long-standing in the region and have become increasingly globalised. The fact that conditional inclusion in Latin America – and elsewhere – has tended to focus on aesthetic experiences (e.g. visual representations, music, dance, cuisine) makes the role of artists in challenging racism particularly important.

In what follows, we explore some key concepts – racism and anti-racism, art, politics and affect – before briefly outlining the racial formations of the three countries in question: Argentina, Brazil and Colombia. The Introduction ends with some reflections on the collaborative methods we have employed, followed by a brief outline of the chapters.

RACISM

The concept of racism that underlies this book is broad and flexible. It goes beyond the common approach that sees racism as processes that exclude and stigmatise categories of people defined in terms of selected aspects of phenotype or ancestry or a combination of these elements – that is, in terms of biology or the physical body. On the other hand, it avoids the kind of 'conceptual inflation' identified by Robert Miles (1989: 50–61) in which an ever-increasing number of processes of category-based exclusions – for example, those driven by xenophobia, ethnocentrism and nationalism – are labelled racist. We understand racism to be processes of exclusion and stigmatisation directed at people identified on the basis of a flexible combination of perceptions of appearance, ancestry and behaviour. However, rather than including all such processes, which would spread the net too wide, we see racism as rooted in specific processes that first emerged historically in the conjunctures of conquest and enslavement that began in embryonic form with medieval Arab trading into sub-Saharan Africa. These processes took further shape in the fifteenth century with the culmination of the Reconquista of the Iberian peninsula by Christians and the progressive exclusion of

Jewish and Muslim people on the basis of their *raza* or *sangre* (blood, ancestry), understood as part of an embodied moral and religious propensity, not just a trait that we now might class as biological. And such processes were consolidated over several centuries from the conquest of the Americas by Europeans, begun by the Spanish in 1492, a period during which ideas about appearance, ancestry and behaviour were used in the domination of subaltern and enslaved populations, identified as *indio/índio*/Indian and *negro*/black, by people who increasingly identified as *blanco/branco*/white (Wade 2015). Racism is inherently gendered and sexed because it refers to ideas about ancestry and inheritance, and thus also sexual reproduction and male–female relations (but also, by extension, non-heterosexual relations) (Wade 2009b).

Racism has mutated over time, partly because it is a 'scavenger ideology' (Mosse 1985: 234) that picks up and seeps into diverse forms of categorisation and difference; partly too because of changes in ideas about and knowledge of the relationships between appearance, ancestry and behaviour; and partly because of changes in relationships between racialised categories of people. Thus, just as one example – but an important one – the rejection of biological determinism in relation to race that gathered force after World War II and the horrors of Nazi racial eugenics meant that the language of race-as-biology, which had become dominant in the West from about 1800, was seen by many as politically toxic. Although the term 'racism' is still commonly used everywhere to designate certain practices and processes deemed immoral and unjust, in some countries any use of the term or concept of 'race' became difficult; it was even banned from French legislative language in 2013. A tendency to use a language of culture to talk about differences has become very common (Stolcke 1995), even in countries such as Britain and the USA, where it is still politically acceptable to use the word 'race', albeit popular usage may prefer 'ethnicity'. This tendency has been labelled 'cultural racism', because it very often targets the differences and the categories previously referred to using the language of race. We are seeing here an inflexion of the relationships between appearance, ancestry and behaviour, in which behaviour (culture) takes on a primary role and ideas about appearance and ancestry may become tacit – although they never actually disappear and may be made explicit by some people (Wade 2002, 2017).

The important point is that we recognise that 'race' – and racism – are at issue not so much because of the overt discourse being used but rather because of the specific categories of people that are being targeted, which are the same categories as those constituted during centuries of colonial oppression. The history is what gives us the main clue, rather than the type of discourse. For our purposes, the implication is that the oppression of Indigenous peoples is very much based on ideas about racialised difference and thus unequivocally involves racism, *contra* ideas that, because differences between Indigenous and non-Indigenous people are not always based on phenotype but also on language, dress, place of residence and so on, discrimination against them is classifiable as ethnic or cultural, not racial (see Chapter 2; see also Sá and Milanez Pereira 2020: 161; Wade 2010b: 38).[8] In this book, we address racism as a set of processes that involves categories of people classed as Black, Indigenous, brown – and of course white.[9]

ANTI-RACISM

As we have already intimated, actions may have anti-racist effects without the actors involved using the term 'anti-racism'. Because we started our research by engaging with artists who appeared to us to be explicitly anti-racist, we ended up working with many people who did identify with that label, but some did not. Referring to Denilson Baniwa and Jaider Esbell, Lúcia Sá and Felipe Milanez (2020: 162) state that 'neither Baniwa nor Esbell make direct use of the term racism in connection to their art'. Some artists have used terms such as 'decolonisation' and 'decoloniality' rather than anti-racism, foregrounding historical processes of oppression against their peoples. For example, the curation of museum and art gallery exhibitions undertaken by Brazilian Indigenous artists discussed in Chapter 5 was defined by them as decolonisation, while it was also carried out as an explicit collaboration with the project's anti-racist remit. And, as we have said, some Indigenous artists in Brazil preferred to define anti-racism around questions of land and territory and the threat of 'monocultures', broadly conceived. (This approach perhaps decentres the tendency for the terms 'anti-racism' and 'decoloniality' to foreground

---

[8] On the role of phenotype in racism against Indigenous people, see Ravindran (2021). Our argument is not so much that phenotype may be – and often is – important, but rather that it is the invocation of the category *indio* or *indígena* that signals the presence of racialised thinking.

[9] In the CARLA project we did not take on the challenge of exploring art in relation to racism against Jewish people or people of Asian or Middle Eastern descent (for example, Japanese, Chinese, Korean, Lebanese). See Fernández de Lara Harada (2021), Pridgeon (2020).

the agency of the dominant actors, instead placing Indigenous concerns at the centre.)

But, of course, racism is a major component of the relations of coloniality that decolonial initiatives seek to unsettle and subvert (Lehmann 2022; Quijano 1999). For this reason, perhaps, it is noticeable that the terms 'racism' and 'anti-racism' are relatively commonly used among Indigenous activists – artists and otherwise – in Brazil compared to other areas of Latin America. For example, alongside noting that Baniwa and Esbell do not refer to 'racism', Sá and Milanez describe two meetings organised in 2018 with Indigenous intellectuals, community leaders, activists and students to discuss the topic of racism against Indigenous populations in Brazil, and observe that 'no Indigenous participant in the two meetings had any reservations to refer to the violence, ill-treatment and invisibilisation of Amerindians in Brazil as racism' (Sá and Milanez Pereira 2020: 163).[10]

In contrast, for the female musicians who make up the Colombian group Las Emperadoras de la Champeta (see Chapter 1), the key issues of inequality and exclusion centre around gender and class and the marginalisation of *champeta* music, a genre associated with the working-class spaces of the port cities of Colombia's Caribbean coastal region. A review of the group's YouTube channel reveals that the only reference to race and racism is in a video of a song, 'Pará en la Raya' (Holding the Line), written and performed especially for the CARLA project – and, even then, the reference is only via the posters adorning the studio walls and the video's description, which both mention CARLA, while the lyrics refer to 'abuse' and 'harassment' of working-class women.[11] However, working-class spaces in these cities are associated in the national imaginary with non-whiteness – Blackness, brownness, dark-skinned Indigenous-Black mestizos – while the music itself has unequivocally African origins, albeit of twentieth-century rather than colonial vintage, and is also strongly associated with Blackness (Cunin 2007; Montoya Alzate 2019; Streicker 1995; Wade 2000). When the topic of racism is provided as a frame – for example, in the context of an interview with band leader Mily Iriarte, recorded for CARLA's online exhibition after

---

[10] See also Braz Bomfim de Souza and Milanez (2023), where there is a very explicit language of (anti-)racism. Warren's work with Indigenous activists in Minas Gerais in the late 1990s indicates that this is not a new phenomenon (Warren 2001).

[11] For the channel, see www.youtube.com/@emperadoras/featured. For the song, see www.digitalexhibitions.manchester.ac.uk/s/carla-en/page/las-emperadoras.

some twelve months' collaborating with the project – then explicit links are easily made. Iriarte says:

> Historically, *champeta* has been stigmatised for being a genre, a culture, which is steeped in Afro themes, Indigenous themes. They have denied us our own space, they have wanted to silence us. Our thoughts about racism are that there is structural racism in the city of Cartagena on the Colombian Caribbean, which we have to overcome and we overcome it precisely with *champeta*.[12]

The case of Las Emperadoras seems, on the face of it, different from that of Brazilian Indigenous artists. But there is a common theme of what Tathagatan Ravindran (2020: 976), describing Bolivia, calls 'undecidability in racial discourses', caused by the 'constant alternation between multiple classificatory logics' that is characteristic of Latin American racial formations with the shifting boundaries of their relational racialised categories. Undecidability means that the discourse of race and racism is absent and present at the same time (Wade 2010a; Wade et al. 2014) and this is manifested, in slightly different ways, in the discourses of both Indigenous artists in Brazil and brown working-class women musicians in Colombia, all of whom may, and may not, talk explicitly about racism.[13] Even the 'anti-racism with a class consciousness' explicitly espoused by the Argentine collective Identidad Marrón, which focuses precisely on the coincidence of racial and class hierarchies, has to constantly battle with the undecidability generated by the fact that discourses of class are frequently used to distract attention from racial inequality (Aguiló and Vivaldi 2023).

At any rate, it seems clear – perhaps increasingly so in the incipient official turn to anti-racism of the last decade or so – that providing a safe space that explicitly invites people to frame their experiences of exclusion in terms of racism and anti-racism acts as a kind of release mechanism that gives voice to an underlying consciousness of racism that is still difficult to articulate in public forums and that is often subsumed into the experiences of class and gender inequality with which it is always deeply entwined (Wade and Moreno Figueroa 2021). Indeed, we found that, as a result of engaging with our research, some artists involved in Afro dance in Colombia and in Indigenous and Afro theatre in Argentina began to adopt the label of anti-racism more explicitly as a way to frame their activities.

---

[12] See video interview at www.digitalexhibitions.manchester.ac.uk/s/carla-en/page/las-emperadoras

[13] On the absent presence of race in Europe, see M'charek, Schramm and Skinner (2014a).

This is to say that our approach to defining what activities count as anti-racist is broad and flexible, in two ways. First, the terms 'racism' and 'anti-racism' may or may not be explicitly used as badges or framing devices: we understand activities as anti-racist if there is some sense among the artists in question of the racialised character of the inequality and oppression being challenged, but this sense can be tacit and emergent.[14] Second, while conceptually we understand racism as a set of historically embedded structures that generate and reproduce racialised inequalities in the distribution of power and privilege – rather than simply being a matter of prejudiced individuals or the non-recognition of identity – we also recognise that such structures and actions are in a relationship of mutual constitution (Giddens 1984), as are structures of resource distribution and regimes of identity recognition (Fraser and Honneth 2003). Therefore, anti-racist initiatives that explicitly target individual people's attitudes and, for example, seek to expand their awareness are not to be discounted simply because they do not explicitly frame what they do as a challenge to racial capitalism, coloniality and other such structures. Equally, anti-racist activities that are aligned to capitalist markets can have valuable effects and should not be dismissed out of hand (Ruette-Orihuela et al. 2024). This is important in thinking about the effects that artists seek to produce – which often aim to provoke certain affective and cognitive reactions in their audiences, as well as challenging structures of power – and about how artists may have to make a living by engaging with the market and the state.

ART, POLITICS AND AFFECT

What can art do in terms of challenging racism and fostering anti-racism? In one sense, it can operate in a number of overlapping modalities, such as: combating racist stereotypes and representations (see e.g. Chapters 4, 6 and 7); decolonising the art world by creating institutional spaces, networks and positions of power for Black, Indigenous and non-white people in that world, as practitioners, curators and cultural managers (see e.g. Chapter 5); working with marginalised communities through art practices to bring people together through engagement with art, affirm their presence, combat invisibility and silencing, strengthen identity, and support local struggles for justice and equality (see e.g. Chapters 6 and 7). Art can also be used to communicate and channel

---

[14] For a discussion of this kind of 'racially aware class consciousness', see Wade (2022b).

another entire ontology, that is, a way of being, living and feeling in the world. This mode focuses on challenging an entire system of interlocking oppressions and inequalities – such as racism, capitalism, sexism, heterosexism, anthropocentrism – to propose another way of being in the world, a way of being where racism and other oppressions do not make any sense. These different ontologies are often connected to non-white, non-capitalist and/or non-Christian belief systems with origins in Indigenous or African cultures (Pinheiro Dias 2022). Although this is not something we directly address in this book, this modality was present in many of the artworks and interviews produced for the project. Examples appear in Denilson Baniwa's film *Colheita maldita* (Accursed Harvest); in Ziel Karapató's criticism of Christian conversion in his installation *Prisão de almas* (Prison of Souls), produced for the CARLA-sponsored exhibition *Hãhãw: Arte indígena antirracista* (Anti-Racist Indigenous Art) in Salvador, Bahia; and in the following statement by Daiara Tukano, who, although she publicly labels herself as an artist on her own website, also states: 'I am not an art creator. I am not an artist. It is not about what I create, but how I relate to creation and let creation flow through me and how I can be a channel to something that is much bigger than me. So that's a different relationship with the universe, with the cosmos.'[15]

This rough typology cross-cuts what Paula Serafini (2022: 25–28) identifies as the functions of art for social movements organising against relations of coloniality and associated practices of extractivism. She lists five functions:

(1) denunciation, which involves making people and their issues visible and affirming their legitimacy and relevance;
(2) documentation, which can be the literal creation of an archive, but may also entail the development of narratives that diverge from mainstream top-down developmentalism;
(3) democratisation, that is, the sharing of information and the building of community around alternative narratives;
(4) the deconstruction of dominant naturalised conceptual frames that depend, for example, on classic Western binaries such as culture/nature, mind/body, feeling/reason;
(5) design, which is the creation of new objects and new ways of being.

[15] For Denilson's film, see www.digitalexhibitions.manchester.ac.uk/s/carla-en/page/denilson-baniwa. For the exhibition in Salvador, see https://arteindigena.ufba.br/ and the text by Arissana Pataxó in this book's Final Reflections. For Daiara's website, see www.daiaratukano.com/en, and for her remarks, see Curated Conversation 1 in this book.

Serafini's functions are useful to think with, but they tend to neglect the key theme of decolonising spaces of the art world; they are also rather abstract, whereas the three (or four) modes we have outlined here are easy to relate to concrete art practices.

Beyond these specific modalities and functions, there is the overarching question of what social change can be achieved by artistic practices. At a basic level, as Bernd Reiter (2009: 158) notes, 'Gaining a voice in the public sphere of a society where racism and exclusion have rendered whole groups of people invisible and labelled their cultural and artistic production unworthy of public display is therefore necessarily a highly political act'. Going deeper, Alejandro de la Fuente contends that 'things that are not speakable in other realms become possible in the realm of art' (Gates, Rodríguez Valdés and de la Fuente 2012: 35). Foregrounding the complex relations between art and politics, Doris Sommer says that 'cultural agency' – as manifest in creative activities such as pedagogy, research, activism and the arts – creates 'wiggle room,' displaying a creative preference 'for caginess over confrontation' in the face of opponents' greater power. Art can undermine univocality and single-mindedness (although it can also reinforce them) and provide a 'dangerous supplement to systems that prefer to be left alone' (Sommer 2006a: 5, 13). Looking at socially engaged art projects initiated both by state politicians and by grassroots agents, Sommer finds that they can inspire faith in new possibilities for society, fostering 'unbiased judgement', 'free thinking' and the overriding of 'predetermined conclusions about values and concepts, personal gain, party lines, or moral argument' (Sommer 2014: 87–88). Art often achieves this in indirect ways: Afro-descendant writers in Latin America work 'in restless toggling or counterpoint between two (sometimes more) antagonistic systems, without necessarily wanting to settle accounts or to claim that one side wins and the other loses'; they 'remind us that creativity is more about endless and unresolved processes than about final pleasing products' (Sommer 2018: 320).

Also observing the diverse possibilities afforded by the arts, Diana Boros differentiates 'plastic' art, which is conformist, mainstream and market-oriented, from 'visionary' art, which is transcendent and rebellious.[16] While all art has 'positive societal value', the repetitiveness, overproduction and profit-oriented character of plastic art means it loses its

---

[16] By 'plastic', Boros means artificial and lightweight. This should not be confused with 'the plastic arts', such as sculpture and ceramics, which work with a plastic (mouldable) medium.

transformative power, whereas visionary art 'encourages important political possibilities by reawakening (through [the] rearrangement [of life]) and engaging (through the critical thought that the rearrangement invites) a participant' (Boros 2012: 6). Although plastic art may foment a 'sense of pride and interest in the public, which is vital to a sincere feeling of community', only visionary art 'encourages within people the expansion of their imaginative capabilities, their true independence (knowledge of self) and their sense of empathy' (Boros 2012: 15).

Haunting any optimistic assessment of the political effects of artistic practices is the fact that, while visual culture may be 'a fertile ground for counter hegemonic exercises', it is also 'one of the fundamental resources for hegemony-building' (Adamovsky 2016: 158). Obvious examples include the art promoted by Fascist and Stalinist regimes in the twentieth century. Art can also be harnessed to nationalist projects based on cultural homogenisation, racism and patriarchy. Jacques Rancière thought that art is inherently political because it creates a representation of a given social world and the people in it and establishes a normative framework for what can and cannot be shown and said about these things. In what he calls the 'aesthetic regime of art', also known as modern art, art becomes identical with all of life (i.e. is no longer located above large parts of it as a bourgeois elite phenomenon) and thus can undermine hierarchy through a politics of aesthetics, creating new communities and new social relations. In that sense, artistic egalitarianism is analogous to political egalitarianism. But this does not guarantee that all art is progressive, as the political context can allow for art to be used for regressive and progressive ends; or simply to be interpreted as either regressive or progressive. Rancière equivocates here between seeing art as having a progressive dimension (given by, for example, the fact that almost anyone can access and use language), and acknowledging that art can work in ways that are both progressive and non-progressive or political and apolitical: 'The arts only ever lend to projects of domination or emancipation what they are able to lend to them, that is to say, quite simply, what they have in common with them: bodily positions and movements, functions of speech, the parcelling out of the visible and the invisible' (Rancière 2013: 19). This is important because the affordances of the various kinds of anti-racist art practices described in this book are often multidirectional and multivalent, especially as they circulate among audiences who may choose to read them against the grain of the artists' intentions.

How does affect fit in here? As we have noted, the creative potential in the political and civic domains that is often attributed to artistic interventions is linked to their capacity for generating effects that are not only cognitive and representational but also emotional and affective (Beasley-Murray 2010; Flynn and Tinius 2015; Moya 2016; Sommer 2014, 2018, 2006b; Thompson 2014). In definitional mode and cutting through the diverse and sometimes contradictory ideas about what affect, emotions and feelings are and how they differ, we adopt a simple approach that sees feelings as personal/biographical, emotions as intersubjective social constructions and affect as an embodied reaction that adds experiential intensity to emotions and feelings (and thoughts) (Shouse 2005).

This does not imply that affect is inherently outside discourse and sociality, *contra* Brian Massumi and others.[17] As Donna Haraway (1991) has argued, there can be no pre-social encounter with the body, biology or nature. In that sense, affect is, like emotion, intersubjectively constructed, even if it is not necessarily mediated by language itself. However, it remains useful to retain a heuristic distinction between the sociality of emotions and the embodied intensities of affective reactions. The distinction is important to understanding the impact of art, which mobilises symbolic discursive meanings and emotional reactions, but which also – in some forms more than others – has the power to produce bodily reactions that intensify the experience of those meanings and emotions.

For example, the experience of watching in person a performance of Sankofa Danzafro, the Afro-Colombian dance company with whom Carlos Correa worked, is different, in terms of intensity of embodied experience, from watching the performance on a mobile phone: the loudness of the music, the reverberation of the drums in the body, the close physicality of the dancers' bodies – all these lend a heightened intensity to meanings and emotions. This is partly because, during weeks of rehearsal and collective reflection, the dancers have embodied their own experiences of being Black in Colombia and are using this affective intensity to 'move' each other and their audiences so as to transmit what racism feels like. This sharpens the emotions and meanings and helps generate what Correa calls an 'anti-racist emotionality', which provides tools for combating racism (see Chapter 4). The same applies to the theatre groups with whom Ana Vivaldi collaborated (see Chapter 6). The actors' bodies materialise

---

[17] Berg and Ramos-Zayas (2015), like Leys (2011), reject the idea of affect as a pre-conscious force associated with Massumi (1995) and others, such as Beasley-Murray (2010: chapter 3). Instead they see affect as profoundly social, like emotions, thus blurring any distinction between them, as does Stoler (2004) and as does Ahmed, whose analysis of 'affective economies' is also a 'model of sociality of emotions' (2015: 8, 10).

the histories of Afro-descendant and Mapuche people in Argentina and intensify the emotions around experiences of invisibilisation, exclusion and violence transmitted among the actors and to the audiences.

In sum, while it is clear that art can function to support regimes of power, we explore art in its potential to be 'oppositional, subversive to power, to the conventional order and its paradigms' (Barber 2011: 110). That potential derives in part from the materiality of art, which engages and connects people's bodies and minds; the affective traction of art moves through bodies, individually and collectively, and adds intensities to emotion and meaning. In anti-racism this is important, because racism is often experienced via the body and perceptions of embodied differences – which, it should be noted, are not confined to biological phenotype but encompass such traits as hair styles, body adornments, habits of body movement and styles of speech: elements that straddle the borders between nature/biology and culture (M'charek, Schramm and Skinner 2014b: 471; Wade 2022a: 177–181).

LATIN AMERICAN RACIAL FORMATIONS

Chapters 1, 2 and 3 give detailed accounts of the ways art has figured in the racial formations of Argentina, Brazil and Colombia (see also Wade, Scorer and Aguiló 2019: 13). In this section we give some general context for these formations, also bringing out the way each country is a variation on themes that run through the Latin American region as a whole – and, indeed, through the Americas.

In the Latin American context, Brazil is often seen as relatively 'Black': although about half the population identifies as white in the census, the other half identifies as *preto* ('black') and *pardo* ('brown'), while those who identify as Indigenous are less than 1 per cent of the total.[18] Consequently, after the 1988 multiculturalist constitutional reform and the 1995 admission by president Fernando Henrique Cardoso that the once official image of Brazil as a mestizo 'racial democracy' was not entirely accurate, the main thrust of anti-racist policy in Brazil has been directed at Afro-descendants, often in the form of controversial affirmative action programmes offering race-based quotas in higher education admissions and federal employment (Lehmann 2018; Paschel 2016; Telles

---

[18] Racial demographics are a shifting scenario in Brazil. Between the 2010 and 2022 censuses, the number of people identifying as Indigenous almost doubled from 896,917 to 1,693,535, while those identifying as *preto* and *pardo* grew from 50.7% (7.6% + 43.1%) to 55.5% (10.2% + 45.3%) of the total.

2004). In contrast, as already noted, racism against the Indigenous population is rarely named as such and is marginal to the political agenda, despite the importance of 'the Indian' in the national imaginary (Pacheco de Oliveira 2016; see Chapter 2; see also Ramos 1998).[19]

Yet in recent years environmental and land conflicts have dramatically increased violence against the Indigenous population, with news of assassinations and violent displacement of native peoples having become a daily routine. There have also been numerous cases of Indigenous men and women being publicly abused, being refused service at shops, restaurants and hospitals, or even being expelled from buses, in clear defiance of Brazil's strong anti-racist laws. This mode of racism has become so open that politicians feel free to make disparaging comments about Indigenous people on live television and in the mainstream press, a trend that only increased under president Bolsonaro (2019–2022), alongside frontal attacks on the status of Indigenous reservations and protected areas.

At the same time, Indigenous activism is now stronger than it has ever been. Besides running for official elected positions such as mayors and councillors and organising themselves in NGOs and political groups, Indigenous Brazilians are increasingly using traditional and non-traditional art forms to counter racism: Indigenous authors are publishing their own books; there has been a well-documented surge of Indigenous cinema production; and an increasing number of visual artists and musicians are making use of venues and media channels based in the Global North to express themselves and, in their own words, educate the non-Indigenous population about their own ways of life.

In contrast to Brazil's relative Blackness, a key feature of Argentina is that, especially in the twentieth century, dominant narratives portrayed the country, internally and abroad, as mainly white and Europeanised. In contrast to some other Latin American countries in which national identity was deliberately articulated around ideas of *mestizaje*, representations of Argentina presented it as an anomaly in the region. It was depicted as a nation where the impact of European immigration and the supposed extinction of Indigenous and Afro-descendant populations during the nation-building period at the turn of the twentieth century had produced a racially homogeneous white country.[20]

---

[19] While affirmative action quotas make provision for Indigenous applicants, this was a later addition to the original policy.

[20] Between 1871 and 1914, over 6 million Europeans migrated to Argentina; many returned to Europe, but more than 3 million settled permanently (Schneider 1996: 99).

In recent decades, the rise across Latin America of Indigenous and Black social movements and the associated turn to state multiculturalism – helped in the case of Argentina by a devastating 2001 economic crisis, which unsettled taken-for-granted assumptions about Argentina's European-style modernity, and by the subsequent left-leaning governments of Néstor Kirchner (2003–2007) and Cristina Fernández de Kirchner (2007–2015) – have spurred revisionist historians to question this exceptionalism, relocating Argentina instead as another, particularly whitened, variant on the Latin American theme of *mestizaje*. They have shown that some nation-building discourses gave more room to non-whiteness than previously thought (Aguiló 2018; Alberto and Elena 2016), while evidence suggests that people of Indigenous, African and mixed background were not erased but instead forced to incorporate into an allegedly uniform population. Also, as shown in Chapter 3, in a country where Blackness and Indigeneity are often characterised as having been erased from a national narrative, there is a surprisingly lively presence, especially in popular culture, of Black and Indigenous characters, alongside mixed-race figures, such as the racially ambiguous gaucho and the *criollo* (Adamovsky 2016b; Alberto and Elena 2016; Alberto 2022; Frigerio 2013; McAleer 2018; Merino 2015; Wade 2023).[21]

This indicates that, while whiteness had become seemingly common-sense and taken for granted, in practice it was a complex and contradictory construct: Argentina has been hailed as a 'race-less' country while, in everyday reality, racialised differences are recognised and contribute to the durability of social hierarchies. Racial difference is spoken through a language of class: the term *negro* is used in everyday interaction not primarily to refer to African background but to lack of civility, associated with provincial and working-class origins and, implicitly, mixed-race ancestry (Aguiló and Vivaldi 2023). In recent years, *negro* has also been used to describe immigrants perceived as phenotypically dark (especially Paraguayans, Bolivians and Peruvians).

Argentina's ambiguous and precarious notion of whiteness allowed the emergence of interstitial spaces in which subaltern sectors were able to explore forms of resistance. Argentina's discourse of homogeneity combined with an asymmetric social structure based on race and class were contested throughout the twentieth century by the dark-skinned

---

[21] *Criollo* designates any living thing (person, animal, plant) of non-American ancestry that was born and raised in the Americas and thus bears the stamp of that upbringing (including the possibility of racial mixture).

masses. In recent years, Indigenous groups have also challenged the view of Argentina as a homogeneous white country. The early twenty-first century has seen an explosion of expressive forms that expose and oppose the oblique and circuitous ways in which race is written into the scripts of national identity (Aguiló 2018). Working-class sectors have been developing cultural expressions through which the stigmas historically associated by the white middle class with the *negro* identity and other non-white subjectivities have been exposed, criticised and appropriated as part of new anti-racist strategies. Nevertheless, the fact that whiteness persists as an image of nationhood indicates its status as a project impossible to renounce.

Colombia sits between Brazil and Argentina insofar as it has a small but substantial Indigenous population (about 4% of the national total), which has a strong and long-standing social movement; and it has a medium-sized Afro-Colombian population (about 10%), which has a more recent and less consolidated social movement (Paschel 2016; Wade 1993, 2009a).[22] Dominant portrayals of racial difference align with a common-sense idea of Colombia as a 'country of regions', in which Blackness is seen as located predominantly in the poor and infrastructurally underdeveloped Pacific coastal region – where over 70 per cent of people identify as Black – with an important secondary location along the Caribbean coast, even though substantial numbers of Black people live outside these two regions.[23] Indigeneity is perceived as more diversely located (in the regions of the Amazon, the Pacific coast, areas of the Caribbean coast and the southwest Andes). It is usually seen as rural and peripheral: the substantial urban Indigenous population is ignored in this racial-regional schema.

Although the state has long given some degree of official status to Indigenous peoples, a major change in the state's relationship to ethnic minorities occurred in 1991 when constitutional reform gave further rights to Indigenous people and for the first time also recognised Afro-Colombians, or *comunidades negras* ('black communities'), as an 'ethnic group' with its own cultural traditions. Subsequent legislation, notably

---

[22] The 2005 census indicated that 10.6% of the population identified as Black and 3.4% as Indigenous. In the 2018 census (which the government admitted had undercounted the population), those figures had changed to 6.8% and 4.3%. Black activists contend that both censuses undercounted the Afro-Colombian population.

[23] According to 2005 census figures, about one-third of Black people live in the Pacific coastal region, with another third living in the provinces of the Caribbean coastal region.

Law 70 of 1993, opened the way for land rights for rural Black communities in the Pacific region, among other measures.

Afro-Colombians initially embraced this ethnic definition, despite the fact that it excluded most urban Black people. Recently some sectors have tried to expand the definition towards a more inclusive racialised one that embraces urban Blackness and addresses racialised exclusion from education, housing and job markets. At the same time, Black (and Indigenous) movements have become increasingly concerned with violence and displacement, which have a long history in Colombia, but which from the mid 1990s became much more severe in their impact on Indigenous and especially Black communities. Since then, in worrying lock-step with multiculturalist land-rights legislation, violence and displacement from land have emerged as major issues for these minorities.[24] Displacement has been construed by many Black activists as a violent mode of racism, and anti-racism now includes adopting the structural position of victim (Cárdenas 2012, 2024).

In Colombia, the change is still under way from culturalist definitions of Blackness towards more racialised ones, and from claims for land and cultural rights to claims for protection and the right to life. It is a shift from an indigenist-style concept of Blackness, which tends to background racism and focus on land and cultural rights, towards a Brazilian-style definition of Blackness, based on criteria of appearance and ancestry.

Latin American racial formations have in common a temporal tension between ideas about the future of mixture, assumed to lead towards ever greater indistinction and mestizo homogeneity, and the past of mixture, which evokes its distinct originary ingredients of Black, Indigenous and white people. Since the multiculturalism of the 1990s, and with the current incipient turn to anti-racism, the emphasis on racialised difference has grown stronger, challenging the standard narrative about what the future might hold. This is true of Argentina, Brazil and Colombia, albeit each country displays its own specific conjugation of Blackness, Indigeneity and whiteness.

---

[24] The Consultancy on Human Rights and Displacement (Consultoría para los Derechos Humanos y el Desplazamiento, CODHES) estimates that 4.1 million Colombians were forced from their homes between 1999 and 2012. Of these people, it was estimated in 2009 that 17% were Afro-Colombian and 6.5% Indigenous (Wade 2016). See also CODHES (2013: 20, 24), which estimates 20% for Afro-Colombians and 7% for Indigenous people.

METHODS, POSITIONALITIES, COLLABORATIONS

The CARLA project began in January 2020.[25] As described in the Preface, it was directed by Peter Wade, Lúcia Sá and Ignacio Aguiló, who led teams working on Colombia, Brazil and Argentina, respectively, countries chosen to align with the experience of the directors. In addition to the directors, each team had three core members: a post-doctoral researcher employed by the University of Manchester (and, as it happened, a national of the country they were researching); a country-based academic co-investigator; and a country-based advisor. The project also hired several research assistants in each country (see Preface for details).

From the start, a key aim of the project was to explore a wide diversity of artistic practices relevant to anti-racist and decolonial priorities. The idea was to include both Black and Indigenous art production in the project as a whole, thus building on a growing trend to challenge the traditional division between these two racialised categories in academic research (Hooker 2020; Wade 2010b, 2018). For Brazil, it seems obvious that we should have included Black Brazilian artistic production, given its volume and prominence in artistic and scholarly worlds (de la Fuente 2018). However, this very prominence impelled us from the start to focus on racism against Indigenous peoples, given the paucity of scholarship on the topic; and, if we focused on both Indigenous and Black artists, we feared that Indigenous people would, as is often the case, be relegated to the margins. For Colombia, the team worked in practice mostly with Black artists, and with some mestizo and brown artists such as Margarita Ariza and some members of Las Emperadoras de la Champeta, both mentioned earlier (see Chapter 1). The Argentina team managed greater diversity, building collaborations with Mapuche and Afro-Argentine theatre companies, an Indigenous Qom hip-hop group and an anti-racist art collective, Identidad Marrón, who identify as *marrón* (literally, chestnut-coloured) (see Chapter 3). These country-specific patterns are reflected in the chapters of this book.

The roster of artists we collaborated with emerged from an initial process of scoping, carried out mainly by the post-doctoral researchers with support from the project directors and the co-investigators and advisors in Latin America. This was followed by a longer process in which these researchers approached artists, invited them to collaborate and built up relationships with them over time. As described in the Preface, much of

---

[25] For details of the project, see https://sites.manchester.ac.uk/carla/.

this was conducted online during pandemic restrictions. The roster was thus shaped partly by the networks of the project team and the interest of artists in the project. In all cases, the post-doctoral researchers, each working in different ways with the co-investigator and advisor in their team, built up collaborations with diverse artists, many of which were later reflected in the project's YouTube channel and online exhibition, and a selection of which featured in the project's Festival of Decolonial and Anti-Racist Art, which took place in Manchester in April 2022.[26]

In some ways, the structure of the project reflected prevailing academic hierarchies. In the core team – project directors, co-investigators, advisers and post-doctoral researchers – there was a majority of men and of people who would be seen by most observers in Europe and Latin America as white, although only one person – the overall director, Peter Wade – is male, white and European, while the co-directors Lúcia Sá and Ignacio Aguiló are Latin Americans living in the UK. But there were important elements of diversity: the Colombian co-investigator and advisor are both Black women, while the Colombian post-doc is a Black man. Among the locally-hired research assistants there was also significant diversity, with Indigenous women working in Argentina and Brazil. Not surprisingly, the artists we worked with were predominantly Black and Indigenous, with the exceptions we have noted of Margarita Ariza, some members of Las Emperadoras de la Champeta and the members of the Identidad Marrón collective.

If the structure of the project thus followed, in some respects, a predictable shape influenced by academic and Global North–South hierarchies of gender, race and region, it also reflected to a significant degree changes to those hierarchies caused by the increasing participation of Black and Indigenous people in higher education and in academic employment in Latin America. We also made concerted efforts to build relationships that were truly horizontal and collaborative, in which the artists we worked with could define the direction and shape of the collaboration – artists were also involved as project research assistants in all three countries and one artist acted as an advisor in Colombia. A significant amount of project funds went into supporting activities proposed and designed by the artists; this funding stream was aided by the pandemic, which made it impossible to hold in-person project workshops in each country, thus

---

[26] YouTube channel: www.youtube.com/channel/UCf2aulENOdu3-0KIvIj-R7w. Exhibition: www.digitalexhibitions.manchester.ac.uk/s/carla-en/page/home. Festival (documentary film): www.youtube.com/watch?v=WB1fKmYkP9M&t=3s.

freeing funds to support artists. We also obtained additional funds from the University of Manchester to support public engagement activities, many of which were proposed and/or designed by the artists. Just as important, a great deal of researchers' time – especially that of the three post-doctoral researchers – went into supporting activities directed by the artists. This is reflected, for example, in the documentary *Terra fértil: Véxoa e a arte indígena contemporânea na Pinacoteca de São Paulo* (Fertile Land: Véxoa and Contemporary Indigenous Art in São Paulo's Pinacoteca), co-produced by Jamille Dias, working with several artists and curators; the film *Colheita maldita* (Accursed Harvest), by Denilson Baniwa, working with Jamille Dias and artist Naine Terena; and the documentary *Detrás del sur: Danzas para Manuel. Prácticas artísticas antirracistas* (Behind the South: Dances for Manuel. Anti-Racist Artistic Practices), produced by Rafael Palacios and Carlos Correa.[27]

The collaborations were also reflected in co-presentations at major conferences and in online discussion events streamed on CARLA's YouTube channel, in which Black and Indigenous Latin American artists took part on equal terms. Collaboration is evident in the co-authorship of chapters in this book by artists – Liliana Angulo, Rossana Alarcón, Lorena Cañuqueo, Miriam Alvarez, Alejandra Egido, Naine Terena and Rafael Palacios – as well as in the book's five 'curated conversations', which draw on discussions involving a wide array of CARLA artists, and in the book's Final Reflections. Importantly, these Black and Indigenous authors have contributed to the overall conceptual framing of the book, avoiding a common hierarchy in which Global North researchers deal with 'theory' while Global South participants provide 'data'. Such a simple division between theory and data is barely tenable to begin with and is anyway broken down by the participation of Black and Indigenous artists in the discussions and workshops held during the project, which shaped the conceptual framing of the project, and through their contributions to Chapters 4, 5 and 6, which although they focus on empirical examples also make conceptual arguments grounded in experience. The curated conversations, which foreground the voices of these artists, also have important conceptual dimensions, while the Conclusion contains reflections by artists on their work and on the project overall. The end result is a book that we hope will support anti-racist art and activism, while also making a significant contribution to scholarship.

[27] See https://youtu.be/7VnYH4VgaAE; www.youtube.com/watch?v=8eRIpEIbDag; and https://youtu.be/swza1FF4-gw.

The methods used in the project were therefore very distant from the traditional models of social science in which some people study others, whether through focus groups, interviews or ethnographic participant observation. Of course, these methods did figure in the research as well, and participant observation in particular was an integral part of collaboration. More formal interviews and focus groups were also used when investigating audience responses to artistic performances and products (Correa Angulo and Alarcón Velásquez 2024; Vivaldi and Cossio 2021). But the overall tenor of the project was set by the theme of horizontal collaboration, to which this book acts as a testament.

STRUCTURE OF THE BOOK

The first three chapters, Part I of the book, explore the relationship between art and racial formation in each country. Chapter 1 on Colombia analyses how racialised differences have been represented in artistic practice in Colombia, as well as the relationship between negatively racialised artists and the art world. The authors show how, in the nineteenth century and into the twentieth, white and mixed-race artists tended to represent racialised subalterns in ways tinged with primitivism and paternalism, without racism coming into clear view as a social issue. However, by the 1930s and 40s, Black artists and writers were using their practice to critique social inequalities in which racism was identified as an important component. The chapter then focuses on Black art practice, analyzing its increasing politicisation and exploring the work of the Colombian artists who collaborated with CARLA to show how their diverse art practices have addressed racism in increasingly direct ways.

Chapter 2 looks at how contemporary Brazilian Indigenous art is rising both in production and public recognition and how it has opened new spaces for a 'contest of imaginaries' in Brazilian society, expanding possibilities for the expression of Indigenous rights. Anti-racism frequently takes the form of a struggle to defend rights to ancestral territories and livelihoods and to oppose monocultures of all kinds; as well as the creation of spaces for the similarities in life and struggle that connect people across all forms of difference.

Chapter 3 focuses on challenges to whiteness and Europeanness in Argentine cultural production, contending that the arts have acted as an important platform for critiques of the subtle ways in which race is written into the script of national belonging and difference. The artistic corpus examined includes anti-racist expressions by Afro-descendant and Indigenous creators, but the chapter highlights cultural products by working-class artists (mostly mixed-race people who experience an elusive yet systematic racism) and their white middle-class allies, who together have played a central role in the articulation of strategies that, despite not being explicitly anti-racist, have contributed to addressing structural racism. The chapter explores how racial diversity went from invisibility to a hypervisibility that mobilises white middle- and upper-class paranoid fears about the Other, but also how affect and emotion allow alliances in the face of racism.

In Part II, the next three chapters are co-authored by CARLA researchers and artists. They draw on specific art practices and productions to explore conceptual questions of art, anti-racism and affect. Chapter 4 focuses on Sankofa Danzafro's Afro-contemporary dance company in Colombia and how it constructs anti-racist narratives, highlighting the role of affect, which works to assemble collective bodies and discourses. Acting as a site of political enunciation and as a mode of resistance-in-motion, dance generates affective atmospheres that help to make visible and challenge the persistence of structural racism. In particular, the chapter explores *Detrás del sur*, a recent Sankofa dance work, to see how these anti-racist strategies have informed the creative processes behind the work.

Chapter 5 looks at *Véxoa: We Know*, the first Indigenous-only arts exhibition held at the Pinacoteca de São Paulo, and explores how such art can work against the affective dimensions of racism in a number of ways, including disrupting dominant cultural narratives, helping to raise awareness about the diversity of Indigenous peoples, and promoting intercultural understanding and appreciation. The chapter shows how contemporary Indigenous arts in Brazil are unsettling categories persistently associated with native aesthetics, and it demonstrates that Indigenous arts can serve as a form of anti-racist cultural resistance, challenging the dominant culture's appropriation and exploitation of Indigenous cultures.

Chapter 6 examines the construction of theatrical poetics, which question colonial criteria of creativity and build alternative spaces for drama production in Argentina. The focus is on the development of anti-racist staging practices, which go beyond recognition politics, centring the stage as a point of reconnection of subalternised social trajectories and presenting the lives of Mapuches and Afro-Latin Americans in all their complexity.

Finally, Chapter 7 reflects broadly on possibilities for anti-racism in artistic practice, focusing on two types of intervention – challenging stereotypes and working with communities – and exploring how various artworks engage with these modes of artistic action and how they create emotional traction and affective intensity.

Intercalated with these chapters are five curated conversations, which give a direct voice to the experiences and conceptual approaches of a wide range of the artists we worked with. In each case, a CARLA researcher draws on a specific (usually online) discussion or event involving artists and researchers and curates the conversation to bring out key themes and ideas in a concise and punchy format. The first conversation is curated from an online event, 'Anti-Racist Art in the UK and Latin America: A Conversation' (2020), which brings together two Latin American and two British artists. The second draws on an online event 'Decolonising the Arts in Latin America: Anti-Racist Irruptions in the Art World' (2020), involving various CARLA artists. The third conversation draws on two texts (produced in 2020–2021) by members of art collective Identidad Marrón, who reflect on their experiences as curators entering a mainly white art scene. The fourth conversation is curated from discussions involving Brazilian Indigenous hip-hop artists (streamed in 2021), while the last item is based on an online discussion (2021) about anti-racist art practices involving the Afro-Colombian collectives Sankofa Danzafro and Colectivo Aguaturbia. The book closes with texts from a selection of the CARLA artists, who were invited to reflect on their experiences working with the project and offer some thoughts on art and anti-racism.

Curated Conversation 1: Anti-Racist Art in the UK and Latin America

Curated by Peter Wade

Source: an online event, 'Anti-Racist Art in the UK and Latin America: A Conversation' (11 November 2020), featuring Daiara Tukano, an Indigenous Tukano artist and activist from Brazil, who had previously collaborated in a project directed by Lúcia Sá and Felipe Milanez (both members of the CARLA project team); Liliana Angulo, a Black artist and activist from Colombia and an adviser to the CARLA project; SuAndi, a Black artist and activist from the UK; and Ekua Bayunu, a Black artist and activist from the UK. This line-up was designed to enable the exploration of differences and similarities between experiences of and ideas about racism in Latin America and the UK, from the perspectives of Black and Indigenous artists. The discussion was in English and was chaired by Peter Wade with logistical assistance from Jamille Pinheiro Dias. The whole two-hour event can be accessed on CARLA's YouTube channel: https://youtube.com/live/HOPwGVBNMXM.

Question: What does it mean to be anti-racist through art or as an artist?

It can mean challenging (and exploring) stereotypes:

LILIANA: I have been working mainly with images so I work with the history of art in Colombia and colonial representations. Most of my initial work was about stereotypes and how Black people have been represented in Colombian art and also in images in general. ... When I started doing this work, I was working on the word '*negro*' and how we relate to that word, because in Colombia the relationship with that word is very complex. We have learned to embrace it in order to fight in the struggle but also obviously it has all this background of colonisation and slavery and all that, so at the time I was dealing with that in order to understand it. So I used it [the word, the image] on my own body and it was very ambivalent. For me, all these works are very painful, because of how we have learned to live with racism. But for some people it was kind of funny, so it was very ambivalent.

SUANDI: I think there's a very arrogant knowledge about who we are as people by the majority white side of society. There's now an intellectual ignorance where people feel very confident to ask the most ridiculous questions.

EKUA: I have a whole body of work that was around trying to turn stereotypes on their head in terms of a personal thing that I try to live as honestly as I can. ... Stereotypes exist within misinformation and ignorance, but they are powerful and they do impact on people and my responsibility as an artist is actually just to celebrate my truth.

DAIARA: One time somebody asked me if I was a cannibal, if my nation eats people. It was in the federal congress in Brasilia: somebody in the federal congress asked me if I eat people. And another time someone else asked me if I was really an Indigenous person or an Indian – I love this word here – because I was wearing glasses or because I was using a cell phone. There is this really stupid misconception that Indigenous people are supposed to be in isolation in the middle of the forest, wearing no clothes and dying of malaria. We deal with every stupidity of racism and the best way I found is just celebrating who I am and my culture and my people and I don't have time to waste with stupid people, you know. And the misconceptions and prejudices about Indigenous nations are so lame that I prefer to use my energy celebrating who we are and how wonderful we are in our diversity, in our history, identity, territories ... by reaffirming my space and my life. I am just trying to live and breathe and in this breath share what I believe and how I believe we can value and restore the energy of life that we deserve to have as human peoples.

It can involve quite explicit actions linked to social movement organising:

LILIANA: I started traveling and working with a lot of women's organisations and organisations in the Black movement in Colombia, so in that sense I started organising and using art practice to deal with issues in different communities and territories. Recently I have been working with a community in the south of Colombia, Buenaventura, which is the main port in Colombia, and one of their leaders was killed. In Colombia, many leaders have been killed over the decades, but recently, after the peace process involving one of the longest-lasting guerrilla forces in history, this issue has been growing. And people who are defending their territory are in danger and this leader was killed; it also happened because he was defending the territory in an area that has big macro-economic development projects for the port. So we worked on his archive – the archive he had created in order to defend the territory – and with the leaders and the community we continue that work.

The art world in general can be a site of struggle:

SUANDI: I realised just what a powerful voice it [art] was and in a way – and I don't want anybody to think I am naive – I also learned what institutional racism was, even though we didn't call it that then. So the arts for me have always been a battlefield but the same time it's been a hugely wonderful supportive experience.

And the art world can be seen as just one domain in a wider social landscape:

DAIARA: I believe we're talking about racism all the time, because we are facing racism all the time. We are facing the story and the narratives of colonisation and trying to dismantle it a little bit, with all the weapons that are available and all the technologies that we can. And art is just one of those spaces, which is also a space for fighting over politics, for fighting over power, and for being present. Reaffirming our Indigenous identities is an act of rebellion in the face of all the discourse of colonisation that tries to make us part of the past or death. We are alive now, we are here, we are as contemporary as everybody and we have a very powerful memory. We are originary peoples, we are defending our rights, our territories, our epistemologies, our way of approaching existence; and we are defending our own truth.

This connects to a wider sense that anti-racism can be immanent in the simple act of being as a Black or Indigenous person or artist. SuAndi observed that 'speaking personally not all the art I make is made to tackle racism; I think as artists we make art because we want something inspired'. And Liliana added that a constant explicit focus on racism and being explicitly anti-racist could be 'tiring' and that working with communities could address such issues in a different way: 'In recent years I kind of got tired of racism and I just focus on the world with the communities and so, yeah, that means the projects are made with them and we work together.'

Ekua questioned what it meant to 'practice' anti-racism through art:

It feels to me that it's possible that we don't 'practice' our anti-racism. There's something weird about that statement. We live constantly with racism as an oppressive force – and as women we live in the intersection of gender-based oppression. ... For me, it's like anything I produce, because of who I am, is Black art, you know. And some people object and they say there is no such term but I think I'm really attached to it because I want to value and celebrate it. I can't imagine that I ever pick up and go 'at this moment I'm not fighting racism and at this moment I am fighting racism'. ... We need to look at fighting racism as a much more global concept. I mean the anti-racist action of just self-care, of love, of being, of the joy of dance, of just breathing and holding your grandfather or your granddaughter ... these are anti-racist actions as far as I'm concerned.

For Daiara, anti-racism means contesting violence and violation, in a context in which 'every time that an Indigenous anything appears, it is the target of many attacks' and in which the 'saying that a good Indian is a dead Indian [is one that] we deal with all the time'. Yet that process of contestation can take forms that go beyond denunciation and can attempt to 'counter colonialism' by reaffirming 'another way of relating to the universe', which avoids 'anthropocentric thinking'. In Daiara's view, although she identifies as an artist on her website (www.daiaratukano.com/en),

> I am not an art creator. I am not an artist. It's not about what I create, but it's how I relate to creation and let creation go through me and how I can be a channel to something that is much larger than me. So that is a different relation to the universe, to the cosmos and how we approach and understand what is the function and the nature of art itself. So maybe questioning and decolonisation and counter-colonisation is, for me at least, all about also questioning the end of anthropocentric thinking.

Question: What does it imply to work in the institutions that control the art world?

On the one hand, it is seen as necessary to interact with institutions in a critical way, which may also mean engaging with them:

DAIARA: If we are talking about anti-racist art, maybe it's just reaffirming the idea that art is in itself a racist space and that it is marked by very racist institutions, like the academy, like the museums, the galleries ... it is a space that has been created just to reaffirm white superiority. The museums are like the most representative spaces of colonialism. And the collections and the exotification of other cultures that are not European cultures, and the narratives that are set in the academy, are very racist. And this is still today a very important tool in promoting ethnocide and genocide. So by making a step into that space, reaffirming a different identity and a different discourse, a different relation to society and a different historical discourse, is by itself a rebellion and is by itself an anti-racist move.

LILIANA: I agree in that the academy, museums, archives and botanical gardens are all institutions that are that were created by colonialism and are at the base of what we understand as culture and as art, knowledge, science and all that. So in that sense I think most of the work that we do has to do with undermining the power behind those concepts.

Liliana recounts an experience with a museum collection in the city of Medellín, in which the only item relating to a Black person was a bill of sale for an enslaved person. In that sense the collection was an expression of racism: 'I mean everything is validated by Colombian art history and there were many representations of Black people made by white artists and in very subtle ways those representations maintain the oppression because they use art to represent oppression and the people being oppressed'. In that same experience, in which she was also working with local community organisations, they came across work by a Black artist, Rodrigo Barrientos (1931–2013), who was little known in Colombia and had migrated to Europe.

LILIANA: It was an experience for everybody to understand how the power of the museum works and how you can relate to that. So we have worked with archives, because in Colombia it is terrible that there is no memory of our ancestors, because memory is obviously written by the people in power, so Black painters were completely erased from art history in Colombia. So in that sense the archives give an opportunity to find that memory and do a process of reparation using art.

SuAndi says that

We fight racism just by producing work that we understand and we hope the audience will look at and question and ponder and wonder but we definitely need to have comrades to do that and some of those comrades are in the arts institutions.

On the other hand, artists perceive real threats and limitations:

EKUA: I've witnessed people who are still working within institutions and the damage it does to them – or what I perceive from the outside as damage.
SUANDI: I know Black people employed by the institutions who have really, really suffered. It's very difficult from the outside to give the support to somebody who's on a staff team where they're constantly being questioned about their ability, their judgments, their opinions. You just hope you can be there for them if they're brave enough to say it's really bad in here and I need help. And I don't blame anybody that doesn't feel they want to say that because it might make them seem as though they're failing.
LILIANA: It is really hard because in Colombia the way racism works is very tricky because it is part of our structure [as Black people]; I mean it's completely institutionalised. So when you walk those corridors, you have your own mind saying that you probably don't deserve to be there and all that, because it's how we have been raised. And it's also because of how people interact in these positions of power, so they all feel that they have the right to be in that seat and to look at you as if you don't.

Tokenism is also seen as a major threat:

LILIANA: I give lots of lectures at conferences and things but I think that's sometimes about them wanting to have a token Black voice. For a long time, I had a struggle with tokenism: there was this practice of people calling me just to kind of validate some curatorial work or something. I'm not always sure they're happy they did invite me to be that token Black voice because I might not always speak in the manner that they wanted me to speak in. But I think every opportunity to speak should be taken, and remember that when we do speak as individuals we represent all Black people, whether that's right or wrong, so we have to be careful and consider what we say and what we do.

EKUA: I have had conversations with the big galleries in my city [Manchester], which scrambled to make statements in response to Black Lives Matter and to look at their programming, saying this is the time, the time is right, come and talk to us. ... But from my perspective it was, like, I'm not interested [unless] we innovate and we come in as equals and you hand over some power to us within this space. I'm not coming in to shape or flavour or to make you more comfortable with your programming because it doesn't create long-term change.

Ekua recognises the 'powerful impact of just being in them [institutions]' as a Black or Indigenous person, 'just existing, just walking down the street in our body', but says it is also necessary to consider 'the work that we can do against the backdrop of the emotional toil that that takes'. She also wonders 'about the sustainability of us working within those institutions without there being a real overhaul and [wonders] how much the visa can be very temporary':

Having worked within those institutions, the changes that you can make can be incredibly temporary, because often we are not in positions of a great deal of power in terms of longevity of planning, longevity in terms of control. ... It's like we are constantly having to reinvent the battleground that we're fighting on.

Sustainability is also an issue for Liliana:

The development project of this mayor [of Bogotá] is huge because it's the first time there has been a little bit of affirmative action. To have an article in that document that says that ethnic groups have the right in Bogotá to have a space, to have the their own voices, to sit at the table, to agree budgets with the authorities of the city – that's huge. But it has happened before that when people gain something, then somebody else gets into the city government and everything is erased. We have experienced that and it is very hard when you have worked for years to gain something and then everything is just erased by somebody – just very easy, in a second.

And insofar as working with institutions also means addressing audiences beyond Black and Indigenous communities, there are also potential problems to be managed:

SUANDI: We are brave when we step out and we're brave when we go to seminars and conferences and pitch our work, because the eyes that are assessing it do not look like our eyes. [But] I can't give out the energy to a white audience that might be offended by it [my work], that is not my job. I'm not going to defend my work to a white audience because I think we've been forced into a defensive position for far too long as a Black community – and I mean that in the global sense of the word – and we do not have to apologise anymore.

PART I

ART AND ANTI-RACISM IN THE NATION

1

Unveiling Racialised Difference in Colombia

Insights from Artists and Artistic Practices

Peter Wade, Mara Viveros Vigoya, Carlos Correa Angulo, Rossana Alarcón and Liliana Angulo Cortés

INTRODUCTION

In this chapter we analyse how racialised differences have been represented in artistic practice in Colombia, as well as the relationships between Black, brown and Indigenous artists and the art world. The first two sections of the chapter begin with a brief look at the colonial period and focus on the nineteenth century and the first half of the twentieth: for these periods we address the representation and participation of Black and Indigenous people. We take examples from visual arts and literature – plus music and dance for the early to mid twentieth century – as realms in which racial difference featured in readily identifiable ways. We show how white and mestizo artists tended to represent racialised subalterns in ways tinged with 'primitivism' and paternalism – although some displayed socialist sympathies in depictions of social inequality, in which such subalterns appeared as oppressed workers, without racism coming into clear view as a social issue.[1] However, by the 1930s and 40s, Black artists and writers were using their practice to critique social inequalities in which racism was identified as an important component. In the third section of the chapter, we turn our attention entirely to Black art practice – primarily music and visual arts, but also touching on oral literature and film – and we analyse its increasing politicisation from mid

---

[1] 'Primitivism' here refers to an international but Eurocentric artistic trend dating from the late nineteenth century that aesthetically idealised and romanticised people and places – usually non-Western – deemed 'primitive', that is, simple, unsophisticated and pertaining to a supposedly pre-modern time (Price 2001). In Colombian national histories of art, the term has a more restricted meaning and refers to an artistic trend of the 1960s to 1980s.

century, which was linked to international currents such as Négritude and Black Power. Also important was the burgeoning Black social movement in the country, which had incipient expressions in the late 1960s and gathered strength with Colombia's 1991 constitutional reform and multiculturalist turn. The fourth section of the chapter focuses on the period since 2000 and explores the work of the Colombian artists – mostly but not exclusively Black – who collaborated with us in the CARLA (Cultures of Anti-Racism in Latin America) project; our aim is to show how their diverse art practices have addressed racism in increasingly direct ways.[2]

FROM COLONIAL NEW GRANADA TO TWENTIETH-CENTURY COLOMBIA

The focus of this section is on the way racial difference figured in the Colombian art world from the creation of the new republic in 1810 until the mid twentieth century, that is, during the long and varied nation-building processes that included the early establishment of key national institutions and a later period of modernising industrialisation and national integration. First, however, we briefly address the colonial antecedents of the relationship between racial difference and art (González 2003).

If we look at visual arts, colonial artists were a rather heterogeneous group that included a small elite – who tended to be whiter – and a mass of artisans who did more routine work and tended to have more Indigenous and Black ancestry (Solano D. and Flórez Bolívar 2012). Both types of artists worked mostly for the Church – creating paintings, carvings, sculptures – although some also did work (mostly portraits) for private clients. The artistic professions were regulated by guilds, and although Black, Indigenous and mestizo artists were members of artists' guilds and confraternities (Rivas Pérez 2021), the status and prestige of these organisations were associated with the socio-racial quality of their members. Therefore, in the Spanish colonies there were certain tendencies towards 'whitening' in that artists with obvious Black and Indigenous ancestry might try to downplay or hide their socio-racial origins (Deans-Smith 2009). However, some mestizo artists were part of the elite, such as the

---

[2] This chapter's sections reflect its multiple authorship. The first section was led by Wade; the second by Wade and Viveros; the third by Viveros; and the fourth by Correa and Alarcón. All four sections were shaped by the incisive revisions suggested by Angulo Cortés.

Mexican painter Juan Patricio Morlete Ruiz – famous for his *casta* pictures, depicting diverse racially mixed types (*castas*) in the colony – who was a member of the Academia de San Carlos in New Spain. In New Granada (now Colombia), the well-known painter Salvador Rizo Blanco, a key member of the Expedición Botánica (1783–1816) and right-hand man of its director José Celestino Mutis, was of African descent ('*pardo*' or brown) and was in charge of purchasing enslaved people for the expedition.[3]

After independence, the emphasis of elites in Colombia, as in other Latin American nations, was on establishing a national identity that could not only claim a degree of individuality and distinction – and political sovereignty – on the regional and global stage, but also demonstrate that it was moving towards the modernity associated with the world's leading powers in Western Europe and North America. This created a certain contradiction in racial terms: 'modernity' as defined in the Eurocentric perspective of the time was associated with whiteness; whereas the nation's distinctiveness arguably lay in its racially heterogeneous population, largely composed of Black, Indigenous and mestizo peoples who were defined as inferior by Eurocentric ideas steeped in scientific racism (Appelbaum, Macpherson and Rosemblatt 2003; Gotkowitz 2011; Leal and Langebaek 2010; Pérez Vejo and Yankelevich 2017; Stepan 1982).

Part of this contradiction can be seen if we explore the visual art of the period: for example, the illustrations produced for the Comisión Corográfica, a scientific expedition that, in the 1850s, set out to take stock of the human and natural resources of the young nation of New Granada under the leadership of the Italian-born geographer Agustín Codazzi. Between 1850 and 1853, the Commission's three artists produced more than 170 illustrations, of which two-thirds were done by the Colombian artist Manuel María Paz.[4]

The images they produced were varied but were generally in the style that scholars have labelled *costumbrista*, romantic and sometimes

---

[3] The Botanical Expedition aimed to inventory the natural resources of New Granada. The case of Rizo emerges from a revisionist history of the expedition, product of the project 'Un caso de reparación. Un proyecto de revisión histórica y humanidades digitales' directed by Liliana Angulo Cortés for the Museo de Antioquia, 2015–2016. See http://uncasodereparacion.altervista.org/ and www.youtube.com/live/yn71alfO64Q?si=sNX9qIc3P3OEtbE2.

[4] Paz was preceded by Carmelo Fernández, from Venezuela, and, in 1852–1853, by the Englishman Henry Price. 151 of the illustrations are preserved in the National Library of Colombia: https://bibliotecanacional.gov.co/es-co/colecciones/grafica/publicacion/comisi%C3%B3n-corogr%C3%A1fica.

dramatic, which was in keeping with the travel literature of the time (Acevedo Latorre, Saffray and André 1968; Muñoz Arbeláez 2010; Saffray 1948; Wiener et al. 1884).[5] The majority of illustrations in the travel literature were crafted by artists who had never been to the country and who worked on travellers' notes. But some travellers – among them the Spaniard José María Gutiérrez de Alba (2012) and the German Alexander Von Humboldt (1810) – and many Colombian artists, including the Commission's artists, worked in the field and this informed their *costumbrista* emphasis on local life, generating many opportunities to represent racial diversity.[6] This was done in various ways.

For example, Ramón Torres Méndez (1809–1885) was a prolific painter who also taught the key Commission artist Manuel María Paz. He is usually classified as *costumbrista*, due to his focus on the working-class poor, both rural and urban, mainly in Bogotá. But his images are notable for the light colour of his subjects' skin and their often European-looking features. Only rarely does he show Black people: for example, *Champán en el Río Magdalena* (Raft on the River Magdalena, 1860) shows the *bogas* (boatmen) as clearly Black.[7] Although his painting of *Indios pescadores del Funza* ('Indian' Fishermen of Funza) is the only one of sixty-three pictures to use explicitly racialised terminology in its title, his *Mujer campesina de Gachetá en viaje* (Peasant Woman from Gachetá on a Journey, 1860) shows a woman with markedly Indigenous features, while in his *Jinetes de la ciudad y del campo* (City and Country Horse Riders, 1860), the racialised dimensions of class difference are clearly visible.[8]

In contrast, among the 480 images created by José María Gutiérrez de Alba (1822–1897), some thirty-five use the word *indio* in the title and five the word *negro*. Many more show regional scenes that include Black

---

[5] *Costumbrismo* is a term of European origin, referring to art, above all Latin American art, that describes local, everyday customs and lifeways, often in ways tinged with romanticism and paternalism.

[6] Images from Gutiérrez de Alba's manuscript *Impresiones de un viaje a América, 1870–1884* can be found at https://babel.banrepcultural.org/digital/collection/p17054coll16/search. For images from Humboldt's book, see https://nrs.harvard.edu/urn-3:DOAK.RESLIB:27417444.

[7] Ramón Torres Méndez, *Champán en el Río Magdalena (Colombia)*, aquatint 26 × 33 cm, colour: Banco de la República, Bogotá. https://colecciones.banrepcultural.org/document/coleccion/63a069235d96b8790f36dda5.

[8] These images, from his *Album de cuadros de costumbres* (Paris: A. De la Rue, 1860), can be seen at https://archivobogota.secretariageneral.gov.co/noticias/accede-al-importante-album-dibujos-sobre-costumbres-colombianas.

people, such as *Lavanderas de Nóvita, Chocó, Cauca* (Washerwomen of Nóvita, Chocó, Cauca, 1875) – actually copied from *Vista de una calle de Nóvita* (View of a Street in Nóvita, 1853) by Manuel María Paz, the Comisión Corográfica artist (see Figure 1.1). The same pattern applies to the 151 images from the Comisión Corográfica that have been archived: thirty-three images show Indigenous, Black and mestizo people, of which eight have titles with the word 'mestizo'; twenty-two have the word *indio*; four have a word that explicitly refers to Blackness (*negro, mulato, zambo, africano*); and five are local scenes prominently featuring Black people, for example, *Vista de una calle de Quibdó* (View of a Street in Quibdó, 1853) and *La marimba, instrumento popular: Provincia de Barbacoas* (The Marimba, Popular Instrument: Province of Barbacoas, 1853).

Three things stand out in these images. First, Indigeneity is a much more prevalent theme than Blackness, doubtless because at that time Indigenous people outnumbered Black people (Smith 1966), but also because Black people were seen as less important in the nation (Wade 2010b). Second, both Indigenous and Black people are generally portrayed as poor and barefoot, usually in rural settings, an image that was strongly reinforced by the Commission's texts, which established a clear socio-racial hierarchy associating whiteness with civilisation and non-whiteness with backwardness and primitiveness. Third, the images reflect the strong link between race and region that the Comisión Corográfica created, for example by depicting Black people as located mostly in the Pacific region (Appelbaum 2016; Restrepo 1999). Overall, while Blackness and Indigeneity are by no means always invisible in these images, they are portrayed in stock and limited ways and there is no sense of a challenge to racial hierarchies.

Turning briefly to literature, we can see parallel trends. The paternalist way Black people were portrayed in Jorge Isaac's romantic novel *María* (1867), set in pre-abolition New Granada, is often seen as *costumbrista*. Although slavery as an institution is decried in the novel, as it was in many Latin American nineteenth-century anti-slavery novels (Jackson 1975), enslaved people are portrayed as contented, well treated and passive. (This kind of romantic *costumbrismo* is an enduring feature: it appears as late as 1929 in Tomás Carrasquilla's *La marquesa de Yolombó*, set in colonial New Granada.)

Quite different from the mainstream work of white writers was the poetry of the Afro-Colombian Candelario Obeso (1849–1884), which presented the worldview of the racialised subaltern classes of Colombia's

FIGURE 1.1 *Lavanderas de Nóvita, Chocó, Cauca* (Washerwomen of Nóvita, Chocó, Cauca), painting by José María Gutiérrez de Alba, 1875 (Colección de Archivos Especiales, Biblioteca Virtual de la Red de Bibliotecas del Banco de la República).

Caribbean coastal region, where Obeso was born and raised. In 1866, Obeso moved from his birthplace, Mompox, to study in Bogotá, where he joined the local literary circles; he also took up various jobs back in his native region, and in Panama and France. Although it had little impact at the time, the work that later became his best known, *Cantos populares de mi tierra* (Popular Songs from My Land, 1977 [1877]), established the beginnings of a Black poetic tradition in Colombia, pre-dating the better-known poetry associated with Hispanic-Caribbean poets such as Nicolás Guillen (Prescott 1985). George Palacios (2010) argues that Obeso founded a 'minor literature', in which he challenged the dominant forms of Spanish language, attempting to convey the characteristic accent and modes of speech of the Black and mestizo inhabitants of his native region, as well as their everyday experiences. His poetry contested the social exclusion that they and he faced in Colombia, where the dominant imaginary represented Bogotá as 'the Athens of South America', which safeguarded 'the purity of the language', the 'correctness' of diction and the 'enlightened vocation' of its rulers, poets and orators (Jáuregui 1999: 574), and which depicted Obeso's home turf as a backward territory (Múnera 1998). Obeso's poetic mission claimed a legitimate space in the nation for Black people, thus subverting and reformulating the national project in ways that prefigure anti-racism.

MID TWENTIETH-CENTURY COLOMBIA: NATION AND RACIAL DIVERSITY

The 1930s and 1940s were marked by political projects of national integration and modernisation – based on expanding education and extending the reach of the state into the rural and urban working classes – and a corresponding artistic nationalism (Bushnell 1993; Muñoz-Rojas 2022; Universidad Nacional de Colombia 1984; Uribe Celis 1992). Underlying these political projects was the ideology of *mestizaje* (racial and cultural mixture), according to which Black and Indigenous peoples would gradually disappear into a mestizo majority. However, in this period, intellectual and cultural processes made visible what the ideology of *mestizaje* had hidden until then: the Indigenous and, especially, the Black presence in Colombian dance, literature, music and popular culture (reified as 'folklore' by scholars). There emerged a new socio-cultural consciousness marked by what is known as *indigenismo*, *negrismo* and Négritude, and various artistic-cultural expressions played an important role in redefining the meanings of what it meant to be Latin American, Black and Afro-Colombian, and in beginning to challenge racism.[9]

This period of national integration was expressed partly in artistic *indigenismo*, although never at the levels seen in Mexico and Peru. This artistic trend was driven almost entirely by white and mestizo intellectuals and artists, among whom challenging racism was not a priority. At this time, there was little Indigenous counterpart to the emergence of a cohort of Black intellectuals that, as we will describe, helped drive a parallel current of Négritude/*negrismo*, elements of which were alive to racial injustice.

Continuing with our focus on the visual arts, an example of *indigenismo* was the group Los Bachué, formed in 1930 by a group of left-leaning white and mestizo artists and writers (Troyan 2008).[10] The name alluded to the movement's aspiration to represent Indigenous people and referred to a Chibcha goddess who had been depicted in a 1925 sculpture by Rómulo Rozo (1899–1964), a Colombian artist who became a Mexican national (Troyan 2008). A founding figure of the group was Luis Alberto Acuña Tapias (1904–1993), who produced paintings of ancient and mythical Indigenous figures, thus locating Indigeneity as Other and belonging to the past. Contributing to this sense of Otherness was the fact that Acuña sometimes depicted Indigenous people naked – for example, in his *Bachué* (1937) and *Chibchakun, el que sostiene la tierra sobre sus hombros* (Chibchakun, He Who Holds the Earth on His Shoulders, 1937).[11] Influenced by Mexican muralists, the Bachué group sought an inclusive national identity based on Latin American, not European, realities, while their leftist ideals of

---

[9] The terms *indigenismo/indigenista* were coined in the 1930s by a Mexican intellectual (Giraudo 2017). They refer to an intellectual, artistic and political current in Latin America that valorised – and according to some, romanticised – a nation's Indigenous heritage and aims to protect its Indigenous populations, while also guiding them towards assimilation (Giraudo and Lewis 2012). *Negrismo* is a term coined by scholars to describe a mainly literary movement promoted from the 1920s, first by white Spanish Caribbean writers who valorised (and arguably appropriated) Afro themes and later by Black writers from the region (Badiane 2010). Négritude was the name chosen by three Black students from France's colonies who founded a literary, philosophical and political movement in 1920s Paris: Aimé Césaire (from Martinique), Léon Damas (Guiana) and Léopold Senghor (Senegal). Different from *negrismo*, this movement expressed a radical critique of colonialism and racism, rethinking Black identity in pan-African terms.

[10] For more information on this group, see http://proyectobachue.org/ and especially http://proyectobachue.org/wp-content/uploads/2016/10/bachue-pagina-web.pdf.

[11] Some of his works can be viewed online at www.diccionariodecolombia.expert/diccionario-enciclopedico/acuna-tapias-luis-alberto/.

FIGURE 1.2 *La república*, mural by Pedro Nel Gómez, 1937 (© Fundación Casa Museo Pedro Nel Gómez, by permission).

social justice underpinned support for Indigenous and working-class struggles. The search for authentic roots for the nation embraced not only Indigenous peoples but also peasant and mestizo populations – as imagined by the artists – for example, the sculptures *Anciana campesina con pañolón (rasgos indígenas)* (Old Peasant Woman with Headscarf [Indigenous Features], undated) and *Muchacha campesina* (Peasant Girl, 1950), both by Josefina Albarracín. While *indigenismo* was a predominant influence for the Bachué artists, there were a few representations of Black subjects: for example, the sculptor Hena Rodríguez produced *Cabeza de negra* (Black Woman's Head, 1945).

Cultural *indigenismo* was an influence on Pedro Nel Gómez (1899–1994), a visual artist renowned for his huge murals inspired by Mexican muralism and socialist thought (Gómez 2013). For example, in his vast mural *La república* (1937, 8 × 11 metres), adorning an entire wall of the Council Chamber in Medellín's city hall, now the Museo de Antioquia, motherhood is represented by an Indigenous woman carrying her child (see Figure 1.2). The influence of the Mexican muralists on Gómez was evident in his attention to poverty, exploitation and displacement, with some attention to mining and its domination by foreign capital. But there is little direct attention to racial difference. The workers, miners and peasants he portrays in *La república* are phenotypically not very different, in a racialised sense, from the managers and professionals in the painting; the main difference is that the former categories are often shown semi-clothed or naked (like some of Acuña's Indigenous figures), while the latter wear suits.

The same cannot be said of the work of another muralist, Ignacio Gómez Jaramillo (1910–1970), who, like Pedro Nel Gómez, was influenced by

Mexican muralism and socialism. Commissioned to paint murals to decorate the National Capitol building in Bogotá, he created *La liberación de los esclavos* (The Freeing of the Slaves, 1938) and *La insurrección de los comuneros* (The Rebellion of the Commoners, 1938), both referring to themes of social justice and featuring brown and Indigenous figures; *La liberación* also features many Black people, mostly semi-naked (Solano Roa 2013). Conservative elements in Colombia were highly critical of the murals of both Gómez Jaramillo and Nel Gómez for their depiction of nudity and for their supposed lack of artistic value, but also for their socialist tendencies. It is not clear to what extent the murals' reference to the racialised character of social injustice was an element in the conservative reaction. But murals by Gómez Jaramillo were plastered over in 1948 and some of those by Nel Gómez covered with curtains in 1950, to be uncovered only in the late 1950s when the political context was more liberal.

If racial injustice was not a theme in *indigenismo* and was of uncertain status in these murals, it got more of an airing by the Black artists of this period – mainly writers, dancers and musicians. However, this airing was an ambivalent part of a Colombian version of the Spanish Caribbean literary *negrismo*, which emerged at this time, the product of two processes. The first was the growing number of Black intellectuals from the Caribbean and Pacific coastal regions and the Cauca Valley, many of whom migrated to the big cities for education. The second trend was the often paternalistic acceptance by white and mestizo intellectuals of elements of Black artistic expression, which were treated in a romanticised manner that aligned with *negrismo* and international trends in artistic primitivism (Price 2001). Much of this was reflected in the national popularity of musical styles associated with the Caribbean coastal region, such as *cumbia* and *porro*, which, despite being subject to some cultural whitening as they became commercialised, did not entirely lose the Black symbolism that was, in fact, central to their popular appeal (Wade 2000).

Some of the romantic and objectifying tendencies associated with *negrismo* were also evident in visual art, where primitivist perspectives were also prominent. *Mulata cartagenera* (Mulatta from Cartagena, 1940) by the painter Enrique Grau (1920–2004, born in Panama) is a realistic depiction of a sexualised Black woman, although it is not typical of his work.[12] The painting's realism and subject matter made an impact and it

---

[12] For example, compare Grau's painting of the Afro-Colombian artist, Delia Zapata Olivella: www.facebook.com/101428403525343 1/posts/delia-un-retrato-de-enrique-grau-para-su-querida-amiga-delia-zapata-olivella/4394210853927382/.

received a mention at the Primer Salón Nacional de Artistas Colombianos (First National Colombian Artists' Salon) in 1940, an achievement for a Caribbean painter realistically depicting a Black woman. The painting raised the profile of Blackness as a vibrant element in the nation. However, in terms of combating racism, it can be argued that this type of painting reproduced stereotypically sexualised images of Black women.

In the realm of literature, some Black writers from both coastal regions eschewed the paternalism and primitivism associated with *negrismo*. Writers from the Pacific coast region included Arnoldo Palacios (1924–2015), born and raised in the province of Chocó, who moved to France in 1949 and lived there until his death. In the novel *Las estrellas son negras* (The Stars are Black, 2010 [1949]), set in Quibdó, the provincial capital of Chocó, he described the psychological damage caused by racism and, unusually for the time, established a direct correlation between US and Colombian forms of racism (Pisano 2012: 95). The novel and its powerful social critique were largely ignored in Colombia until the Ministry of Culture published a third edition in 1998. Something similar happened with Carlos Arturo Truque (1927–1970), also from Chocó, who, in short stories written in the 1950s, used a social realist style to present the lived realities of the racialised subaltern classes of his region (Truque 1993). Truque was also mostly ignored until the 1990s. In the 1950s, too, the Chocoano poet Hugo Salazar Valdés (1922–1997) was appointed director of the magazine of the Teatro Colón, deputy director of the National Library and head of the cultural outreach programme of the Ministry of Education. Laurence Prescott (2007: 145) states that Salazar's poems are a testimony to 'the struggle of the Blacks of the Pacific for a dignified life within Colombian society'.

Writers from the Caribbean coastal region had a greater impact; in the 1960s this was amplified by the enormous influence of Gabriel García Márquez, whose writings made famous a magical realist image of the region, even if this muted its racial Blackness (Bryan 1988). Blackness was more evident in the poetry of Jorge Artel (1909–1994), who was born in Cartagena and continued to be based in the region until his death, apart from travels in the Americas between 1949 and 1971; in 1940 he published *Tambores en la noche* (Drums in the Night). However, Jacques Gilard (1986: 41) characterised his poetry as displaying a 'very conventional *negrismo*': by making frequent references to music and dance, he evoked a sensual rhythmicity for his native region (Prescott 2000).

Rather different were the siblings Manuel, Delia and Juan Zapata Olivella (1920–2004, 1926–2001 and 1927–2008, respectively), also of

Caribbean coastal origin, who devoted themselves to literature, music, dance, visual arts, activism and party politics for many decades – all supported by cultural and historical research. Manuel and Delia Zapata Olivella radically contested the prevailing version of *mestizaje* as a process of whitening the nation, seeing it instead as a force for real, but as yet unrealised, democracy (Jackson 1988; Viveros Vigoya 2013). They affirmed the value of Black and Indigenous cultures and drew attention to racism in the country. Manuel conducted research on Afro-Colombian culture and *mestizaje* and brought musicians from his native region to Bogotá, but he channelled his efforts mainly through his literary work, which achieved national and international fame. An early example was *Chambacú, corral de negros* (Chambacú, Corral of Blacks, 1967 [1963]), which challenged Cartagena's racist order by giving a socially realist depiction of life from the perspective of Black people in a marginalised neighbourhood in the city (Ortiz 2007).

Meanwhile, Delia published articles in magazines and journals such as *Páginas de Cultura, Colombia Ilustrada, Revista Colombiana de Folclore* and *Revista de Etnomusicología*; she also researched and taught traditional artistic expressions of the Caribbean and Pacific regions at the Instituto Popular de Cultura in Cali (Valderrama 2013), while her dance company, Danzas Folklóricas Colombianas, toured nationally and internationally. Delia's research in what was known as folklore – a category rooted in European traditions in which urban elites studied subaltern rural people (Muñoz-Rojas 2022) – went beyond 'the reification, collection, preservation and classification of traditions and cultural practices of Afro-Colombian peoples', traits characteristic of a *costumbrista*, positivist and romantic vision of folklore research (Valderrama 2013: 271): she sought to make visible the relationship of her work with her African roots and with racial inequalities (Valderrama 2013: 267), even if, at the time, acknowledging African ancestry meant risking a loss of prestige (Prescott 1996: 111).

Art practice, research and anti-racist activism went together in the work of Delia and Manuel. With other Black students living in Bogotá, they participated in the organisation of the Día del Negro (Black People's Day) on 20 June 1943, in solidarity with protests against the lynching of Black trade unionists in Chicago, but also highlighting the lack of freedom and equality of the Black Colombian population. On this occasion, poems by Obeso and Artel were recited and *cumbia* was danced. Manuel was a founding member of the Club Negro (1943) and the Centro de Estudios Afrocolombianos (1947) which, despite being ephemeral, had a great influence on the discussions and debates taking place at the time, linking them to the questions being asked by Black peers in other regions about race, identity and imperialism. At the same time, these organisations were strategic spaces for affirming the place of Afro-Colombian values and cultural manifestations in the national imaginary and for challenging the racism of Colombian society and its image as a potentially inclusive mestizo nation (Pisano 2012; Wade 2016). These Afro-Colombian intellectuals pointed out that the yardstick by which 'racial prejudice' and 'discrimination' were being assessed at the time was misleadingly determined by a comparison with race relations in the segregationist United States; and they deployed notions of equality and democracy that had in fact been advocated by Afro-Colombians since the early days of the republic (Lasso 2007).

The work of constructing Black identity was evident in other research that sought to revalue Afro-Colombian lifeways and led to the emergence of an Afro-Colombian counter-public in which questions of racism and Black/Afro identity were discussed (Valderrama 2018). Folklorists and artists from the Pacific region, such as Mercedes Montaño (1912–1999), Margarita Hurtado (1918–1992) and Teófilo Potes (1917–1975), as well as Lorenzo Miranda (1935–) from Palenque de San Basilio in Colombia's Caribbean region, shared with Delia and Manuel Zapata an interest in researching and promoting Afro-Colombian music, dance and oral traditions, and in using their work to denounce racism in Colombia (Arboleda Quiñónez 2011; Valderrama 2018). This work ran alongside the more academic efforts of Black anthropologists such as Rogerio Velásquez (1908–1965) from Chocó and Aquiles Escalante (1923–2002) from Barranquilla, who began to turn Black communities into a topic of interest for anthropology. Other artists and cultural promoters from the Pacific region, such as the poet Benildo Castillo, the dancer and singer Alicia Camacho Garcés and the musician Petronio Álvarez, made other forms of knowledge visible, channelling them into various artistic genres.

These artists and researchers contributed to the strengthening of Black cultural identity in Colombia. Long before the formal recognition of Afro-Colombians as an ethnic group in the 1991 constitutional reform, their various contributions articulated their understanding of 'folklore' as part of a political struggle to resignify the cultural representation of racialised subaltern groups. Afro-descendant music and dance (recognised as also bearing Indigenous influences) – long seen from a dominant perspective as an object of shame and evidence of racial inferiority and moral inadequacy – was finally being positively recognised as valid cultural expressions, and this was an important achievement for the Afro-descendant community, redefining their existence beyond their physical characterisation.

To summarise thus far: we have shown that artistic reference to racial difference took various forms. In the hands of state agents, it could be allied to projects of cartography and governance; in the hands of white and mixed-race intellectuals, it could have elements of primitivism and paternalism, but could also be aligned with a socialist emphasis on social equality, in which dark-skinned and Indigenous people figured as oppressed workers, without racism itself being identified as a problem; in the hands of Black artists and writers, it could be harnessed to critiques of social injustice in which racism was understood as an integral element.

THE POLITICISATION OF BLACK ARTISTIC PRACTICE

In the second half of the twentieth century, the Afro-Colombian diaspora continued to weave networks and build common spaces around culture, generally in central Andean cities and mainly in Bogotá. From the 1960s onwards, political organisations emerged in communities of Black migrants to the Andean cities, focusing on questions about the 'racial condition' of Black people and 'their participation in the construction of the country' (Arboleda Quiñónez 2011: 162). In 1975, the Primer Encuentro Nacional de la Población Negra Colombiana (First National Meeting of the Colombian Black Population), held in Cali on 21–23 February, brought together 183 delegates from across the country to discuss the political and social problems of people of African descent (Wabgou et al. 2012: 99). This led to initiatives to promote affirmative action in education, denounce racism and defend ethnic rights in the political sphere, which continue to be at the centre of Afro-Colombian organisational processes.

Two years later, the organisers of the Primer Congreso de Cultura Negra de las Américas (First Congress of Black Culture of the Americas), which took place in Cali, Colombia, in 1977, described the conference as undertaking 'a double task in the battle against neo-colonialism: education and politicisation at the same time' (Valero 2020: 48). They sought to promote strategies for awareness-raising and change for Colombian Black communities through cultural practices. While some panels in the Congress discussed the need to decolonise art and aesthetics in order to produce their own cultural forms, others pointed to the lack of Black intellectual and cultural reference points as a manifestation of racism.

During this congress and the subsequent ones in Panama (1980) and São Paulo (1983), Black culture emerged as 'fuel for Négritude as ideology' (Arboleda Quiñónez 2011: 192): that is, as having an eminently political character and being a contested field for the definition of Black identity (Valero 2020).

For Santiago Arboleda Quiñónez (2011), Carlos Valderrama (2013, 2018) and Francisco Flórez Bolívar (2015), the cultural consolidation of this period is what made possible the first organised political expressions of Black culture and identity. This occurred in conversation with events in the United States, where, between 1968 and 1975, African American activists were putting into global circulation concepts such as 'Black power' and 'Black is beautiful', promoting racial pride and the creation of cultural and political institutions around the cultural expressions of Black communities (Arboleda Quiñónez 2011: 158; Laó Montes 2010: 294). This had a great impact on Afro-Colombian youth, who appropriated these concepts to legitimise their positions as political subjects. Referring to an Afro-Colombian cultural renaissance, Arboleda Quiñónez (2011: 206) mentions the example of the 'cultural front of southern Valle [province] and northern Cauca [province]' which, in the late 1970s and the 1980s, held meetings that not only consolidated their relations but also led to the questioning of Eurocentric aesthetic canons that devalued Black cultural and artistic expressions.

During this period, thinkers, artists and cultural promoters came together around local festivals, such as those in Palenque de San Basilio and Tumaco, to showcase Black and Afro-Colombian culture, still considered exotic by mainstream audiences. In 1987, the first Festival of Currulao (a Pacific-region music genre) was held in Tumaco – it still exists today, despite economic limitations – bringing together music, theatre, dance and oral literature, as well as cultural promoters interested in Afro-Colombian artistic production. In the same year, the Green Moon Festival was born on San Andrés Island under the slogan 'a fraternal embrace in the form of race and culture', showcasing the music, cinema, gastronomy and religious and sporting expressions of San Andrés communities and of the Creole culture of the English-speaking Caribbean. A year later, in 1988, the first Encuentro de Literatura Oral del Pacífico Colombiano (Meeting on Oral Literature of the Colombian Pacific) took place in Buenaventura, organised by the poet and writer Alfredo Vanín Romero under the slogan 'So that the people do not lose their memory'. Approaches like these express the emerging awareness of the importance of oral tradition – and, ironically, the need to register it in literary form (see, for example, Vanín and Pedrosa 1994) – as a counter-hegemonic version of official history, or as 'history that does not grow old', in the words of Manuel Zapata Olivella (1983). This perspective allowed the bringing together of 'scattered pieces of Afrodiasporic thought, which allowed people to collate and contrast versions, maintaining their diversity, but above all to elaborate new meanings of the past, the present and the future, based on these other sources of history' (Arboleda Quiñónez 2011: 207).

The reform of the Constitution in 1991 brought with it the recognition of a 'multicultural and pluriethnic' identity for the country and of Black communities as an ethno-cultural group (Political Constitution of Colombia, 1991, Art. 7). In this new context, legislation was also created that addresses culture and ethno-cultural diversity as elements for the achievement of peace: Law 70 of 1993, based on collective ownership of land, a fundamental principle of Black culture in the Colombian Pacific region; a 1993 law establishing a Ministry of Culture to manage state cultural policies; and the General Law of Culture of 1997, which specifies the uses of cultural expressions in cultural policy, including to mitigate violence.

These reforms led to a new inclusion of Afro-Colombian culture, and particularly music, in some spaces of the cultural market. An example is the growing presence in popular music of elements from the Pacific region and the proliferation of groups that have taken up the music of that region, which for a long time, unlike Caribbean music, had been rejected as being linked to primitive atavism and the incapacity to progress (Wade 2000). In recent years, this music has featured in state cultural programmes and policies and is present in events such as the Petronio Álvarez Festival of Pacific Music, which has been held in Cali since 1997, and the Green Moon Festival, which was revived in 2012. At the same time, some musicians have fused the musical legacy of the Pacific, the traditional genres of the Caribbean and the native music of San Andrés with elements of contemporary urban music, creating sonorities that are both global and rooted in local traditions.

The new multicultural policies have sought to mobilise traditional music, including Afro-Pacific music, to combat violence in the country, although ironically 'the emergence of multiculturalism was closely linked to the intensification of violence in the country' (Birenbaum Quintero 2006: 14). However, the display of Afro-Pacific music on state stages in order to 'make our essential affinities prevail over our passing differences' – in the words of President Samper (Birenbaum Quintero 2006: 15) – has demanded its spectacularisation. Consequently, local aesthetic logics have been eclipsed, separating musical practices from their ritual functions, and conditioning their recognition to a certain domestication of their differences in order to affirm what Samper called 'shared characteristics' over and above the ruptures implied by the relations of enslavement and exploitation to which Black populations of this region were subjected.

Another example of this new Afro cultural presence on the national scene is the surprising national recognition in the new millennium of *champeta*, a musical genre from Colombia's Caribbean region, previously stigmatised with racist stereotypes and seen as breaking conventions of propriety (Cunin 2003). Indeed, in 2001, Sony released a CD with a telling title: *La champeta se tomó a Colombia* (Champeta Has Taken Over Colombia).

Afro music, in all its diversity, because of its association with 'escape' or *cimarronería* in the face of Western hegemonic values, has gradually become a resource for political mobilisation that brings together various social causes.[13] Ángel Quintero (2020) argues that the freedom and spontaneity of Afro rhythms and dance, as well as their dialogical and heterogeneous character, can be dissociated from stereotypical imaginaries and used to foment a new type of anti-individualist sociality. We could say that these musical practices deconstruct sense conventions, deploying *sentipensamiento* (feeling-thinking) in an integrated way that is far removed from Eurocentric aesthetic norms that tend to separate feeling from reason. This gives them an anti-racist potential insofar as they allow an embodied and integrated apprehension of the effects of racism and create a sense of community through sharing these music and dance expressions. However, it is worth remembering that this potential can best be developed in relative freedom from the hegemonic discourses of multiculturalism and the neoliberal logic of cultural policies that instrumentalise these musical practices as 'technologies of peace' and make citizens responsible for reducing violence (Ochoa 2003).

Turning to the visual arts, in contrast to what happened in literature, music and dance, it was not until after 1950 that the first representations of Afro-descendants by Afro-descendant artists were produced, marking a transition from being objects to subjects of representation. One of the first Afro-descendant artists to follow this path was the painter Heriberto Cogollo, who was born in Cartagena in 1945 and has lived mostly in

---

[13] *Cimarrones* were enslaved people of African descent who escaped slavery and set up autonomous communities beyond the control of the authorities. The *cimarrón* has become a political symbol of Black resistance.

France since 1966. He was one of the members of the renowned Grupo de Los 15, a group of artists at the School of Fine Arts in Cartagena which, between the 1950s and 1960s, proposed disruptive artistic initiatives in the local art scene.[14] Cogollo, who is no stranger to 'revealing his own identity' and his African roots, inspired by his contact with Europe and North America (Obando Hernández 2018: 104), began in the 1970s to do research on aspects of the body and spirituality that masterfully express the difference between looking at the complexity of the African physical and spiritual body from the outside and from the inside.[15] Despite being a renowned artist with an extensive international career, he was until recently largely unknown in Colombia.

In the new millennium, we find references to the Black presence in the Colombian visual arts in various publications: *Nuestros pintores en París* (Our Painters In Paris) (Mendoza, Gómez Pulido and Jordán 1989), with a chapter devoted to Heriberto Cogollo; *El arte del Caribe colombiano* (Medina 2000); the essay 'La imagen del negro en las colecciones de las instituciones oficiales' (The Image of the Black Person in Official Institutional Collections) by Beatriz González (2003); and the curatorship of the exhibition *Viaje sin mapa: Representaciones afro en el arte contemporáneo colombiano* (Journey without Maps: Afro Representations in Contemporary Colombian Art) by Raúl Cristancho and Mercedes Angola (2006). This exhibition was 'A first approach to the visualisation and positioning of contemporary plastic [arts] production in Colombia' (Cristancho and Angola 2006: 2) and it marked an important milestone in the history of Afro-Colombian art by breaking the silence about Afro-descendant artists and by highlighting how the mainstream politics of representation in modern art have been shaped by the cultural hierarchies of the Colombian socio-racial order. The curators brought together a generation of artists who were beginning to work with a clear awareness of being subjects of their own representation – among them Liliana Angulo Cortés, Fabio Melecio Palacios Prado and Lorena Zúñiga.[16] Liliana Angulo Cortés has explored photography, installation and sculpture, and has worked with archives that reveal the power relations structuring visual representations, territorial control, constructions of masculinities, and the way power is inscribed in the bodies of Black

---

[14] For some of his work, see www.heribertocogollo.com/COGOLLO/Site_officiel_du_peintre_Heriberto_Cogollo.html.

[15] See the paintings on pp. 107–110 of Obando Hernández (2018).

[16] On the first two artists, see Giraldo Escobar (2014) and https://fabiomelecio.wixsite.com/mdmg.

FIGURE 1.3 One of nine images from the series *Negro utópico* by Liliana Angulo Cortés, 2001 (© Liliana Angulo Cortés, by permission).

women. Using exaggeration, parody and exoticising stereotypes, she has denounced the violence to which Afro-descendants are subjected (see Figure 1.3). She has also curated various exhibitions that reflect on the collective and personal meanings of Blackness in Colombia, and on the history of hopes, desires and resistances related to processes of racialisation (Viveros Vigoya 2021).

In 2013, the exhibition ¡Mandinga sea! África en Antioquia (Goddammit! Africa in Antioquia) (Maya Restrepo and Cristancho 2015) continued this exploration of the presence of Afro-descendants in Colombian art, their role and the ways they have been represented and have represented themselves.[17] This exhibition included artists such as Heriberto Cogollo, Fabio Melecio Palacios and Liliana Angulo Cortés. Younger artists also featured, such as Fabio Arboleda, a painter, musician and rapper who draws on the language of graffiti to portray Afro-descendant urban subcultures; Lloreida Ibargüen who, in her work *Trabajo de negro* (Black People's Work), translates mining work to the present day, showing the bodies of construction workers – of which her father was one – for whom 'urban tunnels are substitutes for the old mining tunnels'; and Servando Palacios, who uses self-portraiture and elements of clothing fashion from Afro-Colombian popular culture to explore, embody and question different facets of Black identity (Maya Restrepo and Cristancho 2015).

Likewise, after thirty years of state multiculturalism, changes are beginning to occur for the first time in the audiovisual sector in relation to the Afro-descendant population as a subject for a new generation of women and men who work individually and collectively, contributing to the current dynamism of Afro-descendant artistic practices. Some of the collective processes have been developed by Afro-Colombian organisations. Thus, the Corporación Afrocolombiana de Desarrollo Social y Cultural (Afro-Colombian Corporation for Social and Cultural Development, CARABANTÚ), with the support of the Centro Popular Afrodescendiente (Afro-descendent People's Centre, CEPAFRO), in 2014 developed the Kunta Kinte Ethno-Educational Afro Film and Video Showcase, which in 2016 became the International Kunta Kinte Afro Community Film Festival. Its objective was to create an ethno-educational film forum to critically analyse the situation of human rights, racism and territoriality of Afro-descendant communities, and the implications for community life in Medellín. The showcase also sought to promote reflection on and recovery and strengthening of Afro-Colombians' historical-ancestral roots in all their diversity.

To date, nine editions of Muestra Afro (Afro Showcase), exhibiting Afro-Colombian audiovisual art and film, have taken place, most recently in November 2024.[18] The 2021 version, organised by Bogotá's Cinemateca and the collective Wi Da Monikongo (the Afro-Descendant

---

[17] *Mandinga sea* (roughly, goddammit!) is an idiom that expresses frustration by referring to an African ethnonym.

[18] https://cinematecadebogota.gov.co/actividad/toma-afro-9deg-muestra-afro.

Audiovisual Council of Colombia, created in 2017 and present since 2018 in the Muestra Afro showcases), emphasised the spaces for participation and training that dialogue around Afro-diasporic audiovisual, cinematographic and artistic expressions, in particular Afro-feminist and Afro-futurist filmmaking.[19] These showcases made visible and strengthened the participation of people working in the Afro audiovisual sector in Colombia and articulated this with global Afro-diasporic production.

Through varied tactics and aesthetic techniques, the artistic-cultural processes described in this section have radicalised the constrained form of self-recognition offered by multiculturalism and have renewed the arts scene with projects that seek to combat racism. For Black people, self-representation has meant opposing the imposition of an official history that has ignored or stereotyped their performances and cultural productions; creating, recreating and resignifying Colombian Black history and culture in all its polyphony, based on their own experiences and with their own aesthetic resources; struggling to acquire social agency and political and cultural representativeness within Colombian society; in other words, using their collective creative power to denounce, to criticise and to think of alternative ways of ordering the world. These kinds of projects have blurred the increasingly indiscernible frontiers between activism and art, generating a kind of transterritoriality, in which the creative power of activist practices and the politics of artistic practices with their micropolitical resistance have been mobilised, disrupting the dominant meanings and the sensory organisation of the Colombian socio-racial order.

ARTISTIC PRACTICES AND ANTI-RACIST STRATEGIES

In this section, focusing on the Colombian artists with whom we collaborated in the CARLA project, we analyse how the dominant political climate in Colombia since about 2005 has made the articulation between art and activism more evident and given greater visibility to anti-racist art practice. During this period, a far-right political tendency, promoted by the political forces of Uribism, implemented a form of governance based on maximising 'security' and encouraging foreign capital, which was oriented towards extractivism, corporatism and the privatisation of public goods.[20] This reaffirmed mechanisms of political and legal control, while

---

[19] See https://cinematecadebogota.gov.co/noticia/6a-muestra-afro-mas-alla-costumbres-y-tradiciones and www.widamonikongo.org/.

[20] *Uribismo* is the political current based on the ideological and governmental project of former Colombian president Alvaro Uribe Velez (2002–2010). See López Bayona

also introducing new forms of criminality and violence perpetrated by state actors and their proxies at levels from the regional to the highest spheres of government.

As a consequence, social conditions, in terms of human rights protection and the satisfaction of basic needs, became notoriously precarious in the country. The governance involved new technologies of violence and forms of necropolitics (Mbembe 2003) that multiplied the actors involved in the conflict and resulted in the violent displacement of small-scale agriculturalists from their lands and, to a disproportionate extent, of Afro-descendant and Indigenous populations from their territories, contributing to a deterioration of their living and working conditions in both rural and urban areas (Palacios Valencia and Mondragón 2021; Vergara-Figueroa 2017).

From the 1990s, artistic practices in Colombia had already been undergoing incipient changes in their forms of circulation and expression, their spaces of creation, their social commitment and their strategies for engaging audiences. For example, there was a shift from the private sphere and a search for individual aesthetics to what María Margarita Malagón-Kurka (2010) terms 'indexical art', which engaged overtly with themes of politics, trauma and violence, and involved artistic processes that were more collective, participatory and community-based. Abstraction gave way to everyday references, accessible to wider audiences. The works of Fabio Melecio Palacios and Liliana Angulo Cortés, mentioned earlier, are outstanding examples of how the violent and racialised social order began to be questioned critically on the basis of everyday experience. Overall, the period from 2005 to the early 2020s was notable for its prolific collective artistic projects committed to social transformation, not only of Afro representation in art, but also of the value attached to the artistic practices of Afro and other non-white populations in Colombia.

In this context, which moved from a critical framing of the representation of Blackness to a much broader questioning of racism and the legacies of colonialism in Colombian society, artists from various disciplines, self-identifying mostly as Afro-descendants but some also as mestizos, converged on a series of projects and collaborations characterised by their anti-racist orientation and strong commitment to social justice. Their unifying premise is that artistic practice plays a crucial role in dismantling manifestations of racism in racialised social orders.

(2016). From 2022, with the arrival of the new president, Gustavo Petro, a left-wing government started implementing new policies to reverse the effects of previous right-wing political projects.

Furthermore, these artists pose questions to audiences about Afro otherness in Colombia, no longer only from the location of the rural Black community but also from urban contexts.

One example of this collaboration around anti-racist artistic work is Colectivo Aguaturbia, consisting of Afro-descendant artists and cultural agents. In 2016, this collective organised an encounter of artistic practices under the title IRA (Imaginación Radical Afro), which brought together visual arts, animation, audiovisual production and performances in the city of Bogotá. The Aguaturbia collective expanded the initiative proposed by the *Viaje sin mapa* exhibition (see previous section) in that it not only sought to bring together issues of Afro representation in art and culture in Colombia, but also proposed ideas for organised anti-racist actions, drawing on Afro artistic networks, which aimed to transform art spaces for Black people in urban contexts.[21] Artists such as Wilson Borja, Loreta Meneses, Laura Asprilla, Paola Lucumí, Liliana Angulo Cortés, Leonardo Rua and Natalia Mosquera, among others, affirmed the strategy of 'imagining' other ways of being for Afro people in spaces, such as Bogotá, where the white–mestizo social configuration consigned Afro people symbolically to the place of eternal outsider.

The anti-racist artistic practices we will discuss here include Black poetry, Black popular music, performance and 'living arts', contemporary Afro dance, illustration, photography, visual arts, audiovisual production and works based on archival activism and genealogical research.[22] Although their aesthetic languages and artistic disciplines are diverse, the anti-racist strategies employed by them can be analysed in terms of three overlapping and intertwined pathways: subversion, irruption and engaging with publics to produce emotional and affective reactions.[23]

In relation to the first strategy of subversion, Benjamin Barber (2011: 110) observes that some analyses of art conceive of it as 'oppositional, subversive to power, to the conventional order and its paradigms'. Although we understand that art can also be aligned to regimes of power, the character of the artistic practices among the artists that we review here is

---

[21] See www.digitalexhibitions.manchester.ac.uk/s/carla-en/page/agua-turbia; see also Aguaturbia's Instagram site: search for colectivo_aguaturbia.

[22] According to Inma Garín Martínez (2018: 5), the 'living arts' designate performative arts events that bring together characteristics such as direct artist–audience contact, social target, questioning of the concept of art, multisensoriality, research and unconventional venues. Living arts include but go beyond traditional performative art practices, drawing on a wider range of practices and disciplines (e.g. architecture, anthropology) and seeking to challenge standard paradigms.

[23] On engaging publics, see Correa Angulo and Alarcón Velásquez (2024).

subversive, as it is intentionally focused on constructing aesthetics that destabilise stereotypes about Afro people and question the racial order in relation to narratives of national identity, constructions of beauty, the criminalisation of social protest, and the racialised effects of the armed conflict. These works employ subversion around representations of the Afro body by highlighting the physical and symbolic violence that results in its erasure from history, its violent elimination and its exoticisation and sexualisation. Often a vital spur to wanting to be subversive is feeling *inconforme*, literally being dissatisfied, but more widely experiencing a sense of 'non-conformity' and being at odds with prevailing trends, which acts as a creative input. As Frantz Fanon (1986) famously observed, in a racist society Black people frequently experience their bodies as a location for this sense of being at odds: the affective traction produced by an artistic focus on the body is thus especially powerful. Working through and on the Black body and the strictures to which it is subject can produce strong resonances in audiences who may also have experienced their bodies as sites of (racialised) dislocation.

An example of this is offered by the choreographer Rafael Palacios, who founded the Afro-contemporary dance company Sankofa Danzafro in 1997:[24]

What led me to create Sankofa was inconformity with the way dances of Afro origin were represented in Colombia. Especially in the National Folkloric Ballet. I was dissatisfied with the sexualised and exoticised representation of the dances of Afro communities and decided to look for my own language, one that would show Afro dances in their dignity and knowledge (Rafael Palacios, personal communication, November 2020).

More recently, Sankofa Danzafro has been increasingly oriented in an explicitly anti-racist direction, blurring the frontiers between corporeal and intellectual research, training and choreographic creation (see Chapter 4). The company has elaborated a dance narrative and a sensory experience that surprises, disrupts, affects and sometimes shocks in order to destabilise a single, crystallised narrative of Blackness and challenge complacent images of 'beautiful and erotic dancing Black bodies'. As Palacios says, in Sankofa's work the bodies occupy the stage not only to be seen, but also to be heard – in ways that question the racist scaffolding of the society in which they live.

---

[24] See www.digitalexhibitions.manchester.ac.uk/s/carla-en/page/sankofa and https://bienaldanzacali.com/companias/sankofa-danzafro/.

Margarita Ariza Aguilar, who works with visual arts, performance and live arts, expresses a similar inconformity with regard to how the racial order pervades the family sphere. This results in an everyday racism that, while not producing effects as violent as the murder and displacement of Black (and Indigenous) people, generates the intimate violence of internalised racism (Hordge-Freeman 2015; Moreno Figueroa 2010; Pyke 2010). Ariza's 2010 project *Blanco porcelana* (Porcelain White) challenged the everyday norms of beauty, expressed within the family, that valued the whitest phenotypes, encouraged the use of cosmetics that promised *el tono perfecto* (the perfect tone) and instilled values such as *prudencia* (prudence) in young women (see Figure 1.4).[25]

When my son was born, I received some of the cards that were given in my family to welcome newborns. These cards said things like 'he didn't come out very white ...' and things like that. At that moment, I felt uncomfortable and I began to see how unhappy I felt with all those beauty practices and all the socialisation I had been subjected to in my family to look and be whiter. A whiteness that I was never going to achieve, no matter how hard I tried. That is how the art project *Blanco porcelana* was born, which questions the aspiration to achieve whiteness and the everyday forms of racism that come from the legacies of colonial origin that we have in our families and that are then reproduced throughout our society (Margarita Ariza Aguilar, personal communication, April 2021).

Yeison Riascos, an artist from Buenaventura who works with photography and drawing, also makes reference to inconformity, this time in relation to the articulation between the everyday spheres of Afro identities, the racialised order and its relation to much more deadly racialised violence. His photographic work *Descendimientos* (Descents, 2014) concerns twelve young Black men from Buenaventura on the Pacific coast who were massacred with impunity by paramilitaries in 2012 and were given little public recognition (see Figure 1.5).[26] Riascos says:

My inconformity with this oblivion led me and my friends who posed for these photographs to recreate *Descendimientos*. Here [in Buenaventura] violent deaths have become a daily occurrence. We still can't talk about that here, but I felt dissatisfied and that's why this is not only a denunciation by me, but also by those who posed for the work. We knew it could have been any one of us.[27]

[25] On *Blanco porcelana*, see Ariza (2015), available at https://issuu.com/margaritaarizaaguilar/docs/bp-jun29, and https://blancoporcelana.wordpress.com/.
[26] https://baudoap.com/cobertura/los12depuntadeleste/; see also www.digitalexhibitions.manchester.ac.uk/s/carla-en/page/yeison-riascos.
[27] Yeison Riascos, online conversation, 'Racismo y Fotografía', CARLA, 9 September 2021, https://youtu.be/Nwwoo7yxyvE?si=-pBlaziwNkmdPlxQ.

FIGURE 1.4 Drawing from *Blanco porcelana* by Margarita Ariza Aguilar, 2010 (© Margarita Ariza Aguilar, by permission).

The artistic practices of Rafael Palacios, Margarita Ariza Aguilar and Yeison Riascos constitute a subversive anti-racism because they challenge different facets of the racial formation that make them feel *inconforme*. Palacios develops a narrative language in dance that combats stereotypes

FIGURE 1.5 Photo from the series *Descendimientos* by Yeison Riascos, 2014 (© Yeison Riascos, by permission).

using an Afro-centred aesthetic and recovers the knowledge embodied in the dances of Afro communities in Colombia. He critically reviews the daily expressions of racism faced by young Afro-Colombians in Medellín, in the realm of dance and the wider society. His works *La ciudad de los otros* (The City of the Others, 2010), *La mentira complaciente* (The Complacent Lie, 2017) and *Detrás del sur: Danzas para Manuel* (Behind the South: Dances for Manuel, 2021) create intersections between anti-racism, the affirmation of identity and Afro-referentiality through narratives that push audiences to question racialised stereotypes of Black dancing bodies, while the physical and sensory experience of the performance aesthetics lends an affective intensity to this questioning. In the same way, Yeison Riascos with his works *Descendimientos* and *Rostros divinos* (Divine Faces, 2012) seeks to decentre colonial representations of Judeo-Christian religiosity, materialising such representations in Afro bodies in order to weaken the Western imaginary of religiosity and whiteness and to make visible the marginalisation of Afro communities in ecclesiastical contexts. And finally, Margarita Ariza, with her project *Blanco porcelana*, interrogates more subtle and insidious manifestations of racism involved in the representation of whiteness in family contexts, while her later project *Black Enough?* (2016) explores subtle racism in the way presidential leaders have been represented in Colombia.[28] The common intention is to question audiences about their own racialisation in conditions of privilege or disadvantage.

The second pathway – that of irruption – may also be spurred by feeling *inconforme*, but it takes a specific form. The works of the Afro-Colombian poet Pedro Blas Julio Romero and the Afro-feminist poet Ashanti Dinah Orozco, from Cartagena and Barranquilla respectively, are committed to speaking from a place of enunciation informed by Afro epistemologies, challenging the field of poetic production where Afro referents are seen as 'second-order'. Their anti-racist approach consists of breaking – irrupting – into a literary narrative that omits non-Western references to the motifs of world literature and that creates a profound individualisation of creativity and an exhausting anguish for individual participants disenchanted with their time. The irruption of these Afro poetics creates a pathway towards a 'contemporary critical debate on the analysis of a textuality unprecedented in terms of its artistic and political

---

[28] *Black Enough?* concerns the history and legacy of Juan José Nieto (1804–1866), the only Black president of Colombia, who has been sidelined in Colombian history and whose appearance has been whitened in portraits. See www.digitalexhibitions.manchester.ac.uk/s/carla-en/page/margarita-ariza and https://adaariza.wordpress.com/2019/11/14/black-enough/.

significance, which represents a new place of transnational enunciation' (Maglia, Rocha Vivas and Duchesne Winter 2015: 1). Both writers use poetic language and allusive imagery to circumvent literal-minded rational readings and engage readers on a subliminal plane, generating emotive responses with affective intensity sharpened by the irruptive quality of their imagery. Affect can be traced by attending to the intensity and the rhythm of the poetic discourse (Knudsen and Stage 2015) that generates images rooted in the Afro-religious world. Pedro Blas enriches his poetic universe with images such as 'el diablo piel de abdomen de salamanquesa' (devil with gecko-belly skin) and 'Muchacha de las aguas, Gimaní' (water-girl of Gimaní), which recreate different aspects of the working-class Black neighbourhood of Getsemaní in Cartagena (see Figure 1.6).²⁹ The combination of Afro-religious references and allusions to the history and present of the neighbourhood allow him to raise a voice against cultural appropriation, gentrification and the chiaroscuro of heritage policies, and the continuing presence of coloniality in local spaces and their racial conformations.

Similarly, Ashanti Dinah constructs a strong poetic universe framed by references to Yoruba and Afro-Cuban religiosities.³⁰ Questions of meaning, the place of existence and communion with the cosmos – archetypal tropes in world literature – are addressed through highlighting intimate relationships with ancestors and the dead, communion with nature and its role as a messenger of the ancestors, and an everyday rituality expressing an ecological philosophy that fuses time and space into a continuum and blurs the boundaries between the human and the non-human.

These strategies of irruption can also be found in works of 'artivism' (artistic activism). Examples include the works of graphic artist Wilson Borja such as *Color piel* (Skin Colour, 2008), *Terato* (Monster, 2012), *Muestra afro* (Afro Showcase, 2018), *Reparaciones* (Reparations, 2022) and his illustrations for the poems of Ashanti Dinah (2022), all of which challenge the regime of visuality and representation of the Afro in the field of animation and illustration.³¹ Irruption also characterises what might

---

[29] See the collection *Obra Poética* (published by Universidad de Cartagena, 2009; also published in 2010 by the Banco de la República as part of their Biblioteca Afrocolombiana collection). See also an interview with Julio Romero at www.digitalexhibitions.manchester.ac.uk/s/carla-en/page/pedro-blas and information about Hanna Ramírez at www.digitalexhibitions.manchester.ac.uk/s/carla-en/page/hanna-ramirez.

[30] See www.digitalexhibitions.manchester.ac.uk/s/carla-en/page/ashanti-dinah-poems.

[31] See https://wilsonborja.com/projects; www.digitalexhibitions.manchester.ac.uk/s/carla-en/page/wilson-borja; and Phoebe Hopson, Wilson Borja: Artivismo – where art and activism meet, *Bogotá Post*, https://thebogotapost.com/wilson-borja-artivismo-art-activism-meet/21407/.

FIGURE 1.6 *Muchacha de las aguas, Gimaní*: digital image created by Hanna Ramírez, 2021, to accompany the eponymous poem by Pedro Blas Julio Romero (© Hanna Ramírez, by permission).

be called 'art-chivism', understood as the critical revision of archives from an artistic standpoint to highlight racial injustice, social exclusion and the marginalisation of minoritised groups. Works undertaken by Liliana Angulo Cortés in this vein include the 2015–2016 project *Un caso de reparación: Un proyecto de revisión histórica y humanidades digitales* (A Case of Reparation: A Project of Revisionist History and

Digital Humanities), which explored the relationship of enslavement and Afro-descendants with the colonial-era Botanical Expedition;[32] and the 2022 project *Rodrigo Barrientos: disfrazado de hombre blanco* (Rodrigo Barrientos: Disguised as a White Man), which uncovered the previously ignored fact that Barrientos was a Black painter.[33] These projects were part of Angulo's Ethno-Education Laboratory, which she established during a guest curatorship at the Museo de Antioquía (Chacón Bernal 2021). Both Borja and Angulo seek to influence and question the field of education and diverse spaces such as museums, university art education, ethno-education and the production and use of images.

Paralleling the tactics of irruption used by Sankofa Danzafro, the female *champeta* group Las Emperadoras, from Cartagena, intervenes in the field of Black popular music to affirm the presence of women in *champeta* music, which had been dominated by Afro-descendant working-class men. Las Emperadoras broaden the field of anti-racist activism by intertwining it with a critique of sexism and the under-representation of women. Las Emperadoras subvert the image of women as passive participants in music, showing not only their capacity for agency as composers, singers, and samplers, but also presenting performances far removed from the hyper-sexualised stereotypes of Black women that are widely purveyed, including by some Afro artists.[34]

This last example indicates that strategies of subversion and irruption are often juxtaposed and intertwined in artistic practice: not all subversion involves irruption, but irruption often has subversive effects. This is also evident in the case of Sankofa Danzafro, where the difference between subversion and irruption is often blurred. The intent is to subvert taken-for-granted racialised orders, but this is achieved by the irruption of the dance performances onto the stage and into the audiences' sensory apparatus.

Turning now to the third pathway of engaging with publics, the critical interpellation of the public in different forms (as audiences and as communities) is a political intention that characterises all these artists. The Afro-Colombian Cultural Corporation for Social and Cultural Development, CARABANTÚ, mentioned in the previous section, is a good example of the use of art, in this case film, as a tool for engaging Afro communities in the process of emancipation and ethno-education.

[32] See note 3.
[33] See www.digitalexhibitions.manchester.ac.uk/s/carla-en/page/liliana-angulo.
[34] See www.digitalexhibitions.manchester.ac.uk/s/carla-en/page/las-emperadoras.

Recently, with the support of the Wi Da Monikongo collective (also mentioned earlier), they have worked with children and young people to produce a series of short films, screened during the International Kunta Kinte Afro Community Film Festival 2021. The films were made by Afro children and adolescents in Medellín and told stories about their neighbourhoods, with a focus on highlighting the leadership shown by Afro community members.[35]

This kind of artistic practice has contributed to broadening the forms of audience participation, turning members of the public into co-producers of collective narratives that document, accompany and express social discontent. In particular, the social protests that took place in 2017 (a civic strike in May and June in the city of Buenaventura), in 2019 (a national strike on 21 November) and in 2021 (widespread protests in May and June) were scenarios in which the politicisation of artistic practices became a common platform for the spontaneous and passionate expression of a new emerging political subject in Colombia: the young people that made up La Primera Línea.[36]

Examples of the active role that artistic practices played in the 2021 protests include the collective graffiti in the main avenues of cities such as Medellín and Cartagena, street theatre in Barranquilla, and *batucadas* (street dances with drums) and sit-ins with street concerts in Tumaco, Pasto, Bogotá, Medellín and Cali. In addition, the protests included artistic interventions such as the collective creation of the multi-coloured ten-metre Monumento a la Resistencia in Cali and the painting of graffiti and images onto the huge 1960s national monument, Los Héroes, in Bogotá.

Artists and collectives such as Margarita Ariza, Sankofa Danzafro, Las Emperadoras de la Champeta, Yeison Riascos, Liliana Angulo and CARABANTÚ, among others, engage in artistic practices that can be defined as social, community, participatory, public and contextual art, whose main aim is to pursue, 'above and beyond aesthetic achievements, the benefits of social change and the participation of communities in the realisation of the work' (Palacios Garrido 2009: 199). These works establish artistic practices that question conventions in art about the individualistic nature of creativity and relocate creative acts in their

---

[35] See www.digitalexhibitions.manchester.ac.uk/s/carla-en/page/carabantu.
[36] La Primera Línea (the Front Line) referred to people, mostly young, who formed a line of defence against the violence of the security forces during the protests. Several people in the Front Line suffered the loss of eyes from rubber bullets, some were killed by the security forces and others were arrested and indicted.

social context, with community participation and with aims of social transformation.

These creators include in their artistic practices the question of the impact of race on the lives of Afro-Colombian people, highlighting how racialisation works in the systematic reproduction of exclusions in the country. The way artistic work has been linked to these social mobilisations in Colombia reflects the erosion of the boundaries between art and social activism. There is a displacement of the conventional terrain of modern art, shifting attention towards the social context, involving audiences, and including the participation of communities that have their own aesthetic and political sensibilities about creative acts. This is a form of participatory expression that decentres assumptions and debates about authorship in art, subsuming them into the political intentionality of community-oriented social transformation (Nardone 2010).

This transformation of artistic practice in Colombia has made it possible to rethink the ways in which racism and the relations between race and artistic practice are addressed in the country. Instead of tracing references to Afroness and Blackness in art, concerns are focused on how these themes are enunciated outside the institutional and formal channels of artistic expression, generating durable discursive and political presences that express identities in cultural and artistic forms that affirm the value of difference.

In relation to the pathway of engaging the public, these artists seek to affect people by challenging assumptions about the raciality of Afro people. These strategies of questioning audiences can generate distinct affective-emotional responses that can unsettle an unprepared viewer. For example, in relation to the reception of Sankofa's work, in the context of a focus group, one viewer mentioned:[37]

A hook [is created] that has to do with the rigour of their aesthetic format, and which means that this message [the hidden nature of structural problems such as racism] can be conveyed. Suddenly, some unwitting person who goes to see something very aesthetic and very artistic realises that there is a [process of]

---

[37] During March and April 2021, CARLA researchers in Colombia undertook audience studies using digital ethnography methods with focus groups and interviews. The focus groups were made up of social media followers of Sankofa Danzafro and the organisation Champeta Patrimonio Inmaterial (dedicated to achieving the status of intangible cultural heritage for *champeta*). Four focus groups were conducted, two on *champeta* and two on Sankofa Danzafro, and six interviews were done with followers of both artists. The groups were composed of people between eighteen and fifty years old, most of whom were of Colombian origin and resident in the country.

reflection in the background, which is very important. And that is what is interesting: to take them [audience members] like that, without warning, and then let them reflect and let whatever happens happen in their consciousness (participant, Focus Group 2, April 2021)

Reactions of discomfort can be generated among audiences by anti-racist artistic practice, as well as emotions of empowerment and empathy:

How uncomfortable to be called racist to your face, without using a single word. I feel that after the performance there was like a tense energy in the Pablo Tobón Uribe [theatre] (participant, Focus Group 2, April 2021).

There was strength and empathy, adrenaline and strong heartbeats, in a positive sense, when I saw them. It filled me with hope (participant, Focus Group 2, April 2021).

Anti-racism in Colombian art practice is present today in a range of aesthetic forms – music, illustration, literature, dance and performance – that situate the question of racism in the context of other material aspects of systematic exclusion. In their practice, artists shift towards a commitment to collective pedagogy for social transformation, employing aesthetic codes that are taken from everyday contexts and re-signified through reflections on inequality, racism and rights in society. Artistic practice not only interrogates, but also represents a collective feeling of transcendence of the exclusions experienced by racialised subjects in Colombian society.

CONCLUSION

This chapter started with a broad look at the representation of racialised difference in Colombia until the end of the nineteenth century, showing how Black and Indigenous subjects were represented as backward and lacking 'civilisation'. The participation of racialised subaltern artists in artistic production during this period was limited and has been subject to historiographical erasure (which recent critical interventions into the archives are seeking to correct – for example, by highlighting the African ancestry of Botanical Expedition member Salvador Rizo Blanco). The work of the poet Candelario Obeso, who did participate in the literary world and has been recognised, shows that, while prevailing trends of *costumbrismo* certainly influenced his work, with its focus on local characters and customs, there was also a powerful strand of what we might today label as anti-racism in his assertion of the value of Black lifeways. We next showed how in the first half of the twentieth century, tendencies labelled by scholars as *indigenismo* and *negrismo* had the ambivalent effects of highlighting the Indigenous and Black presences in the nation while simultaneously limiting them with romantic and primitivist perspectives. However, Black artists and intellectuals – more numerous than Indigenous ones at that time – often managed to escape the confines of conventional *negrismo* and promote a racially-aware social justice agenda: Manuel and Delia Zapata Olivella are key examples.

In line with the work of CARLA in Colombia, we then moved the focus to Black artists, tracing the increasing politicisation of their postures from the 1950s and the more explicit attention to racism that came with the influence of international currents, such as Négritude and Black Power, and the continuing increase in numbers of university-educated Black people. The multiculturalist reforms of the 1990s opened some space for debates about racism, but funding and support for 'cultural diversity' ultimately diverted attention away from anti-racism. The role of music, already significant in earlier decades, has continued to be important and it reveals the value of a less direct approach to racism that works by affirming Black presence, autonomy and agency.

Our account in the final section of the chapter on the work of the Colombian artists who collaborated with CARLA reinforces the value of a heterogeneous anti-racism: explicit challenges to racist stereotypes and racist aesthetics go alongside forceful assertions of Black agency and autonomy; critical attention to the way Blackness is represented in art goes alongside initiatives to create spaces for Black autonomy within institutional contexts, such as museums and archives, and projects that involve collective participation, including by people who do not identify themselves as artists: the work of Liliana Angulo Cortés in museums and archives is a good example. Anti-racism has become a more explicit frame for these kinds of artistic practice, but what counts as 'anti-racist' may be judged in flexible and inclusive ways.

2

The Cosmopolitics of Indigenous Anti-Racist Art and Literature in Brazil

Lúcia Sá, Pedro Mandagará and
Felipe Milanez Pereira

As Guarani curator Sandra Benites eloquently put it, 'there are folks who think that Indigenous peoples do not suffer racism. How so? Racism in Brazil started against the Indigenous peoples, it started with all this exclusion, with this erasure. It started with them saying that the Indigenous peoples were not human. What is that [if not racism]? What other word would one use to describe it?' (Benites 2021).[1] Indeed, although historians have long recognised that racism in the Americas is a product of European colonisation, with Amerindians being its first victims, the last decades' prolific scholarship on racism in Brazil hardly mentions Indigenous peoples. By the same token, the main thrust of anti-racist policy in Brazil has been directed at Afro-descendants, while racism against the Indigenous population is rarely named as such and is marginal to the political agenda, despite the importance of 'the Indian' in the national imaginary.

Tuxá anthropologist Felipe Cruz has argued that although racism against Indigenous peoples in Brazil is not different from racism against Afro-descendants (in other words, it usually includes physical and/or verbal abuse, dehumanisation, refusal to offer services, etc.), the way in which racialisation happens is different. Racialisation of Indigenous peoples, according to Cruz, often involves de-authorisation, that is, the denial of someone's Indigenous identity (Cruz 2019: 159). De-authorisation can happen in any context in which Indigenous peoples or individuals are perceived by non-Indigenous as differing from preconceived ideas of Indigeneity: this includes, for example, Indigenous persons making

---

[1] All translations from the Portuguese are our own, unless otherwise stated.

use of modern gadgets, adopting aspects of a Western lifestyle, speaking Portuguese or simply defending their own rights. In other words, the mere fact that Indigenous peoples are in contact with the non-Indigenous (notwithstanding the fact that such contact, to begin with, was often not voluntary) makes them, in the eyes of certain non-Indigenous Brazilians, 'not Indigenous enough'. According to that logic, then, the only way of being 'Indigenous enough' would be to revert to a time prior to contact with non-Indigenous people.

As a result of de-authorisation, Indigenous persons become invisible as Indigenous subjects and racism against them is also rendered invisible. This happens in spite of the fact that de-authorisation is often accompanied by other processes of racialisation that are frequently experienced by other non-white groups: Indigenous peoples are also called dirty, savages and infantile, their cultures and knowledge are dismissed or considered inferior and their spirituality is deemed as superstition. More often than not, racism against Indigenous peoples is based on this paradox: those who refuse to 'modernise' are labelled as 'savages' or backward and are therefore pressurised to change or 'modernise', while those who do adopt certain non-Indigenous life styles are deemed 'not Indigenous enough' by the same sectors of society that would see them as 'savages' had they not adopted those changes (Sá and Milanez Pereira 2020: 169). In the words of Cruz, 'if this racialisation attempts effectively to proclaim the ephemeral existence of the Indigenous condition, it is successful in the sense that it renders invisible not only the Indigenous persons themselves, but it also manages to operate without being noticed, that is, by rendering the racial dimension of Indigenous peoples also invisible' (Cruz 2019: 160).

De-authorisation has probably become more common since the last decades of the twentieth century, as a backlash to the strengthening of the Indigenous movement after the 1988 Constitution, which made Indigenous peoples more visible as the main defenders of their own rights and interests. But the process in itself is not new. The arrival of Europeans in the territory now called Brazil started a process in which, according to European colonisers, the Indigenous peoples were destined to disappear, to stop being Indigenous. In the 'Carta a el-rei Dom Manuel' (Letter to King Manuel), the first document ever written by a European about Brazilian natives, the knight Pêro Vaz de Caminha, acting as scribe for Pedro Álvares Cabral, reputed to be the European 'discoverer' of Brazil, explains to Manuel I of Portugal that the natives encountered by the Portuguese had no religion of their own and would most likely be willing to become Christians and subjects of the kingdom. They were, according to Caminha, a blank slate ready to be written on by the process of colonisation. In the years that followed that first landing, the original population of millions of natives was decimated by diseases, extermination and enslavement. The survivors were expected to abandon their ways of living, in a process that was seen as inevitable, as Indigenous peoples were deemed as 'savage' and not compatible with 'civilisation'.

REPRESENTATIONS OF INDIGENOUS PEOPLE IN THE ARTS

Representations of Indigenous peoples in literature and visual arts differed little from this view. The eighteenth-century poem O Uraguai (1769), by Basílio da Gama, criticises the Jesuits for their oppression of the Guarani in the south of Brazil. But the poem's Indigenous heroes, Cacambo, Sepé and Lindóia, all die at the end, with the Guarani survivors being promised civilisation by General Gomes Freire de Andrade, a real-life official in the Marquis of Pombal's anti-Jesuit government and the true hero of the poem. A few decades later, José de Alencar's Romantic foundational novels O Guarani (1857) and Iracema (1865) would further popularise the idea of sacrificial Indigenous heroes. O Guarani's protagonist, Peri, sees his beloved – a white woman, Ceci – as a quasi-supernatural being beyond his reach and ends up risking his life in order to save her from destructive floods. If the end of this novel is ambiguous (with the white woman in his arms, Peri perches in a palm tree that is then carried away by the flood waters), the ending of Iracema is less so, as the eponymous Indigenous heroine dies of sadness after being abandoned by her inconstant Portuguese lover, Martin, but not before giving birth to Moacir, whose name, 'son of suffering', is meant to represent all Brazilians. Alencar celebrated the Tupi and Guarani by relegating them to the past, to the role of ancestor cultures whose inevitable destiny had been to convert to Christianity and become 'civilised' as part of the new nation.

Some of the best-known Brazilian paintings from the Romantic era also depict Indigenous sacrificial heroes. One example is Victor Meirelles's *Moema* (1866), which depicts the death of the heroine from Santa Rita Durão's epic poem *Caramuru* (1781). In Meirelles's painting, the corpse of a rather light-skinned Moema is in the foreground, lying on a beach illuminated by pale yellow sunlight, which presumably refers to the dawn of Indigenous cultures (see Figure 2.1). In a very similar style, *Lindóia* (1882), by José Maria de Medeiros, portrays one of the most famous scenes from *O Uraguay*: the death of the heroine. As in

Indigenous Anti-Racist Art and Literature: Brazil

FIGURE 2.1 *Moema*, painting by Victor Meirelles, 1866 (courtesy of Museu de Arte de São Paulo).

Meirelles's *Moema*, a fair Lindóia occupies the foreground, having just committed suicide using a poisonous snake.

Throughout most of the twentieth century, public policies and academic studies continued to foretell the demise of Indigenous peoples, who were expected to disappear as a result of both violence and assimilation. Even sympathetic scholars, such as anthropologist Darcy Ribeiro, proclaimed the imminent disappearance of Indigenous peoples, caused by capitalist expansion into their territories and the loss of their ability to carry out traditional cultural practices (Ribeiro 1970). The arts, for the most part, continued to echo this view. The avant-garde novel *Macunaíma* (1928), by Mário de Andrade, is a good example. The novel is in many respects a revolutionary inversion of the colonialist model, as its protagonist, 'the hero without character' Macunaíma, leaves his native Amazonia to travel to São Paulo and teach the *paulistas* new ways of being (Sá 2004). However, like most literary Indigenous heroes created by non-Indigenous writers, Macunaíma dies at the end and his people are said to disappear entirely, their language and stories having to be repeated by a parrot. In his first and most successful novel, *Maíra* (1976), Darcy Ribeiro also presents us with a pessimistic view of the future of Indigenous peoples, as the god of the fictitious Mairum culture decides to capitulate in his battle against the Christian god.

These are just some examples of what is perhaps the most prevalent trope in depictions of Indigenous peoples in the arts. From the beginning of colonisation to the last decades of the twentieth century, the racialisation of Brazilian Indigenous peoples nearly always seemed to include the stigma of imminent disappearance. To be Indigenous is, according to this particular definition, to be always on the brink of extinction.

DE-AUTHORISATION AND LAND

At the heart of these processes of de-authorisation is the issue of land. Since colonial times, de-authorisation has been used by state powers and non-Indigenous landowners as a way to deny, explicitly or implicitly, the right to ancestral territory. In his letter, Pêro Vaz de Caminha assured the king of Portugal that the lands they had just found were fertile and 'everything one plants will grow'. In other words, if the Indigenous peoples were a blank slate that would gladly accept the Christian religion and be subject to the Portuguese crown, then the territory where they lived would be available to the king. As ownership by the Crown slowly gave way to private ownership, with land titles being distributed by the Crown and, later, by the monarchic, republican and local governments of independent Brazil (as well as being extensively falsified by land-grabbers), de-authorisation became ever more prevalent. Recognising someone as Indigenous is to acknowledge that their ancestors were there before the colonisers arrived. It implies, therefore, a recognition of their right to the land where their ancestors lived. Refusing to identify someone as Indigenous, on the other hand, is to deny their right to ancestry and to land. In the words of Cruz: 'As a reminder that those territories had been occupied before European conquest, these peoples were extremely dispensable and in fact, had to be exterminated, civilised or whitened in order for the colonial enterprise to be successful. In this sense, Indigenous racialisation was grounded on an alleged fragility, since the only fate for this race was disappearance' (2019: 153).

A very current version of this logic is the resurrection of the racist legal argument called 'time frame' (*marco temporal*). 'Time frame' originally emerged as a 'thesis' in the Federal Supreme Court during the trial for the demarcation of Raposa Serra do Sol Reservation in Roraima (Amazon) in 2009. At the time, one of the ministers (judges) of the Supreme Court defended limitations to the originally proposed extension of the Indigenous reservation by arguing that Indigenous peoples should only be granted rights to land they occupied at the time of promulgation of the

1988 Constitution, which occurred on 5 October. Since then, landowners and anti-Indigenous lawmakers have repeatedly attempted to turn this 'thesis' into actual legislation and, after the election of Jair Bolsonaro, the 'time frame' argument gained momentum as the most recent attempt to inscribe de-authorisation into law. It has gathered strong support from the mainstream press and considerable parts of the non-Indigenous population, who are willing to believe the 1964–1984 military dictatorship slogan of 'too much land for too few Indians' or simply accuse Indigenous peoples of being 'fake Indians'.

Not surprisingly, the 'time-frame' argument has been the subject of fierce opposition and intense mobilisation on the part of the Indigenous movement. Although Indigenous peoples of Brazil always resisted colonisation through organised rebellions and wars against invaders and land-grabbers, the current pan-Indigenous movement in defence of legal rights and ancestral territories started in the 1970s, initially under the umbrella of the Catholic organisation CIMI, Conselho Indigenista Missionário (Indigenous Missionary Council), which sponsored meetings among regional Indigenous groups to discuss needs and demands. By 1978, several regional Indigenous organisations were coming together against the military dictatorship's proposal to 'emancipate' Indigenous peoples – a cynical suggestion of liberation that in reality would allow the commercialisation and trading of Indigenous lands. In 1980, a group of Indigenous leaders founded UNI, União das Nações Indígenas (Indigenous Nations Union), which would become the most successful pan-Indigenous organisation in Brazil: their skilful negotiating guaranteed the inclusion of fundamental Indigenous rights in the post-dictatorship 1988 Constitution, especially articles 231 and 232, which respectively granted Indigenous peoples the right to keep their traditional practices, beliefs and territories, and to defend their own interests. Indigenous leader Ailton Krenak's performance in the 1987 constitutional debates, in which he delivered a speech against the violation of Indigenous rights while painting his face in traditional style, has become the most iconic moment of the Constituent Assembly.

The Constituent Assembly was followed by a period of relative stability under a neoliberal democracy that nevertheless sponsored the increasing extraction of natural resources and deforestation. The election of ex-military Bolsonaro as president in 2018 brought back the rhetoric of the 1970s' dictatorship in favour of a supposed 'emancipation' of Indigenous peoples, and violent, undisguised and systematic attacks against Indigenous rights, land-grabbing and invasion of Indigenous territories. On the judicial and political front, these attacks have supported the 'time frame' argument, trying to push it into law.

Indigenous mobilisation against the 'time-frame' and other forms of violence and racism has happened on the political and juridical fronts (with Indigenous lawyers and lawmakers pressing to overturn attempts to officialise it) and on the streets. The ability to maintain or recover original land and territory has always been at the core of Indigenous activism. For most native peoples in Brazil and the Americas, land rights are often synonymous with the ability to follow traditional practices and beliefs. Most Indigenous peoples see themselves as guardians of forests, rivers and mountains, which they regard as their relatives and ancestors. For these reasons, in the last two decades Indigenous peoples have been at the forefront of environmental activism in Latin America. A common slogan in Indigenous activism in Brazil is that Indigenous peoples belong to the land instead of the land belonging to them. It is not surprising, then, that during the Bolsonaro government there were massive demonstrations when the 'time frame' proposition was being voted on in Congress, in addition to the demonstrations and encampments that happen every year (for example, the Free Land Camp that happens every April in Brasília). On the political front, the Indigenous activist Sonia Guajajara ran for vice-president in the 2018 presidential elections with a platform that defended 'good living' or *bom viver* (on the ticket of Guilherme Boulos, the candidate for PSOL – Socialism and Liberty Party). In the same year, a Wapichana woman, Joênia Wapichana, was elected to the national Congress, together with many Indigenous mayors and councillors in local elections. In the 2022 Congressional elections, although Joênia was not re-elected, Sonia Guajajara and Célia Xakriabá were, doubling the Indigenous representation. Immediately after coming into power in 2023, president Lula da Silva appointed Guajajara as head of the newly-created Ministry for Indigenous Peoples and Wapichana as president of FUNAI (National Foundation for Indigenous Affairs), the first-ever Indigenous person to assume that role.

INDIGENOUS RESISTANCE THROUGH LITERATURE AND VISUAL ARTS

Along with juridical, political and street activism, the arts have emerged (particularly since about 2020) as a new and powerful arm of the Indigenous movement. Several creative fields – literature, visual arts, cinema and music – have joined the legal and juridical battle in defence of

Indigenous rights and traditional territories, by exposing to wide audiences the physical and legal attacks made against Indigenous peoples during Brazil's long history of colonial and colonialist violence. At the same time, the arts are also working in areas that go beyond the reach of the legal and the juridical. Their collective work has been using epistemic tactics that challenge colonialist conventions and knowledge systems. These epistemic changes start with their mere presence in spaces that have traditionally excluded Indigenous cultural production and Indigenous bodies, such as literary festivals, bookshops, museums, art galleries and universities. In what many Indigenous artists have dubbed *retomada* (reclaiming, occupation), Indigenous writers, filmmakers and visual artists have been main features in festivals and exhibitions in the galleries and museums of the most important cities in Brazil. Their presence in these spaces not only challenges what Sonia Guajajara described as the feeling of being constantly made aware that we 'are in the wrong place, that we were not meant to be there' (2019), but also questions established notions of what literature, cinema, music or visual arts are or should be.

Needless to say, all Indigenous groups had their own artistic production before the arrival of the Portuguese: this included narrative and poetry (in oral forms), visual arts (basketry, feather art, body painting, ceramics, architecture), music and dance, and many groups continue these practices today. These art forms are usually collective and play various roles in the communities, being related to activities such as cooking, fishing, hunting, planting, giving birth, providing spiritual protection, rituals, healing, dreaming and so on. Some of these art forms, particularly narrative ones, have long registered the changes brought about by colonialism and protested against those changes. From the end of the nineteenth century, narrative forms also began to be printed and published, though usually under the name of a mediator, often a traveller, a priest or an anthropologist who listed the authors as 'informants'. It is only since the late 1980s, and more widely from the 2010s, that Indigenous peoples from all over Brazil have started to sign their own works individually or collectively, as well as to make use of Western media and genres to target non-Indigenous audiences. The writer Daniel Munduruku explains that individually signing works of Indigenous literature is a phenomenon that dates back to the rise of the Indigenous movement in the wake of the Constituent Assembly, in the mid 1980s, and that has become more ubiquitous with the entry of young Indigenous women and men into universities, particularly with the creation in 2012 of quotas for Indigenous students in public universities.

The first writer to describe herself publicly as an Indigenous author was Eliane Potiguara, who started to publish poetry in the mid 1980s, at the same time as taking a very active role in the Indigenous movement. Born in Rio de Janeiro from parents who had to abandon their traditional territory in Paraíba, Potiguara has highlighted the fight of those who were obliged to leave their land and hide their culture, particularly women. 'Brasil, que faço com a minha cara de índia?' (Brazil, What Do I Do with My Indian Face?), first published in 2004, is one of Potiguara's best-known poems. It delves into the issue of identity for Indigenous people who are supposed to have lost their culture: 'Brazil ... what do I do with my Indian face / and my spirits / my strength / my Tupã / and my circles? // What do I do with my Indian face / and my *toré* [ritual] / my sacredness / my *cabôcos* / and my land?' (2018).[2]

Along with Potiguara, Daniel Munduruku and Olivio Jekupé are the best-known names in contemporary Indigenous literature from Brazil. Originally from the state of Pará, in the Amazon, Munduruku lives in the countryside of São Paulo and is one of the main organisers of Indigenous literature events in the country, from weekly interviews and podcasts to conferences, festivals and workshops. He is also a prolific writer and his production includes Indigenous versions of Brazilian history that analyse colonisation from the point of view of the colonised (2017), as well as traditional tales, usually published in well-illustrated editions that target mostly young readers. Jekupé is a Guarani from the Krukutu village in the outskirts of São Paulo and, like Munduruku, has published an extensive list of books directed at young readers. Both make a point in presenting their works regularly at elementary and secondary schools, as they believe that a function of Indigenous literature is to educate non-Indigenous people about Amerindian cultures.

Since the 2010s, the Brazilian publishing scene has seen the arrival of another type of Indigenous literature: theoretical or philosophical essays that find acceptance among academic readers, particularly those involved in environmental issues. One example is Davi Kopenawa and

---

[2] Tupã (Thunder) is the creator or supreme being for many Tupi Indigenous groups. The 'circles' refer to the Toré ritual, which includes dancing and singing in circles to the rhythm of the maraca. *Cabocos* is short for *caboclos*, which literally means persons of Indian–white mixed heritage. In popular language in Brazil, *caboclo* and *caboco* are often used as synonyms for 'Indigenous', and it is in this sense that the term is used by some Indigenous activists, often to refer to Indigenous ancestors. Caboclo is also the name of an Amerindian deity in some strands of the Afro-Brazilian religions Candomblé and Umbanda.

Bruce Albert's *The Falling Sky* (2013), which was originally published in French (2010) and later in Portuguese (2015). Considered one of the most important books recently published in Brazil, it is an attempt (in some sense, not dissimilar to Munduruku's or Jekupé's) at teaching non-Indigenous audiences (or whites, as they are called in the book) about Yanomami culture, explicitly as a way to deter Western extractivism in the Amazon forest. Kopenawa and Albert's book is important because it is the first book-length testimony by an Amazonian shaman and the first ever to offer a thorough analysis of Western extractivism from the point of view of an Indigenous Amazonian native. In addition, *The Falling Sky* offers key theoretical and philosophical insights into Yanomami ways of seeing the forest and points to conceptual differences between Indigenous Amazonia and Western ways of thinking, particularly with regard to what is normally called 'nature' in Western traditions. *The Falling Sky* has also become an important inspiration for Indigenous artists and activists, as a written Indigenous source that confirms and brings together philosophies and ways of living common to various Indigenous peoples of lowland South America, while being strongly grounded on specific Yanomami beliefs. At the core of these philosophies is the idea that humans are part of affective networks that involve not only their own species, but other living and dead beings, and what Western languages tend to refer to as 'spirits' (which is a much more complex concept in Yanomami and Amerindian thought and includes the 'spirits' of non-human beings) and even entities that Western science considers 'inanimate', such as rivers and mountains.

In a related genre, Ailton Krenak has published a series of very short books based on the oral interventions he has made in the last few years, challenging Western capitalist assumptions about, for example, the importance of work, the meaning of 'humanity' or why the idea of 'the future' is not found in native Brazilian cultures. Published by the prestigious Companhia das Letras (with some translated into English), these mini-books have reached a wide readership interested in alternatives to the political establishment (Krenak 2020a, 2020b).

The dramatic rise in publication of Indigenous authors in the last five years is challenging assumptions long held in Brazilian society about what it means to be Indigenous. As the academic and popular success of authors such as Kopenawa and Krenak demonstrates, Indigenous literature has the ability to invert the still popular nineteenth-century socio-evolutionist view that Amerindian cultures and points of view are backward, savage, inferior and therefore destined to be 'improved' and to 'progress' or disappear: these books' success lies precisely in their radical approach to pressing contemporary issues, such as climate disaster and social inequality – an approach that is seen not as something from the past but, on the contrary, as presenting potential solutions for the future.

INDIGENOUS VISUAL ARTS IN THE AMAZON: JAIDER ESBELL AND DENILSON BANIWA

The cultural field that has seen by far the most dramatic changes in production and public recognition is contemporary visual arts, which will be the focus of the remainder of our analysis.[3] In the last four years, some of the most prestigious art venues in the country have held exhibitions featuring works by artists such as Arissana Pataxó, Daiara Tukano, Denilson Baniwa, Glicéria Tupinambá, Gustavo Caboco, Jaider Esbell and Naine Terena, among many others. Like the writers mentioned earlier, all of these artists participate actively in the movement for Indigenous rights in their communities and at a national level, and their works are often thematically and organically linked to those movements, being also frequently produced for and exhibited at activist events, including events protesting against the 'time frame'. Some of these artists define themselves as 'artivists', as did Jaider Esbell, whose tragic death in 2021 shook both the art world and the Indigenous movement in Brazil. In a television interview on the occasion of the opening of the 2021 exhibition *Moquém_Surarî*, which he curated, Esbell declared: 'I am not a visual artist. What I try, maybe, is to do politics, cosmopolitics'.[4] In the fields of philosophy and history of science, the term 'cosmopolitics' is usually associated with Isabelle Stengers' essays compiled, in English, in the books *Cosmopolitics I* (2010) and *Cosmopolitics II* (2011).[5] It is impossible to know whether Esbell's use of the term was directly connected with her work, but in any case, Stengers' use of 'cosmopolitics' to refer to an 'ecology of knowledges' resonates well with Esbell's critique of the limitations of Western thought.

Several examples of Esbell's cosmopolitics can be found in *Carta ao velho mundo* (Letter to the Old World, 2018–2019), an artwork that consists of physical interventions into a 1972 Brazilian publication

---

[3] Indigenous cinema and popular music, too, have seen an increase in production and visibility in the last decade, but due to lack of space, we will not be discussing them here. However, in this book, see Curated Conversation 4 on Indigenous Guarani rap.

[4] See www.youtube.com/watch?v=yBhGwqjOa-s.

[5] The first collection was published in French in 1996 with the title *Cosmopolitiques I*.

titled *Galeria Delta da pintura universal* (Delta's Universal Gallery of Painting, a volume that drew on an older Italian multi-volume set called *Enciclopedia universale dell'arte*), which, in spite of its over-inclusive title, did not feature any Indigenous art. Esbell intervened in the volume by redacting, drawing, painting and writing on every single one of its 477 pages.[6] Many of those interventions denounce violence committed against specific Indigenous leaders by land-grabbers; others mention the poisoning of food from mercury contamination caused by mining in the Amazon rivers and the environmental destruction caused by extractivism and large-scale agriculture. Several pages make reference to colonialism, the enslaving of Indigenous peoples after the arrival of the Portuguese and the persecution of native religions by Christians.

But Esbell's interventions are not limited to direct denunciation. Many of them put into practice his cosmopolitics by questioning, from his Indigenous Macuxi perspective, various Western cultural assumptions. Several pages of the book, for example, had their written text occluded by drawings of animals. Taking the place of an alphabetical historical narrative that celebrates 'art history' in Western terms, these animals stand for another kind of teaching, for an alternative narrative that is not necessarily human-centred and that is based on affective ties between humans and other kinds of beings. His intervention into Andrea del Castagno's *Crucifixion and Saints* (c. 1441), for example, includes drawings of birds pecking at the cross (see Figure 2.2). At first sight, the animals appear to create a humorous, potentially disrespectful commentary on one of the gravest, most serious icons of Western culture: Christ's crucifixion. Although that may of course be the case, the animals also help us to imagine another narrative, not necessarily humorous: as in so many traditional Amazonian stories where animals save humans or proto-humans from danger, the birds could be there to help free Christ from the cross, while adding Amazonian animal protagonism to a biblical story.

As mentioned, Esbell was never comfortable with being called a 'visual artist'. He wanted to go beyond 'mere visuality' (Esbell 2018b: 37). In his own words, his work was designed to 'be in the soul of whoever is nearby' (*é projetado para estar na alma de quem esteja próximo*, 2018b: 115); in other words, it was designed to *affect* those around him. This desire to affect entails layers of 'extrapolated senses and dimensions', a loss of control and a feeling of 'being in a non-place, sensing a non-image, not finding time/space, not finding form' (2018b: 115). For

[6] See www.jaideresbell.com.br/site/2019/03/20/carta-ao-velho-mundo/.

FIGURE 2.2 Intervention into Andrea del Castagno's *Crucifixion and Saints* by Jaider Esbell, from his *Carta ao Velho Mundo*, 2018–2019 (© Galeria Jaider Esbell de Arte Indígena Contemporânea, by permission).

Esbell, then, his art should affect viewers by freeing them from expected forms and putting them in touch with unexpected, other, non-Western forms of knowledge.

This can be seen in his acrylic painting *Feitiço para salvar a Raposa Serra do Sol* (A Spell to Save Raposa Serra do Sol Reservation, 2019). Raposa Serra do Sol is an Indigenous territory that took a long time to be demarcated – the process only ended in 2008, after several years of judicial disputes, which included the coining of the 'time frame' thesis and a lot of actual violence against Indigenous peoples in their territories. The marks of centuries of oppression caused by agro-industrial exploitation in the region are still there – in the young Indigenous people who never learned their native languages (because their elders were forbidden to); in the land that mostly became pasture due to cattle ranching; and in the illegal gold-mining enterprises that have damaged the environment. If Raposa Serra do Sol needs to be healed by a spell, those are some of the symptoms. The painting portrays the assistants who will help to carry out the spell: that is, the animals. Several animals are represented, connecting the painting to the series of Macuxi (and other Indigenous Amazonian) narratives that involve the 'father' or other ancestor of some creature – usually a talking ancestor, from a time before humans existed. Some of these animals have the appearance of a known animal – there are fish, a jaguar, an armadillo, the heads of some birds. Others are not so recognisable and look like molluscs or even bacteria. They all inhabit the same plane – there is no perspective that organises them and leads the viewer to distinguish the foreground from the background. And yet the painting appears to form a whole, in a way that resembles a map, as if the spiritual powers of the lands and waters of the Raposa Serra do Sol were being 'mapped', to be called upon when casting the spell.

In this painting and in other works by Esbell, Raposa Serra do Sol is both the Indigenous land and a symbol for anti-racist struggle. The fight for demarcation encountered powerful reactionary resistance in the state of Roraima and in several national organisations (such as the Brazilian armed forces). More than a decade after the demarcation process ended in 2008, it was still common to see stickers on car windows in Roraima's capital, Boa Vista, with sayings such as 'Down with the demarcation of Raposa Serra do Sol' or 'I support the island-type demarcation'.[7] These were not displayed only by large-scale farmers or by people who would profit directly from the use of the land. It became an ideological struggle

---

[7] Island-type demarcation splits up Indigenous territories into small 'islands' of land.

with racist tones: much of the regional media would either repeat the classic de-authorising slogan that the Macuxi were fake Indians or reproduce the myth of the 'Indian who does not work' as an 'argument' against demarcation. Besides the obvious racism, this 'argument' presupposes the Lockean notion that ownership of land comes from working it, one of the ideological drives and part of the liberal justification of colonialism. By picturing Raposa Serra do Sol in terms of the animal spirits that inhabit its lands and waters, Esbell opposes this utilitarian view of territory.

In 2020, Esbell exhibited a pair of giant colourful snakes intertwined around the pillars of Santa Tereza bridge in Belo Horizonte as part of the street-art festival CURA. Titled *Entidades*, a word that for many Indigenous and Afro-Brazilian peoples can mean 'spirits' or supernatural beings, the snakes were subsequently on display in Porto Alegre and on the lake outside the São Paulo Biennale pavilion in 2021. Very colourful during the day, and illuminated from within at night, like giant lanterns, the snakes became a popular attraction in the three cities where they were exhibited, with people of all ages travelling especially to their location to be photographed near them. Yet not all reactions were positive, as some people also threatened to destroy the snakes and, particularly during the Belo Horizonte and Porto Alegre exhibitions, their author became the target of vicious abuse on social media, mostly from attackers who described themselves as adherents of evangelical Christianity (a movement that has gained force in Brazil and that has much support in the country's congress and senate). Such strong reactions are related to the different symbolic meaning attributed to snakes in Christian mythology (which sees them as embodiments of the devil that caused Adam and Eve to be expelled from Paradise) and in Amazonian Indigenous traditions (where they are often associated with the big Amazonian rivers and seen as ancestors and relatives of humans).

The racist attacks against Esbell's sculptures are a clear example of the epistemological and affective shock that Indigenous art is able to provoke in Brazilian society. Not that these attacks were necessarily extraordinary: evangelical Christians have been known to burn down Indigenous prayer houses and Afro-Brazilian Candomblé venues. In the case of Esbell's snakes, what is interesting is the agency attributed to the artworks themselves, whose mere existence in a public space was deemed a threat – in other words, the snakes were seen as able to affect a desired moral order. For some evangelical Christians, there is no place for spiritual or epistemological manifestations in public spaces other than their own form of Christianity. Moreover, those who support the censoring of

Indigenous spirituality or forms of knowledge in public spaces are also likely to accuse Indigenous peoples of being 'fake Indians'. The only alternative for Indigenous peoples, according to this logic, is hiding or conversion, becoming 'non-Indian'. Esbell's monumental sculptures brought Indigenous cosmogonic beliefs into the public view, affirming their existence in bright colours, forcing them to be seen and commented on in the media. And forcing racist hatred to become visible.

Like other Indigenous artists, Esbell's artistic practice went beyond a single medium – besides painting, he also wrote fiction, curated exhibitions, founded an art gallery, hosted radio programmes and podcasts. Moreover, he theorised constantly about contemporary Indigenous art, a concept he was highly invested in, through speeches, interviews and in programmatic texts. The result was a kind of never-ending performance, registered in hundreds of social media posts and videos in the years before his untimely death. He had a sense of mission, of being a representative both of native artists and of his people, the Macuxi. As he once said, 'representativeness is intrinsic' (Esbell 2018a) – that is, he could not avoid being a representative, but if he had to be one, then he also had to constantly destabilise the ways in which Indigenous peoples were perceived in Brazilian society. He had to fight de-authorisation with his own ever-performing body and his art. It was as if he was trying to use the potentialities of several media to capture a cosmology that went beyond what could be seen, read or heard, and which could, to use his words, 'penetrate the soul' of his viewers. This is the meaning of cosmopolitics in Esbell's work: if political change is to happen in the Amazon and involve Indigenous peoples, it has to include an understanding of and affective connection with the various cosmogonies that make up the Amazonian world.

Esbell is not the only Indigenous artist to invoke ancestral cosmogonies in their work. In a talk for the University of Zurich immediately following Jaider Esbell's death, Denilson Baniwa told the traditional story of the three prawns, ancestors of the Baniwa. Set in a time prior to the existence of humans, the story describes how the prawns were originally recovered by the primordial jaguar grandmother from the bottom of the river, inside a finger bone of one of her grandson's victims, whose remains had been thrown in the water. Fed and well cared for, the three prawns (called 'those from inside the bone') went on to transform themselves into several other creatures (e.g. woodpeckers, crickets) and to initiate the transformation of the universe. They turned fruit into the animals we have today and into proto-humans, the 'people who knew everything' (Cornelio and Wright 1999). Baniwa has depicted the prawns

FIGURE 2.3 *Camarão – Tapuya* by Denilson Baniwa, 2021 (© Denilson Baniwa, by permission).

in some of his digital art as luminescent beings, set over what appears to be a satellite image of water, for example in his *Camarão – Tapuya* (see Figure 2.3). In his talk, he compared the task of the original prawns, which was to repopulate a world that had been emptied by the constant wars caused by the jaguars, with the work of contemporary Indigenous artists, who have to reconstitute a world that has been nearly emptied of Indigenous perspectives:

Today's struggle is an intellectual war against the narrative told by Western art, a narrative that was created by virtue of silencing us ... Many things I learned came from art, like the history of 'humanity' and the history of contacts. The history of winners is told through art and that is why Jaider and I and other Indigenous artists realised how important it was to exert our right of reply through art. We are like the three prawns who go around planting worlds and spreading seeds by means of different codes. (Baniwa 2021)

The comparison is illustrative of the affective connections that characterise contemporary Indigenous art: artists work in constant communication and consultation with each other and with other Indigenous activists and leaders. These processes certainly include a great deal of intellectual exchange, but they also rely strongly on affective ties based on love and respect. Indigenous individuals in Brazil refer to each other as relatives (*parentes*) and it is precisely this concept of family that can best translate their way of working together. Similarly to families, there is often the need to overlook or negotiate differences, but those differences are seen as less important than their shared history of being on the oppressed side of colonialism, as well as the experience of being and doing things together. Gustavo Caboco recently referred to it as a 'methodology of going together' (*ir junto*), of speaking for, and in consultation with, the collective.

In one of Baniwa's images, the bright orange prawn has a human inside its body. This image is part of a series of works – some of them digital, others acrylic paintings – that depict individual animals (a peccary, a frog, a beetle, a tortoise, a snake, a vulture, a fish, an alligator) each with a human inside its body. The images invoke the 'fathers of animals' already mentioned, who, at the beginning of time, were all human like us. But ancestral time in Amazonian Indigenous cosmogonies does not usually refer to a period that is past and gone, but rather a time that can coexist with the present and that is periodically reinstated through ritual and through the work of the shaman. In most Amazonian cultures, shamans can transform into other animals and in that guise they are able to see the world that those animals see. This is done with the purpose of healing, solving conflict, deciding future actions and, above all, maintaining the equilibrium among all living things.

For Baniwa and Esbell, the work of visual artists is akin to the task of the shaman: Indigenous artists have to transit between different worlds and translate these worlds to one another. Dressed as a jaguar-shaman, Baniwa has made several performances in different parts of Brazil and outside the country. These performances have a healing and didactic purpose aimed at non-Indigenous society: they fight the invisibilisation and de-authorisation of Indigenous peoples by confronting non-Indigenous society with 'Indians' in spaces where they are normally not seen. In doing so, they aim to heal the contemporary maladies of non-Indigenous societies, such as pollution, monoculture and climate catastrophe. In 2018, followed by other Indigenous artists and collaborators, Baniwa 'hacked' (his word) the thirty-third São Paulo Biennale. In the final edit of the performance, uploaded onto Baniwa's site, we see him looking at a few exhibits before buying a book at the gallery bookshop titled *Breve história da arte* (A Brief History of Art). In the next scene, he addresses an audience in front of a large-scale ethnographic portrait of two Selk'nam men from Tierra del Fuego. 'Brief History of Art', he says, holding the book, 'so brief that I cannot see Indians in it. So brief, that it does not include Indigenous art'. Pointing at the photograph, he asks: 'Is this an Indian? Is that an Indian? Is this how you want Indians to be? Stuck in the past, with no right to the future? They steal our image, they steal our time, they steal our art. Brief history of art. Theft. Theft. Theft. Theft. White art. Theft. Theft. Indians do not belong just to the past.'[8]

In another talk in the same year, Baniwa described the jaguar-shaman as a 'herald of the new times, who makes Indigenous memories become present and active in all places' (Baniwa 2018). This link between memory, tradition and contemporary art is central to the works by Esbell and Baniwa. For example, both have reworked drawings from pre-Cabraline petroglyphs, often through the use of recent technology, as in Baniwa's projections on skyscrapers in the city of São Paulo in an event protesting the election of Bolsonaro to power in 2019. A 2022 solo exhibition of Baniwa at the Goethe Institut in Porto Alegre included a mural in which a traditional Arawak longhouse (*maloca*) was surrounded by various animals in the style of ancient petroglyphs. Painted in bright colours over a black background, the mural was reminiscent of Esbell's works (it was most likely a homage to Esbell). The animals surrounding the house in a dark sky looked like constellations, establishing a clear connection between the cosmic order of the universe and the complex designs in the

---

[8] See www.behance.net/gallery/77978367/Paj-Onca-Hackeando-a-33-Bienal-de-Artes-de-Sao-Paulo.

Baniwa *maloca*. The architecture of the *maloca* was also similar to the shape of a frog, one of the animals displayed.

By establishing a continuity between pre-European art and contemporary Indigenous art, Baniwa and Esbell offer a response to de-authorisation and to the freezing of Indigenous peoples in an imaginary past. They also reaffirm the uninterrupted presence of Indigenous peoples in the territory now called Brazil, reclaiming Indigenous rights to ancestral lands against 'theses' such as the 'time frame'. Such rights are based on current and prior occupation but also, crucially, on affective ties between living Indigenous peoples and a network that includes all ancestors and their spirits, as well as the spirits of animals, plants, forests, rivers, mountains and so on. In many of his performances, the jaguar-shaman distributes flyers saying that the specific location of the performance is Indigenous land (*Terra indígena*). During an intervention that happened just a few months before the pandemic outbreak in 2020, on Paulista Avenue located in the most distinguished business zone of São Paulo, Baniwa recited a poem reminding the audience that all that the rich buildings framing the landscape were built on colonial territory over sacred Indigenous land: 'All colonial territory / Is ancestral land, first of all / When all the scum is scraped off / Plastic, asphalt, metal / Untold stories in History / Oxygen fills the blood / Those who have always been from here know / São Paulo has always been / Indigenous land'.

THE NORTHEASTERN COAST: THE ART OF ARISSANA PATAXÓ AND GLICÉRIA TUPINAMBÁ

If the connection between de-authorisation, invisibilisation and land-grabbing permeates the historical and present experience of most Indigenous peoples in Brazil – and in other parts of the Americas as well – working as a particular marker of anti-Indigenous racism, perhaps nowhere in Brazil is this more true than in the northeast region. Centuries of continuous colonial violence forced many Indigenous groups to forget their language and hide their traditions and spiritual beliefs, as described by Potiguara in the poem cited earlier in this chapter. The *retomada* (retaking or reclaiming) movements that took place after the 1988 Constitution saw many groups in the northeast, among them the Pataxó and Tupinambá, reclaim their ancestral lands while recovering and fostering the use of language, rituals and traditions. Northeastern Indigenous groups suffer constant physical violence and harassment, as

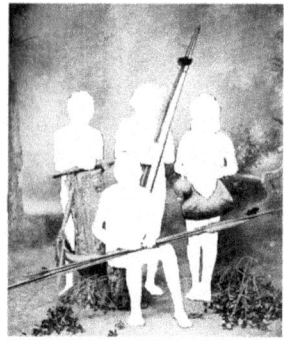

FIGURE 2.4 *Indigente, indi(o)gente, indigen(a)-te* by Arissana Pataxó, 2020 (© Arissana Pataxó, by permission).

well as frequent accusations that they are 'fake Indians' who do not legitimately have the right to their land. These groups are well organised and mobilised, and since the 2010s they have seen an impressive surge in artistic interventions.

Arissana Pataxó's work *Indigente, indi(o)gente, indigen(a)-te* offers a poignant comment on the implication of the arts (in this case, photography) in processes of historical violence against Indigenous peoples in the Americas (see Figure 2.4). The work consists of a triptych with interventions into nineteenth-century black-and-white portraits of Indigenous persons (two of them in antique frames). In two of the portraits the individuals are sitting down, posing with blankets covering the lower part of their bodies. The middle photograph includes four persons holding typical Indigenous artefacts (bows, arrows, maracas, etc.). The portraits do not differ from other nineteenth-century ethnographic photographs apart from one detail: in her intervention, Pataxó erased the faces and the naked parts of the bodies of the posing subjects. They are blank, or rather blanked-out, portraits. The title of the triptych plays with the apparent – but etymologically ungrounded – connection between the words 'indigent' and 'Indigenous'. In Brazilian Portuguese, the word 'indigent' means pauper or destitute, as it does in Latin, but it is also a legal and journalistic term used to describe unidentifiable dead bodies, particularly in the expression *enterrado como indigente* (buried as someone with no identity and no relatives).

The original portraits, taken in Paris by E. Thiesson in 1844, belonged to the Museé de l'Homme's collection of Botocudo (Krenak) photographs, which are now housed in the Musée du Quai Branly in Paris.

Little is known about the individuals who posed for the portraits, but it can be assumed that they were among the various Indigenous individuals who were taken to Europe in the nineteenth century to be exhibited and/or studied as exotic humans. The original photographs emphasise the naked upper torso of men and a woman (the exposed breasts sexualise the woman for non-Indigenous viewers) and body piercings and ornaments. Photographs of Indigenous persons were common from the early days of the camera and many studies have discussed the topic at length, with emphasis being placed on the violent coloniality of such practices (Bell 2011). For our purposes, it is enough to say that this type of photograph did not usually identify the subjects, beyond minimal information about their ethnic group. In most cases, the Indigenous people photographed were meant to represent 'the Botocudo', 'the Bororo', and so on (if not the generic 'Indian'). Pataxó's intervention equates the lost identity of the photographed subjects to the lack of identity of destitute dead bodies which are buried without a name, without relatives or friends – in other words, cut off from any affective connections. By removing their faces from the portraits, she makes the violence explicit: these are portraits without faces, without markers, without identity. In other words, the photographs of unidentified Indigenous individuals that populate European museums have transformed those individuals into 'indigents', unknown corpses, separated from their life history, their family, their community – in the same way that the photographed individuals themselves were separated from their communities when taken to Europe to be exhibited and studied.

By linking the word *indigente* to *indígena*, Pataxó also interpellates the racist dehumanisation of Indigenous individuals by Western knowledge practices, a fact that becomes even more explicit with the poetic transformation of the word *indigente* into *indi(o)gente* (Indian [is] human). The last part of the title/poem, *indigen(a)-te*, calls the viewer to 'indigenise yourself' – which can be read in different ways: for Indigenous viewers, it can be presumed to be a call to reconnect with one's Indigenous roots, to become 'more Indigenous'. For non-Indigenous viewers, it is probably an invitation to learn Indigenous ways of being or to become an ally, to create affective links with the Indigenous world. This last element of the title allows us to extend the reading of Pataxó's erasure of the faces and undressed parts of the bodies beyond nineteenth-century photographic practices. The blanking out of Indigenous identity in the portraits can then be read as a comment on the forced erasure and invisibilisation of Indigeneity in Brazil's colonial and recent history through de-authorisation, a process faced by all Indigenous peoples, be it the Krenak of the photographs or the Pataxó: Indigenous peoples have either to hide and/or erase their Indigenous markers or have their Indigenous identities de-authorised, de-recognised, erased by others. The way out of that process is to *indigenar-se*, to 'indigenise oneself', to assume, in other words, one's ancestral roots.

Ancestral memory plays a crucial role in the work of Glicéria (also known as Célia) Tupinambá, who describes the process of creating her *Manto Tupinambá* (Tupinambá Mantle) as a 'cosmo-agony':

> I was in a cosmo-agony. My body felt itchy and, when I closed my eyes, I went back to that time. Three images would come: one of a woman in the village, sitting, knitting the mantle; the other of the mantle in the ship; and a third one of the mantle leaving the ship, going through the harbour and walking towards an alley and, in that dark street, it would vanish, disappear.[9]

The three images she describes tell the story of the ritual mantles used by the Tupinambá people in sixteenth-century Brazil. Those were sumptuous mantles made of feathers that included a body-length cloak and a headpiece. Only eleven of those mantles are still extant, all of them in European collections, taken by ships to European destinations centuries ago. None remained with the Tupinambá people of Bahia.

According to Glicéria Tupinambá, the sixteenth-century mantles were still alive in the oral culture of her people when they saw the mantle again. The elder Dona Nivalda visited an exhibition in São Paulo, in the year 2000, in which one of the original mantles was displayed, on loan from a Danish museum. Dona Nivalda petitioned for the mantle to be given back to the Tupinambá people and, although the request was denied, this inspired Glicéria to make a new mantle in 2006 as an offering to the *encantados*, the supernatural or spiritual beings that are part of the cosmology of her people, and to make other versions afterwards. The creative process involved travelling to France to see a mantle in the Musée du Quai Branly collections and studying images of the other mantles, but above all it involved talking to the *encantados* in dreams and visions. This is what she describes as 'cosmo-agony' – a trance-like state of deep, visceral communication with the ancestors and, crucially, with the mantles themselves: 'I am not the one who weaves the mantle: the mantle weaves itself'. The mantle, she adds, 'guided her' in making its return to the Tupinambá in Bahia, where it acquired a life and a

---

[9] See https://revistazum.com.br/revista-zum-21/a-visao-do-manto/.

FIGURE 2.5 *Manto tupinambá* by Glicéria Tupinambá, 2020, for the project Um Outro Céu (© Glicéria Tupinambá/Um Outro Céu, by permission).

purpose for its people (see Figure 2.5).[10] The new mantles perform an epistemological repatriation of the cultural artifacts stolen by European colonialism. The old mantles that are preserved in Europe will remain there as a kind of cosmogonical penance for the colonial violence her people suffered:

> I was reading some books and I understood that our people were enslaved, we were taken away from our lands, like the Black peoples, and taken to another continent, without ever going back to Brazil. Our people were lost in the immensity, but not the mantle, it is a record, it is there, still, and they are obliged to take care of it, to preserve it, spending billions to do so. If we were to ask for the mantle back it would be to return it to Nature, to make it not exist anymore, because its function is to return to Nature. Being there, it becomes their penance and, if we were to bring it back, we would forgive them, but we do not intend to forgive. It is just the time, the time that was established by Tupinambá law. So they are going to carry this punishment for the rest of their lives, if it depends on us, the Tupinambá of Serra do Padeiro. We do not want to bestow this forgiveness.[11]

---

[10] See www.brasildefatoba.com.br/2023/04/24/mantos-tupinamba-a-retomada-de-territorios-invisivei; https://umoutroceu.ufba.br/exposicao/manto-tupinamba/.
[11] See https://revistazum.com.br/revista-zum-21/a-visao-do-manto/.

As we can see, Glicéria's description of her creative process and of her people's relationship with the mantle is steeped in an emotive vocabulary (agony, penance, forgiveness) with echoes in Christianity, specifically the story of Christ's suffering. But similarly to Esbell's rereading of Christ's crucifixion, Glicéria's description actually subverts the narrative of sacrifice and forgiveness: agony refers not to Christ, but to a process of trance that allows her to communicate with the very Tupinambá *encantados* that centuries of Christian missionary activity tried to expurgate, and with the mantle itself (whose agency and sentiency would not be recognised by conventional Christianity either). Likewise, 'penance' is a punishment reserved not for Christ but for the European museums, that is, the heirs of the colonial agents responsible for severing the Tupinambá mantles from their affective connections with their own people.

CONCLUSION

If racism against Indigenous peoples is characterised by de-authorisation, that is, the denial of Indigenous identity and/or the pronouncement of their imminent disappearance, anti-racist Indigenous art and literature, as the examples in this chapter demonstrate, is a reaffirmation of Indigenous existence in the present and in connection with ancestral territory. This involves not only denouncing violence, land invasions and legal attempts to curtail Indigenous rights, but also what Jaider Esbell described as cosmopolitics: being part of affective networks that include live and dead humans, animals, plants, mountains, rivers, 'spirits' and ancestral artefacts. Affective networks, that is, that constantly challenge, at an epistemological level, the anthropocentric logic of capitalism.

3

Challenging Whiteness and Europeanness in Argentine Cultural Production

Ezequiel Adamovsky, Ignacio Aguiló, Alejandro Frigerio and Ana Vivaldi

As part of its collaborations with CARLA, in 2022 the anti-racist collective Identidad Marrón, made up of people who define themselves as descendants of Indigenous people, peasants and migrants, carried out an intervention at the Museo de la Cárcova, in Buenos Aires, aimed at making visible the persistence of structural racism in Argentine art.[1] The choice of museum was not accidental: exhibited in its rooms, among other plaster casts, are copies of works from the great European museums such as the Louvre and the Galleria dell'Accademia, brought to Buenos Aires to educate national artists in European aesthetic canons. The intervention of Identidad Marrón consisted of a series of performances by artists identifying as *marrón* (brown) in some of the rooms where these casts are exhibited.[2] The mere presence of their non-white bodies interrupted a space conceived according to Greco-Roman canons of beauty. They thus exposed the way in which racism and Eurocentrism defined the constituent artistic policies and discourses of Argentine art.

As in Argentina, in much of Latin America the classical European canon has functioned as a model when institutionalising a national art form. However, in most countries of the region there were attempts to hybridise these European ideas with elements that were perceived as more 'autochthonous', linked to mestizo, Indigenous or Afro-descendant peoples. Although it was a problematic and controversial matter, most

---

[1] Identidad Marrón literally means Brown Identity, but the collective chose not to use terms commonly used to refer to brown people in Latin America – such as *moreno, pardo* and *prieto* – in order to escape the colonial baggage attached to such words.
[2] See www.digitalexhibitions.manchester.ac.uk/s/carla-en/item/939.

Latin American nations recognised the mediation of non-European factors in the shaping of their cultural imaginary, albeit in a subordinate position. In the Argentine case, on the other hand, the national culture, as conceived by the ruling elites of the late nineteenth century, obliterated any possibility of heterogeneous visions of the nation. The narrative that these elites proposed deliberately rejected *mestizaje* and promoted, instead, the idea of Argentina as a white and European country (Geler 2010; Quijada 2000). According to the official discourses of the time, which persisted through the twentieth century, white and European Argentina was the result of two simultaneous and interrelated processes: the mass arrival of immigrants from Europe and the progressive 'extinction' of native peoples and Afro-descendants due to wars, diseases and their supposed racial 'weakness'.

The whitening of Argentina in the late nineteenth century and the early twentieth was not merely an ideological construct. At a time of great transoceanic migrations, Argentina was the Latin American country that received the most immigrants as a proportion of its local inhabitants. But despite the transformative impact of overseas immigration, Argentina never experienced a total Europeanisation of the population. Afro-descendants, native peoples and so-called *criollos* remained very numerous, especially among the working classes and outside Buenos Aires and the centre of the country. The term *criollo* is an important one, as it became a common denomination for many people of mixed-race origin. *Criollo* is most often used in Hispanic America to mean someone of Iberian ancestry born in the Americas.[3] In Argentina, the term's usage broadened following the onset of European immigration in the late nineteenth century, and as a reaction to it. It came to encompass people and cultures predating overseas immigration, yet not identified as Afro-descendant or Indigenous. The term maintained this ambiguity, signifying whiteness – because of the long-standing association of *criollo* with Spanishness – while also suggesting a certain presence of non-white, particularly Indigenous, elements (Chamosa 2010). In some ways, *criollo* was analogous to 'mestizo', especially in a context where *mestizaje* was overtly rejected.

Because of the colonial heritage as well as the political and economic directions taken by Argentina after independence, these inhabitants were the ones who received the worst educational and labour opportunities

---

[3] In Brazil, however, the Portuguese word *crioulo* means a person of African ancestry. (The term's literal English translation is Creole, usually defined as mixed-race.)

and remained in a subaltern social position. In the late nineteenth century and the early twentieth, they were also forced to adopt a civic ideal of nationality that excluded any ethnic-racial difference and assumed the European character of the social formation, which implied for them a silent but systematic racism (Adamovsky 2012; Frigerio 2008; Geler 2010, 2011; Lamborghini, Geler and Guzmán 2017). Non-white people were integrated into a lower class stripped of any racial reference (Adamovsky 2012; Ratier 2022). In other words, everyone was simply 'Argentine', without differences. But since the official narrative asserted that Argentines were descendants of Europeans, those who did not fit this national type because of their skin colour or because of their Indigenous, Afro-descendant or mestizo ancestry were forced, by the actions of the ideological state apparatus, to embrace a form of Argentineness that, in practice, condemned them to subaltern positions, socio-economically, politically and culturally (Briones 2005; Geler 2016). The Argentine nation-state project devised at the end of the nineteenth century was thus based on a double axis: if on the one hand the reproduction of social disparities maintained structural racism (among other forms of discrimination and marginalisation), on the other, it promoted what Michael Omi and Howard Winant (1994) call a form of 'racial common sense' that denied any racial inequality under the pretext of the supposedly homogeneously white and European character of the nation.

Although the pressure exerted on non-white people to accept their subaltern social position and forget their ethno-racial markers was intense, it is important not to assume that they had no agency at all. On the contrary, those who suffered from structural racism and the whitening mandate developed various forms of resistance. Sometimes this involved distancing themselves from ethno-racial identities to embrace other forms of identification (political, territorial or class) in order to improve their life chances and deal with a profoundly unjust social order. A head-on challenge against racism was not always possible, but these people continued in multiple ways to show the limits of Argentine whiteness as a project. In the 1930s, in the context of large migrations of peasants (mostly mestizos) to Buenos Aires and other central cities, these tensions became more acute – and especially with the coming to power of Peronism in the 1940s, which we will discuss later, and as the working classes became politically vocal.

Sergio Caggiano (2012) points out that the 'visual common sense' in Argentina trains the eye not to read as 'racial' differences in phenotype that are nevertheless clearly evident. As Alejandro Frigerio (2006) shows, only people with stereotypically and very pronounced African features are perceived as Afro-descendants in Argentina. Similarly, outside of rural or community settings, Indigenous people are often thought of simply as *criollos*. This explains, in part, the fact that the idea of a uniformly white and European country has coexisted with a demographic reality that, in the public arena and in daily interaction, constantly contradicts it, given the ethnic-racial heterogeneity of the population. But this 'not seeing' (what Caggiano calls 'invisualisation') is neither systematic nor constant: in certain contexts, differences in skin colour can quickly become very noticeable. A middle- or upper-class white person is likely to immediately notice the phenotype of someone they pass on a deserted street at night if they have a dark complexion. And, while this does not mean that he or she will encode that difference in terms of defined ethno-racial identities (white, Afro-descendant, Indigenous, etc.), this illustrates how phenotypic difference influences forms of social stratification and classification in Argentina, despite the constant affirmation that all Argentines are white and European.

This example also shows how fear and other negative affects can be mobilised by racial factors. In fact, the notion of a 'civilisation' besieged and sometimes invaded by 'barbarism' has been a constant trope in Argentine history, which has been deployed by the dominant sectors to interpret different political and class conflicts and conjunctures. And although these notions have changed over time, they have generally had racialised underpinnings (Gordillo 2020). Thus the usual invisibility of racial diversity in dominant discourses has been punctuated by momentary hypervisibilisations of such differences, which activate visceral anxieties and fears and provide affective bases to justify repressive and/or reactionary political projects. As we shall see, the racialisation of Peronist sympathisers in the 1940s or, more recently, the alarm over a nonexistent 'terrorist' organisation of the Mapuche people in Patagonia are examples of this.

But beyond these moments of hypervisibilisation, whitening discourses have mean that racial difference is alluded to through other markers of difference, such as education, geographic origin and, above all, social class. In fact, the term *negro* in Argentina is used generically to refer to poor people (of whatever skin colour and ethnic origin, even if they are phenotypically white). In the colloquial language of Argentines, *negro* is used to talk about the poor much more frequently than to refer to people of African descent; it generally has a primarily classist, rather than racial, connotation. The term refers to what Lea Geler (2016) calls *el negro popular* (a Black person of the working classes) and Ezekiel Adamovsky (2012) calls the 'non-diasporic black', to differentiate it from an Afro-descendant.[4] At the same time, although not always the case, the implicit stereotype that a poor person will have brown skin often works in practice. Class and race are intertwined.[5]

Efforts to impose the idea of a white and European nation were quite successful in terms of public acceptance of the image, but this did not prevent what elites were trying to exclude – mestizo, Indigenous, brown and the Afro-descendant people and elements – from finding forms of expression outside dominant structures and discourses, and sometimes even within them. In the arts, the figure of the gaucho – typified as a brave, unruly, nomadic cowboy, often brown-skinned – is emblematic of this process, as we will show. The cultural sphere constituted a space of struggle in which some of the most fundamental criticisms of the idea of Argentina as a white and European nation took place. In this chapter we outline the relationship between the arts and the struggle against racism in Argentine history, with a focus on specific relevant examples. We will examine various anti-racist artistic experiences and the tensions (and sometimes hybridisations) they have had with a high culture that thought of itself, originally, in European terms, but that could never escape its relationship with the non-white (partly for reasons of guilty fascination).

Our account will include anti-racist artistic expressions articulated around racial subjectivities with a specific ethnic memory – particularly Afro-descendant and Indigenous – but it will go beyond that. This is due to the fact that, precisely because of the characteristics of Argentina's racial formation and the power of the myth of the white and European nation, Afro-descendant and Indigenous artistic expressions have been less prominent than in other Latin American countries, for example Brazil and Colombia. But, on the other hand – and here it is possible to point out a specific characteristic of the Argentine case – the artistic production of working-class sectors has played a central role in the articulation of strategies that, despite not being explicitly anti-racist, have

---

[4] Alejandro Frigerio (2006) was the first to propose a distinction between *negro* and *negro mota* to refer to the double valence of the term in Argentine racial formation. *Mota* refers to tightly-curled African-type hair.
[5] Similarly, white people in Argentina rarely define themselves as such (as they might in some Latin American countries or in the United States). It is more frequent, instead, that they self-identify as 'middle class' or 'European', which implies a white complexion. Thus, although the construction of whiteness as a norm – and therefore neutral – has been studied in various contexts (Garner 2007), in Argentina it has specific characteristics.

strongly contributed to challenging structural racism. Either directly or through the mediation of middle-class – or even upper-class – artists, the working-class or 'non-diasporic' *negros* mentioned here managed to have a considerable impact in formulating alternative ways of thinking about the nation and to reinstate the presence and value of non-white people as part of it.

In order to deal with the diversity of materials, we propose a typology in terms of how they position themselves in the face of racism, comprising three categories: visibilising, vindicatory and anti-racist.[6] The visibilising category includes practices that grant artistic presence to ethnic-racial groups that are invisible in the narratives of the nation, although they may do so with stereotypical, exoticising or inferiorising images (e.g. that infantilise or bestialise). In this sense, they cannot be considered anti-racist and, in fact, may contribute to racism. However, in the Argentine context, they take on a different weight due to the centrality of discourses that minimise the very existence of racial diversity. Vindicatory artistic practices present favourable images that contest the mostly negative valuation that Argentine society attributes to subaltern ethnic-racial identities, without fundamentally questioning racism or only doing so obliquely. These vindicatory cultural productions can be related to what Mónica Moreno Figueroa and Peter Wade (2022) call 'alternative grammars of anti-racism' – that is, those dynamics that do not explicitly focus on racism or anti-racism, but that address broader structural inequalities in which the role of racial difference is indirectly acknowledged. Not all vindicatory artistic practices are produced by non-white artists but, in the cases in which this happens, the affirmation generated by self-representation takes on a specific gravitational weight, as it implies taking control of symbolic and political representation and, ultimately, of subjectivity (Fanon 1986). Finally, anti-racist discourses *stricto sensu* denounce, with varying degrees of regularity and explicitness, the racism suffered by subaltern ethnic-racial groups.

Most of the anti-racist artistic practices *stricto sensu* have developed in recent years as a result of the impact of multiculturalism in Argentina. However, it is also important to consider the role that vindicatory cultural products have played in the national imaginary. A good part of the struggle against racism in Argentina has been expressed less as a head-on

---

[6] To which we could add a fourth category, that of the stigmatising discourses of the artistic production of the second half of the nineteenth century linked to Romantic-liberal sectors and the subsequent conservative republic.

challenge than as a heterogeneous set of rather oblique, denotative, implicit initiatives that have revalued brownness, and its associated cultural forms and ways of life, and undermined the idea of a white and European nation (and therefore, the superiority of whiteness) without attacking it explicitly. Many of these initiatives were led by people – be they professional artists or just ordinary people expressing themselves artistically – who did not necessarily subscribe to any specific racial or ethnic identity, nor did they have distinctive ethnic memories or even a physical appearance that would make them victims of possible racist aggression. Rather than projecting our own expectations about what form anti-racist cultural expressions should take, we will attend instead to the ways in which the people who create cultural products relate to racism.

THE CONSTRUCTION OF THE NATION-STATE

The beginning of Argentina's independence process in 1810, and its formal declaration of independence in 1816, brought drastic changes in interethnic relations. In 1813 the so-called caste system[7] was abolished, and an 1821 electoral law of the province of Buenos Aires – soon imitated by almost all provinces – established the right of suffrage for any free male, of whatever colour, social status or even literacy. For the free male population – which included a large number of Afro-descendants and Indigenous people living in white-controlled cities – this meant a horizon of equality before the law that was quite radical for the time. Racial discrimination continued, but no longer on a formal or legal basis. Those who had been enslaved had to wait much longer. In 1813, a 'free womb' law was decreed and there were later prohibitions on the slave trade, but the abolition of slavery would come only in 1853 (or 1860 for the province of Buenos Aires).[8] Moreover, the emergent state controlled only half of Argentina's current territory during that time. Parts of the Pampas and the Chaco, and the entirety of Patagonia, were under the control of independent Indigenous communities, with whom the Argentine state maintained ties but on whom it also periodically visited military violence.

The triumph of the Buenos Aires liberals over the interior provinces in 1862, after decades of internal conflict over how to organise the new nation, was preceded and accompanied by strongly racist narratives and

---

[7] The colonial system known as the *sociedad de castas* (society of castes or breeds) differentiated institutionally between multiple socio-racial classes of people, based on criteria of lineage, phenotype, occupation and reputation.
[8] Free womb laws decreed that children born to enslaved mothers were free.

discourses, including in literature and essays, where Afro-descendants, Indigenous people and mestizos were demonised. Paradigmatic examples of this are 'El matadero' (The Slaughterhouse, 1838, published in 1871) by Esteban Echeverría and *Amalia* (1851) by José Mármol, widely considered in Argentina, respectively, to be the first national short story and novel. *La cautiva* (The Captive, 1837), an epic poem by Echeverría, recounted the capture of a white woman and her husband by Patagonian Indigenous people, symbols of the perceived threats to white society (Malosetti Costa 2022). In 1845, Domingo F. Sarmiento published his book *Facundo*, of enormous influence in Argentina and the rest of Latin America, in which he read the political conflicts and development possibilities of the time as an ongoing struggle between 'civilisation' and 'barbarism'. In this view, the former was rooted, in part, in whiteness and Europeanness, while the latter flourished in the rural world of the gauchos and the Indigenous and mestizo lower classes.

From 1879 onwards, the national army quickly and violently occupied the territories of the Pampa and Patagonia (and eventually the Chaco in the northeast) that had been under the control of Indigenous peoples. This was part of a process of consolidation and modernisation of the state and the Argentine economy, which sought to insert itself definitively into the international system as an exporter of raw materials for industrialised countries, particularly the United Kingdom. With the rapid urbanisation of the Pampa region and the mass arrival of immigrants in the following decades, the advance of the project that the elites called 'progress' or 'civilisation' seemed assured. The narratives of Argentine modernisation that flourished at this time presented Indigenous cultures and the African presence (and soon also the gaucho world) as things of the past, of which only fast-disappearing relics remained. At the end of the century, the idea of a completely white and European nation seemed at first sight convincing.

At the intellectual, literary or academic art level, for the time being, there was little possibility of opposing the racism of official discourse or the idea of a white and European Argentina, which was in fact partly promoted in official cultural production. Between the 1850s and 1880s, on the other hand, the Afro-descendant community of Buenos Aires (known as *afroporteños*) maintained an appreciable presence in the public sphere, including via several newspapers of their own in which they defended themselves against racial prejudice. There were also Black poets, such as Horacio Mendizábal, Mateo Elejalde and Casildo Thompson, who published explicitly anti-racist works. After this period, however, due to the pressure for acculturation coming from the dominant sectors (and from part of the Afro-descendant community that sought integration into the national project), the Afroporteño community entered a long period of invisibility in the public domain (Geler 2010; Lewis 1996).

In this period, Indigenous cultural production began to be classified within the incipient ethnographic collections of the Museo de la Plata and the Museo Etnográfico de Buenos Aires, both recently founded (Podgorny 1999). These collections followed the criteria of European rescue anthropology that sought to generate archives of 'cultures' supposedly in imminent disappearance. They were organised by region and did not record the authorship of the objects collected. The collections were supplemented by raciological studies of Indigenous people who were taken prisoner in the military outposts and kept in captivity in the La Plata Museum (where many died), and by the examination of Indigenous skeletal remains exhumed without consent.

In popular culture at the turn of the century, especially in the cities, there were extraordinarily vivacious expressions of the heterogeneity of the lower classes, where immigrants from many nations, internal migrants, *criollos*, Indigenous people, mestizos and Afro-descendants coexisted. Although they did not have an explicit anti-racist message, unique cultural expressions emerged that highlighted ethnic diversity. Examples of this are carnival and tango (which at the time showed their African roots more clearly than would later be the case): they both reaffirmed the presence of the non-white as part of the nation and subtly undermined the official whitening messages.

In turn, the enormous success of José Hernández's poem *Martín Fierro*, published as a cheap pamphlet in 1872, deeply marked Argentine culture, especially among the lower classes. This particular type of popular *criollismo*, produced mainly by white upper- and middle-class *letrados* (men of letters) but aimed at lower-class audiences, turned the gaucho – precisely the figure that official discourses had considered as belonging to the barbaric past – into a hero of the people and an emblem of the nation. The phenomenon points to a distinctive tension in Argentine cultural identity: even as official discourse promoted a white, European ideal, there persisted a widespread desire, cutting across social classes, for cultural authenticity rooted in more autochthonous traditions. For the working classes, *criollismo* provided a means to assert their presence in national culture. For white elites and middle classes, it offered a way to claim cultural legitimacy and connection to an imagined authentic national past, while maintaining their social position. This complex dynamic helps explain how *criollismo* could become a powerful national emblem while simultaneously challenging aspects of official racial narratives. In popular *criollismo* culture, the gaucho hero was frequently portrayed as a dark-skinned, often mestizo, individual who associated with Indigenous and Afro-descendant people and coexisted with them as part of the same *criollo* world that these stories exalted (Adamovsky 2019). And it is not a minor fact that some of the most famous creators in the *criollo* genre – such as Gabino Ezeiza, who was a famous *criollo payador* (wandering minstrel) – were themselves of African descent.

FROM THE CENTENNIAL TO THE FIRST MASS CULTURE (1910–1943)

Between 1880 and 1914, just over four million people, mostly Europeans, arrived in Argentina, of whom 70–75 per cent stayed permanently (Adamovsky 2020; Brown 2011). The narrative of Argentina as a white and European country relied on the role that the enormous overseas immigration would have in 'dissolving' all remnants of the non-white population. But the elites expected migrants from northern Europe, home to the 'race' that was supposed to lead the world's march towards progress. Those who arrived, instead, were mostly Italians and Spaniards of humble origin and, in many cases, with anarchist or socialist leanings.

The need to assert dominance over these foreign-born masses and to reaffirm the social order in the face of revolutionary ideas drove an intellectual movement of a nationalist bent that became more prominent after 1910, drawing on celebrations for the Centenary of the May Revolution. In this context, three voices stood out. Manuel Gálvez reaffirmed the Spanish and Catholic heritage of the cultural traditions of pre-immigration Argentina. Leopoldo Lugones promoted a cult of nationality centred on the gaucho, who as we have seen was already admired by the lower classes. But the gaucho he claimed was a mythical, almost Greco-Latin gaucho, who epitomised the supposedly superior values (nobility, patriotism, virility) that characterised, in his opinion, Argentina's national type prior to immigration (Adamovsky 2019). Finally, Ricardo Rojas did criticise the idea of white and European Argentina by advocating for a mestizo national tradition that combined the European with the Indigenous, although he conceived of the latter as a spiritual legacy and an aesthetic substratum of Argentineness, rather than as a biological contribution to contemporary Argentines. However, none of these three authors was interested in recovering the Afro cultural legacy. These intellectuals, part of a trend known in Argentine intellectual history as 'cultural nationalism', opened a new scenario of revalorisation of the local vis-à-vis the European; but this did not mean the end of racist prejudices, which remained very present.

Despite its limitations, this debate paved the way for other, more profound challenges. The impact of the ideas of writers such as Rojas and Lugones was felt by visual artists, who from the 1920s onwards chose to paint Indigenous or mestizo characters set in scenes from the interior of the country and also gauchos and *criollos* from the Pampa region, in whom mestizo features or brownish skins could often be distinguished (Penhos 1999). Cesáreo Bernaldo de Quirós stands out in this sense (see Figure 3.1). Also influenced by leftist ideas and anti-imperialism, Antonio Berni represented the Argentine working people as having racially diverse bodies (see Figure 3.2).

During this period, wherein Argentina exhibited a pace of modernisation and urbanisation exceeding the Latin American average, popular culture and mass culture (produced by middle-class creators but aimed at various audiences) contributed to rendering the heterogeneity of the nation visible. Popular *criollismo* deepened the connection which it had been making between the gaucho and non-whiteness. Although many of these images and representations relied problematically on stereotyped images (such as the famous illustrations of gauchos by the artist Florencio Molina Campos), they contributed to making diversity visible and, consequently, implicitly questioned the idea that the Argentine people were white and European. In the first decades of the twentieth century, two of the most famous Argentine comic strips emerged, both with non-white protagonists: *Las aventuras del Negro Raúl* (1916, by Arturo Lanteri), inspired by the Afro-descendant dandy Raúl Grigera, and *Patoruzú* (1928, by Dante Quinterno), about a Tehuelche Indigenous man of great fortune and superhuman strength (Alberto 2022; McAleer 2018). Although both reproduced grotesque images of Black and Indigenous people (both characters were presented as unintelligent), in Patoruzú this was combined with admirable characteristics such as heroism and altruism.

The only explicitly anti-racist approach in the arts at that time came from Martín Castro, an anarchist *criollo payador*, who in 1928 wrote a long gaucho narrative poem entitled *Los gringos del país* (The Country's Gringos), published shortly after as part of the collections of cheap booklets of gaucho adventures made available for popular consumption. The poem was a veritable counter-history of Argentina, told from

FIGURE 3.1 *El lancero colorado/El poncho rojo* by Cesáreo B. de Quirós, 1923, from the cover of *Nativa*, a nationalist magazine (photo by E. Adamovksy, courtesy of the Biblioteca Nacional, Argentina).

Challenging Whiteness and Europeanness: Argentina

FIGURE 3.2 *Manifestación*, painting by Antonio Berni, 1934 (© The Berni estate, by permission).

the point of view of the Indigenous people, dispossessed and oppressed by Europeans and their descendants for 400 years. The gauchos that Castro exalted were of *trigueño* complexion (literally, wheat-coloured, i.e. brown) and direct descendants of both Indigenous people and the 'white' Argentines in turn descended from Europeans, who were their enemies (Adamovsky 2019).

Also in the 1920s, the folk music of the northwest region acquired the status of a commercial genre and by the following decade there was already an established circuit of artists. The lyrics of some of its songs, especially those of Atahualpa Yupanqui and Buenaventura Luna, reinstated in the national imaginary the presence of mestizo and Indigenous populations. For musicians, having native lineage and brownish complexion even functioned as a mark of authenticity (Chamosa 2010; Adamovsky 2019). In the 1930s and the beginning of the following decade, moreover, people in the world of tango recovered memories about the music's Afro-descendant roots (made invisible in the previous years), while two Afro rhythms from the Rio de la Plata region were revalidated: *milonga* and *candombe*. Although less prominent, local jazz also gave rise to a revalorisation of Blackness. The world-renowned guitarist Oscar Alemán, who had a very dark complexion and presented himself as Afro-descendant, shone in this period (Karush 2016).

Thus, by the early 1940s, state and school messages, which affirmed that the nation was white and European, coexisted in tension with a powerful popular and mass culture, which produced images of the Argentine that reinstated the presence of non-whiteness and, at times, affectively revalued it. The fact that these cultural productions were largely created by members of the same middle class who, from other places, simultaneously promoted the image of a white Argentina, explains why the clash of visions remained latent. With the partial exception of Martín Castro, Argentine racism was not yet openly discussed by cultural creators, nor was the idea that the nation was or should aspire to be 'white' challenged head-on.

PERONISM AND THE EMERGENCE OF THE CABECITA NEGRA (1943–1955)

The emergence of Peronism in the mid 1940s caused an upheaval in the idea of Argentina as an extension of Europe. As a political movement, it served to unify and articulate different sectors of the population, including both white people of European descent and others of mestizo or even Indigenous descent. The latter were, in general, provincial migrants who, attracted by job opportunities in the cities from the 1930s onwards, had progressively settled in the urban peripheries, particularly in Buenos Aires (Ratier 1971). Although workers of all aspects and ethnic origins supported Juan Perón, it was the provincial migrants who became metonymic signifiers of the entire Peronist movement and the urban proletariat (Grimson 2017).

Faced with the growing unity and voice of the working classes, a powerful anti-Peronist movement was formed almost immediately among the middle and affluent sectors. They now had to share public spaces with dark-skinned internal migrants, who were derogatorily called *cabecitas negras* (little black heads), and who now ventured beyond the periphery and into traditionally white areas of the city. Among the white and European middle and upper classes, this produced affective reactions and intensities that were channelled into emotions of different kinds – in particular, fear and disgust – and that nourished moral and political discourses. The anti-Peronists aimed from the beginning to discredit their adversaries not only in political terms but also morally, aesthetically and racially. They branded their enemies as vulgar, dirty, irrational and unable to adapt to the conventions of urban modernity. But these differences were also essentialised and racialised: Peronists were also attacked using racial categories such as mestizo, *negro* and *indio*; they were accused of being 'hard haired' (i.e. with African-type hair) and, especially, of being *cabecitas negras*. Thus, from its genesis, anti-Peronism was not only structured around ideological issues but also had an affective substratum articulated around racial issues.

Peronism, meanwhile, remained strictly within a discourse of class and did not respond explicitly in the terms in which the opposition framed the discussion. Its rhetoric was expressed in a class language that posed the conflict as a struggle between the working people – without distinction of race – and the oligarchy (Garguin 2007; Milanesio 2010). The problem of differences in skin colour was not a topic for Peronists, nor was there an explicit vindication of the brown-skinned Argentine. In fact, where racism was mentioned, it was rather to deny that it existed in Argentina. The denunciation of Argentine racism, the vindication of the *cabecita negra* and its transformation into an icon of Peronism and the deep roots of the nation would take place only after the overthrow of Perón in 1955 (Adamovsky 2019). As in previous periods, the idea of a white and European Argentina was discussed implicitly and indirectly in the sphere of mass culture and through a language of visuality and aurality. Although the propaganda apparatus of the Peronist state continued to represent the Argentine people through European-looking bodies, a greater presence of images that featured mestizos was evident in these years (Adamovsky 2016). One example is the use of the mestizo figure 'Juan Pueblo' in a poster promoting Perón's Five Year Plan (1947–1951) to modernise and industrialise the country (see Figure 3.3; the text reads 'The vigour of a strong people is a giant step towards national recovery').

The representation of Black Argentines was much rarer, though notable examples exist. One such case shows Perón with an Afro-Argentine child in an illustration for a story titled 'Chocolate', about an Afro-Argentine boy who was bullied at school, published in the regime's main propaganda magazine, *Mundo Peronista* (Peronist World) (see Figure 3.4). While this image could be interpreted as patronising and its title problematic, it nevertheless challenges local racism: the white state school uniform, the company of other (white) boys and Perón's affection acknowledge the Black child as part of the nation at a time when dominant discourses denied the existence of Afro-Argentines.

As before, popular *criollismo* continued to channel these debates. The same happened with music of mass consumption. To give just one

FIGURE 3.3 A mestizo 'Juan Pueblo' in a promotional poster for the Five Year Plan, *El Laborista*, 10 June 1947, p. 8 (photo by E. Adamovksy, courtesy of the Biblioteca Nacional, Argentina).

example, the biggest hit record in Argentine history was a 1950 song, 'El rancho'e la Cambicha' (Cambicha's House), performed by Antonio Tormo, strongly identified with the Peronist regime (Chamosa 2010). The lyrics describe in the first person the preparations of a man who is about to go to a rural *boliche* (popular dance) run by a woman known as Cambicha. Without being expressly anti-racist, its celebration of popular festivities and of the positive affects related to the enjoyment of music and dance, conflicts, albeit indirectly, with the ideal of the white, European people. The lyrics contain words in Indigenous languages: *cambicha*, in fact, is the feminine diminutive of *cambá*, which in Guaraní designates people with dark or black skin.

While there were allusive and indirect ways of thematising ethnic-racial differences, during these years there was no specific militancy along these lines. Afro-Argentines did not have a public voice, as they had had in the nineteenth century, although they did have private spaces in which they maintained their own cultural practices, such as the dances of the Shimmy Club of Buenos Aires, which operated from the 1920s to the 1970s (Frigerio 2008). A development worth noting is that in 1946 the Kolla

Challenging Whiteness and Europeanness: Argentina

FIGURE 3.4 Juan Perón with an Afro-Argentine child, illustration from *Mundo Peronista* 84, 15 April 1955, p. 32 (photo by E. Adamovksy, courtesy of the Biblioteca Nacional, Argentina).

Indigenous people achieved unprecedented visibility in the national press when they organised the so-called Malón de la Paz (Peace Raid), a march on foot from Jujuy to Buenos Aires to reclaim their ancestral lands. It was the starting point of an indigenist movement in the country, which developed more strongly in the 1970s (Lenton 2010).

CONSERVATIVE REACTION AND POLITICAL RADICALISATION (1955–1976)

In 1955, a coup d'état deposed the government of Perón, who went into exile until 1973. During this period, in which the Peronist Party was banned, military regimes alternated with civilian governments of weak legitimacy. The overthrow of Perón constituted an anti-plebeian reaction that sought to defuse the capacity for action of the working class and, given the veiled racial substratum of the political conflict, to restore the pre-eminence of what was seen as the true Argentina, rooted in middle-classness and Europeanness. In a scenario that combined the proscription of Peronism and the continuation of racism, the first explicit public debate on skin-colour discrimination in Argentina took place (racism had been openly discussed before, but only in reference to Jews). In the 1950s, authors such as Jorge Abelardo Ramos and Arturo Jauretche wrote widely circulated essays linking the anti-Peronist reaction to the interests of the oligarchy, to imperialism and to the racist views which, according to them, were held by a substantial part of the middle class. In the 1960s, authors of the 'new left' such as Juan José Sebreli also took up the topic of the oblique racism of those who identified themselves as being middle-class and of European descent. Reversing the negative charge that it had had among the anti-Peronists, sectors of Peronism now vindicated the idea of *cabecitas negras* as an emblem of plebeian Argentina and authentic nationality. The fact that Peronism was the party of the *cabecitas negras* was now proof of the popular roots that the party proudly claimed. To this scenario was added the transnational influence of the decolonisation process in Asia and Africa, the civil struggles of African Americans and, particularly, the proliferation of left-wing anti-imperialist movements in Latin America inspired by the success of the Cuban revolution. All of this gave greater resonance to the anti-racist struggle and projected the vindication of Black and Indigenous America.

In the arts, the affirmation of the non-white Argentina had numerous examples, of which we can mention only a handful. The well-known short story 'Cabecita negra' (1961) by Germán Rozenmacher, a writer of Peronist leanings, describes, from the perspective of a racist white, middle-class character named Lanari, the paranoid fears of the Buenos Aires petite bourgeoisie regarding immigrants from the interior. The story narrates, from Lanari's point of view, an ambiguous and tense situation the protagonist experiences when two people he perceives as *cabecitas negras* momentarily occupy his apartment. The end of the story, in which Lanari is convinced of the need to use the army to 'crush' all the *cabecitas negras* and *negros*, anticipates the Argentine bourgeoisie's support for the militaristic and repressive tactics used by the state in dealing with the working classes in the 1970s; it makes visible the role of racism as the affective basis of that coercive turn.

Challenging Whiteness and Europeanness: Argentina 115

FIGURE 3.5 *¡¡Basta!!* poster by Ricardo Carpani, 1963 (© Verónica Carpani, by permission; photograph by Sergio Redondo, courtesy of TAREA-UNSAM).

In the visual arts the most obvious example is the work of Ricardo Carpani, who devoted much of his work to the illustration of political pamphlets and posters that supported working-class causes. The bodies he chose to represent the Argentine people deliberately showed non-European features (see Figure 3.5).

Cinema also raised the issue of racism as an integral part of the narratives of Latin American emancipation of the time. For example, the pinnacle of Latin American political documentary, Fernando Solanas and Octavio Getino's *La hora de los hornos* (1968, The Hour of the Furnaces), denounces the structural racism suffered by native populations and chooses to show non-white bodies (and a soundtrack that includes Afro-derived rhythms) to represent the oppressed Latin American population. However, it relapses into patronising views of Indigenous people as backward, apolitical and in need of guidance and leadership from urban revolutionaries, reproducing some of the paternalistic attitudes it seeks to criticise.

Finally, popular music was rich in evocations of non-whiteness as part of the nation. In particular, folkloric music – which during this period achieved an unprecedented popularity – affirmed Indigenous legacies and the connection of things Argentine with the cultural spaces of mestizo Latin America. While songs often relied on problematic indigenist tropes that romanticised Indigenous people as noble savages or relegated them to a mythical past, they nevertheless helped challenge the idea of Argentina as exclusively white and European. The repertoires of singers Mercedes 'La Negra' Sosa and Daniel Toro are good examples.

In the early 1970s, the fervour of the working classes also reached Indigenous peoples, who started initiatives to coordinate the struggles of different peoples. Afro-Argentines, on the other hand, continued to have no public voice as such. The lower classes mobilised as never before, but there was no activism specifically focused on anti-racism in these years. However, as we have seen, cultural, trade union, social and political militancy did not completely avoid the issue.

DICTATORSHIP, NEOLIBERALISM AND DEMOCRACY (1976–2003)

The military dictatorship that was installed after the 1976 coup d'état and remained until 1983 sought the total dismemberment of the working classes as political actors through a programme of terror and political repression, economic disciplining and the weakening of social ties and other notions of solidarity. It also attempted to reaffirm a vision of national identity anchored in whiteness and European origins. The repression dismantled incipient Indigenous efforts at coordination and also affected the cultural sphere. Many artists were murdered, disappeared, exiled or forced to keep a low profile to avoid reprisals. Among those mentioned here, Ricardo Carpani, Mercedes Sosa, Fernando Solanas and Octavio Getino went into exile; Daniel Toro remained in the country, but his songs were banned.

The return of democracy in 1983, together with the impact of discourses of multiculturalism sponsored by international organisations, opened up new opportunities for Indigenous communities, which in the 1980s reorganised and presented claims in terms of human rights, in line with the international prominence such rights had acquired during the brutal military regime (Briones, Cañuqueo, Kropff and Leuman 2007). Together with historical demands for ancestral land, this implied a greater emphasis on issues of ethnicity, identity and recognition, which was often expressed at the cultural level. Communities everywhere began to recover their languages, music and traditions. The Mapuche singer Aimé Painé was one of the most outstanding voices in this regard. Although she never managed to record an album, she performed in the country and abroad, working tirelessly as an artist and activist to make Mapuche people aware of their own history and culture and to make them visible among other non-white groups (Navarro Hartmann 2015). The demands of native peoples attracted the attention of white artists. For example, Argentine cinema dedicated many films to Indigenous peoples during this period, among which stand out *Gerónima* (directed by Raúl Alberto Tosso, 1986) with the Mapuche actress Luisa Calcumil in the leading role, *La deuda interna* (The Internal Debt, directed by Miguel Pereira, 1988) and *El largo viaje de Nahuel Pan* (Nahuel Pan's Long Journey, directed by Jorge Zuhair Jury, 1995). Only in the twenty-first century did an incipient movement of cinema made by Indigenous peoples themselves emerge, generated by their participation in training workshops for young communicators (Torres Agüero 2013) and inspired by the boom in Indigenous audiovisual production in the rest of Latin America (Schiwy 2009; Córdoba 2011; Soler 2017).

The first post-dictatorship government (under Raúl Alfonsín, 1983–1989) ended in hyperinflation and a deep economic crisis. His successor, the Peronist Carlos Menem, who governed until 1999, implemented one of the most drastic neoliberal adjustment programmes in the world, which raised poverty and unemployment levels to record highs and provoked a crisis of representation. The weakening of the state's integrative capacity opened the door to a profound questioning of the myth of white and European Argentina and the emergence of alternative identities. The drastic impoverishment experienced by the middle sectors (supposedly 'white and European' people) during the 1990s – and intensified by an extreme economic crisis in 2001 – caused increasing anxieties. Rooted in the persistent affective substratum of racism in Argentina, these fears were often expressed through racial language and were codified in terms of a symbolic 'darkening' of the nation, given the historical association of mestizo, Indigenous and Afro elements with poverty (Aguiló 2018). As Alejandro Frigerio (2006) demonstrates, references to the 'Latin Americanisation' and even the 'Africanisation' of Argentina were common in political and media discourse during the 2001 crisis. At the same time, the crisis led to Argentine racism being discussed more frequently in the media.

In the 1990s there was a marked process of re-ethnicisation, which included the reappearance of native groups such as the Rankulches, Huarpes or Selk'nam, which had been declared extinct (Gordillo and Hirsch 2010). The 1994 reform of the National Constitution included, for the first time, the recognition of the pre-existence of native peoples in Argentina before colonisation, adding to international recognition (such as International Labour Organization treaty 169), and advancing on the provincial recognition that had been achieved in some regions (Carrasco 2000; Briones 2005). In 1995, the Instituto Nacional contra la Discriminación, la Xenofobia y el Racismo (National Institute Against Discrimination, Xenophobia and Racism, INADI), was created with the principal objective of receiving complaints about discrimination and prosecuting citizens accused of acts of discrimination or hatred. Although both Indigenous recognition and the creation of INADI were propitiated by international contexts of expansion of multiculturalist policies as new forms of international governance (see Briones 2005; Hale 2005), these movements would have been impossible without the pressures of national organisations and activisms (Lenton 2010). At this time, associations of Afro-Argentines also began to reappear, aiming to make their presence visible and revalue their cultural legacy (Frigerio, Lamborghini and de Maffia 2011).

In popular culture, from the 1990s onwards, there was also an increase in the reaffirmation of native peoples, although mostly by non-Indigenous people. This was most noticeable in music. The fifth centenary of Columbus's arrival prompted critical commemorative songs by two of the most important names in national rock, León Gieco and Los Fabulosos Cadillacs: respectively 'Cinco siglos igual' (Five Centuries Without Change) and 'Quinto centenario' (Fifth Centenary). Other rock bands produced similar content at the time, such as A.N.I.M.A.L. (acronym for Acosados Nuestros Indios Murieron Al Luchar, Our Indians Died Fighting), Almafuerte, La Renga and Malón. In the realm of folk music, the Mapuche singer Rubén Patagonia stands out. However, with the exception of Patagonia, none of these musicians identified as Indigenous, and most of their mentions of native peoples reinforced the idea of Indigenous peoples as located in the past.

The band Todos Tus Muertos, led by the Afro-descendant and Rastafarian Fidel Nadal – son of Enrique Nadal, a film director and early leader in the fight for the recognition of Afro-Argentines – had great commercial success with *Dale aborígen* (Go, Aborigine, 1994), an album that mixed Afro-Latin rhythms with rap, punk, reggae and ska. The album included several denunciations of racism, although focused on international figures such as the Zapatistas, Malcom X, Patrice Lumumba and Nelson Mandela.

In *cuarteto* music – a popular music from the province of Córdoba – Carlos 'La Mona' Jiménez, the genre's top star and, aside from Nadal, the only artist among those we mention in this section who has a phenotype read by many Argentinians as Afro-descendant, praised the 'skin of my race, Black race' in his highly successful album *Raza Negra* (1994). In another of his compositions, 'Por portación de rostro' (2006, Because of the Face, i.e. racial profiling), he also alluded to the racism suffered by those with 'dark skin'. The fact that Jiménez is considered an icon of the *negro popular* indicates that, despite their being usually differentiated, sometimes there is room for overlapping between plebeian Blackness and ethnic Afro identity.

The most pointed anti-racist approaches in the musical realm of this period were seen in so-called *cumbia villera*, in which also, for the first time in the twentieth century, signs appeared of 'Blackness' becoming an emblem of defiant pride among the working class. *Cumbia villera* is a subgenre of *cumbia* created by musicians coming from low-income and precarious neighbourhoods, called *villas* in Argentina (Cragnolini 2006; Semán and Vila 2011, 2012).[9] It became an unexpected success in the late 1990s and early 2000s, with lyrics that often narrated, in the first person, the alleged daily experiences of the *pibes* (young men) of the slums. Themes of alcohol and drug consumption, leisure time, delinquency and misogynist and heteronormative sexuality in *villera* lyrics, added to the poetic importance of ideas of marginalised territories and the preference for a look based on sportswear, earned the music comparisons with gangsta rap, by which it was in fact inspired (Martin 2008).

One of the innovations of *cumbia villera* was to make visible the fact that the working class suffered not only a form of class violence but also racist violence. It contributed to an affirmation of the *negro villero* (heir of the *cabecita negra*), stigmatised from above, as a positive identification. The band Meta Guacha presented songs in which they identified themselves as *negros*, antagonistically opposed to those with 'light skin' and put forward visions of popular joyfulness related to Blackness. Pablo Lescano, one of the best-known artists of the genre, has the proud phrase *100% negro cumbiero* tattooed on his chest and it is common for him to harangue his audience at concerts by shouting 'Las palmas de todos los negros ¡arriba!' (all the *negros* put their hands in the air!), eliciting enthusiastic responses from his followers. By exposing the racial dimensions of the material and symbolic violence systematically experienced by

---

[9] *Cumbia* originated as a traditional Colombian folk genre, associated with the country's tropical Caribbean region and its dark-skinned inhabitants. From the 1940s, it became a commercial genre all over Latin America.

young people in poor neighbourhoods, and by proposing strategies for appropriating and reversing these forms of racialisation, *cumbia villera*, despite its other problematic aspects (e.g. its gender politics), constitutes an important phenomenon in the recent anti-racist cultural production of Argentina.

THE RECENT SCENARIO (SINCE 2003)

The institutionalisation and recognition of ethnic-racial collectives that took place at the end of the 1990s and the turn of the century generated a context that allowed for the growth of ethnic-racial organisations, the expansion of rights and forms of recognition and the provision of certain resources. But it also generated new challenges. It is relevant to mention two. In relation to both Indigenous peoples and Afro-descendants there was a demand for 'authenticity', even when self-recognition was the fundamental criterion, used for example in the census. The registration of Indigenous communities, for instance, requires a socio-historical report proving that the collective has verifiable ties to an Indigenous nation and that it is a social unit. At the same time, very light-skinned people who identified as Afro-descendants encountered resistance to being recognised as such (Geler 2016). Cultural representations thus became mediated by the demand to demonstrate 'authentic' difference in order to achieve recognition. Any aspect that was seen as ambiguous gave rise to doubts about authenticity (Briones 2005; Vivaldi 2016).

With the arrival of Kirchnerism in 2003, the demands for more pluralistic visions of the nation coming from different spheres – Indigenous, Afro-descendant and migrant activists, the working classes and progressive sectors – found even more echoes in the state. The government developed ambitious cultural policies in this respect, especially after the inauguration of Cristina Kirchner as president in 2007. The clearest example was the organisation of the celebrations for the Bicentennial of the May Revolution in 2010, which included large-scale events by the experimental theatre company Fuerza Bruta. Kirchner's government systematically emphasised the contrasts between these celebrations and those of the 1910 Centennial. The Secretary of Culture, Jorge Coscia, wrote:

> In 1910, the ruling elite celebrated its supposed condition as a white, homogeneous, Europeanised nation, relegating everything that could have a local, *criollo* or Indigenous flavour to a second, third plane ... (T)his Government does not consecrate just one way of being national, as was the case one hundred years ago ... We celebrate diversity as our most valuable specificity. (2011: 30)

One of the central moments was the Bicentennial Parade, which attracted two million people along its route through the avenues of Buenos Aires. Through nineteen tableaux, this parade of floats represented major milestones of Argentine history and popular culture, from a sensory and affective perspective rather than a narrative and chronological one. In other words, rather than promoting a particular interpretation of Argentine history and nationhood in line with the traditional official vision, the event sought to generate an emotional response in the public through audiovisual stimuli and the energy generated by the crowds of people in the public space.

The first scene of the parade symbolised the native peoples. It consisted of three floats carrying Indigenous performers from different native nations, with their traditional costumes, masks, paintings and tools.[10] The second, entitled 'The Argentine Republic', showed dancers dressed in the colours of the national flag, suspended in the air from a crane, representing the homeland.[11] The two female dancers selected to share this role had been deliberately chosen for their mixed-race features. Hanging from a harness, the young women danced to the rhythm of *carnavalito* (a northern folkloric genre with a strong Indigenous Kolla influence) and *candombe* – as well as electronic music – to emphasise the ethnically heterogeneous character of the nation. A group of dancers and musicians accompanied the float. Musical allusions to the quintessentially plebeian celebration (carnival), in its Andean and Afro-descendant manifestations, were combined with the young women's constant encouragements to the people to join in the dancing in the street. All this accentuated the staging of the nation in a multicultural and subaltern key and the event as a popular festival, mobilising various emotions, particularly joy (Citro 2017). Some of other floats in the parade showed different episodes of Argentine history, in some of which Afro-descendant actors participated. Alongside European immigrants, there was even room for the visibilisation of others, such as Bolivians and Chinese.

According to the official plan, the order of the first two floats should have been the reverse – first the Republic, then the Indigenous peoples – but a last-minute glitch forced the change to be improvised. President Cristina Fernández de Kirchner later admitted: 'What had to happen happened, which was fairer and more historically rigorous, the originary peoples at the beginning' (2019: 256). In this almost accidental

[10] See www.youtube.com/watch?v=NhjP2nF7FUk.
[11] See www.youtube.com/watch?v=oWxrU-PsTdo.

way, the parade proposed a refoundation of the nation located in Indigenous cultures and not in the Revolution of 1810. And although the scene fell back on a conception of Indigeneity essentialised and located in the past – the public television narration systematically used the imperfect tense to refer to the originary peoples, while the costumes and scenery of the floats had almost no present-day references – the fact that the performers were, to a large extent, Indigenous distanced it from the indigenist nativism of cultural manifestations of other decades (see Ko 2013).

Despite its positive elements, the opening by the Kirchnerist government to resignifications of Argentina in multicultural terms that had been introduced during Menemism sometimes came into conflict with Indigenous and Afro-descendant organisations, in part because of the attempted capture, by the state apparatus, of the discourses and affective energies of these associations and, in the case of native peoples, by the continuation of neo-extractivism, agribusiness and the conflict over land (Svampa 2019). However, in general, Kirchnerism marked an important contrast with previous official discourses and cultural policies by contributing to the distancing that society had already begun, on the way to the 2001 crisis, from the image of a homogeneously white nation. The impact it had on the field of artistic production was substantial: anti-racist messages and the vindication of the non-white as part of the nation seeped everywhere, from literature to cinema and TV, from music to popular celebrations (e.g. Citro and Torres Agüero 2015).

None of this means that the more traditional views have dissipated. Racism continued stubbornly and even acquired a more aggressive tone, as the voices questioning it multiplied. The coming to power of the liberal-conservative Mauricio Macri in 2015 implied, in part, an attempt to return to an idea of nation of European genealogy. The audiovisual production of the state under his presidency reversed the previous tendency to represent Argentina through varied bodies, with a strong presence of non-whites. Under his successor Alberto Fernández (2019–2023), by contrast, the state developed anti-racist policies through INADI and the Dirección Nacional de Equidad Racial, Personas Migrantes y Refugiadas (National Directorate of Racial Equity, Migrants and Refugees), created in 2020 and directed by Carlos Álvarez Nazareno, an Afro-descendant activist.

In the midst of these implicit struggles about the ethnic-racial profile of the nation, there have been interesting developments in the field of culture and activism, some of which became sites for collaboration for the CARLA project. One such is the Mapuche Theatre Group El Katango (see Chapter 6). Founded in 2002 in the Patagonian city of Bariloche by the Mapuche theatre maker, teacher and researcher Miriam Álvarez (co-author of Chapter 6), El Katango was formed in the space for political debate and theatrical creation called the Mapuche self-affirmation campaign *Wefkvletuyiñ* ('We are Re-emerging' in Mapuzugun). Another CARLA collaborator is the theatre company Teatro en Sepia (TES), founded in 2010 (again see Chapter 6, co-written by TES director Alejandra Egido). TES seeks to break the historical indifference and invisibility of the Afro presence in Argentina through the performing arts. Although TES and El Katango emerged in the context just described, in which legal recognition had allowed ethnic-racial collectives a way of working with the state while society as a whole was beginning to accept Argentina's ethnic-racial plurality, both theatre groups still had to confront invisibilisation, racist stereotypes, the essentialisation of identity and racist structures of territorial dispossession and the criminalisation of Mapuche people, as well as marginalisation in the urban space and labour segregation for Afro women.

To the panorama of artistic initiatives that made visible the claims of Indigenous and Afro peoples, a new element was added in 2019 with the founding of Identidad Marrón, the anti-racist art collective with which we started this chapter, which in a very short time gained a place in public conversations. The novelty of their approach lies partly in the introduction of the term *marrón*, which they chose as a deliberate act of reclamation and political visibility. While *negro* has historically been wielded as a class-based slur, there has also been a tendency to resort to words such as *trigueño* (wheat-coloured), *moreno* or *morocho* when referring to people with darker skin tones – terms that have been used to sidestep explicit discussions of race. By embracing *marrón* as a new term for classifying people, the collective deliberately sidesteps the old familiar euphemisms, forcing a more direct conversation about race and identity in Argentine society.

The other novel aspect of Identidad Marrón's approach is that they aspire to an anti-racist policy that relies not on discrete minority communities but on the majority that makes up the working classes, who have brownish skins and non-white features but who are often unaware of their precise ethnic origins. Identidad Marrón aspires to give voice to the *marrones*, who, according to its definition, are the numerous people of Indigenous, mestizo, migrant and peasant origins who live in the cities. Its activism is located in what they term an 'anti-racism with class consciousness' which aims to combat racism at all levels, especially in the world of culture, while recognising the imbrication of racism and classism. Their initiatives include artistic interventions such as the one mentioned in the introduction to this chapter, as well as street actions, workshops and media and social media campaigns. As part of their collaboration with CARLA, in addition to visual works produced for our virtual exhibition, a book compiling their texts and initiatives was published (Identidad Marrón 2021).[12]

In sum, over the last two decades, although white and European Argentina persists for certain sectors as a horizon of nationality that is impossible to renounce, recent years have exposed even more than before the inability of this narrative to serve as a point of reference for large parts of society. The horizon of anti-racism and the affirmation of non-whiteness as part of the nation are moving forward in a very evident way. In 2020, the anti-racist protests that the assassination of George Floyd detonated in several parts of the world also impacted Argentina, and public debate about the existence of structural racism in Argentina increased further.

As a coda, it is important to note that the election of far-right libertarian Javier Milei as president in late 2023 marks a concerning change of direction for Argentina's trajectory towards greater racial recognition. Milei's rhetoric actively celebrates European heritage and Argentina's supposed exceptional whiteness in the Latin American context. His praise of controversial historical figures such as Julio Argentino Roca – responsible for the military campaigns against Indigenous peoples in Patagonia – combined with his ultra-free-market ideology and commitment to intensifying extractive industries suggests that Indigenous peoples and other racially marginalised groups, as well as the working class, will be disproportionately affected by his policies. The cultural and political gains achieved by anti-racist and ethnic minority organisations and artists over the past decades, and the resilient networks of resistance that have emerged, will surely be tested by this reactionary turn. The coming years will likely see increased tension between official discourses that attempt to restore myths of white Argentina and grassroots movements and artistic expressions that insist on the nation's racial diversity and demand concrete actions against racism.

---

[12] The 2021 book is part of CARLA's online exhibition, where it can be read and downloaded for free: www.digitalexhibitions.manchester.ac.uk/s/carla-en/page/identidad-marron.

CONCLUSION

In this chapter we traced a long history of artistic productions whose relationship with racism we described using three categories: visibilising, vindicatory and overtly anti-racist. Although, as we have pointed out, it is only in recent years that an anti-racist culture *stricto sensu* has been consolidated in Argentina, we have proposed seeing certain vindicatory expressions as implicitly anti-racist, even though they have not always been interpreted by others as such. The peculiar manifestation in Argentina of racial hierarchies combined with the persistent denial that they existed – and, thus, that racism was a problem – forced us to pay attention to the oblique, allusive, non-confrontational ways that local creators tried to deal with the reality of ethnic-racial discrimination. In particular, the phenomenon of generic 'popular Blackness', not diasporic or related to any specific ethnicity, drove us to go beyond more easily identified anti-racist dynamics, such as the affirmation of minority identities and the defence of their rights. If anti-racism in Argentina is now expressed in a verbal, direct and confrontational way that seems totally novel, it is also true that a much older genealogy can be traced, which we have outlined here.

Having concluded this overview, it should be noted that a majority of the intellectuals and creators who put forward vindicatory views in public were white, middle-class males. Only in the current, more actively anti-racist, context do we see Indigenous, Black and *marrón* people, including women and trans and non-binary people, at the forefront of the debate. Neither Ricardo Rojas, Martín Castro, Antonio Tormo, Jorge Abelardo Ramos, Ricardo Carpani nor León Gieco are perceived in Argentina as non-white, nor were they lower class. However, alongside them, often in the same artistic fields, other artists whose bodies did manifest racial differences added their creations of anti-racist tenor. Among others, we have mentioned Buenaventura Luna, Atahualpa Yupanqui, Aimé Painé, Daniel Toro, Fidel Nadal, 'La Mona' Jiménez and Meta Guacha. There is nothing strange in this confluence: for a long time white people were in the best position to mount a defence of the *cabecitas negras* without paying the cost of being seen as such. But, in addition, the struggles for the ethnic profile of the nation were intertwined with class differences and with national politics, in particular with the Peronism versus anti-Peronism cleavage. This scenario was conducive to some white people becoming involved in the vindication of non-whiteness. The outcome of this struggle affected them directly.

Certainly, some of the creations contributed by white artists are purely visibilising, and ambivalences and blind spots can be found in relation to racial hierarchy: for example, paternalism, the reproduction of certain stereotypes and a tendency to visualise the subject in reference to rural but not urban spaces, or in the past rather than the present. There was also a certain preference for Indigeneity, with little room for Afro-descendants. But there was also room for vindicatory discourses with anti-racist potential. All in all, there is no doubt that the debates, sounds and images produced by some cultural products generated by white people contributed powerfully to making racism visible in Argentina and were part of the same scene that fed the creations of non-white artists.

Curated Conversation 2: Decolonising the Arts in Latin America

Anti-Racist Irruptions in the Art World

Curated by Ignacio Aguiló; translated by Peter Wade

Source: an online event, 'Descolonizando las artes en Latinoamerica: Irrupciones antirracistas en el mundo del arte' (Decolonising the Arts in Latin America: Anti-Racist Irruptions in the Art World) that took place on 29 July 2020, featuring Denilson Baniwa (Brazilian Indigenous artist), Miriam Álvarez (Mapuche theatre director), Ashanti Dinah Orozco (Afro-Colombian poet), Arissana Pataxó (Brazilian Indigenous artist), Alejandra Egido (Afro-Cuban and Afro-Argentine theatre director) and Rafael Palacios (Afro-Colombian dance company director). The event was in Spanish and was chaired by Carlos Correa Angulo, with assistance from Jamille Pinheiro Dias. The conversation can be accessed on CARLA's YouTube channel: https://youtube.com/live/5-xs-DR7Yr0.

CARLOS CORREA ANGULO: This colloquium is entitled 'Decolonising the Arts in Latin America: Anti-Racist Irruptions in the Art World'. We will be talking with artists from different parts of Latin America about their work from a decolonial and anti-racist perspective. We will have the participation of Miriam Álvarez, director of the Mapuche Theatre Group El Katango, and Alejandra Ejido, director of the Afro-descendant company Teatro en Sepia, both from Argentina. From Colombia, we will have the poet and Afro-feminist activist Ashanti Dinah Orozco, as well as Rafael Palacios, founder and director of the Afro-contemporary dance company Sankofa. From Brazil, they will be joined by Arissana Pataxó and Denilson Baniwa, Indigenous visual artists. I ask you please to introduce yourselves.

DENILSON BANIWA: First of all, good afternoon to you all. I am from the Baniwa people, who come from the territory called Alto Rio Negro, on the border of Brazil with Colombia and Venezuela. I mean these people live in the three countries. I am part of the Brazilian Indigenous movement, fighting for the rights of traditional peoples and their territories, and from this position I present myself to the world. My artistic work is based on my cosmovision as a member of the Baniwa people and on their resistance to European invasions, occupation and colonisation of our lands, especially in Brazil. In this sense, my work reflects on the construction of a country born from the domination of traditional peoples, which continues into the present.

An example of this is my intervention in one of the iconic monuments of São Paulo, Brazil's main city. This is the Monumento às Bandeiras, which pays homage to the *bandeirantes*. The *bandeirantes* were a paramilitary group from the Portuguese colonial period who were hired to hunt down Indigenous and Black people escaping from slavery, and whom the official Brazilian culture positioned as national heroes. My intervention consisted of projecting onto the monument images of a large Portuguese caravel sinking, from which emerges a forest of mythical and spiritual beings. The purpose of this work is to reconfigure the history of Brazil from the perspective of the originary peoples, who until now have had no voice.

MIRIAM ÁLVAREZ: I call myself a Mapuche theatre maker and also a teacher of theatre. Having grown up as an urban Mapuche and having studied theatre made me want to represent these silenced histories of the Mapuche people. The Mapuche people are a pre-existing people who occupy the territories that are today under the sovereignty of the Chilean and Argentine states. The formation of these states divided our people. I live in the city of Bariloche, in Argentine Patagonia, which is a border city, because we are very close to Chile. And that exemplifies the realities we Mapuche live in, because we have to negotiate with different state and political entities and with very different realities.

ASHANTI DINAH: Good afternoon to everyone and thank you for opening this much-needed platform that calls for a kind of aesthetic justice for the world of art in general. My name is Ashanti Dinah and I was born in the Colombian Caribbean. I see myself – and this is my political identity – as an Afro-Caribbean woman, [who is] always in relation to the Caribbean meta-archipelago, in that polyrhythmic and syncopated identity that those of us born in the Caribbean have. For many years I have been an activist with some [experience of] leadership at the national level. I started very young, at the age of fifteen, when I joined the Angela Davis organisation in Barranquilla, my home town. When I came to Bogotá, the city where I currently live, to study for my master's degree, I refocused my interests not only on the ways in which Afro-descendant characters appear in canonical works, but also on Afro-descendant literature – especially Black women writers who speak with their own voice and use their identity from that position.

And then I also took up my own voice as a Black woman, as a woman of African descent. I didn't get there very quickly; we know very well that identities are constructed, they are dynamic and they are found along the way. I learned to be a Black woman through dialogue with white feminists and I understand what it means to be a woman and Black at the same time. After publishing several magazine articles and essays, I was finally able to publish my first collection of poetry last year, entitled *Las semillas del Muntú* [The Seeds of Muntu], which is part of a trilogy. It was very well received. I am currently working on the second book of poems in the trilogy, called *Alfabeto de una mujer raíz* [Alphabet of a Root-Woman], which recently received an honourable mention in a call from the Ministry of Culture for unpublished works by Afro-Colombian authors.

ARISSANA PATAXÓ: I am from the Pataxó people and currently live in Santa Cruz Cabrália, in the Indigenous territory of Coroa Vermelha. The Pataxó people live in the states of Bahia and Minas Gerais, mainly in urban areas, and we also have Pataxós in Rio de Janeiro, Salvador and Brasilia, who have moved there to study at university and work on Indigenous policy. My artistic work is linked to education, as I have been a primary school teacher since the age of nineteen, working mainly in the community of Coroa Vermelha.

I started to get involved in the art world in 2005, when I took a course in visual arts at the School of Fine Arts of the Federal University of Bahia. At first, my intention was not to become an artist, but to acquire technical knowledge. However, I realised that I needed to enter the artistic field in order to address Indigenous issues, where there was a total lack of understanding of our culture. This was particularly evident in academic environments, which are theoretically spaces of knowledge and learning, but show a great fragility when it comes to understanding the Indigenous world.

ALEJANDRA EJIDO: It is a pleasure to share this stage with such restless and interesting creators. I am Cuban, trained in the performing arts in Havana, and I have always been committed to working on social emergencies on stage. I worked in theatre companies in Barcelona, dealing with issues of gender violence. When I arrived in Buenos Aires, I noticed the absence of Afro-descendant theatre and Afro-descendant issues in general and I began to focus my work precisely on filling this gap. Gradually this work began to focus specifically on the theme of Afro-descendant women and their oppression. For the last ten years I have been directing Teatro en Sepia, a company that focuses on Afro-descendant and Black women's experiences.

RAFAEL PALACIOS: I am a dancer and choreographer trained in traditional African and Afro-contemporary dance techniques in Africa and Paris. When I founded Sankofa in 1997, my aim was to create a space that would allow us to deepen the knowledge that the dancing body can give us, capable of connecting with its past, its identity and its origins, in order to understand who we are in the present and, above all, to formulate strategies that will allow us to lead a better life in the future.

Dance has many qualities, secrets, codes and wisdoms that we, Afro-descendants, can examine and reformulate for a better life. We can discover not only who we are, but also how to communicate with the rest of society and create intercultural dialogues. Through dance, we seek to be heard in a society that has often stereotyped the Afro-descendant body, condemning our dance practices to a place of eroticism and exoticism, without recognising that through every movement we make as Black people, our history, our culture and our vision of society are manifested.

JAMILLE PINHEIRO DIAS: I would like to ask you how your artistic work relates to the notion of internal colonialism.

DENILSON: Brazil tends to identify itself with Rio de Janeiro and São Paulo, and this has marginalised the rest of the country, which functions as a kind of colony of these centres. Brazil has grown from this core, where the majority of the population is of European origin. It is a model of a country that, by concentrating power in Rio de Janeiro and São Paulo (areas that represent the Brazil that does not want to be Brazil, but a copy of Europe), excludes the Indigenous peoples, the Quilombolas and the Blacks.[1] We Indigenous people are forced to leave our places, as I left the Amazon, to occupy spaces in an art world controlled by Europeans. But this is the only way to confront this colonisation and create new perspectives based on Indigenous visions, otherwise we will continue to be invisible. As a friend of mine says, we have to place some artistic 'bombs' in certain places in order to explode colonised thinking and build another way of thinking from the ruins.

ARISSANA: I adopt the identity of artist as a strategy to address Indigenous issues in spaces that exclude us. In general, recognition comes after being validated by institutions in São Paulo and Rio de Janeiro. This is not only external, but also within our communities. My first award did not come from an institution in Bahia, but from Rio de Janeiro, and this led to recognition in other parts of the country. Unfortunately, this dynamic continues, as Denilson mentioned.

RAFAEL: In Colombia, as in Brazil, internal colonialism hinders the recognition of peripheral cultural and artistic practices. The production of cultural managers and artists from the Colombian Pacific is rarely recognised in the capital and when it is, it is considered folklore or local expressions without artistic value. These are the conditions handed down by colonialism. As artists, we are not so much interested in fighting for spaces to be opened for us, but in creating and validating our own practices.

MIRIAM: Yes, in Mapuche theatre we face similar challenges. At best, our practices are seen in terms of folklore. We are asked to essentialise Mapuche representation. In Buenos Aires, for example, people expect rituals, ceremonies and Mapuzugun [the Mapuche language]. For them, the Mapuche are something of the past, almost extinct, because the general perception is that Argentina is a white, European country. However, our presentations try to communicate our current reality, which is also shaped by the present and the urban experience. We are not interested in being part of the artistic elite of Buenos Aires. We reach out to the Mapuche population in the peripheries, bringing theatre to those who do not have access to it.

---

[1] Quilombolas are people who live in settlements called *quilombos*, originally founded by Black people who escaped enslavement.

ASHANTI DINAH: In Latin America, when it came to identity formation, there was a whole class of conservative and feudalist political and economic elites who proclaimed themselves white and, in this sense, white-mestizo. A segregated, anti-popular and stately creole aristocracy monopolised state affairs and also shaped national or canonical cultural and artistic practices. The construction of the nation was articulated around a philological obsession with Colombian identity that linked power to the written word. It is no coincidence that the main political leaders were also writers who, through their essays and literature, validated a colonial grammar centred on Catholic and Hispanic whiteness.

The tradition of contestation was born with Candelario Obeso, who mocked the canon, its whiteness and its idiomatic correctness, even dedicating some of his works to people like Miguel Antonio Caro and Rufino José Cuervo, who represented this conservative elite. Obeso begins to write in the way that people in the Caribbean express themselves, especially the rural population, producing what I call a syntactic dislocation that denounces what the dominant powers consider a deformed and vulgar use of language. My work reclaims this contested voice that defies the segregation produced by literature and the canonical arts.

ALEJANDRA: I live in the capital of the country, Buenos Aires, which is also one of the great capitals of theatre. And I see that the theatre audience here does not necessarily ignore what happens in the provinces, but they do ignore Afro-descendants and, of course, Afro-Argentineness. The narrative that Blacks died in the wars of independence and the epidemics of the nineteenth century remains dominant. We foreign Afro-descendants are ignored. Afro-descendants, like the originary peoples who preceded the nation-state, are not recognised in Argentine culture, except from a rather superficial folkloric perspective, which is reflected, for example, in the proliferation of intercultural festivals.

I was surprised by Miriam and Rafael's attitude of not wanting to be part of the mainstream art movement. I feel that it is impossible for people of African descent to work in a completely self-organised way, without infrastructure. But I am intrigued by their perspective and will think about it more.

CARLOS: I would like to ask how you integrate anti-racism in your artistic work. Do you consciously think about anti-racism as an artistic strategy?

RAFAEL: Sankofa's artistic quest is to explore our own knowledge, but also the oppression of our bodies. We dance to achieve our emancipation, to be heard, to activate liberatory processes, and all of this is related to anti-racism. Our artistic practice questions the exotic and sexualised representation of our bodies on stage, as in the case of *mapalé*, a dance with Afro-Colombian roots that has been misrepresented because it has been reduced to an imaginary of savagery and eroticism, with dancers in loincloths and covered in oil. In our work, *La mentira complaciente* [The Complacent Lie], we denounce this form of representation and reclaim this dance as our own, focusing on its historical context and its meaning for Afro-Colombian peoples. We want the white public to know why these dances were born and why they were created and preserved by our peoples.

To go back to a point Alejandra made earlier, it is not that I am not interested in being part of the Colombian art scene. Of course I am interested, because we have the right to express ourselves and to be seen and heard as Black men and women in our country. What I am saying is that it is not the others who validate me. We, with our own explorations and our own categories and ways of expressing what we do, can say what kind of art we are making. It is an art that is linked to social processes, an art that provides solutions for the daily lives of the people and communities from which these cultural practices come. Each of the works we create in Sankofa seeks to disrupt and undermine the structural racism that we face every day, from the moment we get up to the moment we go to bed, from the moment we are born to the moment we die.

MIRIAM: In our Mapuche performance practices we try to have an impact on two levels. On the one hand, we reach out to the Mapuche population, who generally do not go to the theatre. This means that we have to go to them and present and disseminate our art in a way that invites and motivates them to experience it. On the other hand, we want to install in society in general a reflection on Mapuche themes and, in particular, to bring people into contact with Mapuche stage practices. In works such as *Pewma* ['dream' in Mapuzugun] we deal with the Indigenous genocide in Patagonia, an event that structured social relations in the area where we live.

To talk about Indigenous genocide in the academy or in Argentine artistic practices is to break with a strategic silence in this country. For our Mapuche people, it is a very painful subject because it is not something distant. My great-grandmother was nine years old when the Conquest of the Desert took place, as the military occupation of the territories was called, which was a great massacre. She is not a distant person in my life, because she is the person who raised my mother. So in my family there are silenced stories about the genocide of the Indigenous people. In *Pewma* we investigate the silences of our relatives. This is an example of how we think about racism.

ASHANTI DINAH: I think it is very important to consider the process by which one arrives at an anti-racist poetics. There are many writers of African descent who have never articulated an anti-racist discourse, which I regret. Perhaps they did this as a strategy of insertion into the art world, or to avoid being stigmatised as militants or activists by hegemonic literary criticism. But I start from a very important fact, which is that Hispanic American literature is marked by the racialisation of Afro-descendant characters, who are always located on the side of the barbarian in the antinomy of civilisation and barbarism. We must fight against the racism of a hegemonic canon that perpetuates stereotypes and racism, not only in the representation of Afro-descendants, but in the tyranny of a certain form of diction, writing and speech. The contrast is what Franz Fanon called zoological language, because according to racist grammars we do not speak and communicate, we babble and shout. Our anti-racist poetics seeks to counter the categorisation of our ways of expressing ourselves as inferior and to restore the dignity of our language as a legitimate language.

An anti-racist poetics seeks to give voice back to the Black community, with Black characters telling their own life stories from their perspective and with their own way of expressing themselves. In my work there is a defence of African symbolic memory, which includes the spiritual or religious, not as something barbaric, but quite the opposite. It is necessary to appeal to Ubuntu or Uramba, as it is called in one area of the Colombian Pacific, to return to the ancestral wisdom of the older women. Finally, I would like to stress the importance of an intracentric perspective, where we look at ourselves rather than seeing ourselves through the Eurocentric gaze. I don't need to ask permission from Vulcan or the Greek gods because I have Xangó and my Orixás.

ARISSANA: In Brazil, it is true that the image of Indigenous people has largely been constructed through the arts, whether in literature, cinema or other artistic expressions. Unfortunately, this representation has often been based on folkloristic stereotypes, far removed from the reality and diversity of the more than three hundred ethnic groups and two hundred Indigenous languages present in the country. Although we have the defence of land rights as a common agenda, we are different nations that have been homogenised under a single figure: the 'Brazilian Indian'. Artistic practice provides a valuable platform to deconstruct these stereotypical images that have been constructed over time through artistic production itself. It also opens up spaces for dialogue between nations and communities, as well as with Brazilian society, allowing Indigenous voices to be heard and contributing to a more authentic and diverse representation.

ALEJANDRA: Our dramaturgy tries to decolonise theatre by focusing on characters of African descent, mostly women, who have rarely been in the limelight. But it is also a way of disrupting other currents, such as feminism, because by focusing on the experience of Black women, we are talking about the fact that we are different kinds of women. For example, our play *No es país para negras* [This is No Country for Black Women] came out of research we did in an Afro-descendant neighbourhood in the greater Buenos Aires area. We performed our plays in a house where local Afro-descendant women usually gather. After our performances, we would talk amongst ourselves.

After three months of performances in that house, we noticed that there were themes that systematically came up in all our conversations. So, we interviewed 140 Afro-descendant women, which allowed us to learn about their socio-economic realities. We then produced a new play, *No es país para negras 2*, which reached a diverse Afro-descendant audience and generated a very interesting debate. We address issues that no one talks about, such as how sexual diversity or love relationships are experienced from an Afro-descendant perspective. The challenge for Teatro en Sepia is always to work with limited resources, without a physical space.

DENILSON: As for how art can transform and decolonise, I would like to add that art is essential to rethinking coloniality, but the approach must be holistic and multidisciplinary. This is because colonising thought itself comes from all artistic expressions: literature, music, dance, film and visual arts. Although I work with the visual, I believe that it is necessary to combine all the arts in order to structure a [form of] decolonising thought that communicates broader ideas. This more interdisciplinary perspective can go where each artistic discipline alone cannot. We will only make a difference if we start writing books and creating visualities from this Native American, African American, Afro-American, ecological-originary thinking, from all these worlds that have always been on the margins of the Western world.

PART II

ARTISTIC PRACTICES, RACISM AND ANTI-RACISM

4

Resistance in Motion

Dance and Anti-Racism in the Afro-Contemporary Dance of Sankofa Danzafro

Carlos Correa Angulo and Rafael Palacios

Nobody dances to look ridiculous. There is a grace in dance, some skills that make the body show off its full rhythmic potential, but we cannot stop there. Afro-contemporary dance is performed by individuals whose bodies have experienced historical conditions of structural racism. When these individuals dance, their bodies express their resistance to these exclusions.
Rafael Palacios

INTRODUCTION

A fascination with aesthetic aspects and with the graceful movement of bodies has dominated our views of dance. Dance is characterised by a 'regime of visuality', in Rafael Palacios's words, which pushes both spectators and dancers to share the enjoyable sensations linked to observing bodies that move with music.[1] In the West, dance is often seen as entertainment, stirring something within us, transmitting energy or exuding transgressions. However, early anthropological approaches to the world of dance in non-Westernised societies demonstrated that, alongside music, dance was integrated into a broad system of social relations that supported religious and ritual practices (Boas 1930; Chernoff 1979; Hanna 1988; Robb 1961). Dance was also central to

---

[1] This chapter has benefited from the participation of Rafael Palacios, director of Sankofa Danzafro. His comments and conversations have significantly nurtured its content. Any inaccuracies are the responsibility of myself, Carlos Correa. Naming Palacios as co-author is an attempt to reduce asymmetries in the research process and to promote thinking and writing collaboratively. At times Palacios's voice will be more present, at others my own. We hope to have achieved an honest and polyphonic text.

collective celebratory expressions that reinforced processes of identity boundary construction.

Since the 1970s, dance has garnered interest in anthropology, leading to four basic approaches that remain today. The North American Boasian approach sought to record native dances and introduced philosophical concerns about movement, power and race. The folklorist approach, developed in Germany and France, was concerned with describing and formally classifying dance, but lacked a historical component. The linguistic approach to dance was characterised by formal descriptions of movement patterns. And finally, a more holistic approach included analysis from social anthropology, medical anthropology, cognitive science and cultural studies, exploring the connections between dance and factors such as ethnicity, sexuality, gender, body, migration, identity and transnationalism (Kringelbach and Skinner 2014: 6–8). This approach views dance as an 'embodiment of social life' (Hughes-Freeland 2008: 1) that is both aesthetic and political, both narrative and performative.

An ethnography of dance begins with the premise that dancers, choreographers, spectators and researchers inhabit aesthetic systems rooted in cultural conventions (Kaeppler 2000). Dance ethnography focuses on how participants name and describe movement and conceptualise dance and its purposes. It analyses the formation of 'affective atmospheres' (Anderson 2009), which produce effects on audiences and dancers, and it investigates the relationship between movement and embodied knowledge (Reed 1998).

This chapter delves into dance in relation to ethno-racial elements, the representation of identity and the development of anti-racist agendas. The focus is on how the Colombian Afro-contemporary dance company Sankofa Danzafro develops anti-racist narratives through a particular aesthetic and a political positioning that criticises racism's impact on Black lives in Colombia. Among Sankofa's anti-racist strategies are i) challenging stereotypes about Afro-descendant people, emphasising the importance of 'listening' to the message of the dance, rather than highlighting the aesthetic visuality of the performance; ii) exploring how the embodied knowledge present in Afro-Colombian traditions can be used as a creative resource and a source of 'Afro-referentiality'; and iii) combining traditional and contemporary Afro-Colombian rhythms and movements to create musicality and choreography within an anti-racist narrative framework. We will identify these strategies in a recent Sankofa Danzafro choreographic creation, *Detrás del sur: Danzas para Manuel* (Behind the South: Dances for Manuel [referring to Manuel Zapata Olivella], 2021).

We start by viewing dance as a 'place of enunciation', both political and aesthetic, which aims to break into the racialised social space of art and ideas of race, particularly concerning Black people in Colombia (see Chapter 1). In theories of enunciation, discourses are ways of intervening in the world through language (Van Dijk 2019). However, discursive meanings are not transparent; they depend on the context of communication, on extra-linguistic factors – social, ethnic-racial, political, emotional, and so on – and on the relationships among speakers and listeners. Therefore, discursive meanings exhibit a certain opacity (Benveniste 1971). Our focus is on how Sankofa Danzafro's dance moves between this opacity and the transparency of its messages. This interplay of opacity and transparency characterises anti-racist proposals based on dance, which also depend on the degree of engagement between the company and its audiences.

We approach Sankofa's work from the perspective of what Jacques Rancière (2000) calls 'artistic practices' linked to political processes of the production of subjectivities that seek to destabilise established orders of the 'sensible' (that which is sensed and which makes sense) and its visibility in art and society (Rancière 2005). In terms of a 'place of enunciation', we argue that Sankofa's work has a discursivity that is both performative and narrative (Austin 1990), and is characterised by a bodily and spatial materiality (Butler 1993), reflected in the spaces and acts of dancing. From a discursive perspective, performance contributes to the construction of affective atmospheres (Anderson 2009; Wetherell 2013) in which the assemblage of bodies, movements and aesthetic elements generates anti-racist effects.

We reflect, first, on the role of movement and engagement in constituting the 'affective atmospheres' that produce an 'anti-racist emotionality'. Next, we discuss different perspectives that shape the politics of the category 'Afro' in its relation to Afro-contemporary dance and anti-racism in the work of Sankofa Danzafro. Third, we describe the anti-racist strategies that guide the construction of Sankofa Danzafro's narratives, focusing on the work *Detrás del sur: Danzas para Manuel*.

THE JOYFUL SONG OF THE PARROTS: BODIES AND TOGETHERNESS – AN ANTI-RACIST EMOTIONALITY?

In the spring of 2021, following the most challenging period of the COVID-19 confinement, mobility began to be restored in Colombia. Although life had not returned to normal, people could now travel and

FIGURE 4.1 Sankofa Danzafro dancers in their rehearsal retreat in Tumaco, March 2021 (© Carlos Correa Angulo, by permission).

see friends and family. Carlos Correa was able to accompany the dancers and director of Sankofa Danzafro as they left the city of Medellín for an artistic retreat in Tumaco, a town surrounded by tropical rainforest on the southern Pacific coast of Colombia. We went there to finalise the choreography and music for *Detrás del sur*. Over twenty-two days, the members of Sankofa formed, as dancers would say, 'one body' (see Figure 4.1).

Sankofa's dancers are young Afro-Colombians whose families come from rural areas of the Pacific and Caribbean regions of Colombia. Most of them have been directly or indirectly impacted by the armed conflict and violence in those territories, without this defining their identities. In fact, these events are rarely mentioned when the group is together (although some of Sankofa's artistic creations tackle these themes, for instance, the 2018 piece *Fecha límite* [Deadline]).[2] Some were born in the city of Medellín and others have migrated alone or with their families to the city in search of better opportunities or fleeing violence. Among the dancers, we can find stories with elements in common where family tragedies, structural violence in the region of origin and experiences of racism intermingle with personal entrepreneurial projects, attachment to certain musical styles and religious traditions (including a type of

---

[2] An extract from this work can be seen from minute 3'30" in the video *Festival of Decolonial and Anti-Racist Art – A Documentary*, https://youtu.be/WB1fKmYkP9M.

Afro-Catholicism particular to Colombia's Pacific region). There is also lots of dancing, laughter and endless parties, with an abundant repertoire of Afro-urban rhythms and genres that they enjoy and reference in their personal dance explorations or with other companions. The most popular genres include salsa choque, exotic, popping, break dancing, funk, locking and krumping.[3]

The dance performance *Detrás del sur* was inspired by the book *Changó, el gran putas* (Changó, the Biggest Badass, 1983) by Afro-Colombian intellectual and writer Manuel Zapata Olivella (see Chapter 1). The book narrates the genesis of Afro-descendant communities in the Americas. Not easily classified as a novel, *Changó, el gran putas* adopts an epic style that, in the words of the book's prologue writer, Darío Henao, summarises 500 years of the history of Black people in the Americas by re-interpreting historical facts through 'mythical realism', a style that combines 'imagination and myth to reconstruct the memory of Afro-American peoples using the Yoruba cosmology of the Bantu peoples of sub-Saharan Africa' (Henao 2010: 12). Because it narrates this history using Afro religious, spiritual and epistemic frames of reference, the novel has recently been recognised by literary historiography in Colombia as an expression of the anti-racist work that Zapata Olivella developed over more than four decades. It makes extensive use of 'Afro-referentiality', one of the anti-racist strategies adopted by the Black movement in Colombia.[4]

Rather than being an adaptation of Zapata Olivella's book, *Detrás del sur* is an embodied and danced version of the book based on reflections provoked by its reading. Sankofa's choreographer and dancers experienced an 'affective connection' with the book's depictions of exodus, struggles, the geographies of pain, helplessness and the need to come together that are experienced by the book's characters after being violently uprooted from their place of origin in Africa and forced to settle in the Americas. According to some writers on anti-racism (Ahmed 2005; Eddo-Lodge 2021), affective connection is what characterises the

---

[3] These are all Afro-urban rhythms. Some, such as salsa choque and exotic, were developed in Colombia by urban Afro communities. Others reveal the influence of US African-American culture.

[4] In Colombia, 2021 was officially declared a year of homage to Manuel Zapata Olivella, highlighted as the most brilliant mind of Afro-Colombianism in the twentieth century and a symbol of anti-racist struggles in Latin America: see www.elpais.com.co/cultura/2021-tambien-es-un-ano-para-leer-a-manuel-zapata-olivella.html

durability of a global Black community with an Afro-diasporic consciousness imbued with the trauma of enslavement and the struggle for freedom.

During the retreat's working days, which lasted up to eight hours, Rafael Palacios organised several exercises of exploration and creation based on the book. Dancers, musicians, and others present experienced the creation of affective atmospheres, which were characterised by ambiguity and indeterminacy when people tried to describe their affective-emotional states (Anderson 2009). There was also a 'non-conscious experience of intensity' (Shouse 2005) that at times generated emotions connected to personal memories of painful events and everyday experiences of racism. Carlos Correa recorded the creation of these affective atmospheres in field notes:

> We are all in the open-air studio on the beach in a reading session on the first part of the book *Changó, el gran putas*. This part deals with the subject of curses. It begins with the singing of a mysterious character, Ngafúa, who begins to narrate with the kora, a stringed instrument, the tragedy of the exodus of enslaved Africans. The narrator introduces an atmosphere of suspense, preparing us to listen to the terrible story he is about to tell, which recounts the exile of Africans enslaved and taken to a different and distant land. As we move forward, Ngafúa reveals that the 'Trata', the title of the book's second chapter, is the result of the curse of Changó, the orisha [god or spirit] of thunder, lightning, justice, virility, dance and fire, according to the Yoruba religion. The only way to get rid of this curse is for the exiles to stay united through *muntu*.[5] The very orisha that cursed them would also go with them to America, as a captive and as a liberator. We fall silent and think about the curse. We talk about what a curse feels like, how we know that a person or a family is cursed. The conversation fills with familiar examples. As one person speaks, the others listen and begin to get impatient, some begin to sweat, others appear troubled, looking down at the floor, as if remembering something. The director asks the dancers to begin to explore the sensations they are experiencing. They should do it using movements, something that comes from within, something that we are aware of. They need to embody, to put into movement what they are feeling at this moment, what the reading has aroused, and for this they only have the body. 'To heal the curses you first have to be aware of them', he says. They all begin to think about their own curses, the ones they and their families have been struggling with for years. They all look at each other. They begin to tell stories about their family members. 'My father was killed ...': one dancer refers to the violent death of her father, an Afro-Colombian

---

[5] *Muntu* literally means 'person' in many Bantu languages, but the concept transcends this meaning, since it includes living and dead people as well as the animals, vegetables, minerals and things that serve them. More than entities or persons, material or physical, it alludes to the force that unites persons with their ancestors and descendants in the present, past and future (Zapata Olivella 2010: 649).

like her. 'That's why we don't go downtown [in Medellín] anymore because if it wasn't the police giving us problems, it would be the thieves', a young male dancer said with tears in his eyes; he recounted how they were abused by the police in public places, him and his friends, young Black men.

The dancers positioned themselves around the sides of the studio, concentrated and began to make movements to the rhythm of the music that the musicians were playing ... with their eyes closed, as if held in a trance. Most of [the dancers] hold their heads in their hands, others writhe as if they were shaking something off. One of the dancers hugs herself and cries, another shivers as if she were cold, one dancer takes big strides as if running away from something. One dancer starts to move her belly, another seems to want to vomit and holds on to the uprights of the studio. Some of them speak openly of racism, identifying all these things as what happens to people who are like them, to Black people. All of them have sad expressions on their faces, they are self-absorbed, some with moist eyes, others looking distressed, there is an *indefinable current* that unites them and at the same time keeps each person in their own space. The atmosphere of the room becomes gloomy, there is grief in the air that becomes heavy and suffocating. Only the roar of the sea a few metres away is audible.

After several minutes, the director stops the music. He asks: 'What emotions do you feel when doing this exercise?' 'How do we break the curse then?' one of them answers, crying. 'After being freed from the curse, what comes next?' two dancers ask at the same time with moist eyes. Finally, they feel encouraged to verbalise the vague sensations they experience in the body but do not know how to name. 'I feel rage', says one. 'I feel pain'; 'uncertainty'; 'I feel like an orphan'; 'despair'; 'I have no hope'; 'rage'; 'I feel I don't want to hear any more, I am full of rage, it is unfair that we have to live with this curse', finally says one of the senior dancers while trying to hold back tears.

We have a break. Broken sobbing can be heard. We resume reading after we gather again and have all calmed down a bit. Faces gradually return to their calm expression. We resume reading. We read about the *muntu*, the remedy for the curse, according to Zapata Olivella's book. The *muntu* is divided into 4 categories: *kintu, kuntu, hantu* and *muntu* that mark the relationship between human beings, ancestors, animals, plants and objects. *Muntu* is understood as 'a vital force' that holds all things together. This principle of unity that marks African religious thought was fundamental for survival and adaptation to the new environment in America, we read. When we mention each of the parts that make up the *muntu*, we come to the *kintu*, which refers 'to animals, plants, minerals, inanimate things and their communion with human communities' (Sierra Díaz 2016: 28).

Just then, a flock of parrots enters the studio. They begin to sing loudly and their singing silences us. We don't know where they came from, we didn't notice when they arrived, they are just here now singing very loudly and looking at us. After a few minutes, they fall silent. We resume reading. We mention the *kintu* and the parrots began to sing again loudly. Next, the place filled with a cool breeze; some feathers floated down in the middle of the studio; we were all in a reverential silence. It was as if the parrots were greeting us. The atmosphere becomes light, the air is filled with a fragrance like Indian orange blossoms, a wild flower whose scent we had not noticed before. Bodies relax. Everyone feels like getting up and touching the parrots, but no one does. We let ourselves be enveloped by their joyful song. They are there, affirming their presence and companionship. We feel a communion that we cannot explain. Rafael tells them that they must achieve *awareness of emotions*, of the inner space that we all have inside; the problem is that we spend too much time distracted by what is outside. 'All gods curse their children', he continues. 'The story of Changó is of a deity who cursed his children, but gave them the key so that they could make their way through the pain and seek their freedom. That is what we have to do. Freedom is impossible if we do not join together, as a single body, with the same pain, but also with the same temperance, just like these little parrots that are here today and sing to us, refusing to be ignored' (Carlos Correa, field diary, 23 March 2021).

The formation of affective atmospheres involves 'ways of naming collective affects' (Anderson 2009: 78), which have the ability to be transmitted from one body to another and between human and non-human entities (Brennan 2004). This transmission occurs in spaces charged with affective forces, as 'currents' emerging from 'bodies affecting other bodies and yet exceeding the bodies they emerge from' (Anderson 2009: 78). The analytical distinctions between affect, emotions and feelings are not entirely clear (Shouse 2005). In the ethnographic episode here, several elements converge that are part of the so-called affective turn characterised by an 'interest in embodiment, emotions, and aesthetics ... and the in-between-ness: in the capacities to act and be acted upon' (Caze and Lloyd 2011: 3).

Among dancers, musicians and Sankofa's director, the conscious exploration of emotions leads on to the formation of narratives wrapped in an anti-racist emotionality. The allusion to events of everyday racism mingled with reflections on the uprootedness and exile of people in *Changó, el gran putas* brings about the establishment of an affective atmosphere charged with meaning, on the one hand, and affective 'intensity' on the other. We argue that the affective dimension of creating *Detrás del sur* has several phases in which each dancer first engages with the novel, then with their experiences of daily racism, next with other dancers and, finally, with the affective atmosphere formed by relations between human and non-human entities (dancers, birds, music, sound, movement, corporealities, space, territory, etc.).

Our argument, in line with Anderson (2009: 79), is that dance is an 'aesthetic object' that displays an 'affective quality' with a gradation of 'intensity' specific to a given context. Dance works with emotionality and affectivity in the same way as with the tension between the subjective and the objective. There is a back-and-forth between two oppositions, 'narrative/non-narrative and semiotic/asignifying', with emotion being associated with narrative and signification, and affect with non-narrative and asignifying (Anderson 2009: 80). The dancers' initial difficulty in expressing in words what they were experiencing with their bodies is illustrative of this tension between the narrative and the non-narrative, the verbal and the nonverbal, the cognitive and the bodily, emotion and sensation. We encounter these tensions when we investigate embodied phenomena of movement, such as dance, from the perspective of affectivity.

During the creation process of *Detrás del sur*, there were different intensities of engagement that formed affective atmospheres, configuring an Afro-referential anti-racist emotionality that emerged from the collective space generated by sharing experiences of racism. Sankofa Danzafro's anti-racist strategy analyses the bodily sensations and emotions generated when the traumatic experiences of everyday racism are intentionally embodied. Knowing how racism is *felt* through movement, body memory and intersubjective experience is the first step in developing a dance-based anti-racist consciousness among the company's members.

Engagement is a process charged with affectivity. In the process of creating *Detrás del sur*, there were different degrees of engagement that are configurations of anti-racist affectivity. The first register of engagement occurred with the reading of Manuel Zapata Olivella's book, which situates the origins of Afro-descendants in the Americas in a collective experience of pain that is deeply emotional and leaves traces in the bodily memory. Second, there was an engagement with the characters in the book and their stories. These stories are characterised by the collective 'trauma' of enslavement and by collective struggles for freedom, adaptation and the creation of new conditions to live in a situation of domination. Trauma and tenacity, pain and bravery, mourning and courage are mixed together. These feelings can be defined, according to Eric Shouse (2005), as sensations 'that have been checked against previous experiences and labelled', and that allow 'making sense of the world from experience and not from representation' (Besserer Alatorre 2014: 13).

An intersubjective relationship and affective connection is formed between the Black dancers and fictional characters who share traumatic experiences of racial discrimination and a common struggle against domination and racism. This emotional identification is preceded by an experimentation with sensations, music and movements that create a spatialisation of affectivity. In this phase of engagement, the aesthetic-material interaction between dancers, music and movements involves movements that embody the sensations produced by racism, felt as the 'curse' that connects their own life experiences with those of historical fictional characters with whom they share a common origin. The work of exploring sensations through body and movement is what Shouse (2005) calls 'affect', whose 'abstractivity' makes it transmissible in ways that feelings and emotions are not.

Now, one of the ways in which affect circulates and impacts on others is through assemblages of bodies (Anderson 2009; Massumi 1995). Dancers' individual explorations lead into collective explorations of a shared sense of being part of a painful event that is both historical and contemporary. The interaction with the music and with elements of the environment such as the roar of the sea, birdsong and weeping contribute to an anti-racist emotionality that forms when individual sensations are made conscious as the dancers come together and can then be described in emotional terms – anger, pain, uncertainty, etc. This anti-racist emotionality makes conscious the painful emotions that racism provokes in the lives and histories of Black people and embodies them in order to remove their paralyzing force. To do conscious work with emotions through the body is to learn to control them. Racism works with a surreptitious emotionality, producing discriminatory events and racialisations that reproduce racial stereotypes and structural racism. When the Sankofa dancers in *Detrás del sur* choose to inhabit the place of the emotional pain that racism causes, as a historical and contemporary experience, they are undermining its manifestations and, consequently, dealing with the problem. Thus, examining how racism feels in the body is a way of confronting it from a conscious emotionality, which seeks to counteract racism by working with the body and its capacity to construct narrativity through dance.

THE 'AFRO' IN AFRO-CONTEMPORARY DANCE AND ANTI-RACIST PERSPECTIVES

The definition of 'contemporary' has been the subject of debates both within and outside the field of dance (Siegmund 2003). When and where does the contemporary begin in dance? Does the contemporary refer to a temporal, technical or aesthetic notion?

According to Adeline Maxwell, the consensus is that contemporary dance emerged from a break with the aesthetic ideals and techniques of classical ballet, when Isadora Duncan, Lote Fuller and Ruth St. Denis in the USA, alongside Rudolf Von Laban, Mary Wigman and Kurt Jooss in

Germany, proposed various innovations – for example, dispensing with the pointe shoes in ballet, making movements on the floor – that led to new forms of dance, which 'quickly moved from experimentation to academization' (Maxwell 2015: 23). Contemporary dance became institutionalised as a supposedly 'universal' dance with its own aesthetics and ways of creating narratives and rhythmic patterns.

Sankofa defines its project as 'Afro-contemporary'.[6] Although it shares with contemporary dance a temporal frame that places it in 'the now', for Sankofa being contemporary entails challenging the racism experienced by Black people today. In Afro-contemporary dance, the 'Afro' is a contested field where notions of difference and particularity overlap. Eduardo Restrepo (2021: 21–22) identifies four meanings around the term Afro. First, Afro can subsume 'Black' by emphasising racialised aspects of difference. Second, Afro can refer to ancestry, kinship and a community of common origin. A third emphasis is on 'traces of Africanness' that might be identified in the transnational Afro-diasporic community. Finally, Afro refers to cultural traits characteristic of Black communities, without these necessarily being African in origin.

Behind the politics of naming and conceptualising such ideas as 'Black', 'Afro', 'African origin', 'Afro-diasporic', 'African', and 'Afro-descendant', there are both racialisation mechanisms and sensibilities that underlie political subjectivities (Lao-Montes 2009). Some meanings of 'Afro' become dominant for certain contexts, while others quickly fall into disrepute or disuse, depending on the confluence of national and international actors, who may be internal or external to Afro-descendant mobilisations (Wade 2013).

In the field of contemporary Afro dance, where Sankofa Danzafro is located, anti-racism is expressed primarily by the decision to be explicitly 'Afro' through the embodied practice of dance. This means that contemporary Afro dance seeks to be associated with affirmations of Afro identity at local and Afro-diasporic levels. Transnational ethnic affiliations play with the overlapping political meanings of Afro. Thus, for example, in the case of Sankofa Danzafro, at times the Afro is emphasised as belonging to an Afro-diasporic community, at other times there is an open affirmation of common ancestry, or the racialisation of a re-signified Blackness, or

---

[6] Whereas contemporary dance, arising in response to a crisis of modernity in the arts, establishes an aesthetic rupture in relation to classical ballet, introducing new rhythmic patterns, forms of expressiveness and body movement, it still works with a Eurocentric ideal of the body. It mainly responds to Western concerns about self-renewal and searches for new ways to express the inner being of the fragmented subject.

an ethnic affirmation that politicises 'Black culture'. These moorings and displacements of the meaning of Afro in the positionings of Sankofa and its dancers are emphasised according to the contexts of interlocution, whether those are funding institutions (almost always state-owned) or festivals and tours with their diverse audiences.

The contemporary aspect of Afro-contemporary dance is framed by the intention to explore, based on the current conditions in which dance is performed, the traditions – the past – that influence its dramaturgy and narratives. As discussed at the conference 'African Contemporary Dance? Questioning Issues of a Performance Aesthetic for a Developing and Independent Continent', held as part of the JOMBA! Contemporary Dance Experience festival (Durban, 2004), the term 'Afro-contemporary' seeks to establish a methodology for critically examining tradition and engaging it in a dialogue with the challenges faced by African societies (Douglas et al. 2006: 107–112). In simpler terms, Afro-contemporary dance is seen as a creative technique.

The JOMBA! conference debates about Afro-contemporary dance, involving renowned African choreographers, are echoed in the ideas of Rafael Palacios. For Palacios, tradition is not an immutable flow coming from a static past. Rather, he conceives it as a dynamic space for the exploration and deep understanding of Afro-descendant cultures. In various conversations, Palacios has emphasised tradition as a 'place to return to through investigation'.

> There are traditions in Afro-Colombian dances that need to be examined, investigated. Some of these dances emerged during colonialism and were a way of aspiring to and imitating European ways of dancing, their aesthetics, the appearance of those white bodies. But there are other dances that satirise, parody and resist those ways of dancing. They combine movements and rhythms of African origin, mixed with rhythms and languages developed in Colombia by our Afro communities. (Palacios, personal communication, 24 March 2020)

This critical approach to the past is fundamental in Afro-contemporary dance and is of vital importance for Sankofa as a company. The word *sankofa* originates in the systems of thought of the Akan people of present-day Ghana: it means going back to the past, to the roots, as a way to understand the present and envision the future. *Sankofa* is symbolised by a bird whose feet are pointing forwards, while its head is turned backwards to grasp an egg with its beak. Thus, revisiting the past is a way of creating one's own history, which is constructed from the perspective of Afro peoples in all their heterogeneity and uniqueness. The politics of history, which arises from examining the past, is an essential condition to face the problems that currently affect the Afro-diasporic community.

The director, choreographer and dancers must therefore investigate tradition, enquire into its meanings, contextualise its uses, and not simply 'learn the technique'. The investigation of tradition is the first step in an anti-racist process of decolonising dances and bodies and liberating their potential. A critical examination of tradition leads to an awareness of the aestheticised racialisations that persist and are reproduced by Black people themselves in some of their dances, albeit with the aim of dismantling them, locating their origin and showing that they resulted from a process of domination that tamed subjectivity and shaped the expression of Black identities. From this anti-racist perspective, the expression 'decolonising the body' refers to exploring the forms of domestication of the body in Afro dances, a process that can be seen in various elements: these include body postures and clothing that express a relationship of submission (for example, typical costumes of Afro-Colombian dances in which female dancers wear aprons, dance with their heads bowed, assume a posture of servitude, etc.). The domestication of the body is also seen through the surveillance of sexuality, controlling dance as an incitement to sexual debauchery. This idea about dance justified many of the prohibitions of Black dances during and after the colonial period. From these mechanisms of control, the rhythmic capacities and potentials of Black bodies were diminished and subordinated through the imposition of forms of dance considered less 'erotic' and more 'civilised'.

If the 'Afro' in Afro-contemporary dance implies an examination of the past, it also refers to techniques of creation and methodologies of dance research based in Africa. There is a genealogy that locates the origin of Afro-contemporary dance in the Mudra Afrique school, in Senegal, in the context of the struggles for the decolonisation of Africa and a unity based on the 'common destiny' of all Afro-descendants as proclaimed by Pan-Africanism (Adi 2018; Shepperson 1962). Under the premise that through knowledge of the past (one's own history) and awareness of the present one could confront the challenges that the future would bring to African peoples, in 1977 Léopold Sédar Senghor and Maurice Béjart set about the task of founding the Centre Africain de Perfectionnement et de Recherche des Interprètes du Spectacle Mudra Afrique (African Performing Artists Centre for Development and Research, Mudra Afrique). Germaine Acogny, considered the mother of

Afro-contemporary dance, originally from Benin, was appointed director of the Mudra Afrique school, becoming its most emblematic figure.[7]

The Mudra Afrique school as led by Germaine Acogny around African dances can be defined as a postcolonial cultural production, whose intentions, in Acogny's words, were to combat stereotypes about Afro bodies and 'colonial ideologies reinforced by professional dance training institutions' (Swanson 2019: 50). In her ethnography of Acogny's École des Sables, Amy Swanson identified several principles taught there that give identity to Afro contemporary dance: the creation of a movement vocabulary by adopting a known dance structure, but endowing it with an African aesthetic; the inclusion of aesthetics influenced by the natural environment and the surrounding dancers; and the search for traditional knowledge to find routes to narrate the present (Swanson 2019: 50–54). The emphasis on dissociated movement, the transmission of a collective flow of energy when dancing, the undulation of the body, whose central axis is the spine, circular formations and diagonal steps are some of the elements that characterise Germaine Acogny's technique and that are employed by Rafael Palacios in his dance training, along with variations that he has introduced.

The Mudra Afrique school and Germaine Acogny laid the foundation for many African dancers from Senegal, Ghana, Kenya, Benin and Burkina Faso, among others, to enter the institutional system of African dance education with high standards of quality and training. Afro-contemporary dance arrived in Colombia in 1997, introduced by Rafael Palacios; he had had over five years of training in France and Africa, under Acogny herself and Irene Tassembedo, one of Acogny's first disciples, who has her own school of Afro-contemporary dance in Ouagadougou, Burkina Faso. That same year Sankofa Danzafro was born in the city of Medellin, Colombia. By the mid 2000s, under the influence of Palacios, a handful of Afro-contemporary dance companies emerged on the national dance scene, with the main ones located in Medellín, Cartagena, Cali,

---

[7] *Mudra* means 'gesture' or 'sign' in Sanskrit. An early branch of the Mudra School was in Brussels, founded by French choreographer Maurice Béjart in 1970; however, its focus was not on African dances. Germaine Acogny later founded her own school, the École des Sables, in 1998. She wrote the book *African Dance*, in which she laid the philosophical and technical foundations of Afro-contemporary dance. The Mudra Afrique school in Dakar, Senegal, lasted only from 1977 to 1983. However, despite its short existence, several African dancers were trained there and became recognised exponents of Afro-contemporary dance. Among the most prominent is Irene Tessembedo, from Burkina Faso, who was the teacher of Rafael Palacios and has been one of the main promoters and co-creators of Afro-contemporary dance in Europe and Africa.

Barranquilla and Bogotá. Among these, Sankofa Danzafro stands out for its explicit political commitment to the fight against stereotypes, which is at the genesis of Afro-contemporary dance from the Mudra School to the present day. The company's main motto is 'We dance not only to be seen, but to be heard', emphasising the anti-racist character of their works.

Afro-contemporary dance quickly went from experimentation to standardisation after its entry into the market of global dance cultures, characterised by an exoticising fascination with everything defined as 'African', which turned Afro-contemporary dance into a commodity consumed mainly by the USA and Europe, and more recently by Latin America (Kringelbach and Skinner 2014; Maxwell 2015; Samuel 2011; Swanson 2019). Added to this is the danger Rafael Palacios warns against of the 'emptying of meaning', which, by decontextualising Afro-contemporary dance from the subjects and territories where it is practiced, not only loses sight of the political and contested epistemological meanings that are expressed through the dance, but also ignores the racism that Afro dancers face as racialised subjects in the world.

SANKOFA'S CONTEMPORARY AFRO-COLOMBIAN DANCE AND ANTI-RACIST STRATEGIES IN *DETRÁS DEL SUR*

During 2017, while Rafael Palacios was pursuing a master's degree on epistemologies of the South in Ecuador, he directed *La mentira complaciente* (The Complacent Lie). This Afro-contemporary work focuses on how Black people have to 'embody' racialised social stereotypes about their sexuality, histories and identities in order to be integrated or 'consumed' in the art market and especially the field of dance. During the exploratory exercises, the director asked each dancer to experiment with an element that would be part of the dramaturgy of the work: the loincloth. Several of the dancers expressed their concern about having to wear a garment that has symbolised the barbarism that supposedly characterises Black populations. Palacios explained that he wanted them to become corporeally aware of what it means to wear/embody a stereotype that has for so long denigrated Afro populations. The aim was to awaken a degree of attention to corporeality and to the sensations – the autonomous manifestation of affectivity (Massumi 1995) – provoked by the sensation of having to wear a denigrating garment. The dancers would then have to combat those sensations using movement and dance channelled through 'technique' – that is, the dance knowledge they had already learned from traditional dances in their regions of origin – to transform them into something new, endowing them with 'narrativity', that is, with the ability to express contemporary human experience from a specific positionality (Torres Perdigón 2021).

This exercise of bringing attention to sensation allows us to analyse several constitutive aspects of Sankofa Danzafro's Afro-contemporary dance project: working with embodied knowledge in a conscious way; seeing movement as an expression of multiple materialities; co-producing spaces that can be both physical – movements in a place – and intersubjective – shared interior and imaginative space.

One of Sankofa's dancers who has been dancing in the company for more than fifteen years said that he felt suffocated and overwhelmed when he first wore the loincloth. So he decided to turn to prior knowledge he had about a traditional dance, *currulao*, from his home region, Tumaco, a city on the Colombian Pacific coast. Among the genres of *currulao*, there was a work dance that was performed during the rice harvest. The dust from the rice caused the skin to itch and this gave rise to a type of dance that he learned as a child. While he was doing his dance explorations with the loincloth, he felt his own body remembering the movements and body sensations of the rice harvest dance. He began to make movements that connoted annoyance, irritability, discomfort. For example, to the rhythmic beat of male and female *cununos* (a type of conga drum), he would shake and brush invisible dust off his skin, scratch in desperation, pull at his sweaty clothes to remove them, contort himself, make rapid hand and foot movements that then gave way to a state of surrender, only to return with greater vigour, like someone seeking to get rid of an itchy sensation all over his body. All these bodily sensations were associated with the unpleasant feeling of wearing the loincloth. The stereotypes that materialised in the loincloth caused itching. This is what Sankofa Danzafro's contemporary Afro-Colombian dance project is all about: to make use of embodied knowledge to allow rhythmic explorations that challenge the discomfort caused by 'carrying/embodying' racial stereotypes, which can then be contested using conscious and reflexive movement in front of audiences observing Black dances, who receive a message that has to be 'heard'.

Detrás del sur: Danzas para Manuel

According to Derek McCormack (2008), dance analysis encompasses the body, space and cultural geographies, as well as the various ways in which bodies move. Because of this, both dance and 'danced movement' are culturally produced and express an attitude that is both social and political and must be analysed beyond representation and meaning (Thrift 1997).[8] Dance performance does not always attribute a particular significance to each movement. As Rafael Palacios says in the epigraph at the beginning of this chapter, the movements and the cadence of dancing bodies express a pleasant gracefulness that often only relates to the dramaturgy or choreography of the work. However, when it comes to anti-racism in dance, sequences of movement, interpretation of gestures, music and dramaturgical elements such as lights and costumes weave a narrative that delivers a concrete message to audiences. In that sense, to dance is to tell a story.

Detrás del sur: Danzas para Manuel is divided into five acts, mirroring the structure of Zapata Olivella's book. These acts do not obey a spatio-temporal linearity. Instead, they present a narrative unity that emphasises Afro-descendants' contestation of the structural conditions of racism they face. The acts mix together rhythms arising from experimentation with the music of Afro-Colombian communities (of the Colombian Pacific and Caribbean regions) and fusions of Afro-urban rhythms. The names and order of the acts changed during the development of the work, but at this early stage the first act was 'Muntu': it addresses the emergence of the Afro diaspora in the Americas, the role of race mixture as a founding metaphor, and the birth, rebellion and death of Benkos Biojó (associated with the orisha Changó in Zapata Olivella's work).[9] The next act, 'Diaspora' (also called 'The Ship'), symbolises the transatlantic voyage and the dispersion of Africans and their descendants in America. Here an atmosphere of desperation and agitation is depicted, combining strong and emphatic movements with contortions and elevations. The following act, 'Unction', represents the orishas and ancestors in communion with the Afro men and women, highlighting how they bestow wisdom, knowledge and value on the *muntu*. In Figure 4.2, the middle figure represents *muntu*, who anoints the figures on either side, who are the children of *muntu*. The scenes are characterised by movements that

---

[8] We recognise a distinction between 'dance', which refers to the set of techniques and bodily aesthetics related to a cultural, political and social context; and 'danced movement', which refers to the relatively spontaneous rhythmic movement in which shared rhythmic cultural forms are present.

[9] Biojó was a historical figure attributed with the seventeenth-century founding of the Palenque de San Basilio near Cartagena de Indias. Some historians have indicated that he participated in the founding of other *palenques* – as the communities of formerly enslaved escapees and their descendants were called – such as the Palenque de la Matuna near Tolú.

FIGURE 4.2 Scene from 'Unction' in *Detrás del sur* by Sankofa Danzafro, on stage at the Joyce Theatre, New York, 2024 (photo by Steven Pisano © Sankofa Danzafro, by permission).

imitate the atmosphere of flora and fauna, the environment and the integration of humans and nature, one of the characteristics of *muntu* as a philosophy and religious system. Hand movements and extensions of the torso are emphasised, along with jumps and long strides: the choreography conveys a sacred playfulness. The next act, 'Epic 1', represents the struggles with which the children of the diaspora fought to achieve their freedom, the fights and battles fired by rebellion. The movements and rhythms are a mixture of traditional Afro-Colombian dances and African rhythms characterised by rapid beats and explosive percussion; the choreography is based on energetic movements that require dexterity, speed and precision. The movements on stage combine several horizontal planes and the attitude of each dancer denotes pride, vigour and strength. Finally, 'Epic 2' depicts the struggles waged by Black communities in the present against forms of exclusion and racism and the social protests in which they participated during the 2021 national strike in Colombia.

Combating Stereotypes: Message and Performance

So far, we have focused on how anti-racist sensibilities are generated by affective and emotional responses among dance company members

Dance and Anti-Racism: Sankofa Danzafro

FIGURE 4.3 Scene from 'The Birth of a Warrior' in *Detrás del sur* by Sankofa Danzafro, on stage at the Joyce Theatre, New York, 2024 (photo by Steven Pisano © Sankofa Danzafro, by permission).

without addressing the issue of audiences, whose affective responses are also implicated in Afro-contemporary dance's anti-racist perspectives (Correa Angulo and Alarcón Velásquez 2024). As we have noted, Sankofa Danzafro's motto is 'We dance not only to be seen, but to be heard', which means that strategies of creation and performance are ultimately oriented to audiences. As already mentioned, in Afro-contemporary dance – and in dance more generally – a regime of visuality predominates, particularly situated in the gaze of the spectators. As a result, the messages conveyed by the dance are often diluted by the intensity of the spectators' aesthetic gaze on the bodies. These messages are characterised by a tension between the opacity and the transparency of their meanings, which are thus not always clear to the public and are only gradually assimilated. For example, Figure 4.3 is from a scene that, at the time, the dancers called 'The Birth of a Warrior', which shows a woman and the son she has just given birth to: this evokes the (re)birth in the Americas of both Changó and Benkos Biojó, referring to various meanings in Zapata Olivella's novel. These references can be opaque for some and transparent for others, depending on their degree of familiarity with the novel.

Although stereotypes do not operate exclusively in visual mode, they tend to work in the sphere of the visible, which serves as apparent evidence that they refer to 'reality'. In *Detrás del sur*, on the other hand, there is a communicative intention that is expressed not only in the aesthetic choices of the dramaturgy, but also in the invitation to the spectator to 'hear' a message. In one of the musical pieces in Act 3, 'Unction', the vocalist repeatedly instructs the audience 'oíd, oíd' (hear, hear) while the dancers perform slow steps with exquisite elastic movements. This is based on the first lines of an intense poem in the first part of *Changó, el gran putas*: '¡Oídos del Muntu, oíd! / ¡Oíd! ¡Oíd! ¡Oíd! ¡Oíd! / ¡Oídos del Muntu, oíd! / He visto en sueños a Changó' (Ears of the people, hear! / Hear! Hear! Hear! Hear! / Ears of the people, hear! / I have seen Changó in dreams). The command to hear is directed at the children of *muntu*, that is, to Afro people, but on stage, due to the immediacy of the performance, the instruction involves the audience. Similarly, in the first act, 'Muntu', a character emerges from the back of the stage reciting an unintelligible message. He shouts and makes emphatic intonations with his voice; he interpellates the audience, looking them in the face and telling them, 'Listen, understand.' But no one can understand, because the character speaks in *jeringonza*, a Spanish form of pig Latin, incomprehensible to the uninitiated. This choice of language represents the misunderstandings in communication between dancers and audiences.

One of the challenges in combating and dismantling stereotypes is the difficulty of ensuring that audiences 'listen' to the Others who are the objects of stereotyping. The action of listening is made possible by affective charges that underwrite the communicative aspect of the message (Van Dijk 2019). The primacy of the exoticising gaze that focuses on the dancing Black bodies thus makes it impossible to truly hear what is being communicated. The viewer's gaze returns again and again to the bodies, their appearance, their skills, the amazing abilities they demonstrate while dancing: the unspoken premise is, 'They are Black bodies: that's why they can dance like that' (see also Chapter 7).[10]

Sankofa's anti-racist work seeks to break with the gaze and its primacy in the shaping of stereotypes. As Mary Louise Pratt (1997) points out, the gaze is laden with an exoticisation that makes possible the emergence of the stereotype. Víctor Segalen (2017) states that exoticism arises from the operation of the senses, especially those of sight and smell, in a way that

---

[10] The company's audiences are heterogeneous. For example, the exoticising gaze changes when it comes to Black audiences who are involved with debates about racism, coloniality and dance. For details of an audience study conducted during this research, see the next footnote; see also Correa Angulo and Alarcón Velásquez (2024).

distances what is being sensed. Exoticism implies a gaze and, therefore, distance. It arises in encounters that occur in contexts of power inequality and the colonisation of bodies, territories and resources, and that, in the voluminous canon of travel literature, are represented as involving an element of surprise. The genesis of the stereotype is thus based on surprise, although once a stereotype exists, this element disappears insofar as a stereotype implies complete predictability.

Breaking with the exotic gaze is perhaps the most ambitious objective of an anti-racist strategy such as Sankofa's. To this end, in *Detrás del sur*, there is a careful narrative that also generates effects of surprise, but with a very different valence. A spectator of Sankofa's work said this:

> It took me by surprise. Because you expect to find Black bodies doing one thing and suddenly they're showing through dance, something else. We were expecting them to do one thing and they did the opposite. It was a rather uncomfortable and surprising feeling. (Alex, focus group 1, April 2021)[11]

Sankofa's works generate an anti-racist effect on the audience by using the effect of surprise in reverse. Audiences are surprised when they see Black dancers enacting a story that, far from being mere entertainment, makes viewers question how they have imagined Black people in ways that may be deeply stereotypical and that imply unequal power relationships.

In the material and symbolic reproduction of racial systems, not only are discourses generated, but also 'structures of feelings', as defined by Raymond Williams in the 1970s, which link mechanisms of racialisation with emotions and sensations (Berg and Ramos-Zayas 2015: 655; Sharma and Tygstrup 2015). So an emotional dimension shapes the creation of stereotypes and racialised representations that become, with use, conventional ways of knowing and relating to others (Ahmed 2015).

However, racial stereotypes are not always active, just as racism is not always actively affecting Black people all the time, but needs specific spaces and moments for it to operate even without being noticed (Lentin 2016; Moreno Figueroa 2010). There are moments when racial stereotypes are activated and deactivated during the performance, according to

---

[11] Our audience study consisted of interviews and focus groups conducted via Zoom with followers of Sankofa Danzafro, who were contacted through the company's social media channels. The study aimed to learn how audiences received Sankofa's work. Participants included Afro-Colombians and people described in Colombia as white-mestizo. See Correa Angulo and Alarcón Velásquez (2024).

the audience's degrees of connection to the narrative. In the interviews we conducted among Sankofa audiences, some participants emphasised that at first they did not understand what the works were about, but were dazzled by the dancing, the costumes, the lights and the scenery. Then, later during the performance, they suddenly felt that the message of the dance directly challenged them and made them question the image they had of Afro-descendants.

> It's something you don't expect. There's a moment when you realise that the dancers are talking about the racist way they are viewed by white people. Sometimes you feel uncomfortable because it's like you're being singled out. You realise that the whole performance is a message that seeks to show us how Afro people are treated and how they are seen in society. Then you ask yourself about the way you have looked at them up to now. It is not a performance that you go to just to see them dance and have fun; there is discomfort. (Diego, focus group 2, May 2021)

Provoking discomfort in audiences happens when they are challenged about their imaginaries and representations of Afro-descendants. The message makes use of all kinds of histrionic and dramatic resources to achieve this effect, including satire and the exaggeration of erotic behaviour. Being 'heard' is often achieved not with words, but by enacting an anti-racist argument that challenges the audience at the emotional heart of their stereotypical prejudices.

In *Detrás del sur*, the aesthetics can be described as 'typically Afro'. The dancers wear red cloths that wrap the body but leave the men's torsos bare, while masks allude to an iconography that has become representative of Africanness in the global dance market (Samuel 2011). However, this aesthetic gradually paves the way towards a narrative that is told through dance and that has at its core forms of resistance that reveal the agency of Afro-descendant communities in overcoming historical and contemporary vicissitudes. In each of its acts, the work shows Afro communities as subjects of knowledge with forms of self-government and with religious and thought systems that have practical utility in facing the problems of daily life. The performance moves back and forth between past and present-day struggles.

AFRO-REFERENTIALITY AS A CREATIVE RESOURCE

During the creative retreat in Tumaco to develop *Detrás del sur*, a documentary film was made with the title *Detrás del sur: Danzas para Manuel. Prácticas artísticas antirracistas* (Behind the South: Dances for Manuel.

Anti-Racist Artistic Practices).[12] The documentary outlines how Afro-referentiality can be deployed as an anti-racist strategy in the several ways: these include the strengthening of bridges among Afro-descendant people; the centring of *muntu* and *ubuntu*; and the creation of work in *el territorio* (the territory).

Bridging

Afro-referentiality strengthens epistemic bridges connecting Afro-descendant people. The process of making *Detrás del sur* starts with literature and extends to dance, because dance works with the body, which is where the multiple violences of racism are most clearly experienced. The work is based on *muntu*, seen not only as a system of thought and a philosophy of the past, but also as present in reappropriated and updated form in the organisational processes of rural and urban Afro communities in Colombia. The work addresses racism from a historical perspective and updates this discussion for the present. *Detrás del sur*'s anti-racist power derives in part from the intertextuality it establishes between Afro aesthetic objects of different orders – in this case, literature and dance. *Detrás del sur* quotes the literary text, but the text acquires meanings that are co-produced by interpretation through dance. This intertextual dialogue – understanding intertextuality as the concatenation of various discursive formats – consolidates a field of anti-racist enunciation that makes visible the existence of racism and proposes ways to combat it through artistic practice. One such way involves breaking with expectations about literature – usually associated with 'white' spheres of production – and rupturing stereotypes of Afro dance. As for literature, the author Zapata Olivella creates a literary universe replete with messages conveyed by living and dead characters, ancestors and their enslaved descendants, orishas and entities of nature. These messages are not always clear to others; they are encrypted and must be deciphered by those to whom they are specifically addressed. This ecological dimension of mythical realism establishes ruptures with the conventional ways in which nature usually appears in Westernised literature. As Sommer astutely notes (Sommer 2018: 319–320), Afro-descendant literary traditions have always been dedicated to seeking freedom in creative and innovative ways. When it comes to writing, 'freedom lies in the *how*, not the what'. As a strategy in

---

[12] See www.digitalexhibitions.manchester.ac.uk/s/carla-en/page/sankofa.

literary arts, 'complicity' and a sense of restlessness play a significant role in engaging audiences and readers. For its part, Afro-contemporary dance breaks with expectations of what Afro dance is expected to do: entertain. Beyond simple diversion, Afro-contemporary dance conceptualises, situates, explores and elaborates planimetries loaded with meaning.[13]

Muntu and Ubuntu

As an Afro-referential and anti-racist work, *Detrás del sur* makes visible a subject that is dismissed in the hegemonic centres of thought and intellectuality: *muntu* and the philosophies of several African peoples. Often, in discussions of *muntu* or *ubuntu* – organisational, religious and philosophical principles of African peoples that are re-actualised in the Americas – there is a tendency to label them as essentialist or as romanticisations of the past. They are not appreciated as systems of thought and philosophies worth studying rigorously or being of interest to science. *Muntu* and *ubuntu* are concepts in the thought systems of Yoruba peoples that explain and make sense of their human experiences and their being-in-the-world. They are products of their contexts and explain their contexts, as do Aristotelian philosophy or Olmec principles of thought. However, they are considered pre-scientific or pre-philosophical. Making these issues visible situates Afro-descendant people as subjects of knowledge.

El territorio

Afro-referential anti-racism is rooted in ideas about territory. *El territorio* – the territory – is the term the dancers used for the historically Black Pacific coastal region as a whole, with connotations of an ancestral homeland, belonging and ownership.[14] To develop the work in 'the territory' of the Pacific coastal region is a political move more than a romanticisation. Tumaco is a racialised space traversed by multiple forms of raw violence, carried out by drug traffickers, para-military groups, guerrillas, local criminal gangs and smugglers, and leading to a striking degree of militarisation. In interviews, the dancers were asked what it meant to them to create the work in this place.

---

[13] 'Planimetries' is a term commonly used by Sankofa dancers and in formal descriptions of choreographies in dance. It refers to the angles and planes formed by dancers among themselves and in relation to the scenery and the audience.

[14] By extension, *el territorio* is also used by Sankofa dancers to refer to city neighbourhoods, for example in Medellín, where they feel Black people form a community.

It would have been cheaper in Bogotá, because Tumaco is expensive due to its distance, but coming to create in *el territorio* is a way of nurturing the political content of creation. To be here is to identify in these geographies [i.e. these spaces] stories and aesthetic, cultural and emotional elements that give a special meaning to the creation of this work. (Adriana, personal communication, 24 March 2021)

El territorio also contributes sounds, emotionality and a particular sensation of spatiality with which several of the Sankofa dancers are familiar because it is where they come from. These elements enrich the creative process and give concrete meaning to the concepts and aesthetic forms that constitute the work: the music, for example, was composed by Plu con Pla, a band from Tumaco. In *el territorio*, the recursive relationships among community, nature and resources can be appreciated in a way that would be impossible to see in the city. These elements contribute concrete meanings to the notion of *muntu*, which, in its sense of togetherness, feeds powerfully into the work. So, creating dance in *el territorio* generates an anti-racist effect because, using the elements and relationships that have been assembled, dancers burst onto the stage with an aesthetic endowed with concrete and specific content.

AESTHETICS, POETICS AND ANTI-RACISM

The development of an aesthetic that seems relevant and makes sense to Afro communities is one of the anti-racist strategies explored in *Detrás del sur*. While the work is not an adaptation of the literary text, the costume design, the characterisations, the dance movements, the communicative intent and the music align with the tone of Zapata Olivella's epic novel. For example: the bodies of the dancers are covered with bone-coloured ash to represent the children of *muntu*; the red of their tunics alludes to Changó; the white-blue attire of one dancer evokes the goddess Yemayá; the bell-carrying narrator, Ngafúa, represents a common ancestor.

The work takes movements rooted in Afro-Colombian dance techniques and transforms them into steps and movements that are associated with the idea of *muntu* and its pluralistic integration of ecology, knowledge and body. The contortions, the dissociations, the stomping, the undulations of the spine and the direction that the hand takes with respect to the back – these movements generate an aesthetic that affirms the Afro-contemporary technique and the way it resonates with the movements of the flora and fauna in the environment of Black communities in *el territorio*.

The versatile choreography at times leaves aside the movements of strength and thrust associated with Afro dance techniques to give way to softer, slower, more leisurely movements. In the execution of certain dance techniques, the dancers go from delicacy and restraint to more explosive movements that build the narrative and its communicative intentionality. All this forms a poetics that integrates patterns of movement evoking contemporary and traditional ideas of what constitutes Afro.

CONCLUSION

Whether we dance to the rhythm of music or to the rhythm of life, dance is a cross-cultural expression that tells us something about the subjects who dance, their cultural practices and the stories inscribed on their bodies. The message emphasised by Sankofa Danzafro challenges the persistence of racism and its expression through stereotypes, exoticised images and the lack of recognition of Afro referents in current epistemologies. At times, Sankofa Danzafro directly alludes to racism by questioning stereotypes and elaborating narratives that dignify Afro-descent through its works. At other times, it does so through the enhancement of Afro-Colombian identities, their histories, their geographies and their knowledge embodied in dance. In this sense, Sankofa Danzafro's Afro-contemporary dance project has a double purpose: to dismantle the racialisation of the Afro in dance and to decolonise the body by directly combating racial stereotypes about Black people. It does the former by directly questioning stereotypes and the undervaluation of Afro dance by means of conscious explorations generating an emotionality that leads to a narrative that 'has to be heard'. The latter is achieved through a critical review of tradition to see how parts of it reproduce colonial structures that may be present in their aesthetics, movements and performance.

In *Detrás del sur* we can see how the anti-racist strategies in Sankofa's creative processes construct a message that provokes sensations and questions in audiences, especially with respect to stereotypes about Afro-Colombian people, Afro-referentiality as a creative resource and the development of an Afro-representative aesthetic. These anti-racist effects are achieved in the racialised field of dance by an engaging with the audience, to varying degrees, to create an affective atmosphere combining bodily movements and sensations, which is consciously projected onto audiences to surprise and unsettle them. An open question is whether anti-racism in artistic practice is limited to an 'effect' that has the capacity to 'affect' the viewer only in the moment (Besserer Alatorre 2014), or whether it produces a narrative that can survive the fleeting immediacy of performance (Taylor 2002, 2020). What is certain is that the anti-racist narrative constructed by Sankofa not only uses dance as a vehicle, it also employs other elements of discourse. Postings on social networks, synopses of the works in the handbills, the interviews given by the dancers and the director, all contribute to and complement the anti-racist strategies of the dance performance.

Curated Conversation 3: On Curatorship

Curated by Ana Vivaldi and Peter Wade; translated by Peter Wade

Sources: the authors of this text are Abril Caríssimo, Flora Alvarado and América López. They are members of Identidad Marrón, a collective that emerged as a response to Argentina's invisible racism. It aims to create a meeting point and space of visibility for Indigenous and mixed-race people negatively racialised by others in Argentina as *negros populares* (dark-skinned working-class people), who are usually associated with stigmatised *villas* (low-income, informally built neighbourhoods), and whom the collective defines as *marronxs*. *Marronxs* are people with Indigenous ancestry who may or may not recognise themselves as such, as well as the city-born children of campesinos, Indigenous people, and immigrants from the countryside and neighbouring countries. Identidad Marrón promotes anti-racist strategies and affirms the non-white bodies that the myth of a white Argentina has tried to silence.

The statement by Abril Caríssimo was designed as a contribution to a CARLA workshop, held in Manchester in April 2022, with some twenty-five CARLA researchers and artists. Abril was involved in the curation of the Virtual Visual Art exhibit in the section of the CARLA online exhibition dedicated to Identidad Marrón. Ana asked Abril to record a video about curation (https://youtu.be/wWA9rlIzgZg), which has been transcribed and translated here.

The text by Flora Alvarado and América López, titled 'Malonear los museos', was written by them at Ana's request as a reflection on their experience of curating an exhibition titled *¿Qué necesitan aprender los museos?* (What Do Museums Need to Learn?), which ran from 12 December 2020 to 6 March 2021 and was curated by Identidad Marrón and the writers' collective Poetas Villeres (Poets from the *Villas*) for the public state museum Palais de Glace in Buenos Aires.¹ The exhibition included various items from the museum's collections, which served as points of reflection.

Context: the phrase *malonear los museos* is a good entry point for understanding these texts. *Malonear* is a Spanish word used in Argentina and Uruguay meaning to undertake a *malón* (from the Mapuzugun *maleu*, to inflict damage on the enemy). *Malón* is the name given by colonial and Republican authorities to the raids carried out by Mapuche warriors. The term gained special significance during the genocidal campaigns against Mapuche and other Indigenous populations carried out under the name of La Conquista del Desierto (Conquest of the Desert), directed mainly by General Julio Argentino Roca in the 1870s. The campaigns were nominally a response to Indigenous *malones*. The famous paintings *El malón* (1845), by Mauricio Rugendas, and *La vuelta del malón* (The Return from the Raid, 1892), by Ángel Della Valle, capture the dominant image of Indigenous people as the barbarians against whom the forces of civilisation were ranged. One aim of the interventions designed by Identidad Marrón is to *malonear* – 'invade', 'raid' or 'occupy' – the spaces of the venerable institutions created by the forces of 'civilisation', such as museums and galleries, and appropriate them for the expression of *marrón* identities and priorities, including an acknowledgement of the pervasive presence of racism in Argentina.

STATEMENT BY ABRIL CARÍSSIMO, A.K.A. BBYWACHA

Hi, I'm Abril Caríssimo. I work as an artist under the pseudonym Bbywacha and I am a research student in visual arts. I was part of the curatorship of the virtual exhibit [in the Identidad Marrón section of the CARLA online exhibition].

There is a theme that I think is important to highlight in the way we think about curatorship, which perhaps has to do with specific problems in Argentina, particularly institutional ones. And this also involves the idea of translation: the translation of our own work and the translation of our experiences into institutional settings.

For the racialised artist, I feel like there are like two levels of difficulty.² One is that we are trained in artistic institutions that are governed

---

¹ See the exhibition catalogue at www.argentina.gob.ar/sites/default/files/dossier_el_museo_aprende.pdf.
² 'Racialised' as used by members of Identidad Marrón means racialised as non-white or racialised negatively or disadvantageously.

by white structures and schemes of thought. For all that art has been theorised and researched in Latin America, the reality is that, not only in the ways we understand and study art history, but also more generally in the ways we study today's artists, conceptualisations and problems, and the theorists and thinkers that we read to this day – all these are still European and white.

And the problem is that a lot of how we present our own experience in art continues to be under these hegemonic gazes. They are a way of perceiving our own experience so that it continues to be seen from the outside and through the internalisation of this external, hegemonic gaze. [And this] creates a limitation on the ideas that we validate and the themes and aesthetics that we use in our work.

In my journey as an artist and in [the journeys of] other artists, I see that in the process of translation there is a difficulty in how we divide ourselves between two worlds. Between a real, everyday world, where our work is appreciated and understood in self-managed artistic spaces; and an institutional world where it is often impossible for us to translate these works or these dynamics.

And I think [the second difficulty is] the fact that historically, in Argentina, artistic spaces, such as artistic training institutions, galleries and museums, have been mostly occupied by white middle-class people. And the people who criticise and consume art, the people who know about art, surround themselves with very little diversity of experience.

So what makes translation difficult is that they can't necessarily understand or empathise with our experiences or even understand our points of reference. Many of the ways in which we are conditioned to exist in institutional spaces continue to be in terms of ignorant art or young, emerging art, as seen from an external perspective.

Despite being racialised [as non-white] in the same way as a large part of the Argentine population, in institutional spheres we continue to be seen as belonging to another age. The importance of curatorship and institutional critique and racialised production has to do specifically with this, but there has to be an interrogation of how we are categorised, how we are understood to begin with and how we are presented. And this also has to be done from a racialised perspective because, if not, we continue to exist under these super-limited perceptions of what we should and should not talk about in our art. Like the idea that we make art that has no depth or that comes from outside, from the non-institutional [sphere]. The reality is that for the art world and for the racialised artist, these places of curation, these places of institutional critique generally come from outside, they come from spaces like Identidad Marrón.

MALONEAR LOS MUSEOS: STRATEGIES AND CONSIDERATIONS

Text by Flora Alvarado, with América Canela

As part of the exercise of breaking with the racist structures that exist in Argentine society, the Identidad Marrón collective not only denounces the glass doors that invisibly restrict access to cultural institutions such as national museums, but also implements actions to counteract the exclusion of the Indigenous *marrón* population from them. Acting on the premise that 'anti-racism is action' and posing questions such as 'Is art in Argentina only for white people?', the collective carries out numerous activities, including debates on spaces of power, led by *marrón* people who, from a peripheral location, work to ensure the inclusion of their territories, their perspectives and their voices, while questioning their absence in the places considered as historically relevant, which are often also the spaces where decisions and meanings are defined.

The project to decolonise, or *malonear*, museums must take into account various institutional factors: the spaces as such, the collections or archives that comprise them, the public that visits them, the texts that accompany the exhibitions and the way in which they are written, whether admission is free or not, and so on.

Taking culture as a right, the collective sees museums as spaces where people with cultural competences acquired through academic or classroom education should be able to participate, but also the children of workers, peasants and migrants of popular origin, because, as a right, culture should always be accessible to everyone and not just to one social sector.

Questions: Who are the people who go to museums? Do we all go? Should museums be committed to diverse communities or just to the white middle/upper classes?

Forms of exclusion operate quietly when it comes to accessing institutions that present themselves as open and inclusive. This is the case with museums and cultural institutions that are mainly accessed by a social class with certain economic and cultural capital. In addition to economic and class factors, there is also a racial factor, since the sector that occupies museums or cultural institutions (not only as spectators, but also as representatives of these spaces) is predominantly white. Even under progressive policies, racialised people, *marrón* identities and subaltern populations continue to be excluded from real access to culture and its spaces. Reaching museums located in wealthier areas of cities means travel, when distance, cost and time pose challenges that restrict equal access for all. The majority of racialised populations live in peripheral or working-class neighbourhoods, far from these areas. In other words, access to museums is a privilege reserved for a very small sector.

Article 27 of the Universal Declaration of Human Rights states that cultural rights must be guaranteed, including the right of everyone to participate freely in cultural life, to enjoy the arts and to share in scientific advances and the benefits thereof. Access to culture is a right that is being violated for a broad section of the working class, mostly racialised people. In this context, the Identidad Marrón collective faced several challenges in curating the exhibition for the Palais de Glace. Not only did we have to break with preconceived notions about the audiences that usually have access to the museum, we also had to take into account the various barriers we have mentioned (economic, geographical, ethnic-racial). Above all we had to break through the biggest barrier of all: the indifference generated by the absence of racialised people in these places. It meant adopting, as a key principle, a perspective that sees racialised people as active agents in culture, not as objects to be exhibited or subject matter to be presented and represented by an othering or white gaze, but as participating as workers and creators of culture, as bearers of voices and knowledges derived from their experiences and territories. A key challenge was also to raise the issue that museums do not discuss questions regarding access and the social profile of the public they reach. They present themselves as public, free and accessible, but in practice the exclusion of racialised sectors continues to be the reality.

The idea behind the curatorship of the exhibition, the inaugural and closing events and the various activities that took place during the exhibition was to design actions in which *marrón* people could walk through the glass doors of the museums. In this and in line with our key premise that anti-racism is action, we took the position that museums should take responsibility and, more importantly, take action and change their practices through dialogue and collaboration with our collective: understanding the museum not only as an exhibition space, but also as a space that has the potential to repair, to build collectively and to give a place to populations and perspectives that have been historically marginalised and silenced. A fundamental factor is that, in order for this reparation to be real and not just symbolic or temporary, it must take place in dialogue and joint action with the communities concerned.

Question: *How can we create an exhibition that has an impact?*

Creating an exhibition is not just producing materials that generate pleasure, entertainment, or contemplation. For our collective, the curatorial act of conceiving and making an exhibition is an opportunity to put into practice a class-conscious anti-racist perspective on the art world. The primary aim is to extend to the *marrón* population the right to access, the right to culture. It is also a matter of beginning to notice the presence or absence of debates about progressive policies of inclusion, and whether this inclusion is actually made real by working with the populations in question. It is about seeing artistic and curatorial practice as a political act. In this way, putting together an exhibition creates a space that invites reflection and the questioning of preconceived ideas about who makes decisions in museums and the art system, and what happens with their installations and agendas. Furthermore, it is an opportunity to think of an exhibition as a place of encounter between the different populations that might make up its audience, but with particular attention to the racialised population of popular origin.

We tried to create an exhibition that would occupy – that is, *malonear* – the museum, transforming it into a space in which links between different communities are actively developed. The focus was deliberately on *marrón* people in order to reduce the distance between the institution and the racialised communities that do not usually occupy it. This was taken into account in the curatorial process, the inaugural and closing events and the associated activities: guided tours, workshops, audiovisual clips and social media content.

The organisers, the participants in the activities and the artists invited to star in the video clips were racialised people who already had experience in artistic and cultural practices. In this sense, the aim was also to validate and recognise their work and personal journeys, as well as to provide a space for them to meet each other. For many members of the public, on the other hand, it was the first time they had been to an institution of this kind.

The selection of works from the Palais de Glace collection was made on the basis of the bodies represented in the images, the themes they address (racialised labour, access to rights, etc.), the materials they used and the allusions they made to specific places. These works were acquired by the Palais de Glace during various editions of the annual competition of Salón Nacional de Artes Visuales. The works were selected in dialogue with racialised corporealities and realities, bearing in mind that none of the artists who created them belonged to racialised communities. The aim of the selection was to question who has the opportunity to produce artistic works. We envisioned a dialogue between the works of the Palais de Glace collection, the presence of the *marrón* population, the series of video clips, the guided tours and works produced by the Villeres Writers' Collective. The exhibition opened the possibility of a dialogue between works that could have come from artists from popular backgrounds and actions performed in the present that question social imaginaries from an anti-racist perspective.

Museums are places that legitimise discourses and validate knowledge and narratives. Working collaboratively means understanding they can also be seen as a tool that provides reparations to diverse communities, always taking into account the place the museums have historically occupied and their relationship to racialised communities. It means beginning to see museums as potential spaces of reparation, not only by providing a physical space but also by enabling debates, opening their doors to reference points and collectives whose trajectories and histories can be recognised both symbolically and economically. It is a way of building the museum collectively, making a museum that allows for the existence of possibilities beyond the dominant ones.

Question: Who are the creators of knowledge, of truth, of history?

The debate about the differences between arts and crafts is still current today. Art is seen as something produced by creative geniuses, associated with an exclusive sector that possesses innate talents, and linked to a position of power and elite, that is, only for the few. Crafts are associated with a job that is taught and learned, and with manual and mass production; it does not have a unique value because it is mass-produced. In the social imaginary, when we think of the bodies that create arts and crafts, there is also a valorisation based on racial factors. Which bodies are understood as being capable and worthy of producing the works of art, the knowledge and the signs of cultural and intellectual value that can be presented in a museum? In the art system, success is measured not only in terms of quality and productive capacity, but also in terms of the tools and doors that networking gives access to, which intervene in construction of figures taken as representative.

Art is a sign of the political, historical, social and cultural events happening at the time of its creation. It serves as an indicator that, together with theory, create narratives about history and its participants. In Argentina, the primary exponents of the arts have generally been – and still are to this day – of European descent. Those who produced the works that shaped social imaginaries and represented the Argentine nation, commissioned by the state during its process of formation, have been Europeans or Argentina-born white people trained in European art academies. In other words, the gaze that shaped the artworks foundational to the country's history is white and Eurocentric.

Racialised bodies – Indigenous *marrón* bodies – are seen as objects of study, in museums to be analysed, studied and measured. The descriptions in the diaries and illustrations of the European travellers who came to the Americas revealed an anthropological or sociological gaze that objectified, infantilised and animalised Indigenous *marrón* people. From the transporting of Indigenous individuals to the Global North for study, to the theft of cultural artefacts from Indigenous communities, museums retain colonial roots in their history. In this scenario, the representation in art institutions of alternative ways of being for *marrón* bodies represented a break with the social schema in which *marrón* people are not even considered human persons, but objects or animals, and their cultural artefacts, in turn, are considered only as anthropological objects.

Considering racialised subjects as knowledge-producing subjects and creators of art allows us to give space to the diverse voices and knowledges of different communities. Objects are given life and meaning through the people who represent them, in a process of re-signifying and affirming narratives. It is people and their communities, and in this case people who identify as *marrón*, who, by their active presence in museums, can use words and use their bodies to occupy, disrupt and expose structural racism, unequal access and entrenched prejudices. Museums must position themselves as places of exchange, learning and reparation that can make their tools available to communities and collectives to ensure change with real impact.

5

Indigenous Arts and Anti-Racism in Brazil

Perspectives from the Véxoa: We Know *Exhibition*

Naine Terena and Jamille Pinheiro Dias

INTRODUCTION

Discussions about invisibilised artistic traditions have put pressure on what is meant by promoting self-representation in museum practice and art circuits. With that in mind, this chapter examines perspectives around *Véxoa: Nós sabemos* (Véxoa: We Know; *véxoa* means 'we know' in the Terena language), the first Indigenous-only arts exhibition ever held at the Pinacoteca de São Paulo and the first ever to be curated by an Indigenous person in a prominent museum in Brazil. On show from 31 October 2020 to 22 March 2021, *Véxoa* was curated by one of the co-authors of this chapter, Indigenous researcher and artist Naine Terena. The exhibition *Véxoa: Nós sabemos* was part of the OPY project (*opy* means 'prayer-house' in Guarani), a collaborative effort between three distinct institutions: the Pinacoteca de São Paulo, the Casa do Povo and the Kalipety village of the Guarani Mbya people. These institutions – a state museum, an independent cultural centre and a community – joined forces to highlight the lack of Indigenous arts in museum collections, address issues of preservation and knowledge transmission, and envision a different idea of Brazil. The initiative involved various activities, including *Véxoa*, performances, seminars and events beyond the museum's physical boundaries, creating an interaction between museum collections and Indigenous art practices. The OPY project received the 2019 Sotheby's Prize, recognising the excellence of *Véxoa*'s curatorial approach and providing financial support for the exhibition, public programming and research.[1] The

---

[1] This chapter is the fruit of numerous conversations with the many artists who participated in *Véxoa* and with whom we had the chance to engage in a series of online meetings

exhibition marked a shift regarding self-representation in Indigenous arts and curatorship in Brazil. In this regard, this chapter aims to contribute to the discourse on the significant role of Indigenous arts in challenging racism and advocating for Indigenous recognition in Brazil. By reclaiming spaces traditionally dominated by non-Indigenous perspectives, Indigenous artists in Brazil have been challenging colonial and extractive epistemologies in a sustained manner (see Terena 2020).

In a context marked by increasingly open anti-Indigenous racism, propelled and encouraged by Jair Bolsonaro's administration (2019–2022) and the disproportionately severe impact of the COVID-19 pandemic on Indigenous peoples, *Véxoa* represented a milestone in the growing recognition of a generation of Indigenous artists in the prestigious art circuit of São Paulo and in Brazil at large. This generation is introducing a different gaze to aesthetic practices, challenging commonly held assumptions about the supposed appearance of Indigenous arts, the media they are thought to exist in, and the timelines, categories and conceptual frameworks they are expected to conform to. These artists are occupying the cultural sphere as a form of resistance and pedagogical intervention for non-Indigenous audiences, as well as emphasising the interconnectedness of all life forms, the spiritual realm and the environment, challenging anthropocentrism and highlighting the importance of ancestral ties. This generation has also been strategically employing self-representation as a means of countering the invisibilisation of Indigenous authorship in Brazil's art history and creating spaces for conversation on the need to intensify the advocacy for Indigenous rights.[2]

broadcast on the YouTube channels of the Pinacoteca de São Paulo and the CARLA project (see for example '*Véxoa: Nós sabemos* na Pinacoteca de São Paulo e a arte indígena contemporânea no Brasil', online conversation, 30 September 2020, organised by Jamille Pinheiro Dias in partnership with the Pinacoteca de São Paulo, www.youtube.com/watch?v=MoCW6AERCvo&t=2s). We are deeply grateful to them for their time and willingness to share their insights. We also acknowledge the sustained exchanges we have had with Fernanda Pitta, former senior curator at Pinacoteca and curatorial coordinator of *Véxoa*. Denilson Baniwa has been a vital interlocutor and an inspiring friend, as we hope is readily apparent. We extend very special thanks to Pinacoteca's director Jochen Volz, whose hospitality and enthusiasm greatly contributed to this collaboration. Producer Guilherme Barros has been unfailingly supportive and a consistent point of reference at Pinacoteca. Bearing in mind that aspiring to anti-racist practices in the arts necessarily involves looking critically at the distribution of workforce along racialised hierarchies of power, we wish to acknowledge the often invisibilised people of colour who perform the work of cleaning, maintenance, reception and security that keeps museums, galleries and other art spaces functioning (see, among others, Vergès 2019, 2021).

[2] See 'As Artes Indígenas e as Culturas de Resistência', online conversation, 2 December 2020, organised by Jamille Pinheiro Dias in partnership with the Pinacoteca de São Paulo, www.youtube.com/watch?v=MDnwfKJvJmE.

CONFRONTING STRUCTURAL ANTI-INDIGENOUS RACISM

The centrality of Indigenous arts in Brazilian art history narratives makes this process even more pressing, emphasising the urgency of highlighting the contributions of Indigenous peoples in both artistic and societal realms. In line with this, two projects – Racism and Anti-Racism in Brazil: The Case of Indigenous Peoples; and Cultures of Anti-Racism in Latin America (CARLA) – have demonstrated the necessity for further investigation into the particular characteristics of racism against Indigenous peoples in Brazil.[3] This implies the need for renewed approaches to the intersection of anti-racism, arts and cultural production in the country that acknowledge the specific experiences of Indigenous peoples. Both projects have demonstrated that in Brazil, terms such as 'race' and 'racism' have traditionally not often been used to discuss violence against Indigenous peoples; instead, oppression is usually framed in terms of 'ethnicity' or 'culture', often leading to the exclusion of Indigenous peoples from academic and political debates on racism. Furthermore, it is also important to recognise that there is a tendency to ignore the diversity of African enslaved peoples and Indigenous peoples, both victims of racism, with scholars such as Walter Mignolo and Catherine Walsh (2018) arguing that the modern concept of 'race' and modern racism originated with European colonisation, characterised by exclusion, erasure and dehumanisation.

Despite some historical acknowledgment, recent research and anti-racist policies tend to overlook Indigenous issues, focusing more on Afro-descendants, often lumping Indigenous populations into a broad category of non-whites, typically categorised as *pardo* (brown), resulting in the marginalisation of Indigenous issues. As Lúcia Sá, Pedro Mandagará and Felipe Milanez Pereira show in Chapter 2, the racialisation of Indigenous peoples includes 'de-authorisation', denying their Indigenous identity if they do not conform to preconceived notions of Indigeneity.[4] This paradox of being perceived as either 'not modern enough' or 'not Indigenous enough' reinforces their marginalisation. The belief that Indigenous peoples cannot adopt Western tools without losing their identity is a manifestation of this racist paradox, as they face pressure to modernise yet are criticised as 'non-Indians' if they do,

---

[3] The Racism and Anti-Racism in Brazil project (2017–2019) was led by Lúcia Sá with Felipe Milanez. See https://projects.alc.manchester.ac.uk/racism-indigenous-brazil/.
[4] See also Sá and Milanez Pereira (2020).

fossilising Indigeneity as an unchangeable trait tied to non-Indigenous ideas of primitiveness. This notion that Indigenous identity can only be lost and never changed or regained denies Indigenous peoples the possibility of changing their identity, compounded by societal and political rhetoric that deems modernised Indigenous individuals as 'not real'. Consequently, racism against Indigenous peoples is often rendered invisible due to scholarship avoiding its discussion and structural racism erasing the visibility of Indigenous peoples. Furthermore, Brazilian visual arts have historically depicted Indigenous peoples through lenses of disappearance or assimilation or as sources for inspiration. The current generation of Indigenous artists in Brazil is actively challenging these persistent processes of erasure by representing Indigenous peoples as dynamic and present, thereby confronting and reshaping the narrative around Indigenous lives.

VÉXOA'S MULTIDIMENSIONAL APPROACH TO ANTI-RACISM

As emphasised in the 2021 documentary *Terra fértil: Véxoa e a arte indígena contemporânea na Pinacoteca de São Paulo* (Fertile Land: *Véxoa* and Contemporary Indigenous Art at the Pinacoteca de São Paulo), while the inherent politics at work in *Véxoa* might not always be explicit in the artworks selected for the exhibition, they are present in various forms.[5] The political messages embedded in these artworks, though sometimes subtle, are integral to the artists' expressions. The boundaries between the political and the spiritual are porous and mutually reinforcing. We can see this interplay between politics and spirituality in Edgar Kanaykõ's photographs of the Acampamento Terra Livre (Free Land Camp), which since 2004 has been an annual event advocating 'land titling now' for Indigenous peoples, and in the works by the Movement of Huni Kuin Artists (MAKHU), who aim to create art that brings healing to the world. Highlighting the implicit politics within *Véxoa* shows that the exhibition is an exemplary case of how anti-racist action can take many forms. Even when the artists involved do not address racism through explicit condemnation, they do so through advocacy for land rights and environmental justice, critique of anthropocentrism and acknowledgment that other life

---

[5] Documentary produced by the CARLA project in partnership with Pinacoteca de São Paulo, directed by Jamille Pinheiro Dias and Débora McDowell; see https://youtu.be/7VnYH4VgaAE.

forms and spiritual entities participate in creative processes. This multi-dimensional approach enriches the understanding of anti-racist affective operations in art and highlights the necessity for varied strategies. Thus *Véxoa* underscores the power of art as a tool for anti-racist activism, illustrating that both direct and indirect methods are crucial in the collective effort against racial inequality.

As Indigenous activist and thinker Ailton Krenak, one of the artists participating in *Véxoa*, recently argued, the current generation of Indigenous artists in Brazil is making a highly purposeful use of spaces relying on *telas* – a term meaning both 'screens' and 'canvases' in Portuguese – 'making cracks in the walls of museums' and taking advantage of social media and communication technologies as an effective means to broaden and strengthen the rights of Indigenous peoples (Jeronimo 2020: 7). The present era, starting in about the 1990s, can be described as the fourth moment of Indigenous history in Brazil, indicating a historical landmark in the achievement of increasing protagonism by Indigenous peoples.[6] In this fourth era, whose origins date back to Xavante congressman Mário Juruna's use of a tape recorder to register the promises made by politicians around 1982 (Juruna, Hohlfeldt and Hoffmann 1982), Indigenous people pursue their own activities and actions via technologies (all technologies) in a more impactful way, standing out in Indigenous media, literature and the arts.[7] In this era, massive production of counter-information by

---

[6] According to Terena (2019), the first moment was marked by attempts to physically exterminate Indigenous populations. The second moment saw endeavours to culturally assimilate them and extinguish their own cultures; during this time, the rights of Indigenous peoples in Brazil were regulated by the state under a guardianship regime (*tutela*). Under this condition, Indigenous individuals did not fully enjoy citizenship, being subject to paternalistic measures that limited their autonomy and freedom. The third moment began with the 1988 Constitution, which acknowledged and guaranteed the fundamental rights of Indigenous peoples and provided them with comprehensive legal protection. See also Cunha (2018).

[7] The 1980s were also a turning point in the strategic utilisation of audiovisual means by Indigenous groups in Brazil within the context of advocacy, self-representation and self-determination. The Kayapó Video Project, catalysed by Terence Turner, harnessed the potential of video to document challenges shared by different Kayapó villages, such as the construction of dams and protests against governmental actions. The Kayapó Project also held politicians accountable by capturing their statements on film. The project involved the instruction of Indigenous individuals by Turner and others in the operation of video cameras, as well as the skills necessary for filming and editing documentaries centred around their own community. The Video in the Villages project, dedicated to training Indigenous filmmakers, also of great historical importance, was founded in 1986 by Vincent Carelli, with an emphasis on leaving the control of their narratives in the Indigenous people's own hands, creating a powerful tool for advocacy. See Pace (2018).

Indigenous groups and individuals really started to contest hegemonic narratives, mainly through the growing use of social media and other communication technologies – in political and legal spheres as well as in the art world.

THE SOCIAL DYNAMICS OF AFFECT IN ANTI-RACIST ART

We also aim to contribute to a better understanding of what affect is and how it operates in art engaged in anti-racism. Affect has become a popular concept in the humanities, being used frequently in contexts both significant and vague, which has diluted its meaning. The term is sometimes used without clear implications and may be equated with something general such as 'personal' or 'subjective'. Ernst van Alphen argues for the inherently social significance of affect in art, proposing that engaging with affective operations can lead to a more ethical interaction with cultural objects (Van Alphen 2008). He contends that there is a growing need to understand affect and how it operates in art, especially given the information overload and implosion of meaning in contemporary society. For him, affect is often confused with personal feelings but is inherently social. Affects are not personal or subjective; they are social and operate through interactions between people and objects. Sara Ahmed (2004) argues something similar, stating that emotions delineate social and political boundaries, reinforcing who belongs and who is excluded from a given collective identity. Emotions can be transmitted and have physiological impacts, preceding their expression in words.

Van Alphen shows how the work of Cuban-American artist Félix González-Torres marked a shift during the early 1990s from politically charged, slogan-driven art to more personal, affective forms of expression. This shift was driven by the need for new modes of contestation that resonated with the changing socio-historical context. Based on González-Torres's claims, Van Alphen asserts that art using a more personal voice can be better understood as a shift towards affective rather than assertive or didactic communication. For him, the political impact of art now lies in its ability to generate and transmit affect rather than to convey a specific message. Additionally, Van Alphen follows Gilles Deleuze in noting that art stimulates thought through sensation rather than cognitive recognition. By doing so, he argues that art, as a mode of thinking, challenges traditional philosophical distinctions between thought and sensation.

Understanding affect as a social phenomenon is crucial in addressing anti-racism in Indigenous arts. Indigenous arts often carry profound cultural, historical and emotional significance that transcends personal or subjective experiences. By recognising affect as inherently social, we can more effectively engage with Indigenous artworks, understanding them as active agents that transmit collective emotions and social critiques. This approach allows us to move beyond superficial interpretations and recognise the political, cultural and cosmopolitical dimensions of Indigenous arts. It enables us to see how these works operate affectively to challenge racist narratives and foster solidarity among diverse audiences. Acknowledging the social dimension of affect thus enhances our capacity to engage with Indigenous arts in a way that supports anti-racist efforts.

BREAKING THE SPELL

The Pinacoteca is well known nationally and internationally as a prestigious place in which to see masterpieces of Brazilian art dating from the nineteenth century to the present day. A state-funded fine arts museum founded in 1905, it is the oldest of its kind in the state of São Paulo. The starting point for claiming the Indigenous occupation of this space was not only presenting works from the last ten or fifteen years, associated with so-called contemporary Indigenous art, but also the possibility of framing a curatorial approach that would foreground the existence of aesthetic expressions that have always been made by Indigenous people in Brazil, but that have been historically invisibilised. When considering the art canon in Brazil, we notice many voids and omissions resulting from this invisibilisation. Challenging those voids and omissions also involves a refusal of the linear conception of time that circumscribes this notion of 'contemporary' and underlies colonial modernity itself.

When Macuxi artist Jaider Esbell coined the term 'arte indígena contemporânea' (contemporary Indigenous art), he meant it as a strategic approach, highlighting the complex interplay of power dynamics and colonial perceptions concerning Indigenous artistic expression.[8] According to his proposal, this phrase operates as a symbolic space for Indigenous artists to assert legitimacy and navigate the historical and cultural complexities of Indigeneity while challenging conventional boundaries of art and Indigenous representation. Esbell's strategy encapsulates an understanding of Indigenous creativity as both a form of resistance against historical oppressions and a platform for reclaiming autonomy and agency in shaping narratives and cultural discourse. By referring to

---

[8] See, for instance, Esbell (2016, 2018c).

'Contemporary Indigenous Art' as a 'trap for traps', he suggested that it functions as a mechanism to ensnare and confront the various 'traps' inherent in the colonial legacies of the art world (Esbell 2020). Esbell considers that by employing this term, Indigenous artists are strategically positioning themselves to counter prevailing power structures, subvert expectations and assert agency.

Another way to critically address the notion of the contemporary in relation to Indigenous arts would be to refuse a linear conception of time, acknowledging the multiple temporalities inherent in Indigenous forms of expression. This recognition leads us to contend that the notion of contemporary art is intrinsically linked to global power dynamics, particularly to the control and systematisation of time by capitalism (see also Brizuela 2019). Consequently, it is important to acknowledge that the assimilation of Indigenous arts into the concept of contemporary art risks perpetuating a hierarchical regime of temporality, wherein alternative temporalities are marginalised and perceived as less valuable. Saying that Indigenous arts have always been present in Brazilian history and that they should be presented in art spaces according to Indigenous criteria implies questioning a version of history that assumes the vanishing of Indigenous peoples and that was used to relegate Indigenous peoples to the past. In other words, speaking back to a canon that has historically both appropriated and erased the aesthetic force of Indigenous peoples involves interrogating the supposed neutrality of hegemonic temporalities.

Denilson Baniwa, one of the most important artists in the emergence of Indigenous leadership in the arts in Brazil, argues that 'art was used as a colonial spell'. He continued: 'Through art, history is written, history is erased, stories are constructed and destroyed. ... Art was one of the most powerful tools for the domination and erasure of various peoples.' Part of colonisation is the colonisation of art, which has systematically portrayed Indigenous people in 'idyllic, romanticised, sensual and tragic ways', as Baniwa said in an event organised by the Federal University of Minas Gerais (UFMG 2020). For him, art can function as a tool to challenge these stereotypes and rewrite history from Indigenous perspectives – in other words, to break the colonial spell. He mentions artistic and literary works such as Victor Meirelles's 1861 painting *A primeira missa no Brasil*, Pedro Américo's 1877 painting *Batalha do Avaí* and Mário de Andrade's 1928 novel *Macunaíma* as having made Indigenous populations 'occupy a place of simplistic knowledge and savage intellectuality'; taken as sources of 'inspiration for art', they were made into 'fragments of people transformed into Western knowledge'. 'My work consists of challenging this place, occupied by living or dead models, who had no right to negotiate to be there. It is the struggle for the right to respond to arts that are like simulacra, that simulate the realities of the Indigenous, the Black, the poor, of those who live on the margins', he pointed out, illustrating the link between the formation of Brazil's canonical visual culture and racialised hierarchies.

ADDRESSING VOIDS

As one of the largest institutions sheltering Brazilian art history, the Pinacoteca, in the years preceding *Véxoa*, had already been promoting seminars to critically engage with art history in Brazil and its own long-term exhibition of its collection, seeking to rethink the museum's narrative structure and addressing the question of what topics deserved to be presented to its public. In Baniwa's terms, the Pinacoteca was already expressing an interest in challenging its own entanglement with Brazilian art history's 'colonial spell'. In July and August 2017, one of the Pinacoteca's curators, Fernanda Pitta, who would later become a close collaborator as curatorial coordinator of *Véxoa*, led a summer collaborative working group at the Clark Art Institute in Willamstown, Massachusetts, looking at research narrative models for long-term exhibitions of historical art collections. In September 2018, after participating in one of these events, the international symposium Ways of Seeing, Ways of Showing, Naine Terena visited the Pinacoteca's collection with curator Valéria Piccoli. The symposium held discussions about the approach to chronology in the long-term exhibition of the Pinacoteca's collection and realised that there were indeed many voids in how that history was being presented. Terena asked Piccoli about the reasons for such voids, as well as about why Indigenous art had not yet been incorporated into the institution's collection.

Those voids were clear: Indigenous people were represented by non-Indigenous artists in the collection, but the absence of works made by Indigenous artists was striking. Thinking about this absence was the first step in addressing the possibility of making Indigenous artists present in the context of the institution. With the Pinacoteca's overall commitment to making critical changes to exhibitions and displays as part of this process, a more consistent anti-racist agenda was already taking shape. This movement became evident with an exhibition titled *Territórios: Artistas afrodescendentes no acervo da Pinacoteca*

(Territories: Afro-descendant Artists in the Pinacoteca's Collection), curated by Tadeu Chiarelli. Running from 12 December 2015 to 13 June 2016, it celebrated the Pinacoteca's 110th anniversary by showcasing notable works by Afro-Brazilian artists, aiming to highlight and value the contributions of Afro-descendant artists to art history in Brazil. Curated to reflect on the institution's past and present collection, it offered a non-chronological look at Afro-Brazilian artistic production and its context within the museum's collection. May 2017 marked the beginning of the work of Jochen Volz as general director of the Pinacoteca. Volz had acted as the chief curator of the 32nd São Paulo Biennale, *Incerteza viva* (Live Uncertainty), which had taken place from September to December 2016, addressing issues that are vital and urgent to Indigenous peoples and humanity at large, such as global warming, the extinction of species and the loss of biological and cultural diversity. Naine Terena contributed to this biennale, broadening the perspective on Indigenous cultures. This drive to implement an anti-racist agenda at the Pinacoteca continued with powerful solo exhibitions by Black female artists, notably Rosana Paulino's 2018 *A costura da memória* (The Sewing of Memory) and Grada Kilomba's 2019 *Desobediências poéticas* (Poetic Disobediences).

In 2019, the Pinacoteca significantly expanded its collection of contemporary Indigenous art through the Patrons of Contemporary Art programme, acquiring *Feitiço para salvar a Raposa Serra do Sol* (A Spell to Save Raposa Serra do Sol) by Jaider Esbell and a series of pieces by Denilson Baniwa, including *Voyeurs*, *menu*, *luto* (Mourning), *Vitrine* (Display), *O antropólogo moderno já nasceu antigo* (The Modern Anthropologist Was Already Born Old) and *Enfim, 'civilização'* ('Civilisation', At Last). These acquisitions marked a pivotal moment in the museum's recent history, as its only Indigenous art held up to that time consisted of Iny-Karajá dolls made of clay and wax, known as *ritxoko*. The inclusion of Esbell's and Baniwa's works not only diversified the Pinacoteca's collection but also underscored the institution's commitment to recognising and showcasing Indigenous arts.

In October 2020, the Pinacoteca undertook a rehang of its collection, moving away from its elitist past to celebrate Brazil's rich diversity. This overhaul included acquisitions of contemporary works by women, Afro-Brazilian and Indigenous artists, significantly increasing their representation. The museum's collection, previously displayed in chronological order, is now organised thematically across nineteen rooms, juxtaposing eighteenth-century academic portraiture with modernist and contemporary art. This new arrangement aligned with curator Jochen Volz's vision to address the institution's colonial heritage and promote inclusivity. *Véxoa* coincided with this rehang.

In the years prior to *Véxoa*, through partnerships with Indigenous artists and communities, several institutions hosted exhibitions that advanced the self-representation and self-determination of Indigenous peoples, striving to bring Indigenous agency to the forefront of artistic and curatorial practice. Notable among these were *ReAntropofagia* (Reanthropophagy; Niterói, Arts Center of Universidade Federal Fluminense, 2019), *Dja guata porã: Rio de Janeiro indígena* (Walk Well: Indigenous Rio de Janeiro; Rio de Janeiro, Museu de Arte do Rio, 2017–2018) and *¡Mira! – Artes visuais contemporâneas dos povos indígenas* (Look! Contemporary Visual Art of Indigenous Peoples; Belo Horizonte, Espaço do Conhecimento, Universidade Federal de Minas Gerais, 2013–2014).[9] Collectively, these exhibitions emphasised the significance of art in the political and aesthetic struggles of Indigenous peoples, while also challenging the notion that Indigenous cultures are static relics of a mythical past. These events provide context for why *Véxoa* became the first exhibition to be curated solely by an Indigenous person at a highly prestigious museum in the country. Ultimately, *Véxoa* is the culmination of a long process and represents a significant political achievement accomplished by Indigenous peoples.[10]

RESPONDING TO ANTI-INDIGENOUS RACISM THROUGH THE ARTS

In the Brazilian context, anti-Indigenous racism has historically served as justification for land appropriation and colonial violence towards Indigenous peoples.[11] It was later used to justify state-sanctioned violence directed at Indigenous peoples under the military regime as well as after the enactment of the 1988 Constitution. During Dilma Roussef's administration, Brazil's Comissão Nacional da Verdade (National Truth Commission, 2012–2014) recognised Indigenous peoples as among the groups targeted by the crimes and human rights violations during the dictatorship from 1946 to 1988. However, the country's deeply ingrained developmentalism continued to threaten Indigenous lives during the

---

[9] *Dja guata porã* is a Guarani phrase; it can also be translated as 'walk together'.
[10] This process is discussed in depth in Terena and Pitta (2022) and Terena, de Carvalho Freire and Pérez Gil (2022).
[11] See Chapter 2 in this volume.

almost two decades of government by the Partido dos Trabalhadores (Workers' Party), which relied on the advancement of predatory agribusiness and genocidal megaprojects such as the Belo Monte hydroelectric dam. The situation worsened after 2019 with Jair Bolsonaro's openly anti-Indigenous far-right agenda, the increasing power of the rural caucus and their backing of the 'time frame' or *marco temporal* legal argument.[12] In broader terms, we can say that the history of contact between Indigenous peoples and colonisers has been marked by attempts to whiten the population. Historically, there were various moments in which actions were taken to homogeneously integrate Indigenous peoples into the national population, ranging from physical extermination to the imposition of formal education.

Currently, more than 300 Indigenous peoples and about 250 Indigenous languages exist in Brazil, distributed throughout all regions of the country. The trail left by attempts at extermination is clearly visible in the racist construction of the images of Indigenous peoples in the eyes of the non-Indigenous national population. This construction is sometimes encouraged by mass media, textbooks and, more recently, by an enormous amount of fake news spread across popular social networks in Brazil. Such actions attempt to delegitimise Indigenous identity and belonging, with the assumption that Indigenous peoples no longer maintain their cultural traits and, because of that, should adhere to a new reality – a new guise for socio-cultural integration. We have also seen various attacks based on physical stereotypes and the demoralisation of the Indigenous movement and its members. In recent years, discrimination by gender and race, among other forms of difference, has been widely legitimised by the Brazilian population itself, through actions that systematically affect minoritised groups.

This violent and complex historical backdrop recalls the relationship between the building of Brazil as a nation-state and how, despite the many achievements of Indigenous people spanning from early colonisation through to contemporary society, colonial structures persist. Derogatory, racist and Eurocentric imagery is one of the instances in which coloniality unfolds, assigning intellectual and cultural inferiority to Indigenous peoples and shaping ideas about who is seen, who has the power to see, who is represented and who represents. On the other

---

[12] See Chapter 2. Briefly, the legal argument proposed that Indigenous people could claim legal title only to lands they actually occupied on 5 October 1988, when the new Constitution was enacted.

hand, Indigenous people of various ages have been developing their own narratives and disseminating them to broad audiences, appropriating an extensive range of technologies, bringing different forms of knowledge together and gathering arguments to fight for the realisation of rights achieved in the 1988 Constitution and the maintenance of ways of life, as well as the continuity of the process of demarcation of Indigenous lands.

In this context, *Véxoa* emerged as a site where it was possible to discuss Indigenous existences in twenty-first century Brazil through the arts, in conjunction with a reflection on the invisibilisation of Indigenous forms of expression in the history of art in Brazil. *Véxoa* was committed to making space for Indigenous artists as agents and producers of content, not merely as sources of inspiration for non-Indigenous artists. The exhibition's curatorial approach sought to encompass not only 'contemporary' Indigenous arts but Indigenous arts more broadly, calling for a renewed look at the history of art in Brazil, as well as a rethinking of the Brazilian artistic system and museum culture. The rationale behind the exhibition was to showcase Brazilian art created by Indigenous artists. By adopting this approach, *Véxoa* exemplified how Indigenous arts could be an effective vehicle for anti-racist activism, even if in subtle and indirect ways. By foregrounding Indigenous curatorship and artistic expression, the exhibition challenged the traditional Western-centric art narratives that have historically predominated in Brazilian museums. This process was crucial for dismantling the entrenched racial hierarchies and biases that have historically marginalised Indigenous voices in the art world, ensuring that Indigenous narratives are told from Indigenous perspectives. The affective power of the artworks in *Véxoa* played a pivotal role in this approach, encouraging viewers to confront their own biases and complicity in systemic racism, and thereby promoting a more profound commitment to anti-racist action. The following pages provide some examples of how this was performed. Although it is not possible to discuss all the artworks that were exhibited in *Véxoa*, we intend to shed light on some of the strategies that *Véxoa*'s curatorial approach implemented.

CONFRONTING PRECONCEIVED NOTIONS OF AUTHENTICITY

A key aspect of *Véxoa* was the recognition, validation and reterritorialisation of items usually classified as 'artifacts' and 'crafts' that are typically denied artistic status or quality, positioning them as artworks. *Véxoa*

FIGURE 5.1 Gustavo Caboco and his mother, Lucilene Wapichana, 2020, in front of their collaborative works with Camila dos Santos da Silva, Divalda Silva and Juliana Kerexu, from the series *Where Is Indigenous Art in Paraná?* (© Levi Fanan/Pinacoteca de São Paulo, by permission).

placed emphasis on valuing them, the processes involved in their creation and the people who produced them, wherein the context of these works is as significant as the outcome. One of the aspects addressed by *Véxoa* was the critique of expectations surrounding Indigenous crafts, articulating a disjunction between cultural authenticity and external demands. This critique emerged in the collective works of Gustavo Caboco, Juliana Kerexu, Lucilene Wapichana, Ricardo Werá, Camila Kamé Kanhgág and Dival Xetá, particularly in their collaborative series *Where is Indigenous Art in Paraná?* (see Figure 5.1).[13] By incorporating images of animals such as the orca whale and giraffe – beings that are not found in Indigenous territories in Brazil – the artists played with and ironically subverted the expectations of what constitutes 'authentic' Indigenous art. This deliberate inclusion of animals that do not inhabit Indigenous territories in Brazil challenges the stereotypical confines imposed on Indigenous creativity, questioning why traditional motifs such as the anteater or the jaguar are deemed more

[13] For some examples, see https://millan.art/artistas/gustavo-caboco/.

'authentic' than an orca whale or a giraffe, animals foreign to the cultural and geographical milieu of Indigenous peoples in Brazil.

In his text for the catalogue of the *Véxoa* exhibition, 'O ser humano se reconhece como ser humano?' (Do Human Beings Recognise Themselves as Human Beings?), Gustavo Caboco relays a narrative that underscores this irony (Caboco 2020). During an encounter in a Guarani Mbya village, Caboco and Juliana Kerexu responded to demands for non-traditional Indigenous sculptures with humour. They understood requests from outsiders for Indigenous artists to produce figures such as a giraffe or an orca as a metaphor for the broader expectation that Indigenous peoples must constantly adapt and cater to external definitions of their identity. This expectation extends beyond the art realm into their everyday existence, where Indigenous people are often pressured to conform to non-Indigenous norms and aesthetics to secure their livelihood. When Kerexu provocatively asked, 'Do human beings recognise themselves as human beings?', she highlighted the irony of having to assert one's humanity and cultural identity continually.

This critique is further deepened by the irony of commodification in Indigenous arts. The Guarani Mbya bracelets bearing the logo of the Flamengo soccer team, as described by Caboco, epitomise this irony, lying in the juxtaposition of traditional craftmaking with popular commercial symbols. Fundamentally, this irony advances a critique of the expectations placed on Indigenous arts and crafts, questioning the assumption of authenticity dictated by external perceptions and the absurdity of these demands. Through their work, these artists simultaneously reference their cultural heritage and the imposed necessity to perform and transform their identities for external validation. They intervene in the reductionist view that Indigenous arts consist of 'little sculptures', as Caboco emphasised. By challenging the notion that Indigenous arts must adhere to predefined, exoticised categories to be recognised as legitimate art, these artists invite viewers to reconsider their own assumptions about Indigenous arts and identities. Their use of irony becomes a means of empowerment – a strategy to navigate and subvert the constraints imposed upon them, while simultaneously engaging in a dialogue about recognition.

BEYOND QUOTA FULFILMENT

The recognition of the absence or insufficient presence of Indigenous representation in museums and the steps taken to address these voids also lead us to discuss the importance of moving beyond mere inclusion, ensuring the sustained and meaningful integration of Indigenous peoples in the art world. In this regard, the issue of tokenism in art institutions remains challenging, but Indigenous artists are actively working to transform these spaces. Olinda Tupinambá, who participated in *Véxoa* with the film *Kaapora – O chamado das matas* (Kaapora – The Call of the Forests), reflected on this topic during a 2023 talk titled 'The Future Existence of Indigenous Peoples' as part of the programme of the exhibition *Histórias indígenas* (Indigenous Histories) at the São Paulo Art Museum (Tupinambá 2023). She expressed the sentiment that, in certain environments, Indigenous people might feel as if they are merely fulfilling a quota. She acknowledged the risk that institutions might invite Indigenous artists for a period and then consider their obligation fulfilled, as if they have ticked a box. This perception of superficial fulfilment can undermine the meaningful engagement and concern that should ideally underpin the involvement of Indigenous artists. However, as Tupinambá pointed out, many Indigenous artists are making significant strides in utilising these spaces to their advantage. They are not content with mere representation; instead, they seek to bring more Indigenous voices into the conversation, exerting a proactive effort to subvert tokenistic inclusion and push for more substantial and sustained participation.

The process of curating *Véxoa* at the Pinacoteca underscores a similar concern. The purpose of showcasing Indigenous arts should not be treated as a temporary trend. Indigenous arts should not be relegated to a quota but should instead be integrated into the ongoing narrative of art history. Indeed, *Véxoa* was not just an exhibition but also a strategic effort to reposition Indigenous arts within art institutions. It aimed to embed Indigenous artists into the broader conceptual frameworks and timeline of Brazilian art history – a gesture that also disrupts and reshapes this timeline. This approach strove for an integration that acknowledges the depth and diversity of Indigenous arts. It sought to ensure that Indigenous artists are meaningfully integrated into cultural and historical discourse. This ongoing effort demonstrates that while resolving the issue of Indigenous representation in art institutions may be complex, it is indeed worth pursuing through persistent and strategic engagement.

During the live streamings held in partnership between the CARLA project and the Pinacoteca, several participants stressed the fact that for Indigenous peoples, art is not something separate or to be learned in a strictly technical manner for later application. This resonates with how contemporary art makes space for artistically untrained people to have the freedom to express themselves through art, bringing 'the powers of life into art', as Arthur Danto (2007: 126) explains. The fact that the avant-garde movements of the 1960s were keen on bridging the divide between art and life, aiming to eliminate the distinction between high and popular art, demonstrates that. However, one of the distinctive characteristics of Indigenous arts is the idea that art praxis and creativity are intrinsically cosmopolitical, constituted by entanglements between humans and non-humans, that is, an ecology of human, plant, animal, mineral, spiritual and other forms of life.

There is currently an increasing interest among art historians and art researchers in general to acknowledge Indigenous arts within the extensive context of artistic production already canonised by the various artistic movements in the world. For instance, Fernanda Pitta (2021) examines the origin and development of the concept of Indigenous arts in Brazil. She demonstrates that it was initially constructed through the appropriation of Indigenous artistic expressions to build a narrative of Brazilian national art, which has had long-lasting implications for how Brazilian art has been perceived. Pitta argues for a re-evaluation of the role and recognition of Indigenous arts in Brazilian institutions, emphasising the need to navigate cultural differences and avoid subsuming diverse artistic conceptions under a homogenised national narrative. She advocates an 'indigenisation' of art history, which involves honouring the conceptual frameworks and histories of Indigenous peoples rather than fitting them into pre-existing Western-centric models. Pitta critiques traditional art historical narratives that often exclude or marginalise Indigenous art, calling for a shift in its perception and integration into the broader narrative of Brazilian art history and advocating for institutional recognition of Indigenous contributions.

Exhibitions such as *Véxoa* exemplify this much-needed shift, highlighting a recontextualisation of artworks made by Indigenous people and the established canon of contemporary art movements. Such a conceptual framework is sometimes referenced in Brazilian media to broaden the understanding of Indigenous artworks, considering the more than 520 years of contact and resistance. Indigenous arts, which, as we have noted, have often been seen as crafts or artifacts, are now being described as contemporary Indigenous art or even Brazilian art made by Indigenous people. In this context, works from different historical periods with distinct characteristics were displayed in the three rooms dedicated to *Véxoa*, supplemented by music and other artworks in the corridors and Denilson Baniwa's intervention in the car park in front

Indigenous Arts and Anti-Racism in Brazil

FIGURE 5.2 Denilson Baniwa and his intervention in the car park of the Pinacoteca de São Paolo, 2020 (© Levi Fanan/Pinacoteca de São Paulo, by permission).

of the museum (see Figure 5.2). This intervention, called *Hilo* (Hilum), was part one of a three-part work titled *Nada que é dourado permanece*, which referenced Robert Frost's well-known poem 'Nothing Gold Can Stay'. A second part was *Amáka (Coivara)*, for which he stored, in a collection of glass jars, ashes from the National Museum's devastating fire of 2 September 2018. *Amáka* is the Baniwa term for a burned area prepared for planting, following the slash-and-burn agricultural technique known as *coivara*, which involves burning vegetation to clear land for agriculture. For *Hilo*, Denilson initiated a planting and seeding action of medicinal and ornamental plants, flowers and spices in the Pinacoteca's car park, two years after the fire at the National Museum. In this work, Denilson catalysed a mode of creativity that symbiotically gestated art-making with other species, building aesthetic bridges across the web of life. The space previously reserved for cars was thus subjected to a healing process by Denilson and his plant and animal allies. Together, they fostered life in what was supposedly pure aridity among the stone blocks of the urban landscape. Through this *coivara* and fertilisation of the ground at the city's oldest museum, both subjective and physical territories were restored. The third part of Baniwa's work, *Terra preta de índio* (Indigenous Dark Earth), consisted of a video recording of the planting and seeding performed in the outdoor area, broadcast live and displayed in the exhibition room (see also Pinheiro Dias 2021).

Hierarchies between art, craft and artifact were critically examined in the *Véxoa*'s central exhibition room, which presented *apapaatai* – ritual masks of the Waujá people – and pottery produced by Yudjá women. Such hierarchies were also interrogated through the presentation of the jaguars by the Pataxó artist Tamikuã Txihi, made of clay fired in a pit, representing guardians of memory and ancestral knowledge passed from generation to generation. Tamikuã, born in Pau Brasil, Bahia, is a visual artist, poet and leader. She lives in the city of São Paulo, in the Guarani-Mbyá territory in the Jaraguá Indigenous Land. Through her art, Tamikuã aims to promote the physical and spiritual protection of Indigenous people and their territories. Tamikuã's participation in *Véxoa* was particularly symbolic as an anti-racist gesture following the vandalisation of her jaguar sculptures in a 2019 regional exhibition of visual arts in the municipality of Embu das Artes (in the city of São Paulo), in the context of *bolsonarismo* and the resurgence of the far right in Brazil. During that exhibition, her pieces were broken in an anti-Indigenous attack, underscoring the ongoing discrimination and violence faced by Indigenous peoples.

Invited by *Véxoa*, Tamikuã brought her broken jaguars and included new pieces (see Figure 5.3). The decision to exhibit them as they were, broken, recast the damaged pieces as expressions of remembrance and as a testament to over five centuries of resistance. Tamikuã's jaguars stood in *Véxoa* as symbols of strength and protection, carrying their offspring that represent the future. The racist attack on her pieces during the exhibition in Embu das Artes did not deter her; instead, she responded by creating two additional pieces for *Véxoa*, asserting the continuity and resilience of Indigenous practices amidst ongoing struggles. As Tamikuã said in an interview in the documentary *Terra fértil*: 'I left these jaguars as they were; I didn't want to remake them. In that way, the remembrance and memory of the struggle of a people, of the original peoples who have been resisting for more than 520 years, could remain.'

Among the questions raised in *Véxoa*, the most visible were related to art institutions and the absence of Indigenous artworks. The Pinacoteca de São Paulo itself, until 2019, kept just a few Indigenous items in what it classed as its permanent collection, all of which were in fact on long-term loan from other collections – which was one of the points of reflection for its team and management. Why were Indigenous works not part of the Pinacoteca's own collection, which is one of the largest in Brazil?

Indigenous Arts and Anti-Racism in Brazil

FIGURE 5.3 Tamikuã Txihi's jaguars, 2020 (© Levi Fanan/Pinacoteca de São Paulo, by permission).

This exclusion of Indigenous arts, not only from the Pinacoteca de São Paulo but also from other institutions, reflected a strategy of keeping Indigenous peoples out of the sphere of intellectual recognition, given that Indigenous peoples are still commonly seen as relegated to the past, delegated to anthropology and having lost much of their ancestral knowledge. *Véxoa* did not aim to fix the historical neglect of Indigenous arts but instead to provoke reflection about this neglect. The project acknowledged the risk of 'planned obsolescence' for Indigenous arts in Brazil, drawing a parallel to the concept of planned obsolescence in consumer capitalism, where products are designed to become outdated quickly to drive constant demand. Similarly, there is a danger that Indigenous arts might be treated as a fleeting trend. When Indigenous art becomes fashionable, it garners attention from institutions, galleries, curators and critics. However, there is a risk that once the trend passes, they will be ignored and forgotten, much like obsolete electronic gadgets. This cycle aligns with a modernist and capitalist mindset that prioritises continuous innovation for profit. *Véxoa* challenged this mindset, urging for a more sustained engagement with Indigenous arts that goes beyond passing fads. In this way, *Véxoa* sought to intervene in a space that was not restricted to the rise of Indigenous arts in the art market, but was more concerned with establishing the presence of Indigenous peoples in state-managed public spaces, and especially with pushing for public policies for the creation, expansion and maintenance of collections.

Véxoa's narrative arc, then, ranged from works by present-day exponents of Indigenous art, such as Denilson Baniwa, Jaider Esbell and Daiara Tukano, to pieces such as the Yudjá pots and items by thinkers such as Ailton Krenak, who before then was unknown as an artist to a significant part of the art public. The temporality of the exhibited works also brought about a reflection on the process of continuity and the resistance of Indigenous artistic practices, given that the intention of the curatorial approach was not to present innovations, as if Indigenous artists would only have emerged now, but rather, through the time span of the presented works, to reaffirm that Indigenous arts have always existed in the territory now known as Brazil – that Indigenous people had always known how to make art, but have undergone a process of erasure and neglect. This feeling of erasure and neglect seems to have mobilised the performance carried out by Daiara Tukano and Jaider Esbell, entitled *Morî' erenkato eseru' – Cantos para a vida* (Songs for Life), which took place on 23 November 2020. It was presented as a kind of performative cleansing ritual to expel harmful forces from the institution (again, we could think of Baniwa's notion of breaking the colonial spell). During the performance, before going up the stairs of the museum, Esbell emphasised that the moment was important because Indigenous people were entering the Pinacoteca through the front door for the first time. This statement, along with what Krenak said about 'making cracks in the walls of museums', is directly related to the racism experienced by Indigenous people, which is reflected in institutional spaces such as universities, public offices and museums. Esbell and Krenak capture how Indigenous people feel in Brazil when living through daily situations of erasure and racial violence.

Yacunã Tuxá was one of the artists for whom *Véxoa* provided an opportunity to present her art within a prestigious art institution for the first time. Her digital illustrations contributed to the exhibition's framework from both autobiographical and broader cosmological perspectives, including by foregrounding her identity as a lesbian Tuxá woman. Her work navigates a landscape marked by gender-based violence, LGBTphobia and racism. Addressing multiple layers of marginalisation and historical injustice, Tuxá's art highlights the prejudice that Indigenous people face even in supposedly inclusive spaces such as universities, as well as the lesbophobia she encountered within her own community after coming out. By showcasing Tuxá's illustration *Mulher indígena e sapatão* (Indigenous and Dyke Woman), *Véxoa* created a space for critical discussions intertwining race, gender and sexuality within the context of the Indigenous struggle. Broadly speaking, Tuxá's works reclaim and celebrate the diverse identities and histories of Indigenous women, often misrepresented in mainstream narratives.[14] In a different vein, another digital illustration titled *A queda do céu* (The Falling Sky) further exemplifies Tuxá's approach. In this piece, she depicts an Indigenous person holding a copy of the well-known eponymous book by Davi Kopenawa and Bruce Albert. Tuxá emphasises how the weapons of Indigenous peoples today extend beyond traditional tools such as the club and the bow and arrow to include books, which hold legitimacy in the eyes of non-Indigenous people. From this perspective, both books and digital art – her medium of choice – emerge as crucial tools for strengthening her community.

Edgar Nunes Corrêa (a.k.a. Edgar Kanaykõ), from the Xakriabá Indigenous Land in Minas Gerais, participated in *Véxoa* with a series of photographs focusing on Indigenous resistance and traditional ways of living. Like Tuxá, he adopts a present-day medium – in his case, the camera – as a platform for struggle and resistance, likening it to an alternative 'bow and arrow' (Corrêa 2019). By using photography, Indigenous people such as Kanaykõ reclaim self-representation, asserting control over portrayal and safeguarding their heritage. For him, photography serves a dual purpose: it is both a means of documenting traditional ways of living and a tool for activism. On one hand, it captures rituals, singing, body painting and other aspects of Xakriabá daily life from an insider's viewpoint, preserving them for future generations. On the other hand, it raises awareness and galvanises support by documenting Indigenous resistance. Events such as the Acampamento Terra Livre (Free Land Camp), where Indigenous peoples from across Brazil converge to advocate for their rights, are visually documented by Kanaykõ. His photographs from such gatherings serve as visual testimonies of resistance. Thus, his photography not only portrays the Xakriabá community but also contributes to the broader Indigenous movement in Brazil, showcasing the cultural resilience and political activism of these communities.

For instance, in *Guerra nas estrelas para sustentar o céu – Série luta e resistência indígena* (Star Wars for Holding up the Sky – Indigenous Struggle and Resistance Series), from 2017, Kanaykõ portrays a young

---

[14] See 'Mulheres Artistas Indígenas: Questões de Gênero na Produção e Reconhecimento', online conversation, 13 January 2021, organised by Jamille Pinheiro Dias in partnership with Pinacoteca de São Paulo, www.youtube.com/watch?v=AQ0x-9DWB4w.

Indigenous man wearing a *Star Wars* T-shirt in a demonstration, alluding to the ongoing Indigenous resistance against external threats, akin to a cosmic battle depicted in the popular science fiction saga. The fact that the man being portrayed is wearing a *Star Wars* T-shirt is particularly significant; it bridges popular culture and Indigenous struggle, drawing a parallel between the fictional fight against imperial forces in the *Star Wars* narrative and the real-life resistance of Indigenous peoples against colonial and present-day oppressors. The young man's attire symbolises the intersection of Indigenous identities with global cultural elements, shedding light on the dynamic and evolving nature of Indigenous resistance. Other works by Kanaykõ such as *Wawi* and *Wairê* depict traditional Xakriabá body painting, chants and dances, serving as visual records of cultural practices and symbols of resilience, and as a form of resistance against attempts to undermine Indigenous ways of living.

Olinda Tupinambá's film *Kaapora – O chamado das matas* also counters this undermining by illustrating how Indigenous perspectives can challenge stereotypes that have long devalued Indigenous epistemologies. *Véxoa* marked Tupinambá's first opportunity to engage with an art institution. In the film, the artist, from the Tupinambá and Pataxó Hãhãhãe peoples, examines the relationship between Indigenous peoples and spiritual entities. Her work connects this relationship to environmental issues, a concern that Tupinambá has been actively working on through the restoration of degraded areas in the Caramuru Paraguassu Indigenous Land in Pau Brasil, Bahia, where she was born. Non-Indigenous viewers may perceive Kaapora as a myth or legend. However, in her film, Tupinambá portrays her people's connection with the entity, demonstrating that Kaapora is a living and existent being. Portraying Kaapora as real and alive, rather than a myth or legend, is an anti-racist gesture, even if not explicitly named as such.

This example demonstrates the efficacy of diverse, sometimes indirect, anti-racist strategies in addressing structural inequalities and promoting cultural restoration and recognition. Featuring Kaapora as an existent entity in Tupinambá's film is an anti-racist gesture because it validates Indigenous knowledge systems that were historically marginalised and dismissed by colonial narratives. This representation resists stereotypes that reduce Indigenous spiritual entities to mere folklore, affirming their cultural and spiritual significance. Furthermore, by integrating Indigenous perspectives with environmental activism, Tupinambá decolonises ecological discourse, emphasising that Indigenous spiritual ties with the land are vital for planetary care. This approach challenges the racial hierarchies that place Western thought above Indigenous epistemologies, pushing back against their historical devaluation. Furthermore, Tupinambá's political and artistic resistance as an environmental activist, filmmaker and performance artist illustrates the combined anti-colonial roles of the arts and reforestation as forms of aesthetic and epistemic insurgency in the context of the Anthropocene.[15]

CONCLUSION

Véxoa marked a significant milestone in the history of Brazilian art by being the first exhibition entirely curated by an Indigenous person in a prestigious museum in the country. This milestone called into question the long-standing absence of Indigenous artists in museum collections. The exhibition challenged conventional boundaries and distinctions between art and craft, which have often marginalised Indigenous artistic expressions as handicrafts. *Véxoa* not only showcased Indigenous arts but also instigated a necessary critique within the fields of museology and anthropology, addressing inherent racial inequalities in the representation of Indigenous aesthetic expressions. Moreover, it emphasised the need for museums to work closely with Indigenous communities and to consistently incorporate Indigenous professionals within their institutions. This shift, as demonstrated by *Véxoa*, is crucial to ensuring that Indigenous perspectives are represented in both curatorial and administrative processes.

Véxoa aimed to educate the public on the diversity and depth of Indigenous arts, presenting a wide range of works from various Indigenous artists and communities, which was important for its anti-racist impact. The exhibition served as a platform for educating the public about the plurality of Indigenous cultures, seeking to foster long-term change. *Véxoa* not only showcased present-day Indigenous arts but also emphasised the importance of traditional forms of knowledge and practices. By juxtaposing works that incorporate traditional techniques and materials, such as pottery and masks, with works made with present-day tools, such as digital illustration and video performance, the exhibition challenged the racist notion that Indigenous cultures are relics of the past. *Véxoa* also highlighted intersectionality within the Indigenous struggle, showing how issues of race, gender and sexuality compound experiences of marginalisation. By including works by artists such as Yacunã Tuxá, who

---

[15] For more on Olinda Tupinambá's work, see Milanez Pereira and Souza (2022).

navigates both her Indigenous and lesbian identities, *Véxoa* broadened the discourse on anti-racism to include overlapping layers of oppression.

Additionally, the exhibition underscored the role of Indigenous arts in environmental advocacy. *Véxoa* demonstrated how Indigenous arts can be a powerful tool for sensitising, raising awareness and mobilising support for this cause. This approach showed how the fight against anti-Indigenous racism is inherently connected to broader struggles for justice. Furthermore, *Véxoa*'s presence in a major institution such as the Pinacoteca de São Paulo served as a critique of institutional racism within the art world. By highlighting the historical exclusion of Indigenous artists from major art museums, *Véxoa* called for systemic changes within these institutions. It advocated for more inclusive curatorial practices and the integration of Indigenous agents at all levels of the art world, aiming to transform the structures that reinforce inequality in the art world itself. This effort challenged conventional understandings of what counts as art and highlighted the aesthetic diversity of Indigenous traditions. Through its curatorial process, *Véxoa* not only brought visibility to previously unknown artists but also attempted to reframe the standards of artistic recognition. Indeed, in *Véxoa*, the concept of curatorship (*curadoria*) was linked to healing (*curar*), serving as a means of cultural and historical restoration.[16]

Véxoa contributed to the current anti-racism momentum in Brazil to highlight the historical and ongoing role of racism through a nuanced approach, seeking to build broader alliances and to avoid the potential backlash that more explicit racialised demands might provoke. *Véxoa* integrated a structural understanding of inequality, which includes but is not limited to racism. This approach, reflected in the exhibition, aims to address foundational power structures while maintaining a racially-aware sense of justice, showcasing how anti-racist strategies can be effectively implemented within the arts, even without explicit mention of racism.

While naming racism explicitly is often seen as essential for anti-racist action, *Véxoa* demonstrated that it does not necessarily guarantee a comprehensive understanding of racism or effective anti-racist strategies. The perspectives on anti-racism evoked by *Véxoa* reveal that different Indigenous artists have varied approaches to addressing racism. Many

---

[16] See also 'Curando com a Arte Indígena', online conversation, 24 February 2021, organised by Jamille Pinheiro Dias in partnership with the Pinacoteca de São Paulo, www.youtube.com/watch?v=GWIbftdAAlc&t=18s.

focus on broader struggles such as land rights, anti-anthropocentrism and environmental justice, which also have racialised dimensions. This approach resonates with the notion of 'alternative grammars of anti-racism' proposed by Peter Wade and Mónica Moreno Figueroa (2021). Indirect anti-racist methods, as demonstrated by *Véxoa*, can sometimes be advantageous, particularly in recognising and addressing structural racism within art institutions. Through this multidimensional approach, *Véxoa* provided a framework for integrating anti-colonial practices in the arts, emphasising the importance of diverse strategies in the fight against racial inequality.

Curated Conversation 4: The Power of Guarani Rap

Curated by Lúcia Sá

Source: 'O poder do rap guarani', a ninety-minute online conversation with Bruno Veron and Kelvin Peixoto, of Brô MC's (from Dourados, Mato Grosso do Sul), and Kunumi MC (now known as Owerá), of the Tekoá Krukutu (in Parelheiros, São Paulo), moderated by Jamille Pinheiro Dias. The conversation can be accessed on CARLA's YouTube channel: www.youtube.com/watch?v=sqvpH1HpNHw.

Context: the Brazilian rap and hip-hop movement began in São Paulo in the late 1980s, led by Black performers and activists who gathered in a square in the city centre, Praça Roosevelt. The first album, *Hip-hop cultura da rua* (1988), was a collective work led by legendary DJ Thaide. It was soon followed by *Consciência Black* (1989) by Racionais MC's, a group that would spearhead the rapid rise of the genre all over Brazil. As in other parts of the world, Brazil's rap and hip-hop are mostly urban. For example, the lyrics of Racionais MC's, which became emblematic of the genre, centre on youth life in the peripheral areas of the city of São Paulo, featuring topics such as racism, social inequality and drug violence. These themes held clear appeal for Indigenous peoples confronting racism, displacement and violence in Brazil, and in 2009 Brô MC's emerged as the first Indigenous rap and hip-hop group, singing in a combination of Guarani and Portuguese. The region they come from, Mato Grosso do Sul, is characterised by extreme forms of violence and racism against Indigenous people.

JAMILLE: The topic of our conversation today is the power of Guarani rap. Guarani rap is capable of transforming consciousness, contributing to the fight for demarcation and respect for Indigenous rights. It would be really cool to hear from you about this.

Conversation 4: The Power of Guarani Rap

KELVIN: Indigenous rap has emerged in order to give voice to everything that's happening with our Indigenous brothers, for example those who are in the process of re-occupying land, or the people fighting to expel the miners in the Amazon. They carry on their fight there while at the same time we give voice to this fight on the stage so that it reaches high-ranking people. We are often treated as invisible beings. So that's why Indigenous rap, Guarani rap, is important, because it brings up a lot of themes that people are discussing. Brô MC's shows what really happens in our Indigenous communities, Jaguapiru and Bororó, both Guarani, located here in [the Indigenous reserve] Francisco Horta Barbosa.

And it also highlights land re-occupations, because there are three areas of re-occupation that are very close to the community. I have witnessed conflicts between farmers and Indigenous people, and often it is the farmer who wins because they come with very heavy weapons. Many people have already been injured in land re-occupations. One person went blind, others have lost their fingers. This leads people into depression. Not long ago there was a boy whose fingers were torn apart by a bomb thrown by the police to disperse them. And last week they found him dead, hanging from a tree. His parents said that he became depressed because he lost his hands. The press does not show what is happening there. So, we write lyrics that talk about this and also about our daily lives.

BRUNO: So, as Kelvin said, [the state of] Mato Grosso do Sul is where Indigenous leaders are persecuted and killed by farmers and landowners. And nobody says anything about Mato Grosso do Sul. I believe it's because it's a state created for agribusiness. There are a lot of farmers. They kill Indigenous people and say it was an accident. It is like a song we wrote, which says: 'Mato Grosso do Sul is a state built on the dead bodies of Guarani-Kaiowá people.' It's something you don't see in other states, in other places. Here, we live in fear, as if it were a new kind of Iraq. We often wake up to gunshots, like an alarm clock. A bomb going off near you or a tractor called a *caveirão* [big skeleton] tearing down your house. The media doesn't show this reality to people who live in other states or other countries. And Brô, in the midst of this, portrays it through rap, through these rhymes, through these songs, that we use on stage as a protest to spread this knowledge.

Just this week, an Indigenous territory that was demarcated, I think, in 2008 or 2005, will be returned to farmers. It will be a huge eviction of Guarani-Kaiowá families. And we are waiting to see what will actually happen: if they're going to leave, if they're going to resist. We're a bit scared because we have relatives living in these repossessions. And the media doesn't show this, it doesn't show this issue, this reality. One minute you can be alive, next minute you may be dead. It is a state in which Indigenous people are very persecuted. Even Brô MC's, when we go out to sing, we don't announce where we're going. We just leave the village and don't tell anyone. Brô MC's are also persecuted, for singing, for expressing ourselves, for bringing this message, for depicting this harsh reality of Mato Grosso do Sul.

JAMILLE: I would like to hear also from you, Kunumi, because you live in a very different reality at the Krukutu village, in Parelheiros, São Paulo. What are the situations that you try to make visible, through rap?

KUNUMI: Firstly, I would like to thank you very much for this live streaming event. I believe it is really important. For us, the best weapon is music. Mainly rap, which is a style that is not Indigenous, it is a technology of Black people, but which Indigenous people took and started to build MC's. Today, there are several Indigenous peoples already singing in their own languages. Guarani is also a very cool language to speak, and many people can pick up and understand some of the words we sing. And Guarani language fits perfectly into rap. Our reality is indeed very different, there are no longer farms here in the areas on outskirts of São Paulo city. We live in *tekoás*.[1] But we suffer prejudice all the time. We are still fighting for our land to be demarcated. Our leaders fought hard in the past to have schools in Indigenous villages. And today, in many places in Brazil, we have schools in Indigenous villages. This is very good, because we can now talk confidently with each other.

About rap: I had already heard about Brô MC's and once they came near here, to Parelheiros. I was nine years old, I saw their concert and I got really excited. We are very grateful to them, because every story, every musical style has a root, and that root [for Indigenous rap] is called Brô MC's. Today, when I sing, I actually sing more about prayer music. I try to bring prayer into rap. I believe that when I'm rapping, when I'm on stage, I feel the strength of the ancestors helping me. But it's also the same thing when I talk about protest, about struggle. The ancestors are still here, helping us, because the topic may be different, but the ancestry is always here with us, giving us strength.

KELVIN: Our God is Nhanderu, Nhandejara. We put him in our songs, too. Because in our music we say: 'Xe ru, Tupã, aiko ne ndive.' So here I'm talking exactly about our God. So that he always strengthens us and protects us from everything. And we also sing in our own languages. I think that 95 per cent of the songs I sing are in Guarani. My ancestors spoke Guarani-Kaiowá, a language that our people never abandon. I think that the Indigenous blood runs so strong in our veins that we don't need to mix so many things to show the reality that we live, and also the way we live together in community.

BRUNO: Yes, the question of ancestry is something that has been passed on to us from generation to generation. When we are singing on stage, he [Nhanderu] will always be protecting us, looking out for me, for the people who are going through difficulties, for the people who are listening to our message, making them understand our songs. My grandfathers, my grandmother, they always say their prayers, their *guaru*, their *guaxiré*, their songs. So it comes from our family. But fighting for demarcation,

---

[1] Guarani term for their own villages, which must always include green areas for growing medicinal plants and basic foodstuffs, and areas for hunting and fishing.

Conversation 4: The Power of Guarani Rap

being a militant also runs in the family, from my grandfathers who used to fight for land.

KUNUMI: Although I don't know how to ask questions, I'd like to talk about how the situation is today compared to when you started, in terms of your careers.

BRUNO: So, bro, when we started, around 2003, 2000, the hip-hop movement here was very, very small. Here in Mato Grosso do Sul it was difficult to start, we were only well received outside our own state, in São Paulo, Rio, Brasília. Just now, for the first time ever, we did a concert in our city, Dourados. It is like this: if you turned on the radio or TV, you'd hear people saying bad things about Indigenous people. But what they were saying wasn't what was happening in the village where I lived. So, that was something that led me to rap. I said: 'No, I want to make a difference, to take our messages, not only to us Indigenous people, but to other peoples too, be they white, Black, other races. So that they can hear about the social problems we face in our daily lives.'

So, at the end of 2009, we released our first CD. For us, Brô MCs, when we started, all we wanted was to record a little CD and keep it for ourselves. I made that CD at the back of our producer's little house, on a balcony. Since then, seeing that our message through music has reached several places, it's made me believe that it is possible to change things through music. It is possible to encourage other Indigenous people to think like us, to fight the prejudices they suffer. This led me to believe that people together are like sticks: you can break one stick, but when you put more than twenty sticks together they are difficult to break. And when other guys appeared, like Kunumi, Oz Guarani, other Indigenous rap groups, that has given even more strength to Brô's work.

KELVIN: I agree with what Bruno said. When we started we didn't have much faith in being able to spread our songs, and now our rap is everywhere. People, especially from São Paulo and other states, know our songs. And here in the village too, people really enjoy it. Mainly kids, and there are young people who are sometimes inspired by us to try to write. So I think we managed to change things here. Many young people are interested in music. And I tell them we don't have to have just one musical style. It doesn't matter whether it is rap, country music, Paraguayan polka. We have to fit in everywhere, no matter what style we like. And not only music, but other arts, too, for example, theatre, visual arts, paintings. There are a lot of young people here who have talent. We also have people entering the digital world, like games.

This what I always tell them: regardless of where you are, don't leave your culture. Some time ago, there was a boy, about fifteen, sixteen years old, who came to us so we could give him tips. So we talked to him about our ancestry, our culture. It's something we can't leave aside. And that's how we talk. I always say to people who are in the world of music, or art: 'You cannot leave aside your culture, your ancestry, your origin.' Put on a headdress, put on a necklace, feather earrings, body paint. This is ours.

Some people tell us we are the guys, that we are very famous, and I tell them, 'No, I don't feel famous, I don't consider myself famous, because I consider myself a representative of my people, so I can show this reality, show what is happening to our community here in Mato Grosso do Sul, to our relatives, both Guarani-Kaiowá and Terena, all the atrocities.' Also, Brô represented Brazilian Indigenous people in Europe: Bruno and Creb went there to represent the MC's. It is not only the Guarani-Kaiowá that we went to represent, but also all Indigenous people in Brazil and the world.

JAMILLE: I think that much of what you have already shared with us draws attention to racism, to the violence that is so present Mato Grosso do Sul. In what contexts do you observe racism in Mato Grosso do Sul?

BRUNO: So, here, like Mato Grosso do Sul, the city of Dourados was created by landowners, at a time when they wanted to divide Mato Grosso do Sul from Mato Grosso. In anthropological studies, half of Mato Grosso do Sul belonged to the Guarani-Kaiowá. But when they created this [Indigenous] reservation here, with [the communities of] Jaguapiru and Bororó, they created it in a desert, a place where there was nothing. So here, there are two cities sucking the life out of the villages: Dourados, which is behind me, 2 km from here, and Itaporã, 3 km from here. When this village emerged, the intention of white society was to eliminate Indigenous peoples from the Mato Grosso do Sul region. It was supposed to be the end. So, when our ancestors saw that this was a desert, they tried to return to where they had been removed from, where their *tekoá* is. And when they returned, they found a farm, with cattle ranching, with an electric fence. And then prejudice begins.

When this village was created, there was nothing here, just dirt and nothing else. So, the Indigenous people thought: 'We have to plant trees, let bushes grow, let the vegetation emerge again.' They [the landowners] think that the Indigenous people do that because we are lazy, that the Indigenous people just want land to go to ruin, 'the Indigenous guy, that guy over there, wants the land just to let it run wild'. But no, the point is that we Indigenous people have always lived off nature. We lived from hunting and fishing. So, nature provided our sustenance. It provided our livelihood. So, that's what they don't understand. They don't understand our customs.

So, when our ancestors, our grandparents, return to these lands from where they were removed, which is their *tekoá* of origin, through re-occupations, prejudice arises here in Dourados, in Mato Grosso do Sul. The Indigenous people here in Mato Grosso do Sul are called lazy bums. They often call us land stealers, they say we are stealing their land. And the media, radio, TV help spread that message that Indigenous people just want to let the land run wild, not to farm it. The white guy, his thinking is to invest, to make a profit for his pocket. And for us Indigenous people, the land is precious, it is more than money. They don't understand this.

For this reason, there is this prejudice against Indigenous people. When you go to the city, go into a store, people look at you from head to toe, discriminating against you like this: 'Oh, look at this Indian coming in.' Here in Mato Grosso do Sul you see this. It is an issue that Indigenous people suffer on a daily basis. I believe that if Indigenous people care too much about this they will not be able to survive. There have been many Indigenous people who suffered prejudice and then came to the village and committed suicide. You see it all the time, an Indigenous man who committed suicide, who fell into depression because he was humiliated in front of everyone in the city. That's why there is a village, here in Mato Grosso do Sul, known as suicide village, a village where many people committed suicide.[2]

So the media, TV, pass on bad information to non-Indigenous people, to white people. That's why when people come here at night, for example, when they take a taxi to come to the village, the taxi drivers are afraid. On the radio they always say that [Indigenous] villages are dangerous. But that's not true. It's bad information they give about the Guarani-Kaiowá and Terena people here in the Jaguapiru and Bororó villages. Sometimes I listen to the radio. They say things like: 'I don't know why the Indigenous people want the land, since they don't plant anything.' Or, 'You saw, right? They demarcated that land there and we only see bushes there.'

Also, they are so prejudiced against us that they treat us as if we were invisible people. So, they stop us in stores: when we enter a store, the guard is on top of us, as if we were going to steal something. Because, in their view, Indians steal, just take things, thinking that they don't belong to anyone, but that is not the case. I've seen it many times when I enter a store: employees keep an eye on us. When we go somewhere, they walk around, or when we go to get something, they watch us. Or on the other hand: when we enter a place, people think we're not there. They brush past us and don't come and ask if we need anything. When something terrible happens, like deaths, which happen all the time because a lot of fatalities happen here on the highway, they don't really care. When we went on Xuxa's TV programme, an online newspaper said that we were representing Mato Grosso do Sul and Dourados. There were a lot of people who commented saying that we didn't represent them, we didn't represent Dourados, nor Mato Grosso do Sul, because we were

---

[2] On high suicide rates among the Guarani in Brazil, see www.survivalinternational.org/news/9632.

Indigenous, lazy bums, we just liked to invade land, and that we were dirty and smelly.

This discrimination is plain to see, not only in the city, but also in universities throughout Brazil. And I see that our excellent president himself [Jair Bolsonaro] propagated this hatred even more. I think it is the Indigenous people who are holding things together here on the planet, because the Indigenous people are the protectors of the lands, the animals, the forest. It is the Indigenous people who are protecting life. If it were up to white people, the forest, the animals would have been destroyed long ago. And the forest is so important to us that without it we cannot survive, because it brings us the oxygen that we breathe. In Amazonas, you see the fires that happened, the landowners themselves did it, didn't they? To put pressure on the government. Then there's the issue of miners. They are destroying the forest. The Indigenous people, as Bruno mentioned, are not backward. Many white people say that we are backward. We are not. We are protecting something that is good for the world. And in the white world, the only value is greed. This is what happens here in our community, but I think it happens throughout Brazil as well.

6

Poetics and Theatre Research in the Reconstruction of Afro-Latin American and Mapuche Lives in Argentina

Ana Vivaldi, Lorena Cañuqueo, Miriam Álvarez and Alejandra Egido

INTRODUCTION

Our work within the Cultures of Anti-Racism in Latin America (CARLA) project brings into dialogue two forms of subalternity in Argentina: Afro-descendant and Mapuche. The collective research process involved a relational analysis of the plays produced by Teatro en Sepia, an Afro-descendant theatre company directed by Alejandra Egido, and by the Grupo de Teatro Mapuche El Katango (Mapuche Theatre Group El Katango), directed by Miriam Álvarez. This process generated new collaborative theatrical texts and productions. Our analytical perspective combined social sciences and theatre, exchanging methods and staging strategies, and allowing us to develop the political implications of these dramatic creations. The dialogue in theatre and academia between Afro and Indigenous subaltern experiences, both located in processes of racialisation in Argentina, together with the connection between activist spheres and the academy, in which Egido and Álvarez also participate, have produced innovative artistic and research outputs.

Artistically, the collaboration produced two new plays. The first, *Ñiküfnaqkechi waria* (Silence in the City), was directed by Álvarez. Two scenes were produced as video clips from this play, 'Las hierbas' (Herbs), with a performance by Lorena Cañuqueo, and 'Como dos gotas de agua' (Like Two Peas in a Pod), with performances by Egido and Álvarez (see Figure 6.3 later in the chapter). The second play, *Fuego amigo* (Friendly Fire), was written and directed by Egido, with Álvarez also acting.[1]

---

[1] For 'Las Hierbas', see www.digitalexhibitions.manchester.ac.uk/s/carla-en/item/710; for *Fuego amigo*, see www.digitalexhibitions.manchester.ac.uk/s/carla-en/item/711. 'Como

In analytical terms, we highlight here two dimensions that emerge from the anti-colonial and anti-racist work we did using a collaborative methodology. First, from a theatrical point of view, in discussions between the four of us during more than six months in 2020, we analysed the poetic procedures used by Egido, Álvarez and Cañuqueo. Second, from a socio-political perspective, we compared different experiences of racialisation and analysed associated anti-racist strategies. This implied thinking of the stage as a space of reconstruction and a site of construction and redefinition of belonging from which both theatre companies address the different affective responses to violence against, and the forced displacement of, racialised bodies (Da Silva 2007). Both affect and emotions can be read as constitutive of our collective experiences, but affect was understood as embodied knowledge and traces of experience that precede emotions and are experienced via our bodies' perceptual capacities (Sirimarco and Spivak L'Hoste 2018). Affect arises in concrete social situations and generates varied collective capacities for action, and it is particularly important for understanding silenced or unexpected processes such as uprisings and spontaneous emergence (Beasley-Murray 2010). Following Denise Ferreira da Silva, we consider affect in its colonial and gendered dimensions, considering that some bodies are more exposed to forms of violence than others: that is, some bodies emerge from the colonial situation and racialisation as violated bodies (Da Silva 2007). At the same time, different circumstances generate different capacities for self-realisation and empowerment, which can give rise to unexpected re-emergence – of identities, peoples, presences – in adverse situations, with artistic creation being a privileged space for this (Da Silva 2022; Saldanha 2004). This understanding gives us insight into the staged corporealities that we categorise as dissident, and into the way in which affect, by materialising particular poetics, is also a political practice. The theatrical practices analysed here share analytic and theatrical procedures that recreate Afro and Mapuche lives from archives and memories and on stage, challenging their strategic erasure by white European Argentina. But, far from homogenising these experiences, we understand that they have specificities that differentiate them and that we address here.

---

dos gotas' was premiered at the Festival of Latin American Anti-Racist and Decolonial Art (Manchester, April 2022): see https://youtu.be/WB1fKmYkP9M.

DISSIDENT SCENES IN THE WHITE EUROPEAN NATION: MAPUCHE THEATRE GROUP EL KATANGO AND TEATRO EN SEPIA

The processes of racialisation that shape these theatre companies emerged in response to the construction of an Argentine nation-state that aspires, through its discourse and imaginaries, to be European and white. On the one hand, the Argentine elites enacted the project of a nation 'without Indians' through the so-called Conquest of the Desert, which brought together the military occupation of Indigenous territories in Patagonia (and later the Chaco) between 1878 and 1885 (Delrio 2005) and the symbolic representation of these lands as a 'desert', open to be colonised and incorporated into the Argentine nation. The Indigenous people located there were depicted as 'barbarians', justifying their dispossession in the name of civilising progress. This thinking, typical of the nineteenth century, remains in the common sense of Argentina today.

On the other hand, the premise that Afro-Argentines 'disappeared' after the late nineteenth century has sustained the myth of a white, European nation (Frigerio 2006; Geler 2012, 2016). Early on, intellectuals such as Juan Bautista Alberdi and Domingo Faustino Sarmiento argued that Afro-Argentines had died in battle, especially in the Paraguayan War (1864–1870), or had succumbed to various conditions because of their intrinsic vulnerability (Geler 2010). Moreover, in order to sustain this 'disappearance', they applied statistical invisibilisation. The last national census to include data on race was 1827, although municipal censuses (e.g. for Buenos Aires) had racial data until 1895 (Andrews 1980; Edwards 2018, 2020). Despite the fact that Afro-descendants were recognised anecdotally as having contributed to the construction of the nation, they are not valued as members of a nation-building people and are generally considered to have disappeared.

Images of 'barbarism' and 'absence', on the one hand, and a model of society based on the influx of European immigrants imagined as 'civilised' and 'desirable', on the other, structure differentiated citizenships, which, intertwining with ideas of territory, class, gender and age, have performative effects in the present. These are all questioned, staged and reversed in the artistic creations of Teatro en Sepia and the Mapuche Theatre Group El Katango.

Rather than analysing the process of Argentine racial formation here (see Chapter 3 and also Adamovsky 2012; Aguiló 2018; Alberto and Elena 2016; Briones 2003; Frigerio 2006; Geler 2016; Segato 1998), we emphasise that the dominant model of the nation has been challenged by Afro-descendant and Indigenous activism, which between the 1980s and 2000s achieved important dimensions of visibility vis-à-vis the state. This led to legal and institutional recognition, such as the 1994 constitutional recognition of the pre-existence of Indigenous peoples (Carrasco 2000) and the creation of the Instituto Nacional contra la Discriminación, la Xenofobia y el Racismo (National Institute against Discrimination, INADI), which began to officially recognise Afro-descendants in the country (Pita 2021). These policies initiated a process which is not only fragile, but also one in which recognition has to be demonstrated and validated according to state criteria. The artistic projects we analyse go beyond this demand for visibility and begin to investigate the multiple trajectories and lifeways that Afro-descendants and Indigenous peoples have followed from the creation of the nation-state to the present day. The two theatre groups emerged in the 2000s (El Katango in 2002 and TES in 2010), during a period when Argentine society was beginning to recognise its ethnic-racial plurality and when multiculturalist legal reforms allowed the groups to establish a working relationship with the state. However, many sectors of the dominant society and media continue to express surprise at finding 'Blacks' and 'Indians' in Argentina, and stereotypes update the core assumptions of colonial ideologies, such as 'the spiritual Indigenous woman' or 'the happy Black' (Andrada 2016; Morales 2014).

On the basis of their experiences, the two theatre groups arrived independently at the conclusion that the persistence of surprise at Indigenous and Afro presence is not Argentine structural ignorance, but rather an ideology that has produced strategic erasures of Afro and Indigenous people in order to create the perception of a white nation, even among people with Indigenous and Afro ancestry. Surprise is one of the modalities of structural racism, where the bodily reaction to the existence of non-white, non-European people is a visceral reaction, barely mediated by reflection. The Afro-Indigenous presence provokes a corporeal shock in the context of the erasures produced by the assumption that one lives in a white society.

The multicultural policies of the 1990s have not been able to erase the legacy of late-nineteenth-century images of Argentina as a country 'without Indians and without Blacks' and, as a result, both the theatre companies, linked to wider Mapuche and Afro movements, work to internally reconstitute Mapuche and Afro social ties, while also addressing emotionally and affectively powerful erasures and stereotypes, such as those that criminalise or romanticise racialised subalterns.

Mapuche Theatre Group El Katango

The Mapuche Theatre Group El Katango emerged in 2002, in the Patagonian city of Bariloche, in a context of great economic and political crisis in the country. The group is directed by the Mapuche theatre maker, teacher and researcher Miriam Álvarez, and was formed with Mapuche and non-Mapuche members in the framework of the Campaña de Autoafirmación Mapuche *Wefkvletuyiñ* (Mapuche Self-Affirmation Campaign, We Are Re-emerging), which questioned the stereotypical state criteria defining Indigenous identity (Álvarez 2021; Cañuqueo and Kropff 2002).[2] Initially named Mapuche Theatre Project, the company worked with people who were not engaged in theatrical activity: its first play was *Kay kay kay egu Xeg xeg* (The Water Snake and the Earth Snake, 2002). In 2007 the company was renamed the Mapuche Theatre Group El Katango. *Katango* (written with *k* as proposed by one of the grammars of Mapuzugun, the Mapuche language) means 'cart' and refers to the possessions and painful stories that the Mapuche bring with them as they travel; it evokes the survival of families in the countryside and the city (Cañuqueo 2010).

The Campaign and El Katango created spaces for the multiple ways of being Mapuche in the present, trajectories that strengthen the Mapuche resurgence as a *pueblo* (people, nation). The theatre deconstructed essentialised images – depicting rural locations and practices crystallised in the past, condemned to extinction – that had excluded a large percentage of the Mapuche population. Among other things, this made it possible to analyse the violent incorporation of Mapuche territory into the Argentine state and its consequences, including family dismemberments, forced displacements, confinement in concentration camps (Delrio 2005; Pérez 2016; Nagy and Papazian 2011), the arbitrary disposal of people as slave labour for urban aristocratic families (Escolar and Saldi 2018; Mases 2002) and the confinement of entire families in museums (Colectivo GUIAS 2010). These forms of subjugation fall under the United Nations' definition of the crime of genocide, which includes attempts to eliminate entirely or in part an ethnic group or to destroy its reproductive capacity.[3] Even well into the twenty-first century, genocide as a founding event of the Argentine nation continues to be silenced and ignored in academic and

---

[2] See https://hemisphericinstitute.org/en/enco7-home/enco7-performances2/item/963-enco7-mapuche-theater-project.html.
[3] See Convention on the Prevention and Punishment of the Crime of Genocide, United Nations, 1948.

political circles (Delrio 2010; Lenton et al. 2015; Pérez 2016; Trinchero 2005). By working with the body, the stage and dramaturgy, El Katango aimed to recover stories silenced by official history and omitted by previous generations because of the painful burden they represent and the lack of social recognition of these experiences. El Katango works from the bodies of the group members and engages with family histories to access silenced dimensions of experience, such as the memory of ceremonial gestures performed wordlessly and transmitted in the intimacy of the family. By staging elements from a silenced past, El Katango generates forms that support Mapuche re-emergence and connects with audiences, which often include people who are Mapuche or in a process of Mapuche re-emergence (for example, city dwellers in a process of identity recovery).

From the Conquest of the Desert onwards, many surviving families were forced to leave their territories and migrate to the city. This generated a population in cities such as Bariloche that initially did not identify itself as Indigenous and that only in the last two decades has begun to be reconstituted as such in the city, although not all people of Indigenous descent are involved in this process. The process of invisibilisation of the Indigenous population in these urban spaces was shaped by structural racism in the region: in the distribution of land, it is Indigenous people who tend to be less permanent and have less access to public lands, while in the city they remain as others but are not recognised as Indigenous, with the rights attached to that official status. The members of El Katango were initially young people who grew up in the peripheral neighbourhoods of Bariloche and were in a process of identifying as Indigenous through their involvement in cultural practices. In the 2000s, these practices included a network generated by music bands and recitals in the barrios, and the production of fanzines and radio broadcasting material (Kropff 2004). El Katango connected with these movements by engaging with different generations and their urban experiences. While the first generations of Indigenous activism focused on recognition and reparation based on the handover of territories, the Katango generation emphasised the multiplicity of forms of Indigenous activism and on ways of being Mapuche in the city (Álvarez 2021; Briones 2002; Kropff 2004). In this context, El Katango works internally with members of the group, while also inviting audiences in Bariloche and in rural areas to become sensitised to Mapuche trajectories through theatrical practice. El Katango makes visible and engages with a sector that had been left out of the early processes of recognition, including those who had to leave the territory and even hide their identities.

El Katango's activism and theatrical artistic process questions hegemonic folklorising, essentialising and demonising discourses (Álvarez and Cañuqueo 2018; Álvarez and Kropff 2022; Kropff 2010), as even in the twenty-first century the Mapuche population is stigmatised in terms of the civilisation/barbarism binary. These discourses are updated by the mainstream media and by public officials and representatives of economic elites who enable dispossession and violence against Mapuche families and communities. For example, in the recent eviction of the Lafken Winkul Mapu community of Villa Mascardi (Río Negro province), it was argued that the community was preventing the development of tourism in the area.[4] To counter such imaginaries, the theatre group helps strengthen Mapuche social networks, embracing the multiplicity of ways of being Mapuche and investigating the experiences of people who live in the city. Among other strategies, the group leaves the traditional theatre circuits and the spaces usually occupied by the Mapuche political movement (such as assembly spaces or political demonstrations). In addition, it researches its members' own memories in collaboration with historians and anthropologists (Kropff 2010) to recover experiences of forced displacement during the Conquest of the Desert, which is a key focus of El Katango's production. Mapuche performance practices are traversed by the consequences of the genocide by the Argentine state against the Mapuche people, including the loss of territory and the drastic change in the way of life of parents and grandparents who moved from the countryside to the city (Di Matteo 2019). The genocide is approached from the urban experience and its relationship with the countryside and, taking this history into account, the performance practices of El Katango are representations of traces and furrows resulting from territorial dispossession that remain in Mapuche memory. In this way, El Katango (like Teatro en Sepia, as we will see) uses both history and the present to contribute to the reconstruction of the collective.

Compañía Teatro en Sepia

The Compañía Teatro en Sepia (TES) was created in 2010, at a time of economic recovery, expansion of employment, the incorporation of

---

[4] Note how, in this article on the case, inverted commas are used to question the sacred status of the community's *rewe* (a ceremonial object used by the *machi* or ritual specialist): www.infobae.com/politica/2022/10/19/un-altar-mapuche-enfrenta-a-los-vecinos-de-villa-mascardi-con-la-justicia-federal/.

popular sectors through consumption and new ideological currents that opened fissures in the official discourses on nation-building. The aim of director and actress Alejandra Egido, a Cuban and Argentine director who works on the Afro-migrant and Afro-descendant experience, was to use the performing arts to break down the historical indifference that erased the presence in Argentina of the descendants of Africans enslaved in colonial times and of other Afro-descendants coming from post-colonial migrations. The work of TES became an element in emerging anti-racist debates in Argentina because the violence associated with the forced assimilation and erasure of Afro-Argentine and Afro-diasporic populations is not a finished process, but is replicated today in the projection of foreignness onto Afro-Argentine bodies. The dominant imaginary in Argentine society still has difficulties in recognising Afro-descendants as nationals alongside other Argentine citizens.

TES has produced eight plays, including *Calunga Andumba*, by Carmen and Susana Platero, Afro-Argentine playwrights who in the 1970s were pioneers in visibilising the Afro community; *Afrolatinoamericanas: De voces, susurros, gritos y silencios* (Afro-Latin American Women: Voices, Murmurs, Cries and Silences), by Alejandra Egido and Lea Geler, based on archive materials and texts by Afro-Latin American women; and *No es país para negras* (This is No Country for Black Women) by Alejandra Egido. For several years, *Afrolatinoamericanas* was the only play in Argentina written entirely by Afro-Latin American women. TES avoids exoticism and seeks to create a shared space of encounter with repressed narratives, which works with the body, the mind and the word to change the perceptions that erase Afro existence, and which connects with its audiences, for example by narrating the childhood experiences of one of the actresses, when in school other girls did not want to play with her because of racial prejudice. These experiences are made relatable to a non-Afro audience beyond the differences imposed by racist structures.

Among the groups that use art to challenge the denial of Afro presence (including groups such as Tertulia de Mujeres Afrolatinoamericanas), TES has been innovating by deploying artistic strategies that promote (self-)reflection. Through the staging of social issues, TES generates a space for public discussion, providing tools for the empowerment of marginalised populations through artistic reflection. The performances show that racism is not a barrier that can be jumped simply by opening up residency requirements or by the nationalisation of migrants, but is instead a set of relationships that structures Argentine society, that transcends the recognition of identity and is an integral dimension of the multiple inequalities that affect society.

One of the practices in the anti-racist repertoire generated by TES is the reconstruction of Afro-Argentine and Afro-descendant histories and trajectories. Immersing itself in archival material with the help of historian Lea Geler, TES reconstructed Afro-Argentine trajectories that were not 'interrupted' at the end of the nineteenth century, as the dominant narratives suggest, but continue into the present (Geler 2010). The core of 'white European Argentina' is suspended and dismantled by the theatrical staging of TES, which re-embodies the histories and communities that were threatened with dismemberment in the construction of the white citizen body. For Afro-descendants, Afro-Argentines and Afro-migrants, the embodiment of these stories enables a space in which to articulate ways of feeling linked to their experiences of invisibilisation, thus strengthening the creation of communities. A theatrical poetics that works from the body goes beyond the representation of a predefined narrative: it locates these narratives in the body. The actresses' bodies become a space where affects circulate that cannot always be registered in language, and that through the physical work of the actresses in creating these narratives, become present in gestures, movements and bodily sensations – which include laughter (Hurley and Warner 2012).

After an initial period of work on Afro-descendants in general, TES made a decision to focus on the experiences of Afro-descendant women, given the evident lack of images of these women in the public sphere. Lea Geler describes this moment:

> The textual homogenisation of resistance was explicitly avoided in order to make the spectator reflect on the multiple facets of gender/sexual and racial domination, and the multiple ways of confronting it ... This was an artistic-political process of self-representation, both because of the origin of the texts and because the actresses and the director self-identify as Afro-descendants. (Geler 2012: 360)

As Geler argues, self-representation challenges the tendency to conceive of cultural resistance as a homogeneous way of confronting racist structures. The coming together of Afro-descendant voices and actresses on stage includes the diversity of trajectories and knowledges that migrants can add to the Afro-Argentine experience. This multiplicity includes people who arrived in recent Afro-Latin American migrations, generations of African migrants, and Afro-descendants with genealogies dating back to colonial enslavement (Anderson 2018). The exploration of the varied social trajectories and experiences of migrants help break down the particular forms of Argentina's invisibilising racism, and also break down Argentina's isolation – as a 'white European nation' – from the rest of Latin America.

Finally, TES challenges perceptions of Argentineness, since among the Afro-descendant actresses some would be classified, according to dominant perceptions, as 'Argentine': that is, *blanca* (white). Their presence informs the public that phenotype is not the condition of Afro-descendant ancestry, sociability and cultural belonging, or what Geler calls 'being socially black' (Geler 2016). At the same time, being phenotypically white but socially Black unsettles ideas of citizenship and nationality that aspire to Europeanness, insofar as the apparent contradiction affirms Afro existence, in its diversity, as part of Argentine citizenship. In short, the staging and the texts produced by TES generate a bridge between the historical archive, the experiences recorded by first-hand social research and the current realities of the actresses (Geler, Egido, Recalt and Yannone 2018). All these sources comprise a scene that presents the multiplicity of Afro experiences.

***

In the next section, we describe the staging practices of the two theatre groups, including their explorations of gesturalities and bodily and discursive performances, which construct particular forms of theatrical poetics. These practices go beyond contesting representations (although they do this too), as they open spaces for activating Afro-descendant and Indigenous ways of life that invite their audiences to rethink the social fabric and challenge the Europeanising mandate. Forms of difference are not just meanings that can be constructed and refuted in discourse; they are systems that assemble and define access to space and living conditions (Crenshaw 1991).

In a scene from TES's *No es país para negras*, an Afro-Argentine woman narrates a racist question from a schoolmate about the colour of her genitals, followed by laughter. This shared moment reveals the dehumanising impact and invasion of privacy, but also the absurdity of the question. By processing this experience through laughter, both individually and together with the audience, racist habits are challenged. The scene works through affect, connecting the Afro bodies on stage with those of audience members, whatever their racialised status.

Similarly, the work of El Katango in *Tayiñ kuify kvpan* (Our Old-Ancient Ancestry) sensitises Mapuche and non-Mapuche audiences by means of an invitation – not offered from a position of moral-intellectual authority – to share in and become aware of Mapuche people's concrete experiences of the expropriation of their lands (Álvarez and Kropff Causa 2021). When two Mapuche women in an urban setting discuss returning to their homelands and one of them suggests that there is no one there anymore, the other tragicomically responds that all the dead people of their families are there and generates a pause that gives the audience time to process this statement, which is not fiction but a reference to places their audience knows well. This subtle yet powerful scene sums up the violence of displacement to the city and the appropriation of land by settlers backed by the police and the local state. The presence of a Mapuche actress and the authenticity of the story reinforce the invitation to become aware of the experience of the violence used to dispossess Mapuche families of their land decades ago, as an ongoing event and not just a fact of the distant past.

The scene is also a shared affective exercise, transmitted to the audience, an invitation to get involved in the story and to dismantle the systems that generate this violence. This transmission takes place both in terms of rights, which can be discussed and articulated, and in terms of affects that flow from the actresses' bodies to the audience. In both theatres, affect promotes a communality, an invitation to generate a common social matrix that is non-racist and non-expropriating.

Theatre is a particularly important form of creation for thinking about and challenging how racism is produced and reproduced in everyday interactions, how it operates on bodies and what effects it has on them. The stage is more than a space of representation, it is also a space from which to rearticulate forms of life and experiment with new forms. Both directors aim to unpack constructions of 'barbarism' and 'absence' and show their effects on the distribution of acceptable bodies and actions in urban and rural spaces.

MAPUCHE AND AFRO STAGING: THEATRICAL POETICS AND CORPOREALITIES

In this section we analyse El Katango's play *Tayiñ kuify kvpan* (Our Old-Ancient Ancestry), premiered in 2004, which is about relationships with the ancestors and the Mapuche diaspora experience.[5] We also explore

---

[5] The play can be seen at www.youtube.com/watch?v=WDj-F_BGv78. For more analysis, see Álvarez and Kropff Causa (2022).

TES's *Afrolatinoamericanas: De voces, susurros, gritos y silencios*, to analyse the relationship between Black women and the Museo de la Mujer Argentina (Museum of the Argentine Woman) in Buenos Aires, where the play premiered in 2012. These analyses draw on our initial research, in which we discussed how each creator works with non-fiction theatre and against the silences of national history and the archives. We explored how each artist addresses the effects of racialisation on the body, in order to recover the trajectories of Mapuche and Afro people and to empower forms of existence and re-emergence.

Traces of Ancestry

Tayiñ kuify kvpan represents the intersections of ethnicity, territory, gender and class, but also adding the dimension of age, on the assumption that in all complex political processes more than one category of difference is involved (Hancock 2007). *Tayiñ kuify kvpan* emerged from a theatre workshop for Mapuche youth in Bariloche that explored forms of identification as Mapuche among young people.[6] Participants brought up the theme of ancestors, lineage and personal connections with the dead, including dream practices. Miriam Álvarez and the young people then explored the bodily gestures performed in Mapuche ceremonies, such as *jejipun* (prayer ceremony) and *purun* (dance). As there were fragmented memories of these gestures within the group, an activist from an older generation was called in to share her knowledge and experience. With Álvarez's guidance and attention to corporeality and gestures, an intergenerational space for the transmission of knowledge was generated. Stories were reconstructed based on orality and we also sought to reconstruct aspects of the gestures that the young people, non-professional actors, brought to the stage. Research and the reconstruction of senses of belonging were intertwined in the making of the play.

The resulting mise-en-scène is structured in six frames of non-linear action, thus distancing itself from what Bertolt Brecht calls Aristotelian dramaturgy, characterised by a beginning, middle and end, which together form an organic dramatic structure. The performance begins when the audience enters the auditorium. Two of the characters are

---

[6] The workshop was held in a primary school in a low-income neighbourhood. The participants were people under twenty-five years of age, all inhabitants of Bariloche and in the process of self-identifying as Mapuche. Participants worked on theatre practices such as the creation of characters, corporeality on stage and the use of the voice.

already on stage: two old people who represent the spirits of the past, the dead who continue to accompany the living today. Sitting to one side, the old woman knits, while the old man lies dead in the middle of the scene. Then, once the audience is in their seats, tableau one begins, with two young women bringing clothes and food to the *alwe* (spirit). After they have set everything down, the old man stands up, takes the clothes that have been left for him and begins to walk until he meets the old woman, who represents another spirit.

From this beginning, the play is structured around the relationship between the living and the dead. The dead are old people and the living are represented by two young women who have suffered encroachment on their lands, dispossession and poverty. A later tableau features an old woman who saves herself from the army's incursions into her land, but now wanders disoriented. Although she refers to an historical event (the late-nineteenth-century Conquest of the Desert), she is not located in a time that can be considered the past, nor is she included among the dead, but among the living. She is a liminal character who places the genocide and its effects in an on-going present. Her liminality is a bridge between the past and the present, breaking with linear temporality. The experience of this character in the play articulates with *Nawel gvxam* (Story of the Tiger), a traditional Mapuche tale that narrates the return home after the Conquest of the Desert war. The story is told by an old woman, the protagonist, who escapes the invasion and then meets a *nawel* (tiger) that does not attack her, but helps her, and whom she calls *futa lamgen* (big brother) (Golluscio 2006). In the play, two characters appear who encourage the old woman to follow the *nawel*. Next there appears a younger woman, who addresses her as *abuela* (grandmother) and cares for her (see Figure 6.1). She recounts that many local people, including her own mother, have – like the *abuela* – been violently displaced from their territory and forced to move to the city.

The theatrical staging sought to elicit a certain aesthetic identification in the Mapuche spectators, taking into account a process of self-recognition. As we will analyse in detail, the staging constitutes a Mapuche corporeal repertoire by means of a metacultural operation, defined as any cultural action that, while being performed, reflects on culture itself (Briones 1998): that is, a set of practices that begins to be called and understood as 'culture'. The aim was to stage organised forms of behaviour through gestures that were identifiable for the Mapuche audience: the *palig* (a Mapuche game), the *jejipun* (a Mapuche prayer ceremony), the use of traditional dress such as the headscarf for women and the headband

FIGURE 6.1 Scene from *Tayiñ kuify kvpan* with Lorena Cañuqueo and Sofía Curapil, on stage at the Escuela de Arte Municipal La Llave, Bariloche, Argentina, 2004 (photograph by Matías Marticorena, © Archivo de la Campaña de Autoafirmación Mapuche Wefkeletuyiñ, Estamos Resurgiendo, by permission).

for men, and the use of the Mapuche language, Mapuzugun. The work reconstitutes a Mapuche corporeal repertoire elaborated in the 1990s by Mapuche activism that, through a metacultural operation, sought the resurgence of these practices, which had been silenced by decades of state persecution and Christian evangelisation.

Afro Screams and Silences

In 2012, when Teatro en Sepia premiered the play *Afrolatinoamericanas: De voces, susurros, gritos y silencios* (see Figure 6.2), a transition took place: the company became feminist and dedicated itself to the experiences of women of African descent, no longer the Afro community in general. The play resulted from an invitation from the Museo de la Mujer Argentina in Buenos Aires in the year of the bicentenary of independence. As part of the celebrations, the museum planned events that showcased women's participation in Argentine history. But the initial programme included only the experiences of white European-descent women and did not recognise the role of Afro women in the struggle for independence.

FIGURE 6.2 Poster advertising *Afrolatinoamericanas: De voces, susurros, gritos y silencios* for a performance run in 2013 (© Alejandra Egido, by permission).

So the members of TES decided to test the relationship between Black women and the Museo de la Mujer as a feminist space. The idea was to work with two time periods: the historical past and the present day, highlighting the continuity of Afro issues and struggles.

A starting point for the production was the figure of Sarah Baartman, an African woman of the Khoikhoi ethnic group who in 1810 was forcibly taken to Europe and made to exhibit herself naked as a public attraction because of her prominent buttocks (Geler 2012). It was decided that the actresses, all of them Afro, would go on stage with their faces covered, demonstrating that, in the social imaginary, Black women are considered as bodies, without faces or heads.

The rehearsals were moments of collective construction between Alejandra Egido, historian Lea Geler and the non-professional actresses (Geler 2012). The scenes drew on historical materials and contemporary texts by Afro-Latin American women playwrights, some of which directly allude to a situation of Afro 'resistance' or to historical events in the Afro community. Texts were selected that overlapped the historical past and the present, showing the resonances between these moments (an operation already described for El Katango). The performance included personal and contemporary testimonies of the performers delivered through video, as commentaries on the historical and literary texts.

An ecclesiastical legal text recovered by historian Florencia Guzmán structures the plot of the play. This text refers to an early-nineteenth-century divorce trial in Córdoba, Argentina, in which a Creole woman asks the Church to annul her marriage. The woman argued that 'her husband has adulterated the marriage bed, and gives himself to every Black and brown woman who enters his service, whether by purchase or agreement, thus squandering the dowry of his children on enslaved children' (Guzmán 2009: 412). Although the wife brought the enslaved women to give testimony at the trial, where they attested to the violence, including rape, that they suffered at the husband's hands, the Church's final verdict, with which the play closes, was that it did not consider that the evidence given was 'sufficient grounds to authorise the separation of the spouses' (Guzman 2009: 419). The husband's violence was not seen as a problem.

The tension between the white mistress and her husband unites her with the enslaved Afro women who also denounce the master's abuses. But the scene also presents the frictions between these women. While the wife protests at her wounded honour, the Afro women were subjected to enslavement, sexual abuse and the jealousy of the wife. Their positions cannot be equated, an understanding that indirectly challenges the role of white feminism in the present day and shows why an anti-racist feminism is relevant. In rehearsals, actresses improvised around life in a colonial house and the place of women, whether mistresses or enslaved, and improvisations also drew on feminist texts such as Gloria Anzaldúa's *La frontera* (1987) to bring in themes of dissident feminisms, classic feminism and sexual diversity in a context in which mass feminism in Argentina did not take into account Black and intersectional feminism. The play opened up this discussion in Argentina: Egido sums up the staging of the play as 'a thump on the table', put together with urgency and little time. The play was a simultaneous intervention into white feminism, which did not consider racialised differences, and into claims by the Afro movement that did not consider gendered differences and put women between brackets.

At the same time, in order to unsettle the association of Afro people only with colonial times, scenes based on historical texts were superimposed with contemporary accounts given by the actresses. For example, in a scene where the character of Josefa Tenorio, an enslaved Afro-Argentine military woman, reads aloud a letter she addressed to General

San Martín – hero of Argentine independence – asking for her liberty, her monologue is interrupted by a present-day video of the performer, an Afro-Argentine actress, in which she narrates the obstacles she faces in finding a job as a dental hygienist because of her skin colour.

While making visible the Afro contributions to the formation of the Argentine nation in the shape of a military woman – a heroine of independence who still did not win her freedom – the scene also reveals the current situation of Black women in Argentina, where the descendants of enslaved women continue to fight for recognition as Afro and Argentine, in a country that alienates them, and to carry forward the anti-racist struggle for the right to dignified work. The strategy of superimposing the past and the present emphasises the non-fictional character of the work and refutes assertions that Argentina 'is not racist'.

Dissident Afro and Mapuche Corporealities

The Mapuche and Afro-descendant bodies staged in the work of El Katango and Teatro en Sepia both result from a colonial experience, in which, as Yuderkis Espinosa observes (2020), 'the gender order is always racialised and geopolitically mediated'. The theatre groups do not describe a generically embodied coloniality – as, for example, in Walter Mignolo's (2012) analysis – nor even the imposition of sex-gendered categories (Lugones 2010), but rather specific traces of the experience of actresses, drawing on oral history and personal archives. Both historical reconstruction and reflection on the present are embodied. We think of corporealities in terms of their material and symbolic dimensions, and as objects of discipline and reproducers of social structures, but also in terms of their capacity to affect and be affected beyond these structures.[7] When *Afrolatinoamericanas* intersperses narrations of the past with actresses' current experiences, or when *Tayiñ* works with a character who survives the nineteenth-century Conquest of the Desert and arrives in the present where she continues to escape military violence, it not only

---

[7] For the analysis of corporeality in its symbolic dimension, we rely on the work of Foucault (1978) and Butler (1993), and in its affective-material dimension, on the work of Bourdieu (1977), Spinoza (1996), Deleuze and Guattari (1983) and Beasley-Murray (2010). We follow the work of authors who think about the affective dimensions of racialised and sexualised bodies, including Da Silva (2007) in relation to Afro bodies, Simpson (2017) in relation to Indigenous bodies and Segato (2010) in relation to racialisation of the sex–gender axis.

demonstrates the racism of the dominant society, but also highlights the fact that the violence continues.

Taking the body as a space of memories and as a space capable of regenerating Afro and Mapuche lives is a shared focus for both theatre groups. Theirs is not a didactic intervention that explains colonialism, enslavement or genocide in a simplified way; instead they open a space for exploration, first in the intimacy of the groups and then with audiences. For both groups, the creative process starts by investigating the material effects of these forms of racism as they are manifested in present-day structures of expropriation of bodies and territories in Afro and Mapuche communities, with attention to the multiple affective impacts of those processes. By resorting to humour or generating scenes that 'leave the audience frozen and mute', in Egido's words, or by 'moving and unlocking memories through evocations and dreamlike scenes', as Álvarez puts it, the directors question social structures without having a predefined direction or expecting a single response.

When reconstructing corporealities, particular attention must be paid to how they express power relations. In the Mapuche case, the memories of military campaigns and forced displacements form an indispensable part of any 'Mapuche poetics', while in the Afro case the discourse of absence that erases current presences is a necessary referent for the work of making visible a diverse experience, but emphasised in a gendered way. In Egido's words: 'TES revealed the fact that Black women were not only characters of the colonial era, but that we are part of today's society, of today and now.' We cannot only refer to an 'ancestral' Mapuche corporeality or to an Afro woman secluded in the past, because the marks left by the construction of the nation on these territories and bodily repertoires are significant elements for the political work of both theatre groups.

El Katango seeks to generate a new poetics of theatre that narrates the Mapuche reality, while also aligning with specifically Mapuche perspectives on theatrical poetic procedures. To do this, the bodily repertoire that bears the historical marks of subordination to the nation was mobilised to generate self-identification among Mapuche people. Corporeality was elicited through attention to the habitual gestures that have been marginalised in Argentina and within the Mapuche movement itself, but that were repeatedly and wordlessly enacted in the families of the Katango participants, such as ceremonial gestures of gratitude before entering or drinking from a lake, gestures related to cultivating the land, or saying words in Mapuzugun in someone's ear, almost in secret. Some gestures have gender dimensions, such as when women cover their mouths when they speak, as if hiding their words. Gestures and corporeality recovered in the workshops were then put on stage. For example, the performers worked on ways of sitting with the body folded in on itself, which are defensive postures, expressing traces of violence and the feeling of inadequacy in white European spaces. As Álvarez says: 'Although attempts were made to forget and erase the moments of pain, they remained as furrows, as traces that seep into bodies, looks, ways of speaking and above all into memories.'

Miriam Álvarez (2021) uses Marcel Mauss's concept of 'techniques of the body' precisely to refer to this set of bodily repertoires, which, as Ugo Volli (1988) explains, are traditional acts that are culturally conserved and transmitted. There are many peoples who, while maintaining a certain dominance, have had their 'techniques of the body' erased by Western culture. More profound is the effect on dominated peoples, such as Mapuche and Afro people, who have been disciplined through daily violence, and this is precisely the material that El Katango and TES are beginning to explore. In our conversations, Álvarez suggested that observing techniques of the body can reveal gestures and corporealities, which can be integrated into narratives that show how dispossession leaves traces on the body. The aim is to reconstruct not only a scenic story, but also a 'Mapuche way' of installing the Indigenous experience on the stage.

In Teatro en Sepia, Afro women work on how they are interpellated by colonial sex-gender systems and the effects of this interpellation. The plays of TES address the invisibilisation of the bodies of Afro women in Buenos Aires, one of the most 'whitened' spaces in Argentina, and dramatise this to a non-Afro theatre-consuming public, which is astonished at their existence. TES's work reconstructs histories and reconstitutes the social fabric to question Argentina's racial structure. It also generates anti-racist practices: challenging stereotypes; contributing to forms of self-representation; and breaking social oblivion by presenting Afro-Argentine characters and actresses. These operations on stage encourage Afro audiences who go to TES plays to see themselves represented, and challenge white European audiences who, without knowing it, participate in the structures of invisibility.

Our analysis of the work of El Katango and TES on the embodiment of subalternity and the diverse ways this is expressed on stage and in Mapuche and Afro communities led us to identify two areas of common interest. First, the predominance of women in groups led us to pay attention to the operation of gender roles and, in particular, women's roles within the (re)constructions of violated, colonised, racialised and subordinated lives. Second, we were struck by the spatio-temporal location of Indigeneity and Afroness in the national narrative and the challenges to this location from theatrical representations of experiences situated in other spatio-temporal frameworks, deemed relevant by the creators.

Regarding first the question of gender, some of the scenes in *Afrolatinoamericanas* address the hyper-sexualisation of Afro-Latin American women that has existed from colonial times, which had a particularly violent expression in exhibitions of humans in eighteenth- and nineteenth-century Europe and which continues today, for example, in the frequent association of Afro migrant women with sex work. In this play, working between past and present, and between theatrical and audiovisual modalities, the creators tugged on the fibres of the connection between the Afro bodies on the stage and the white feminist audience that filled the hall of the Museo de la Mujer. The work gives voice to the dissident bodies of Afro-Argentine and Afro-Latin American women who are not usually found on stage or in museums, other than as historical objects. The play also engaged with debates within the feminist movement. It made clear that the oppression faced by Afro-Argentine and Afro-Latin American women cannot be explained on the basis of gender alone, as classical feminism does, but is a matrix structured by class, ethnicity, national identity and migration. According to Egido, the affective intensity that circulated in the theatre, generated by the play's themes and the actresses' embodied actions, became evident in a silence that 'could be cut with a knife'. This indicates the effect on a feminist, academic, middle-class audience of being confronted with the reality of intersectional racism that members of the audience may ignore in their everyday lives.

In *Tayiñ kuify kvpan*, there are several female characters who, far from being similar or indistinguishable, present heterogeneous constructions of femininity. In addition to ethnic and gender differences, there is a generational dimension, with old and young people on the stage and in particular the third old woman, a liminal character with valuable ancestral wisdom. This character interacts with the *nawel* (the mythological tiger), performs the Mapuche prayer and communicates with the spirits. She escapes the army's advance and manages to meet one of the young women in the city, to whom she gives advice. In other words, among all the characters, she is the one who empowers herself in a situation of extreme vulnerability, escaping in her slow and painful body, alone and without shelter. In this way, reference is made to different space-times, which are shown to be interconnected: the world of the dead with which the work begins, the ancestor who escapes from military violence by crossing fields and timelines, and the urban world of the young people who took part in the workshop.

With regard to the issue of spatio-temporal location, the play by El Katango presents different territorialities and times in the same scenic space: the land of origin from which part of the Mapuche population was expelled at the end of the nineteenth century, the multiple spaces where people fled from military persecution, and the spaces of reunion in rural areas, which can also be found in the daily life of an urban neighbourhood. In the play, histories were interwoven, showing that the Mapuche are dispersed in their own lands and that it is the link with their ancestors that will allow the reconstruction of the Mapuche people, a heterogeneous, complex and diverse people. The mise-en-scène questions the hegemonic discourse, which restricts Mapuche existence to the countryside and to ancestors disconnected from the present and the city. In place of this, the play suggests a continuity of Mapuche life connecting the past and the present, the countryside and the city, and opening up a common space between young and old. In this sense, mobility evokes not only the distance between places but also their interconnection (Cañuqueo 2015; Vivaldi 2016).

On the basis of these intersectional readings of the plays, we argue that both theatre groups challenge the dominant constructions of race, ethnicity and citizenship of the nation-state. Both groups also decentre dominant models of femininity, including those of mainstream feminism. Moreover, the Mapuche and Afro dissident corporealities present in the plays destabilise any image that freezes the possibilities of existence, while empowering the re-emergence of multiple forms of life for both peoples.

This opening of spaces for multiple ways of being Afro and Mapuche takes a step beyond the activisms of the 1990s that needed simply to assert existence. For example, as we have mentioned, in *Afrolatinoamericanas* at one point the actress appears in a film, with her face amplified on the screen above the stage, looking into the camera and directly questioning the audience. She explains that, as a person of African descent, she tells her perfume-buying clients to remember her, not by name, but as 'the Black Woman of perfumes'. This moment both identifies forms of racism (customers see her generically as a 'Black woman') and ignores the invisibilisation of that racism in Argentina (by encouraging customers to label her in that way, without shame). The woman accomplishes the dual task of asserting herself as 'Black' and as a perfume-seller with a clientele that remembers her. She claims that racial identity as her own, making explicit how white Argentines perceive her and pushing them to recognise their own racism. The interaction creates a connection with the audience, as the actress interpellates the feminist and white European audience of the Museo de la Mujer. The artistic context both denounces and acknowledges as 'normal' the racist act of remembering a Black woman generically and without individuality as *la negra*. On stage the performers reclaim the power of representation, but also engage the audience as participants in dismantling racist structures in everyday life.

For its part, El Katango addresses the specificity of Mapuche urban experiences, which is an area that is difficult to reach for the type of Indigenous activism recognised by mainstream society. The young city-dwelling participants in *Tayiñ*'s creation workshop were not recognised and acknowledged as Mapuche in their daily lives in the early 2000s. El Katango asks: How can the experiences of urban people, descendants of genocide survivors, who are negatively racialised in the city be made public when Mapuche as an Indigenous political identity is still not recognised, and when some people may choose not to identify as Mapuche, because of the violence that affects those who identify as Indigenous? The play, as an artistic and political intervention, engages with this question by working with embodied memories.

Both directors work with bodies and with history to challenge interconnected structures of colonial, racist, patriarchal and class oppression. In this way they not only produce plays with novel themes in Argentine theatre, but also generate political interventions that invite audiences to be part of decolonial practices, as white middle-class feminists, as Afro people, as Mapuche people, as part of a colonising society. The stage is thus a meeting place, a space for experimentation, in which to reformulate a social matrix that is not only white European.

DIALOGUES BETWEEN AFRO AND INDIGENOUS EXPERIENCES

Over recent decades, Afro and Indigenous activists in Argentina (and elsewhere in Latin America and the world), alongside decolonial thinkers, have drawn connections between the colonialism of the conquerors and the emergence of nation-states, something common to Afro and Indigenous experiences. However, connecting Afro and Indigenous trajectories is still a field in need of development. For the moment, academic works that generate rapprochements between these collectives are few, but important (Edwards 2020; Hooker 2020; Safa 2005; Wade 2018). For their part, Afro and Indigenous organisations have spearheaded demands for historical reparations and state recognition, against a background of multiple instances of convergence and solidarity, which acknowledge that the separation of Afro and Indigenous struggles is a legacy of colonial divide-and-rule strategies. Despite this, however, the construction of common relationships often has a peripheral place within their agendas, for reasons that will be mentioned later.

This is reinforced in contexts of multiculturalism with state policies that encapsulate 'Indigenous' and 'Afro' in different institutional spaces, even when there are equivalent expectations on the part of the state that lead, paradoxically, to policies demanding that Afro activisms adapt to criteria of Indigenous legitimacy (Rahier 2020; Wade 2010b). While official recognition has generated spaces for interaction with states, the emphasis on authenticity and the demand to demonstrate 'community' and prove identity have created a political context where distinctions have become more pronounced (Hale 2005). If one of the key advances of Afro-descendant activism and research has been to identify the forms of racism that Latin American nationalisms have long denied, this critical analysis also allows us to rethink the experience of Indigenous racialisation from an Afro perspective. We follow the provocation of Denise Ferreira da Silva (2007), who identifies colonised bodies as more exposed and vulnerable, especially in the Americas, to the powers of European rationality. The exposure of racialised bodies to expropriations and vulnerability (their 'affectability', for Da Silva) is a common aspect of the experience of racism that El Katango and Teatro en Sepia investigate and intervene into, as are the vital forces that, working from the body, reconstruct Afro and Mapuche lives and communities.

It is important to highlight the novelty of this encounter between the Afro and the Indigenous, but also to identify the gap that exists in memories of and historical works on these encounters, which is why in this project we also recreated these encounters, working from small beginnings. However, we do not want to lose the specificities of the distinct projects of TES and El Katango, which are, at the same time, exactly what allow us to establish connections and dialogues. In order to show how 'the Afro' and 'the Mapuche' are represented in the work of Teatro en Sepia and El Katango, we will analyse the links and convergences that emerged from their encounter in the CARLA project. During the first year of the project we analysed plays from each theatre group so as to create a dialogue between them. In what follows, we take the work of the theatre groups to reflect from a Latin American intersectional perspective that is localised and contextualised in Argentina (Viveros Vigoya 2016).

Anti-Racist Theatres, Interwoven Theatricalities

Given the context just described, a constant theme during our research was the search for traces of any Afro-Mapuche encounters, recorded in archives and social memories, and more specifically encounters that had been encouraged by theatrical productions. Except for references to barely visible Afro communities located in proximity to Mapuche territories, bereft of details about encounters and relations, we did not find any specific work.[8] Hence the directors' desire to create plays that would stage such encounters, working in a mode of historical speculation that makes an informed reconstruction of archival gaps and ellipses in memories (Hartman 2019). With the premise of incorporating an Afro character in Álvarez's work and a Mapuche character in Egido's work, both creators wrote their outlines. The writing was individual, but took place in the shared framework of a writing workshop called 'Clandestine Dramaturgy' directed by David Arancibia, a Mapuche playwright based in Chile. During the process, the playwrights exchanged versions, provided information and commented on each other's work. The collaborative work was called *Entramadas* (Interweavings) and emerged, in our words at the time, 'as an urgent and necessary exchange of experiences between two forms of theatre that challenge the erasure of Indigenous and Afro-descendant narratives, gestures, bodies and experiences in Argentine theatre'.

The work that led to the writing of these proposals was preceded by collective reflection on the affective impacts of coloniality on racialised bodies described in the previous sections, some of whose modalities continue in the present. These forms continue to target Afro and Mapuche bodies in ways that have significant similarities. Both Afro and Mapuche bodies can

(1) be denied (i.e. their actual existence);
(2) be made foreign (Afro-Argentines are identified as foreigners from other Latin American countries and Mapuche are often identified as Chilean);

---

[8] Colleagues who are oral historians have mentioned stories in the archive of enslaved people who escaped to Indigenous territories, but not works that focus on this issue. In conversations with social organisations, Lorena Cañuqueo heard mention of people who may have had both Mapuche and Afro ancestry.

(3) be surveilled as 'other' bodies in the space of the city (both theatre companies work in cities that are thought to be white and where the non-white is marked as strange and dangerous);
(4) be recognised only within limited folkloric parameters (Afro people linked to a colonial image, women dressed in white with their hair covered; Mapuche people as rural and wearing traditional clothes), which evoke an illusory past (a harmonious colonial society where Afro people were street vendors and enslavement is invisible, and Mapuche people were in small, dispersed rural communities);
(5) be made hyper-visible in folkloric stereotypes (Afro people as happy and associated with dance and music, not with thought; Mapuche people linked to a stereotypical spirituality) or in images of criminality (Afro people associated with illegality; Mapuche people linked to violence and terrorism).

These points were identified as 'differentiated communalities' in our meetings and in the process of thinking about the motivations and interventions of each theatre group.[9] On the basis of this process of collective reflection, Egido and Álvarez decided move towards theatrical creation.

Entramadas, which speculatively reconstructs stories of encounters and silenced lives, has been an important achievement, because even though each theatre group had been exploring how to stage their productions by combining political and poetic dimensions, working together allowed us to expand this differentiated communality and speculatively reconstruct Afro-Mapuche encounters (resonating with projects such as King 2019). Specifically, it allowed us to represent Afro and Mapuche bodies in a single theatrical work and thus unite us in questioning white Argentina. We arrived at two theatrical creations, noted at the beginning of this chapter: *Fuego amigo* (Friendly Fire) by Alejandra Egido and *Ñiküfnaqkechi waria* (Silence in the City) by Miriam Álvarez. The plays bring together the stories of Mapuche and Afro women, referring to common experiences of oppression (such as forced displacement and forced labour) and common recourse to a sense of humour as a gesture of resistance. We observed that the stories of both collectives could be

---

[9] We speak of differentiated communalities because, although there are experiences that are common insofar as Afro and Indigenous people are the object of racism in the white European racial formation of Argentina, there are specific historical trajectories for each group and for the forms of racism they experience; these are reflected in the specific anti-racist practices of each theatre group.

represented in both theatre groups, making visible that 'we share more than we imagined', as the creators put it. In the plays, Afro and Mapuche people meet and, despite not knowing the particularities of their respective stories, they resonate with each other's experiences, not only empathetically but also because each recognises the traces of colonialism in the other's history.

Ñiküfnaqkechi waria is a play that, at the time of writing, is still under construction. It seeks to question the silence with which both Mapuche and Afro-descendant populations were surrounded after the Conquest of the Desert, an experience linked with successive periods of loss of land and the ongoing dispossession of lands by *criollo* settlers. The women in the play turn to their memory, their ancestral ties and beliefs to give themselves strength to carry on. The joint work generates a common space on the stage that intertwines the experiences of violence and the forms of resurgence of both peoples, a path towards anti-racism and decoloniality that is taking shape as Afro and Indigenous struggles in the Americas are linked to one another (King et al. 2020). When we rehearsed and also when we discussed the theatre groups themselves, we found points of connection that generated a common matrix: the white Argentina that silenced both collectives, the forced mobilities, the violence on bodies and territories.

Thus, in the construction of *Fuego amigo*, as in *Ñiküfnaqkechi waria*, the idea was to represent forced displacements as part of the creation of a broader cartography (Dubatti 2016). In *Fuego*, we see what the urban territory means for Mapuche and Afro-descendant people. In *Ñiküfnaqkechi*, rural territory takes centre stage, but here we also sought, through poetic procedures of expressionism and symbolism, to evoke a territoriality occupied by water. For Afro-descendants, this meant the Atlantic, the ocean crossing and ports; for the Mapuche, it meant water as a place of refuge, of healing and of memory. In one scene of *Ñiküfnaqkechi*, a film of a fast-flowing river is projected and at one point we see that it is carrying photographs, swept along by the current. This river represents water and fluidity in general and evokes a way of seeing Mapuche territory as ever-changing. When this scene, 'Como dos gotas de agua' (Like Two Peas in a Pod), was premiered at Manchester's Contact Theatre in April 2022, the feedback from the audience was striking and included comments from Afro-Colombian artists who were not only moved, but also expressed the uniqueness of seeing two subordinate corporealities with so much in common in Latin America, who, nevertheless, do not usually participate together in artistic projects (see Figure 6.3).

FIGURE 6.3 Scene from 'Como dos gotas de agua' with Alejandra Egido and Miriam Álvarez, on stage at the Contact Theatre, Manchester, UK, 2022 (© Jami Bennet and Shawn Stephen, by permission).

Fuego amigo adds another contribution to this innovative encounter and the differentiated communality of these two plays with its feminist perspective and a futuristic projection. By fictionalising the stories of the protagonists (a Mapuche woman and a woman of African descent) and locating them in an imagined new social order in Argentina based on the realities of the pandemic, it metaphorically evokes the way the health crisis exacerbated existing tendencies while also underlining the corruption of the neoliberal order and highlighting the historical resistance of these subaltern characters in the face of a system in breakdown. The play's protagonists are working together in a near-future scenario as technicians who have been hired to install sensors that measure the presence of viruses in the air at traffic lights. The job requires them to move around, and instead of having cars or motorbikes, they travel on horseback. With the trust that comes from spending long hours together working in a daily routine, they begin to share their personal stories with each other. The Afro woman tells how she was evicted from her home and ended up living on the street, possibly all as a result of racist exclusion from the labour market. The Mapuche woman recounts her eviction from a community school where she worked. It becomes evident that both women are extremely strong, capable of overcoming these circumstances. In contrast to the past experiences that they narrate, both women are electrical technicians and expert horse riders, which challenges the standard view of these activities as masculine. The play then shows them joining forces to bring a legal suit against the Argentine state, thus speculatively raising the possibility of historical and political reparation for colonised peoples. In the scenes depicting the lawsuit, the state's responsibility for the exploitation of the bodies and expropriation of the lands of Afro-diasporic and Mapuche peoples as constitutive processes of the nation becomes evident.

CONCLUSION: THEATRICAL POETICS AND MAPUCHE AND AFRO LIVES ON THE STAGE

The stage, as a space for experimentation, not only allows new forms of representation and narrative but also foments the recomposition and resurrection of Afro and Mapuche lives through the poetic and deeply political language of theatre (Simpson 2017). The artistic practices of the two theatre companies are anti-racist and decolonial because they emerge from (collective) bodies and fragmented territories and because they propose the reconstruction of life against the genocide of Indigenous peoples and the dehumanisation/instrumentalisation of Afro bodies that have generated a hierarchical order of bodies and territories in the nation. The companies also offer a discursive-enunciative anti-racism that challenges the differences produced by structural racism. This challenge is expressed, for example, in the denaturalisation of the common sense that sees Afro bodies in Buenos Aires as 'foreigners' or 'outsiders' and which is the geopolitical reflection of Argentina's model of civilisation. It is also expressed by contesting the discourses of the mainstream media, certain political leaders and the Argentine establishment that characterise Mapuche activism for territorial rights as 'terrorism'. In other words, both companies propose a dialogue among their own collective experiences in the present in order to produce alternative readings in political, poetic and aesthetic terms.

The two companies also have in common the aim to go beyond dramaturgy as metaphor or allegory for something else. The original theatrical and socio-political research they have done reconstructs histories from state archives and from the bodily archives of their communities of belonging. Thinking on the basis of bodies on the stage reminds us that decolonisation, as Eve Tuck and K. Wayne Yang (2012) say, is not a metaphor, and that in the Indigenous context it has to include the restitution of land. In the Mapuche context, following Lorena Cañuqueo (2015), it implies the possibility of living and circulating in a territory without restrictions being imposed on thought. In the case of Afro-descendants, going beyond metaphor is about the possibility of control over the body, the right to mobility and the right to remain in a country, neighbourhood, home. That is to say, perhaps we can think in terms of control of territory and then of bodies, in Mapuche theatre, and in terms of control of the body and then of a diasporic territory, in the theatre of TES.

In a recent lecture, Angela Davis addressed the question of why anti-racist and anti-colonial art should be made in these contexts of emergency (Davis and Dent 2020). Her answer was that art is urgently needed in the face of emergency because artistic practice allows us to process what is being experienced, beyond the analytical rationality of science. Art, Davis asserted, is a space in which to imagine other lives and other futures. TES and El Katango perhaps go a step further. Not only do they imagine, but they also initiate a process of (re)construction, using the poetics of theatre to challenge the historical erasures instituted in Argentine national narratives. Both theatre projects, mainly made up of women, reflect on their experience within the interstices of the movements of which we are part. The stage opens up a space where the bodies of Afro and Mapuche women are linked to their respective past trajectories, breaking into racist structures and connecting the stage with multiple other territories. The stage is thus a place of regeneration and resurgence of Afro and Mapuche lives in their multiplicity.

Curated Conversation 5: *Casa Adentro* (Inside the House)

Anti-Racist Art Practices

Curated by Carlos Correa Angulo

Source: an online event, 'Conversatorio: Casa adentro; prácticas artísticas antirracistas' (21 May 2021) with members of the Afro-Colombian artistic collectives Sankofa Danzafro and Colectivo Aguaturbia (both of which collaborated with CARLA), and guests Peter Wade and Mara Viveros (both members of the CARLA project team); moderated by Carlos Correa Angulo (CARLA Research Associate for Colombia) with the technical assistance of Rossana Alarcón (CARLA Research Assistant for Colombia) and Paula Uribe. A recording of the event can be accessed on CARLA's YouTube channel: www.youtube.com/watch?v=hNtgI6SwbTo.

This discussion explored the concerns and creative processes that reflect on the durability of racialised social orders and the way racism is manifest in various areas of the lives of Afro-descendant men and women in Colombia. We were interested in seeing how artists reflect on these issues on the basis of their anti-racist artistic practices.

Question: How can your dance practice be understood from an anti-racist stance?

RAFAEL PALACIOS (SANKOFA DANZAFRO): I remember that when I was little I always liked dancing. I would hide in a room in my house in order to dance and I would hide because I didn't want my parents, my siblings and relatives to see. I felt embarrassed. For a long time I hid away and danced in a dark room. I would turn on the radio and that gave me a lot of joy and happiness.

[As time went by], I realised that the joy and happiness I had as a child was disappearing because I had to spend time – in order to dance in front of everyone – creating a dignified space for myself: I mean, fighting against all those stereotypes that form around a Black man who danced.

The eroticism, the exoticisation, the belief that for us dance is something easy. And this is not true because in reality dance is a discipline that we have to study in a very dedicated way. So, what began as a feeling of joy ended up being the power to communicate with the rest of the world and creating a space of struggle. I believe that this is where dance and its practice becomes an anti-racist political space. I discovered that, through dance, which gave me enjoyment, I could also express my pain, my nonconformity, my protests, my struggles as a [Black] man in the world, struggles to reclaim my humanity, which they always wanted to take away from me.

For Rafael Palacios, anti-racism in dance is an expression of protest that seeks to subvert stereotypes about Black people and a political enunciation that affirms the humanity of Afro-descendants. For other dancers in his Afro-contemporary dance company, dance is anti-racist when it highlights the importance of the history of Black peoples from an Afro-centred perspective.

ANDREA BONILLA (SANKOFA DANZAFRO): Anti-racism in dance has to do with the importance of recognising history so we can move through time with self-awareness and coherence. It is about recognising the past and the history that we have been denied but which are present in our voices and in our bodies [when we dance]. As Yndira says, you don't necessarily have to verbalise [that you are anti-racist] for it to be possible. There is action in the body and thought. I like to use another term that I am working on and that is *acuerpar* [to embody]. Anti-racist thinking is embodied through dance itself. It is an active voice that constantly deliberates in an Afro-centred way. That's why I don't know if anti-racism has to be against, because sometimes I ask, 'Is it against being in a place?' I prefer to think of Afro-centring as an anti-racist stance.

Question: What does it mean for artists to be anti-racist in a space where there are no such deliberations, for example, in predominantly white-mestizo spaces?

LORETTA MENESES (COLECTIVO AGUATURBIA): To answer this question, first I want to share something about the collective voice that we built in Aguaturbia. Aguaturbia was a collective of Black artists that was formed in Bogotá from 2015, 2016 onwards. Although we are now seven people, before we were twelve. There were poets, visual producers, dancers, and actresses, musicians, writers, visual arts and others. We decided to call ourselves Aguaturbia because of the experience of a friend, Paola Lucumí, who was doing her undergraduate research work. She is the daughter of a mestizo woman and her father is Black and, let's say, she did not grow up with her paternal family. And in her search in [the] Cauca [region], for her paternal family, they told her that she was not from there, nor from here [Bogotá]: she was 'muddy water'. That experience generated some illustrations and Wilson Borja, another artist in Aguaturbia, who is an animator and illustrator, captured all those reflections in some illustrated stories entitled *Color piel* [Skin Colour].

[Through that experience] we realised that we were the Black people in Bogotá, the Black artists who wanted to disrupt Bogotá.[1] We had experienced racism incidents throughout our lives. We called this project anti-racist because Bogotá as the economic, political and cultural centre of the country is configured as a place founded on a deep legacy of racism and colonisation. So Aguaturbia was born with the aim of challenging this racism by making visible, promoting and positioning the artistic production and intellectual perspectives of Black, Afro-descendant, Raizal and Palenquero people, etc., who make up the social fabric of the city.[2] [We wanted to] develop our own language and question the concept of race, gender, territory, using our bodies as referents in these places [in Bogotá]. Finally, we wanted to address issues [such as racism] to bring them into artistic projects in the city.

Question: How do you manage the question of the body in relation to anti-racism?

PETER WADE: When you put the body on stage as an instrument of expression you also expose it to violence, which you are trying to challenge. How do you respond to this ambivalent status, to the mixed emotions that the body as an instrument, as a technique, can produce when used in anti-racism?

ANDREA BONILLA (SANKOFA DANZAFRO): Well, I don't see the body as an instrument, because to see the body as an instrument is to locate it outside of [oneself], [it means] not to inhabit myself, and I think that precisely what happens to us with dance and with art is that we stop being an instrument and become a place, become action. [So] there is a change in that paradigm, in that way of seeing and conceiving the body. The West has taught us to see the body in terms of pain and pleasure, two very marketable locations, but when dance and art allow us to create, to live, to experiment, to bring our voice, to bring our emotions and to be, it is then [that] a different state [of things], an anti-racist state, is produced.

You were talking about the danger of the body falling into spectacularisation and exoticisation. We could always say that, yes, that does happen. For me as a Black woman, Sankofa has strengthened me a lot. I also do capoeira from Angola (the most traditional type of capoeira), which is also a home place for me. It is called Nzinga de Capoeira Angola. That is a place that I have as a Black woman, it is another place, a place that is not socially expected, and since that [place] does not get dislocated, I don't have to

---

[1] Bogotá (the capital of Colombia) is a city with a predominantly white-mestizo population.
[2] Raizal refers to Black people born in the Colombian Caribbean islands of the San Andrés archipelago. Palenquero refers to people from the *palenque* (a settlement founded by people who had escaped enslavement) of San Basilio, near Cartagena.

act out seductive scenes, [for example,] which were very commonplace for Black women in dance before I entered Sankofa.

Question: How do you see the relation between territory and anti-racism?

PETER WADE: In your interventions, you always relate the work you do to 'the territory': anti-racist artistic practice and territory. How would you explain what territory is to people who don't know Colombia? How does it relate to an anti-racist stance?

LAURA ASPRILLA CARRILLO (AGUATURBIA COLLECTIVE): I was born and raised in Bogotá. The collective was created in Bogotá and the meeting of the Afro Radical Imagination [IRA] was held in Bogotá in 2016. So, the IRA allowed us to get a feeling of the territory in Bogotá. The interesting thing is that, despite being born and raised in Bogotá, one perhaps does not recognise Bogotá as the territory. In terms of defining what a territory is, Bogotá is also a territory, but Black people born in Bogotá think of territory more as the place where our parents were born, as the places where the [Black] population is concentrated, not only in cities like Bogotá or Cali or Medellín.³ We think of territory not as the place where I grew up, where I was born, but as the place where I identify with my ancestors, with mother earth, with my true customs.

According to Laura, artistic practice allows the idea of territory to act as a locus of identification in spaces where there is a dis-identification in ethnic-racial and cultural terms. For Yndira, the territory is also a space for healing, drawing on situated artistic practice.

YNDIRA PEREA (SANKOFA DANZAFRO): The territory is the place that saw us grow. Being in Tumaco [creating and rehearsing the work *Detrás del sur: Danzas para Manuel*] was the best thing that could have happened to us during those moments that were difficult for everyone because of the pandemic.⁴ Although they were very exhausting days, because the work was hard – all day dancing, reflecting on the book⁵ – I think we enjoyed it very much and that the territory had a lot to do with it. I had a shoulder injury and I forgot all about it. I mean, I don't know at what point it got better. Dance also heals us, the territory also allows us to create in a different way, it allows us to be inspired. I think that getting to the territory and connecting with the people, with their history, seeing the resistance of these people also helps us. It allows us to create in a different way.

---

³ Many of the Black people living in Bogotá today come from, or are the children of people who come from, Colombia's Pacific coast region, which is 90 per cent Black.
⁴ Tumaco is a city in the southern Pacific coast region.
⁵ Yndira is referring to the book *Changó, el gran putas* (Changó, the Biggest Badass) by Manuel Zapata Olivella – the 'Manuel' of the dance performance's title – which served as an inspiration for the dance; see Chapter 4.

For Laura and Yndira, the territory is a connection with memories that are spatial and corporal. Anti-racism in dance and art that emerges from the territory mean collectively creating an affective network and a political knowledge that have healing effects.

Question: How do you approach the relationship between body, dance, illness and healing in dance and art?

RAFAEL PALACIOS (SANKOFA DANZAFRO): Well, I believe that all human beings like to dance, we like to move the body to a rhythm, a song, a memory, a silence – and that makes us feel good. Just as I was telling you that when I was little, I felt good when I danced, [so] to feel good is to be healthy. But I also believe that there are many dances, specifically for us Afro-descendants, that have ridiculed us, dances that have eroticised and exoticised us. That is the specific case, for example, of the performance of *mapalé* with a loincloth.[6] This is a dance that caricatures us, that makes us look like beings who are only thinking about sexual pleasure and I believe that this also hurts and sickens a community. So when we on stage, we undo that image, we do away with that stereotype. When we get together to dance with each other and to say this is how we want to narrate ourselves, on the basis of the right to feel good, to feel happy, to want to share an emotion through dance – this is when dance heals the body. So, I would say that dance heals and heals us in a very profound way.

According to Rafael, anti-racist dance has a healing effect when it subverts stereotypes that ridicule Black dancing bodies and turn them into a caricature of sexual frenzy. Dance itself is wellness; this is why it is healing.

Anti-racist art also has the potential to be deeply affective, in the sense that it starts from a deeply emotional place, which is sometimes made explicit and becomes transmuted into a space of liberation:

MARA VIVEROS: There is one thing I noticed; I wasn't sure if I wanted to share it. When you were talking about emotions and feelings [during the documentary *Detrás del sur*],[7] someone mentioned melancholy and it made me wonder about melancholy, because melancholy is not mourning for one's own libido or for one's own self. Melancholy is that defensive feeling that seeks to avoid the pain of being constantly handicapped and that struck me because I was trying to imagine what the slave trade implies for those who lived it and the memories that we carry because we are in any case linked to

---

[6] *Mapalé* is a traditional dance often included in presentations of Afro-Colombian 'folklore'. The female dancers often wear very short skirts.

[7] The process of developing the dance performance *Detrás del sur* was the subject of a documentary, *Detrás del sur: Danzas para Manuel. Prácticas artísticas antirracistas* (2021), https://youtu.be/swza1FF4-gw.

those stories. And it seemed very beautiful to be able to move from melancholy, which would be like mourning the power [of the collective], towards something that would be like the re-signification of that power through the art of dance, which results in something healing.[8]

Thus, an anti-racist art is the possibility of healing the histories, lineages and silenced actors that come from the legacy of enslavement. Anti-racist art effects this healing when it makes visible legacies, people, artistic projects and the intellectual thought of Black people in diverse spaces, such as, for example, in central Andean territorial spaces that have excluded, silenced and erased the Afro from their configuration.

LORETTA MENESES (COLECTIVO AGUATURBIA): [We ask ourselves] How do we dance? What does it communicate? Who is drawing/illustrating? Why is it done in that way? Who is declaiming? What is the meaning? What is the message? We recognise that in this city where we live, the lineages deserve to be healed, that our ancestors and our older people, we the reborn[9] need to be cured of everything that colonialism and slavery have left in the bodies of [Black] women and men who were in the end treated as objects; our ancestors and ancestresses. So, we said, 'of course, this is healing'. To be able to live differently in this city and to know that our voice is a political presence even in spaces like the Andean one that has always seen us as a periphery.

---

[8] Mara is referring back to an earlier comment she made about the power of the collective.
[9] *Renacientes* (literally, the reborn) is a term used by some people in the Pacific coast region to refer to people (and other living things) of current and future generations who are embedded in the local environment of the region.

7

Art and Anti-Racism in Latin American Racial Formations

Peter Wade

This chapter will reflect on possibilities for anti-racism in artistic practice. Reviewing the work of the diverse artists we have collaborated with in the project Cultures of Anti-Racism in Latin America (CARLA), we can see that there are many ways artists can embody anti-racist and decolonial elements in artistic practice. For example, they can work towards decolonising spaces, especially institutional spaces, in the art world.[1] They can use their art to communicate or channel another entire way of being, living and feeling in the world, challenging an entire system of interlocking oppressions and inequalities – racism, capitalism, sexism, heterosexism, anthropocentrism and so on.[2]

---

[1] See Chapter 5 for a discussion of the first exhibition dedicated to Indigenous art in an important art museum in Brazil, *Véxoa: Nós sabemos* (Véxoa: We Know), which was curated by Indigenous researcher Naine Terena. See also the online discussion of the exhibition at https://youtu.be/MoCW6AERCvo.

[2] This modality tends to be associated with an Indigenous ontology – with a special relationship with the land and the cosmos at its heart – and the intellectual current around *otros saberes* (other knowledges) and the so-called ontological turn in social theory. See Stephen and Hale (2013) and https://lasaweb.org/en/sections/otros-saberes/; see also Holbraad and Pedersen (2017). An indication of this modality is in the words of the Brazilian Indigenous artist Daiara Tukano, who, although she publicly labels herself as an artist on her own website, also claims: 'I am not an art creator. I am not an artist. It is not about what I create, but how I relate to creation and let creation flow through me and how I can be a channel to something that is much bigger than me. So that's a different relationship with the universe, with the cosmos' (see Curated Conversation 1 in this book). Although linked strongly to Indigenous perspectives on anti-racism, this modality can also be identified in Black-centred approaches. Radical Black perspectives address racial capitalism in its intersectional entirety (Andrews 2018) and Afro-futurism also envisages new worlds that are radically different from existing ones, often invoking the power of technology as a means to achieve this, but also tapping into a spirituality inspired by religions of the African diaspora (Beliso-De Jesús 2015; Nelson 2002).

Art and Anti-Racism in Latin America 241

In the chapter, I focus on two types of affective intervention that I believe help us to think about various ways of doing anti-racism through art. I label the two types as (1) challenging stereotypes and (2) working with communities. I explore how various artworks engage with these modes of artistic action and how they create affective traction. I think these modes of practice have specific characteristics that make a comparison of them interesting and useful. The aim of the exercise is to be productive and helpful in the struggle against racism by providing some tools that scholars, artists and organisations may find useful to think strategically about anti-racism as a practice and reflect on the opportunities and risks that attach to different interventions.

AMBIVALENT EFFECTS/AFFECTS IN ART PRACTICES

The key argument of the chapter is that artistic practices that intervene in the world and mobilise affect towards decolonial and anti-racist ends have ambivalent effects. Challenging stereotypes is a vital and necessary activity; it is also necessary to bear in mind that it brings with it the possibility of reproducing and even reinforcing those same stereotypes. Working with communities to produce artistic works can also risk reinforcing stereotypes and it usually requires funding, which brings risks of co-optation by funding bodies. If the communities are racially diverse, working with them may also dilute a concentrated focus on racism. I argue that, while challenging stereotypes is an important and necessary mode of action, community-based work provides certain useful affordances and possibilities that are less available to modes of practice that focus on challenging stereotypes. The latter modes tend to be more insidiously 'haunted' by the racist meanings and unconscious affective intensities attached to the stereotypes they set out to contest. Working with communities involves multi-stranded social relations that operate across racialised differences and mitigate binary objectifications and stereotyping. In short, artistic practices and interventions can have ambivalent and even contradictory effects, in large part depending on how they are interpreted by audiences and fitted into existing understandings of the world.

The reasons for the ambivalence of artistic interventions are linked, first, to the nature of artistic practice and, second, to the way art is inserted into racial capitalism and structures of coloniality. Regarding the first point, I agree with Alfred Gell (1998) that art objects have agency and create effects in the world through their relational engagement with other objects and people. Gell denies that art objects encode symbolic propositions about the world, but my view is that symbolic propositions can also have relational agency in the world; there is no mutually exclusive opposition between doing and saying. Art objects are also examples of what Sara Ahmed calls objects of emotion, which include material objects, images, and oral and written statements. These objects circulate in the world and, over time, accumulate affective value, becoming 'sticky, or saturated with affect, as sites of personal and social tension' (Ahmed 2015: 11). This happens in ways that tend to erase the history of accumulation so that emotions appear to reside naturally in the objects or in people, obscuring the fact that 'what we feel might be dependent on past interpretations that are not necessarily made by us, but that come before us' (Ahmed 2015: 171). These two theoretical footholds provide a way to explore how artistic practices have effects in the world and they both suggest that, because art objects are relational and circulate in affective economies, they can produce multiple effects. The reason why this multiplicity might be structured as a contradictory kind of ambivalence is linked to the second point: the way art is inserted into racial capitalism and structures of coloniality.

According to Terry Eagleton (1990), with the Enlightenment there emerged an understanding of 'the aesthetic' as a 'discourse of the body' (materiality, the senses, instincts, imagination), but also as a mediator between the body and the mind (reason, rationality) in the process of forming human subjectivities (1990: 13). The aesthetic thus involves both the senses and reason and it is the way in which rationality (the law, reasoned understandings) is incorporated into the affective life of the body, regulating it in accordance with the dictates of rationality and law, while also allowing bodily sensibilities a degree of autonomy. But the introjection of rationality into the operations of the body/senses has historically – under colonialism and racial capitalism – also been the introjection of classism, racism and sexism (often legitimated by science) into socialised bodies, as a way of controlling and regulating them in hegemonic fashion. However, insofar as the aesthetic is rooted *in* the body, as well as mediating *between* body and mind, or affect and reason, it can also be a means of questioning reason and its regimes of governance, from the space of relative autonomy that the body has, even in its constitution through social processes. The aesthetic thus has an inherent and ambivalent duality, located between *reproducing* the status quo and *challenging* it in various ways, which range from simple unruliness to movements for progressive social transformation and which all derive from the lived experience of inequality and oppression.

As noted in the book's Introduction, this duality has been noted by others. Doris Sommer recognises that 'culture' can be repressive and constraining, but thinks that 'cultural agency' – defined as creative activities that contribute to society, such as pedagogy, research, activism and the arts – can inject a 'dangerous supplement to systems that prefer to be left alone' (Sommer 2006a: 13). Focusing more directly on art, Diana Boros distinguishes between 'plastic', conformist, profit-oriented, mainstream art, which, while it may contribute to a sense of community, is repetitive and overproduced, and 'visionary', transcendent and rebellious art, which opens important political possibilities by encouraging within people 'the expansion of their imaginative capabilities, their true independence (knowledge of self) and their sense of empathy' (Boros 2012: 15). The categories Boros uses map roughly onto what Susan Buck-Morss (1992) calls 'anaesthetics', which describes the mind-numbing control of people's lived connection to the world produced by modern media from the nineteenth century onwards, and 'aesthetics', which, in the meaning it originally had before being hijacked by these media, described people's lived engagement with the world (i.e. Eagleton's discourse of the body). For Jacques Rancière, art is inherently political because it creates an image of society, what it and its people look like and what it is permissible to show about them. As such, the political context can allow for art to be used for regressive and progressive ends: 'The arts only ever lend to projects of domination or emancipation what they are able to lend to them, that is to say, quite simply, what they have in common with them: bodily positions and movements, functions of speech, the parcelling out of the visible and the invisible' (Rancière 2013: 19). Likewise, with specific reference to the use of images in anti-racist work, Mónica Moreno Figueroa (2024: 2326) argues that 'anti-racist projects may include the possibility of re-inscribing racist discourse and practice', due to the contradictory ability of images to explain and illustrate, but also ensnare.

This is important for my purposes because the affective affordances of the various modalities of artistic anti-racism that I describe in this chapter are never unidirectional, univalent or unambiguous. On the other hand, neither are they necessarily classifiable as either one thing or another. In fact, a given artistic practice or work can have contradictory effects at the same time, depending on its relational location in a network of articulations and connections. While prima facie it may seem as if anti-racist art should by definition be progressive, according to the intentions of its creators, this is rarely a straightforward matter, if only because things can be read against the grain of these intentions. And these readings are not necessarily conscious or perverse 'misreadings': as mentioned earlier, 'what we feel might be dependent on past interpretations that are not necessarily made by us, but that come before us' (Ahmed 2015: 171). Affective responses tend to 'travel along already defined lines of cultural investment' (Pedwell and Whitehead 2012: 123) and some subjects – such as women and Black people – have become so 'over-associated with affect' that they become the objectified targets of other people's affective responses (Hemmings 2005: 561).

In what follows, I explore two modes of artistic intervention: challenging stereotypes and working with communities. For each modality I look at key examples, exploring the affective dimensions that are generated with this type of artistic intervention and the affects that circulate between bodies and minds; these can be channelled to strengthen anti-racism, but that might also create potentially problematic effects, which are not necessarily avoidable but need to be seen as coming with the territory.

CHALLENGING STEREOTYPES

The stereotype is a simplified image of a category and its component members. While social psychology and studies of human cognition recognise that simplification is a normal part of human categorisation processes, the stereotype has come to mean a preconceived, over-generalised and over-simplified image of a person, situation or thing, which attributes to every instance of a given category the same simple and essential characteristics and thus acts to distort a more complex reality. A stereotype can be a source of bias or prejudice in that it can affect how people behave towards others, whom they expect to align with the stereotypes they hold about them; and how people comport themselves in relation to stereotypes they assume exist about them (a phenomenon known as stereotype threat).

Stereotypes are key components of entire worldviews, deeply embedded in our cognitive systems. When stereotypes are racialised, they act as fundamental and interconnected nodes that bring together elements of a whole regime of representation that supports racialised hierarchies and legitimates discrimination, inequality, violence and, ultimately, death. These images reproduce schemas for thinking about racialised categories of people by orienting perceptions and behaviours in ways that tend to align with them. Importantly, the schemas are robust but not completely rigid: stereotypes can survive multiple 'exceptions', because individual instances are not simply either in or out of a given category, they are more or less close to the prototypical exemplar of it (Hinton 2000).

Challenging racialised stereotypes that reproduce the unequal position of subaltern groups and legitimate violence against them is thus a vital strategy in anti-racism, which has effects at many levels, symbolic and material, and in terms of impacting on issues of recognition and redistribution, and of stigmatisation and discrimination. Such challenges not only help to counter the false conceptions and unwarranted, prejudicial assumptions that generate indignation, pain, anger and death among those they stereotype, they also work to affirm the legitimate presence and value of racialised subaltern groups in the society; they combat invisibility and silencing, and thus also strengthen a sense of identity and human worth, generating feelings of confidence and legitimacy.

It is useful to locate challenging stereotypes in terms of what Paula Serafini (2022: 25–28) says are the five functions of art in the context of decolonial social movements and community organising against extractivism. She identifies denunciation (making visible but also establishing the legitimacy and relevance of what is made visible), documentation (literally, but also in terms of constructing narratives different from those of developmentalism), democratisation (sharing information and building community around these narratives), deconstruction (of dominant naturalised concepts, such as culture/nature, mind/body, feeling/reason), and design (creating new objects and new ways of being). Challenging stereotypes crosses several of these functions: in one sense, it is a form of denunciation, a protest at being misrepresented and stigmatised in ways that legitimate the violence that is often visited upon subaltern racialised people. An example could be contesting stereotypes of Indigenous people – or *indios*, to use the colonial term – as located in the past and in nature and thus as either irrelevant to extractivist projects or destined to be overcome – often with genocidal violence – by the projects' modernist conquest of nature. Simple denunciation is necessary but limited. As Macarena Gómez-Barris (2017: 3) says, 'if we only track the purview of power's destruction and death force, we are forever analytically imprisoned to reproducing a totalising viewpoint that ignores life that is unbridled and [that] finds forms of resisting and living alternatively' – forms that would fall into Serafini's 'design' category.

Challenging stereotypes is, however, also a form of deconstruction, in that it contests a dominant, taken-for-granted representation. And the challenge goes deeper still, towards design, because contesting an image of this kind generally involves creating a different narrative about what it means to be Indigenous in Latin America today. Disseminating the challenge also involves sharing that narrative and, potentially, mobilising people around it, while the challenge implicitly deconstructs nature/culture binaries and creates new objects (e.g. the 'modern *indio*') that point to new ways of being.

Nevertheless, as I have indicated, artistic anti-racism is never unidirectional, univalent or unambiguous. Contesting racist stereotypes in art practice appears to be a progressive and decolonial intervention, but it is haunted by the very racialised hierarchies and colonialities it sets out to challenge (cf. Stoler 2006). Lingering traces remain of the very racist stereotypes being challenged that have accumulated an affective baggage of meanings and past interpretations, which have 'stuck' to them (Ahmed 2015: 11) and traces of which (re-)activate as the artwork circulates and gains agency in different articulations and arrangements of relational networks of people, objects and ideas. Ann Stoler uses the concept of recursion to get at the way regimes of governance and discourse – in her case, colonial/imperial ones – are not erased by regimes that appear to displace them: elements of the old are reworked and redeployed in new ways to achieve some of the same effects through 'processes of partial reinscriptions, modified displacements, and amplified recuperations' (Stoler 2016: 27). Christen Smith, trying to grasp the contradictions of 'Afroparadise' in Bahia, Brazil, where Black bodies are celebrated as part of Brazilian culture while also being subjected to genocidal violence, points at the same phenomenon when she suggests it is necessary to read Bahia as a palimpsest, in which, according to Achille Mbembe, time 'is not a series but an interlocking of presents, pasts, and futures that retain their depths of other presents, pasts, and futures, each age bearing, altering, and maintaining the previous ones' (cited in Smith 2016a: 63). Amade M'charek refers to the same phenomenon when she says that an effect of what she calls 'folding time' is that 'history can be *recalled* in objects. History is never left behind' (M'charek 2014: 31).

These palimpsestual, recuperated, enfolded traces can linger and remain active in different ways. One is that challenging stereotypes often involves giving some visual space and airtime to the stereotype itself, usually with some parodic or satirical intent, perhaps using grotesque exaggeration – as in the controversial work of US Black artist Kara Walker or the early work of Afro-Colombian artist Liliana Angulo Cortés, which focus on the Black body (I will return to this in what follows). Another way of lingering or haunting is when there is a simple inversion of existing meanings, resignifying a trait that is negatively valued in racist hierarchies by giving it a positive value. For example, Mara Viveros Vigoya (2002) found that some Black men in Colombia had appropriated racist stereotypes of them as over-sexed and recast them in a positive way to suggest they were sexually attractive. Similarly, Moreno Figueroa (2024) argues that some Black women in Mexico's Costa Chica region supported what could easily be seen as photographic sexualised objectifications of them, because the images made them feel good and represented. Joane Nagel (2003: 121–124) argues that the Black Power movement in the US resignified racist images of Black men as violent to convey meanings of a virile masculinity ready to defend family and community. Astrid Ulloa (2005) shows that some Indigenous movements coincide with state discourses in promoting images of Indigenous people as close to nature and thus as ecologically-minded guardians of the environment; but being 'close to nature' is also readable as being 'uncivilised'. These resignifications are important but they also provide affordances that allow existing elements of the original stereotype to operate in a racist way in the context of networks of dominant representations.

Haunting and lingering traces can remain even when stereotypes are challenged by constructing new images – for example, the technologically savvy Indigenous person, the urban Indigenous person, the Black professional, the Black woman with a 'natural' Afro hairstyle – which defy the existing regime of racial representation and its hierarchy of values by creating new contradictory elements. But we should not underestimate the power of partial reinscriptions and recuperations, in which past patterns of interpretation made by others are not displaced but recursively reactivated.[3] The affordances provided by artworks are inherently relational – they emerge in relation to agents who use them in the world in various ways (Keane 2018). As such, the effects that artists' works produce in the world can be multiple and uncontrollable. To be sure, it may be obvious to artists that they cannot control how other people view their work. It may be less obvious how deeply rooted the effects of haunting and recursion are and especially how contradictory effects can coexist, perhaps even within the same person.

It is also worth noting that, in art practice, the challenging of stereotypes is quite often done within the institutional structures of the mainstream art world and its audiences and markets, even if the challenge is disruptive or not condoned by the institution. This, of course, is in

---

[3] Many of these ambivalences and complexities are apparent in the use of racial stereotypes in comedy performances. As Pauwel (2021: 91) remarks: 'it may prove impossible to have the counter-hegemonic effects of racial stereotype humour, without also unleashing its hegemonic effects.' See also Weaver (2010) and Wade (2023).

FIGURE 7.1 *Cunhatain, antropofagia musical* (Cunhatain, Musical Anthropophagy) by Denilson Baniwa, 2018 (© Denilson Baniwa, by permission).

large part the whole point of the challenge: the dominant institutions and norms have to be tackled head on. Insofar as these dominant institutions and structures are fertile locations for recursions of coloniality, the risks of haunting are ever present.

Let us explore an example in which this modality of anti-racism is clearly in play. Several paintings by Brazilian Indigenous artist Denilson Baniwa challenge the stereotypical and constraining image of the Indigenous person as tied to the past, to rurality and to primitiveness (Sá and Milanez Pereira 2020).[4] A series of his prize-winning works from 2018 show prototypical *índios*, identifiable as such by their body paint, dress and bead adornments, using video cameras, mobile phones, computers and sound systems (see Figure 7.1).[5]

---

[4] In CARLA, Jamille Dias worked closely with Denilson.
[5] See www.pipaprize.com/denilson-baniwa/ for the following paintings: *Awá uyuká kisé, tá uyuká kurí aé kisé irü* (Those Who Harm with Metal, With Metal Shall Be Hurt), 2018; *Cunhatain, antropofagia musical* (Musical Anthropophagy), 2018; *Curumin* (Memory Keeper), 2018; *Nheengaitá* (Protagonism and Our Voice Needs to Be Heard), 2018.

These paintings engage with dominant images of Indigenous people in Brazil as constantly on the edge of extinction and death, relegated to oblivion by forces of coloniality that combine elements of settler and extractivist colonialism (Pacheco de Oliveira 2016: ch. 2). Western visions of progress and modernity are founded on a notion of the past as something to be transcended, but also as a reservoir of nostalgia, a past that Indigenous peoples are held to embody. Denilson's paintings could be seen as tapping into an Indigenous futurism that, like the work of some North American Indigenous artists, 'urges the viewer to imagine Indigenous futures' (Baudemann 2016: 118). But Denilson's work urges the viewer to see these images as part of the present too. The paintings play with time via what Grace Dillon (2012: 3) characterises as 'Native slipstream', which 'views time as pasts, presents, and futures that flow together like currents in a navigable stream'. Denilson works between *el indio permitido* (the permissible *indio*) – Silvia Rivera Cusicanqui's term for the Indigenous figure seen as acceptable by the dominant classes (Hale 2004) and which elicits in them affective forces of nostalgia, pity and joy – and what might be called the *indio inconforme* (rebellious, challenging, otherwise-minded), which often elicits responses of anger, fear and contempt from elites.

These images should be seen in the context of other pieces of Denilson's work, such as his video *Colheita maldita* (Accursed Harvest, 2022), which likens agro-industrial landscapes to a horror film in which we are all trapped, and his performances as a *pajé-onça* (shaman-jaguar), in which he walks through modernist landscapes (city avenues, art galleries), producing spatial and temporal dislocations and an embodied critique of modernity.[6] Denilson brings together challenges to racist stereotypes and a whole political ecology and ontology to suggest ways of being Indigenous that are urgently relevant to the present and the future.

All these images and performances foreground in one way or another the figure of the *índio*. Of course, this figure is haunted by racist meanings and emotions and my argument is that these can be reactivated as the images circulate. We should recall that mainstream Western society

---

[6] *Colheita Maldita* was produced for the CARLA online exhibition: www.digitalexhibitions.manchester.ac.uk/s/carla-en/page/denilson-baniwa. For Denilson's *pajé-onça* performances, *Pajé-onça caçando na Avenida Paulista* (Shaman-Jaguar Hunting on Paulista Avenue, 2018) and *Pajé-onça hackeando a 33ª Bienal de Artes de São Paulo* (Shaman-Jaguar Hacking the 33rd São Paolo Art Biennial, 2018), see www.youtube.com/watch?v=GtwR1-KopqM and www.youtube.com/watch?v=MGFU7aG8kgI. See also Chapter 2 of this book.

is familiar with images that mix 'the primitive' (often in the figure of the Indigenous person) and 'the modern' (often represented by technology). Michael Taussig (1993) argues that modern Western civilisation has long used the *indio* and his/her supposed fascination with technologies – such as phonographs – to attest to the wizardry of Western technologies that Westerners value so highly but also come to see as routine and second nature. With his/her apparent fascination, the *indio*, seen as close to nature, can vouch for the natural and life-like imitations produced by technologies such as record-players, tape recorders and cameras, which originally astonished Westerners before they became routinised.[7] Taussig contends that Westerners often laugh with pleasure and fascination at what they perceive as Indigenous people's fascination with Western technology (Taussig 1993: 231).

Denilson's paintings flirt with this primitivist tradition in complex ways. The paintings depict Indigenous people as prototypical *índios* – mostly wearing traditional clothing and body paint – but there is little amazement in the way the people in the paintings handle the technological devices; on the contrary they appears as a routine items. For the non-Indigenous viewer – who is arguably the intended audience addressed by the gaze of the subject in the painting – this creates a contradictory effect. There is something familiar and yet unfamiliar about the image; something easily assimilable to a primitivist perspective, yet also profoundly unsettling of it. There is a matter-of-factness about the way technology features in these paintings that, for the non-Indigenous viewer, is at odds with the very traditional depiction of the Indigenous subjects and their surroundings. Both the stereotype of the forest-dwelling Indigenous person and images of the Indigenous person 'fascinated' by the wonders of modern technology fit neatly into the dominant racial formation and thus generate a sense of frustration and anger for some Indigenous people.

Appropriating cameras for political ends, as documented by Terry Turner (1992) for the Kayapó (see Chapter 5), can channel these sentiments into a fight for justice, but making the technology everyday – as the Kayapó also do when they use cameras in their village-based ritual ceremonies, as opposed to their encounters with the state – creates a different affective response; it generates a sense of radical equality by showing that the same technology is 'at home' in quite different surroundings. Denilson's paintings create a sense of both radical (Indigenous) alterity

---

[7] Recall Thomas Edison's reaction in 1878 on hearing his voice played back on an early phonograph: 'I was never so taken aback in my life. Everybody was astonished.'

and radical (technological) sameness. The Indigenous person lives a life that is quite different in some respects from the lives of non-Indigenous people, yet in other respects their relationship to technological modernity is the same – both categories of people are fully at home with technologies, which are experienced as routine.

Despite these complexities, however, I argue that these paintings remain haunted by the affordances they provide for traces of primitivist racism. This is due to the double effect of a key component of the images, on which they depend for their effect, which is the classic depiction of the *índio* as semi-naked and wearing body-paint and beads. These elements remain key indicators of Indigenous status in Brazil.[8] For Indigenous people, they are part of everyday life, spiritual relationships and aesthetics, but they are also important in the way they present themselves to the state, during protests and negotiations, and in the public political sphere in general (e.g. in street marches). As in Denilson's paintings, these indicators make the claim that it is possible to be 'Indigenous' in this way and also be an active part of today's mainstream society. But the effect can also be to reinforce a primitivist view of Indigenous people; the images allow the possibility of a colonial romantic reading of traditional *índios* fascinated by a modernity that is beyond their ken. This reading is not *entailed* by the image: the point is that images circulate in multiple assemblages of people, objects and meanings. People will read the image in ways mediated by diverse connections with other agents and discourses. But the possibility of the colonial recursion exists. It is a catch-22 situation caused by the agency of the artwork in a relational network.

A further example of this complex ambivalence is in the work of the Afro-Colombian dance company Sankofa Danzafro. The company is directed by Black Colombian Rafael Palacios and includes dancers who are all Black in Colombian terms (*negro* or *afro*) and self-identify as such.[9] The terrain of dance is a complex and contradictory one for challenging racism directed at Black people, because dance (and music) are so deeply embedded in the hierarchies of the racial formations involving Blackness. From colonial times, music and dance have been a field in which dynamics of control, subjugation, assimilation, co-optation, appropriation and resistance have played out (Birenbaum

---

[8] See, for example, 'Índios no Brasil – Construindo imagens e desconstruindo estereótipos' (Indigenous People in Brazil – Constructing Images and Deconstructing Stereotypes): https://cartografias.catedra.puc-rio.br/wp/2019/02/22/indios-no-brasil-construindo-imagens-e-desconstruindo-estereotipos/.
[9] In CARLA, Carlos Correa worked closely with Sankofa Danzafro.

Quintero 2019; Feldman 2006; Gilroy 1993; Radano and Bohlman 2000; Wade 2000).[10] This means that dance or music identified as 'Black' or 'Afro' – whether identified as such by performer or audience – can always signify varied things and mobilise contradictory affective forces, such as indignant disgust and (sexualised) pleasure (e.g. by white audiences both decrying and enjoying music they associate with Blackness), admiration and envy (e.g. by white musicians and dancers competing with the supposedly 'natural' talents they often ascribe to Black performers), and despair and pride (e.g. by Black performers facing racism and mobilising against it).

In terms of racism and anti-racism, Black dance and music – and the Black bodies with which they are closely connected – are highly ambivalent spaces, with the potential to both foster and subvert racism in complex ways. As artist Liliana Angulo says in reference to her art installation *Négritude* (2007), which featured a soundtrack of Latin American songs that referred to the figure of *el negro* (the Black man), 'the songs of Afro-Caribbean genres chosen [for the installation] express many of the ideas and imaginaries promoted by the thinkers of the Négritude movement [that began in the 1930s] and they also display many of the stereotypes of racism. It is not something Black and white, because no one in our countries is Black or white.' The fact that these musical styles are 'directed at the body, at enjoyment, at celebration and sensuality' could make them subject to 'being co-opted as stereotype'; on the other hand, this does not detract from their power to be fundamental cultural practices that can also be 'revolutionary, liberatory, challenging, insolent, etc.' (cited in Giraldo Escobar 2014: 151, my translation).

Similar ambivalences have been evident in other representations focusing on Black bodies. Kobena Mercer, for example, contends that the images of white photographer Robert Mapplethorpe from the 1980s, which sexualise Black male bodies, reiterate 'the terms of colonial fantasy' and thus 'service the expectations of white desire'. But while 'colonial fantasy attempts to "fix" the position of the black subject into a space that mirrors the object of white desires', Black readers 'may appropriate pleasures by reading against the grain, overturning signs of otherness into signifiers of identity' (Mercer 1994: 134–136). Nearly forty years later, the same ambivalence inhabits the queer Black art of the late Nigerian-born photographer Rotimi Fani-Kayode. A commentator writes: 'Despite

---

[10] Music and dance also mediate images of Indigeneity, but less powerfully than for Blackness (Mendoza 2000; Montero-Diaz 2019).

being black and insisting his art does not pander to the same stereotypes as Mapplethorpe's, his work is unable to circumvent these stereotypes entirely.' The writer recognises that this is because the power of interpretation lies with the viewer, but still hopefully concludes that, despite this, Fani-Kayode's photographs 'retain subversive potential because both he and the men in his photographs possess subjectivity' (Muldoon 2020). I think the point is that the subversive potential and the inability to circumvent stereotyped readings are both available routes that can be traced in overlapping but different networks.

The controversies surrounding the work of US Black artist Kara Walker traverse the same terrain. While many commentators contend that her work ultimately undermines the stereotyped images of Black people she consistently deploys in scenarios commonly featuring racial and sexual violence (Neary 2015; Seidl 2009; Shaw 2004), others say she does not offer a clear resolution (Schollaert 2014) and fellow African American artist, Betye Saar, who has also worked with stereotyped images of Black women, protested publicly that Walker's art 'was basically for the amusement and the investment of the white art establishment' (PBS 2000). Walker herself says 'One theme in my artwork is the idea that a Black subject in the present tense is a container for specific pathologies from the past and is continually growing and feeding off those maladies' (cited in Neary 2015: 160). This resonates with the recursiveness of the past that I wish to highlight. In this respect, Janet Neary comments that, once Walker produces an artwork, 'she does not have control over her production': her work 'identifies, but cannot fully control or inoculate against, the workings of racial terror' (Neary 2015: 160).

I argue that this kind of ambivalence can be seen in Sankofa Danzafro's fifty-minute production *La ciudad de los otros* (The City of the Others, 2010). The dance starts with music that has a rolling drum-heavy beat, with rhythmic horn riffs and vocals that combine rapping and chanting; the choreography suggests a dance party, including a male-female pair close-dancing with synchronised hip action, and featuring a street-style dance-off between competing crews, overlain by a chanting rap vocal; a solo clarinet comes in with melodies suggestive of musical styles (*bullerengue, cumbia, chirimía*) from Colombia's historically Black coastal regions (see Figure 7.2). For audiences in Colombia and elsewhere in the Americas, this all evokes a sense of ludic Blackness. The next scene shows people strap-hanging in a bus or train, while a solo voice sings over a drum, known in Black regions of Colombia as

FIGURE 7.2 An early scene from Sankofa Danzafro's *La ciudad de los otros*, Battery Dance Festival, New York, 2015 (photo by Steven Pisano, © Sankofa Danzafro, by permission).

a *tambor alegre* or *conuno*, which plays a fairly complex rhythm. This segues into several minutes of an energetic solo male dancer interacting with the drummer, ignored by the other 'passengers' who are now seated on chairs. A change is marked when another drum, the *llamador* in Colombian Caribbean regional terminology, starts playing a single beat under the *tambor alegre*, joined by a *guasá* or shaker, which together provide the rhythm for a male-female couple dance that is clearly a traditional dance from the region (in this case a *bullerengue*, although the non-specialist might identify it as the better-known *cumbia*), a cultural reference reinforced by the appearance, towards the end of this segment, of the unmistakable *flauta de millo* (cane flute) of the Caribbean coastal region.

At this stage, the instruments and much of the music are clearly rooted in the musical traditions of the coastal regions, although the opening dance party scene and the solo male dance interlude introduce a more urban and 'contemporary' dance element that is still recognisably 'Black' for the audience. Meanwhile, the suggestion of an urban transport system and the fact that all the dancers, male and female, wear smart-casual trousers, long-sleeved shirts and ties both contradict the sense of a 'folkloric' performance and frame these traditional elements as, perhaps, cultural oases or memories for Black people living in city environments that they experience as belonging to 'others'. Nevertheless, some basic connections between Black bodies, drum-heavy rhythms and ludic, sensual and energetic dance moves are reiterated throughout.

The performance then moves off into diverse scenes that do not reiterate these familiar connections. One sequence of almost ten minutes has a peaceful feel, with music dominated by the sounds of harp and piano, and bodies moving in synchronised waves, with hands and arms that reach out and stroke. Subsequent scenes evoke urban life and are accompanied by frenetic, rhythmic, metallic electronic music, which at times develops into alarming stress-inducing noises overlying bodies that twist and convulse, struggle and drown, collapse and revive. The overwhelming impression is of people confronting hostile urban/industrial environments, being shut in, going mad, being distraught, arguing, being assaulted, and being observed and checked up on. This aligns with Sankofa Danzafro's own description of the performance, which says that it 'reveals the lack of opportunities for human beings who for generations have been marked by ethnic discrimination and social inequity'. There are also impressions of resisting and defying, expressing oneself individually and freely, interacting collaboratively and in a friendly way with others. There are moments when each dancer has a solo dance break in an enclosed space defined by three 2.5 × 1 metre boards, suggesting confinement, each of which ends with a defiant gesture that says something like, 'This is who I am.' There are other moments when people dance in groups of three or four or all in unison, working together, lifting and supporting each other (see Figure 7.3). This reflects the official description's statement that

FIGURE 7.3 A later scene from Sankofa Danzafro's *La ciudad de los otros*, Battery Dance Festival, 2015 (photo by Steven Pisano, © Sankofa Danzafro, by permission).

'Black and other marginalised communities, always observed through the same lens, demand political power that results in authentic forms of coexistence.'[11]

The overall effect with regard to stereotypes of Blackness is ambivalent. The use of music and dance as a medium to express a positive message about Blackness will inevitably be obliged to navigate existing negative and restrictive stereotypes about Blackness. As noted, some fundamental and familiar affective connections between Black bodily dexterity and elasticity in dance, drum-heavy rhythmicity, and playfulness and sensuality are reproduced in the performance. This resonates with some powerful stereotypes about Black people that are deeply rooted in the hierarchies of coloniality, and which trivialise, sexualise and animalise them. In addition, some stereotypical associations specific to Colombia are also reiterated, linking Blackness to the coastal regions and to traditional 'folkloric' musical styles such as *bullerengue* or *cumbia*.

On the other hand, a great deal of the performance, while it necessarily connects Black bodies to dance and music, addresses themes that break with familiar stereotypes, at least in the Colombian context. Harp and piano music, for example, are not associated with Blackness in Colombia. A more important break is the portrayal of urban Blackness, as, in Colombia, Blackness is typically associated with peripheral rural regions, despite a long history of Black settlement in cities. (This would be less relevant for US or European contexts, where Blackness is stereotypically more urban.) In addition, showcasing in visible and audible terms the trauma and alienation affecting Black people – in short, highlighting racism – challenges traditional images of Colombia as a racially tolerant social formation in which racialised difference is not considered important. The performance makes a case for Black solidarity and cultural specificity – rooted, for example, in traditional music and dance – as a resource for dealing with exclusion, rather than just a resource for the cultural diversity of the nation, defined in the dominant imaginary as an inclusive polity.

Ultimately, foregrounding Black bodies as vectors for anti-racism and decoloniality is inherently an ambivalent strategy (Moreno Figueroa 2024; Ruette-Orihuela 2022). Brazilian Black feminist Beatriz Nascimento noted that 'slavery is present in our bodies, our blood and our veins' (cited in Smith 2016b: 81) and the fact that enslavement restricted Black people to their sheer physicality is one reason why she privileged the

---

[11] See https://sankofadanzafro.org/portfolio/la-ciudad-de-los-otros/.

body 'as a political site' and insisted that 'the quest for Black autonomous space is located first in the corporeality of the body', that 'the body is the territorialization of memory' and that the *quilombo* – as physical and symbolic space – 'is the transmigration of the Black body from the *senzala* (slave quarters) to autonomy' (Smith 2016b: 80, 82).[12] Yet this journey is haunted by traces of coloniality and its racist stereotypes of the Black body, reduced to a *negro permitido* – or more frequently a *negra permitida* (permissible Black woman) (Rahier 2014: 146) – that is, a body for sensual consumption by others.

It is interesting that Liliana Angulo, reflecting back on her work from the early 2000s, which played with stereotyped images of Black people using hyperbole, caricature, parody and satire (see Giraldo Escobar 2014), commented that, for her in 2018, 'stereotypes are no longer a preoccupation' (Valoyes Villa 2018).[13] In an online conversation in 2020, she observed:

I kind of didn't realise it but now I think that I was dealing with the pain I think I was facing. Because when I started doing this type of work I was working about the word *negro* and how we relate to that word. It is very complex in Colombia ... in the sense that we have learned to embrace it in order to fight for the struggle, but also obviously it has all this background of colonisation and slavery. So at that moment I was dealing with that in order to understand it. So I used it on my own body and it was very ambivalent. Because for me all these works are very painful, but some people, because of how we have learned to live with racism, for some people it was kind of funny. So it was very ambivalent.[14]

Since then, Liliana Angulo has moved in other directions, including working with local communities.[15] In the next section, I argue that this kind of work may offer different affordances that sidestep some of the

---

[12] In Brazil, *quilombos* were historically places where Black escapees from enslavement set up autonomous communities; the term also denotes settlements where descendants of these communities still reside today. Symbolically, the term connotes political practices of Black resistance (Nascimento 1980).

[13] Examples of Angulo's earlier work are the series *Negro utópico* (Utopian Black, 2001), https://razonpublica.com/la-raza-como-arte/; and *Negra menta* (2003), www.banrepcultural.org/multimedia/obras-comentadas-negra-menta-de-liliana-angulo. The title *Negra menta* evokes, among other things, the pejorative term *negramenta* (crowd of Black people). For more detail on both series, see Giraldo Escobar (2014: 84–112).

[14] See Curated Conversation 1 in this book. See also 'Anti-Racist Art in the UK and Latin America: A Conversation', https://youtu.be/HOPwGVBNMXM, at 01:42:57.

[15] See, for example, her visual essay 'Rodrigo Barrientos: Disfrazado de hombre blanco' (Rodrigo Barrientos: Disguised as a White Man), a product of collective curation with local Black organisations: www.digitalexhibitions.manchester.ac.uk/s/carla-en/page/liliana-angulo.

ambivalences and hauntings that working with stereotypes involves – although working with communities presents its own challenges.

WORKING WITH COMMUNITIES

This modality of anti-racist artistic practice involves working with people who occupy the lower rungs of racialised hierarchies. This work seeks to affirm presence, combat invisibility and silencing, strengthen identity, and support local struggles for justice and equality. This mode of practice may also aim to build capacity in the communities, both by giving people specific skills and by increasing general self-esteem and confidence.

Regarding the affective dimension of this modality, we can see that racism produces feelings of isolation and alienation among those who experience its negative impacts. If one effect of racism is to produce the internalisation of racialised value hierarchies, this effect is exacerbated to the extent that a person feels they are on their own in dealing with the demeaning judgements they have internalised. Recognising and feeling the collective nature of the experience helps people to grasp the structural character of the oppression they face (Pyke 2010); working with and interacting with neighbours around issues of racialised difference and identity, especially in a creative setting, can generate feelings of solidarity and connection and of aspiration and hope, all of which can be channelled into anti-racist struggles.

These struggles are frequently intersectional, insofar as people do not 'live single-issue lives' (Lorde 1984: 138) and thus, in practice, they find it meaningful to challenge issues around racism, classism, sexism and heterosexism – among other -isms – in ways that acknowledge their connectedness. In particular, racism and classism in Latin America are very closely interwoven, given that in most areas of the region, the spectrums of racialised and class difference tend to coincide strongly (Telles and Project on Ethnicity and Race in Latin America 2014), which is different from the United States and Europe, where the lower strata are majority white. The congruence of racial and class hierarchies in Latin America is important for the effects and affects produced by anti-racist art practices in the community.

An example of this modality is the work that Sankofa Danzafro – the same group discussed in the previous section – did over a four-month period in 2020 with young people, mostly but not uniformly Black, in the working-class communities of Medellín. Within the framework of the Red de Danza de Medellín (Medellín Dance Network), organised by the mayor's office in association with a local university and several cultural organisations, Sankofa Danzafro organised neighbourhood dance 'laboratories' to deliver training, some of it virtual due to the COVID-19 pandemic. Working with Sankofa, Carlos Correa organised the production of a video showcasing the process, which consisted of Sankofa Danzafro members training groups of young people, who then presented short dance routines.[16]

The video shows excerpts of the young people's performances and extracts of interviews with them and the Sankofa dancers. These interviews are short and the context tended to elicit positive statements, but it is clear that the process and, especially, the focus on dance, generated powerful feelings of community. One boy said, 'I like to dance because of the way I am, to make more friends, create companionship.' Another said 'It is important to dance in the neighbourhood, in the community, to rescue young people and rescue others too.' A dancer-instructor said that the end result of the process was 'a work that the children had achieved, in which they managed to join together, seeking the companionship and the family that we always try to find in these processes'. The mother of one girl valued the positive forces the work generated as a counter to forces undermining community. She identified these forces as 'vices' and the COVID-19 pandemic. First: 'It is no secret that we live in vulnerable communities ... where there's a lot of – let's call them vices, other alternatives to choose.' Second: 'The hardest thing we had to face was virtuality: if it wasn't the internet, it was the children who couldn't be together because maybe they didn't have a cell phone or a computer.' In the face of this, she said that, for the children in the project, it was 'beautiful to be able to participate, be able to dance, be able to live and be able to enjoy themselves day by day and feel they are just children'.

Although the word 'racism' did not appear in the video, the trainers saw this community-building as closely linked to Black identity and resilience. One said: 'We address the theme of identity with the children, which is also a question ... that everyone has about how they are seen and how society sees them; and what are the stereotypes that exist in society ... about us, and that damage us physically and psychologically.' Another noted that the young people already had a reservoir of embodied knowledge about dance from their own experiences and that building on this was facilitated because their knowledge had 'a lot of affinity with

---

[16] See 'Muestra final: Laboratorios de creación en casa' (Final Showcase: Creative Labs at Home): www.digitalexhibitions.manchester.ac.uk/s/carla-en/page/sankofa.

FIGURE 7.4 Scene from *Muestra final: Laboratorios de creación en casa*, video, 2020 (from video by Lethal Peligrosos Producciones, © Sankofa Danzafro, by permission).

Afro-contemporary dance techniques: there are many movements that are similar. So we make a connection there.'

In terms of the dancing itself, a key feature was the location of the routines in ordinary cityscapes, such as pavements, the open concrete plaza surrounding a local cultural and sports centre, the occasional green space squeezed in among the roads and houses, and small playgrounds. In these spaces, to the ubiquitous sound of drum rhythms, young people performed energetic and dynamic dance routines in public, sometimes as buses, cars and trucks roared past at arm's length (see Figure 7.4). The drums, the movements and the bodies of the people together constituted a clear assertion of Blackness in the public space of the city – which, it is important to say, is the capital city of a region that is little associated with Blackness and that has a historical reputation for being racist (Wade 1993). Together the dancers, drummers and instructors used sound and body movements to intervene collectively in the affective history of the city of Medellín, adding a dimension in which Black people occupy everyday public spaces – beyond theatres and art galleries – transforming them temporarily, and challenging the long-standing racist views that cast Blackness as uncivilised and thus marginal in a city widely perceived as a beacon of modernity and whiteness.

Spatial arrangements are an expression of, and a means to enact, power relations, involving both control and resistance (Gregory and

Urry 1985; Massey 2005). Where racial difference is imbricated with power relations, spatial structures will necessarily be racialised and racial hierarchies will necessarily be spatialised (Lipsitz 2007; McKittrick and Woods 2007; Neely and Samura 2011; Wade 2020). Space can be seen as 'an active archive of the social processes and social relationships composing racial orders', active in the sense that spatial structures are not just a static representation of the racial order, but, via the located activities of people, actively participate in the construction of that order as a material-semiotic assemblage (Knowles 2003: 83). As an archive, racialised spaces can be sites for control and for resistance and autonomy; as with the discursive realm of stereotypes, processes of recursion mean that spaces can be haunted by traces of coloniality that remain active (McKittrick 2011). But working with communities creates a distributed form of agency that is different from the stereotype-challenging art object, which, although it creates effects and affects in a relational way as it circulates, is more likely to become an object with a life of its own, which can provide affordances for racist readings that are locked into a recursive binary of representations – racist versus anti-racist.

What we see in this video is a vivacious performance of affective intensities that goes beyond the simple representation of identity framed by a binary of hegemony and resistance. It would be possible to see the urban spaces and their temporality as being hegemonic structures that are defied by Black bodies dancing in resistance. But this binary framing does not grasp the everyday, habitual inhabiting of these spaces and temporalities by the dancers, along with their families, friends and neighbours, of which the dance performances themselves are just a snippet. Importantly, we also see beyond the performances to glimpse some of the community networks in which they are embedded: we see families, we see dancers talking about how dance fits into their everyday lives and provides them with support, we see the instructors talking about how they make connections with the young dancers.

Together, the dancing and the music, the bodies in motion, synchronised with each other and the drummers, while also being embedded in everyday relationships in the community, create affective intensities in space and time to suggest that urban places can also be scenarios for living as a Black person in the city – alongside non-Black others. This is not a romantic invocation of the organic community: the idea of distributed agency does not depend on the idea of individuals coming together as one. Rather, it is a scenario of events involving bodies and objects that relate to each other in diverse ways and with diverse affective experiences, according to the event in question – whether it is a dance performance or rehearsal, a street football match, a neighbourly visit or conflict, a school class or queuing in a local shop. Doing artistic work in communities may bring people together around a specific event, but this cannot be separated from other events in which they are also involved together and which produce bodily reactions and investments that are not reducible to simple categories and oppositions (Thrift 2004: 71). Community-based work tends to foreground that people do not live single-issue lives: they encounter each other in the multi-stranded complexity of their everyday living.

The importance of this can be seen if we think back to the issue of stereotypes. To some extent, the same problems of haunting and recursion exist for community-based work as for the modality of challenging stereotypes. For example, people who operate with the racist assumptions that Black people are naturally good dancers or that they spend too much time dancing and not enough time working might be reassured in these assumptions on catching sight of a Sankofa Danzafro dance lab performance on the street. This potential problem exists, but I think that, in specific contexts, community-based interventions are well placed to sidestep them. To start with, these interventions, while they may be funded by institutions (e.g. local government, NGOs), often work outside the institutional spaces of the art world (theatres, museums, galleries, etc.) where the hauntings and recursions of coloniality may be powerfully felt. The way such interventions diffuse through the community, becoming imbricated with everyday life and distributing agency across a wide network, means that stereotypes are rarely stand-alone objectifications: if a young Black person is a dancer, then they are also a neighbour, a friend, a school colleague, a sports team-mate and so on. In a barrio in Medellín (and in other Latin American cities), such links are also likely to cross clearly racialised differences, mitigating the reification of racialised identities and attendant issues of exclusiveness and divisiveness, which otherwise hamper collaborations and solidarities that intersect boundaries of difference. The community focus brings out that people have multi-faceted lives, rather than just being the embodiment of a certain stereotyped image.

Just as the challenging of stereotypes does battle with haunting and recursion, so community-focused strategies face other rough patches on the field of anti-racist struggle that come with the territory and have to be negotiated. There are pitfalls of tokenism and co-optation: material support given by the city authorities for this kind of community-building intervention can entail limitations on autonomy, especially if the interventions are explicitly about reaffirming Blackness and thus readable as exceeding the bounds of *el negro permitido* – for example, by appearing to be not inclusive enough and even 'racist in reverse'. However, by virtue of the distributed agency that attends community-based endeavours, this kind of art practice, especially in Latin American cities, can engage with people in an inclusive fashion, even if the topic is, for example, Afro-contemporary dance. But this in turn heralds another potential problem, which is that, precisely by virtue of distributing agency across racialised difference, there is the risk that the specific issue of racism might slide into the background and be overwhelmed by generalised images of marginalisation and disadvantage. There is a tricky balance to be achieved in terms of highlighting racism in an inclusive way. It may be that working with Afro dance (or other expressions of Blackness) in the community is a medium well suited to doing exactly that.

CONCLUSION

The two modes of anti-racist intervention through art that I have analysed are not mutually exclusive. They overlap and interweave in the work of specific artists and in specific interventions. Sankofa Danzafro's work gives examples of challenging stereotypes and of working with communities. Liliana Angulo Cortés started working with stereotypes and has moved towards working collaboratively with communities and other artists in projects that highlight the work of Afro-Colombian artists who have been marginalised by the art institutions of Colombia. Like many other Indigenous artists in Brazil, Denilson's work – of which the paintings I analysed are a small sample – is intimately connected to Indigenous communities. Within a single artistic intervention the same overlap occurs: the Sankofa Danzafro dance labs, which were an example of working in the community, also indirectly challenged stereotypes.

My argument has been that each mode puts into circulation affective forces in ways that have their own particular strengths and problems. I think that challenging stereotypes is a vital part of the decolonial and anti-racist struggle. I also think that this specific mode of intervention is perpetually haunted by the colonial and racist meanings of the very images it sets out to challenge. This is in part because of the recursive power of the structures and discourses of coloniality, which do not disappear but adapt and transform. And it is in part because of the way art objects circulate in relational networks, where the meanings that have accumulated through histories of coloniality and have stuck to the objects can be reactivated and recuperated in racist ways.

When artistic anti-racist practice foregrounds working with communities, the problem of haunting is less obvious. While the spaces in which the artists and communities work may be shaped by structures of coloniality (e.g. residential and job segregation along race–class lines), the racialised identities that emerge from the work tend to be less subject to objectification, because the agency of the artists and the art objects produced is distributed across a social network in the community that – especially in the context of Latin American cities – is heterogeneous and variegated. The affects that stick to these art objects as they circulate and create effects in the world are therefore likely to exceed the binary of racism versus anti-racism, while the racialised identities that are generated and their representations are also less subject to the hauntings that attend the art objects involved in challenging stereotypes. On the other hand, working with communities raises issues of co-optation by institutional forces and of how to stop the specificity of racism from slipping into the background.

Final Reflections

The book closes with some final reflections from three artists or groups of artists who kindly agreed to offer some thoughts on art and anti-racism and on their experiences with the CARLA project. The text from Arissana Pataxó – the Indigenous Brazilian artist who features in Chapter 2, who contributed to CARLA's online exhibition and who worked with Felipe Milanez as a research assistant in Brazil – was edited and translated from a conversation between her, Lúcia Sá and Jamille Pinheiro Dias. The contribution by Miriam Álvarez, Lorena Cañuqueo and Alejandra Egido – the Mapuche and Afro-Cuban people behind the Argentine theatre companies Mapuche Theatre Group El Katango and Teatro en Sepia, and co-authors of Chapter 6 – was written by them and translated and edited by Peter Wade. The piece from Wilson Borja – the Afro-Colombian graphic artist who features in Chapter 1 and who contributed to the online exhibition – was edited and translated by Peter Wade from audios recorded by Borja.

SOME THOUGHTS ON THE CARLA PROJECT AND INDIGENOUS ART

Arissana Pataxó

I'm always on tenterhooks when it comes to university-related projects because, ever since the expeditions of the nineteenth century, universities have been institutions that go into communities to extract knowledge. In the nineteenth century, naturalists went to find geological riches, medicines and knowledge that they could exploit. In the same way, today the university often seeks out knowledge that already exists in communities in order to transform it into concepts that it presents as new.

When I took part in the first online meetings of the CARLA project, I confess that I didn't really understand the project's objectives. I mean, I knew it had to do with racism, anti-racism and Indigenous art, but it wasn't clear to me what they wanted to do. I also knew that we were going to organise a meeting here in Salvador, and Felipe [Milanez] had invited me to be part of that organisation. With the pandemic, we couldn't organise the meeting, so we decided to use the resources in another way. And then, in the conversations to decide what to do, we felt the need to organise Indigenous artists to move art forward here in Bahia. There was a lot of participation by Indigenous artists, even those from Bahia, in exhibitions in the southeast of Brazil, but there was no such participation in the northeast, especially here in Bahia. That's why we decided to re-articulate the project to include more artists from Bahia, and the way that Felipe found to circumvent the university bureaucracy was to add them as researchers, since these artists were not linked to the university. So for four months, we had this presence of research artists at UFBA [Universidade Federal da Bahia] whose aim was to carry out some artistic work and plan an exhibition in Salvador that would bring the discussion of anti-racist art to the city. The idea was also that we could interact and create a collaborative network of conversations and dialogues. And it happened – what we did made it possible for the artists to work together: me, Glicéria Tupinambá, Yacunã Tuxá, Juliana Xukuru, Ziel Karapotó, Olinda Yawar Tupinambá.

It was from this articulation that we managed to organise the exhibition *Hãhãw: Anti-Racist Indigenous Art*, bringing the project's own concept of anti-racism to the exhibition at UFBA's Museum of Sacred Art, in Salvador, in November 2022, with the participation of artists who had links with UFBA as researchers, as well as others who had already taken part in the CARLA project, such as Denilson Baniwa, Naine Terena and Gustavo Caboco.[1] At first, we didn't call it an exhibition, but simply anti-racist Indigenous art, because we wanted to occupy other spaces, not just the museum. For example, we occupied the cinema of UFBA's Geological Museum, showing films by Denilson, Naine and Ziel, and the public space of the UFBA library, where Glicéria created a mural. We also occupied spaces by means of talks, bringing Juliana Xucuru and Ziel Karapotó to speak at UFBA. We spent six months organising these occupations.

---

[1] For the exhibition *Hãhãw: Arte indígena antirracista*, see https://arteindigena.ufba.br/.

It was only when the exhibition was ready that we were able to see everything that had been produced, despite the short time we had to organise it. Some of us finished some of our artworks the day before, and the dialogue with the museum was very difficult, because they wanted to see the photos of the works before the exhibition, and we had to say 'Calm down, the photos don't exist yet'. For me, that's normal, but they wanted to have the works three months in advance, so they could decide what would go in and what wouldn't, and for them it was a problem to have things at short notice. But we were sure about what we were going to do, what was going to be there. Of course, we also had a lot of uncertainties. Initially, the museum had given us a very small space, because an exhibition by an individual artist was scheduled for the same date. But suddenly they called us to say that the artist had cancelled the exhibition and the space would be open. That's when we occupied it. In other words, when everything seemed like it was going to go wrong, everything worked out and we ended up with this larger exhibition space. At that moment, I thought we wouldn't have enough works, so Yacunã and I brought some more.

After the exhibition was finished, the idea arose that it needed to circulate, to go to other places, and so it did. Under Ziel's curatorship, it travelled to Fortaleza, adding several local Indigenous artists, and from there to the Centro Cultural do Cariri [in Ceará state], where even more artists were added. Then came the proposal to bring it back to Salvador, to the Solar do Ferrão in Salvador, this time curated by Yacunã and with even more artists. If memory serves me right, there were more than twenty Indigenous artists in this final version. A much larger network of artists was created as a result of these circulations. What emerged was a kind of movement, with the younger artists taking on the curatorship of subsequent versions of the exhibition, nominating artists who became part of the group, and everyone, especially the younger ones, learning a lot from this process. Working together, we got know each other's abilities and inclinations, and this is very important because the art system depends on those who make referrals, on collaborative networks.

It was also important that the Brazilian arm of the project focussed exclusively on racism against Indigenous people, because there is already a lot of discussion in Brazil about racism against Black people and little discussion of racism against Indigenous people. And because there is little discussion, there is still the idea that there is no racism against Indigenous people. Even some Indigenous people end up not seeing everything that happens, not seeing the discrimination against a certain group or people as racism, and giving it other names. Over the last few years, I've seen a change and now this discussion about racism comes up more often, but we still need to do more. We suffer racism all the time. I remember, for example, one time when we were demonstrating in Porto Seguro [Bahia state] against one of the PECs.[2] My husband and I were in the bank [making a withdrawal]. We weren't wearing traditional clothing, but outside some people were coming from another village to board the river ferry, dressed [in traditional clothes] and singing. As we were leaving, a man who was also in the bank said: 'They've opened the corral'. My husband asked: 'What did you say?' I held onto my husband and the woman [who was with the man] realised that we hadn't liked the expression he had used and pulled him by the arm. There is a lot of fear on both sides. This is just one example. I could mention many more. We hear a lot of things all the time, and sometimes we swallow and keep quiet, and sometimes we speak.

Through the exchange with other artists from Latin America, promoted by the CARLA project in Manchester, I was able to see that the racism that happens to us is everywhere, and it happens almost always in the same way, with the question of territory being a central issue. Felipe Tuxá makes the point that the denial of our existence – that is, denying that this or that people exists, or denying that a people or an individual is Indigenous because of cultural transformations that are often imposed – is a way of guaranteeing a political monopoly over a territory, over a place. I saw these same issues in the presentations given in Manchester, mainly from the MCs, but also the performance of the women from the Mapuche theatre.[3] These are topics that we often discuss here in schools and communities. Often we don't call it racism or anti-racism, but these are discussions that are always in our midst, this question of the denial of identity and how people see us.

The event [in Manchester] also allowed me to think about other arts. I'd already had a lot of contact with rap. But I hadn't had any experience with theatre and I was very taken with it because I hadn't seen it before, although there are cultural activities in the communities that can be considered theatrical performances, but not in the more academic way that the Mapuche women did it. The use of memory in their work is very

[2] *Proposta de emenda à Constituição* (PEC): a proposed constitutional amendment, such as the ones to limit Indigenous land rights discussed in Chapter 2.
[3] Presentations and performances (by Eskina Qom, Teatro en Sepia and Grupo de Teatro Mapuche El Katango) given in CARLA's Festival of Anti-Racist and Decolonial Art in Manchester's Contact Theatre, 22 March 2022.

important, because although we think we always have to look to the present or the future, the memory of the past, of who we are, strengthens us and makes us better understand our common history.

I don't think that we, as artists, are going to provide any solutions to concrete problems, but I believe that art collaborates with discussions in the theoretical field, helping to break down the racist view that non-Indigenous society has of us. With this, it contributes to making changes in future policies. For example, in textbooks today I have seen a change in the way non-Indigenous schools have dealt with the whole question of the arts, and this has happened through Indigenous arts. And thanks to this, the way of talking about Indigenous people has changed. Textbooks are obliged to address this issue, and they have done so through the works of Indigenous artists, Indigenous writers, Indigenous filmmakers and Indigenous musicians.

Some teachers from pre-school to high school have also sought me out, and through my works, they end up addressing the theme of the Pataxó people and Indigenous themes in general. I think this will create young people with a new way of thinking about Indigenous peoples, who will no longer think that the Indigenous person is the one in [the stories about] Pedro Álvares Cabral [the European 'discoverer' of Brazil], but who will be able to imagine that they will study with Indigenous people, that they can, in the future, have a consultation with an Indigenous doctor, and know that we are part of society, not something excluded. I think art has changed this since we started participating in the circuit [of the art world]. Of course, there is a bubble of people who attend and have access to those spaces, but at the same time the circuit ends up creating visibility, and this visibility leads to discussion in other places, such as schools. So I think that the more we, as artists, create articulations like the one we created with the CARLA project, the more we are together in these collaborative networks, the more power we have to bring these discussions to the arts.

Another change I've seen is the presence of Indigenous art in universities. When I started at university, Indigenous art was unheard of, so when I now see professors inviting me and other Indigenous artists to read texts by Davi Kopenawa and Ailton Krenak, I realise how much the university has changed in the ten years since I started my degree. Before, Indigenous issues were only dealt with in the field of anthropology.

That's why I think education is still a fundamental tool, especially in relation to children. I've noticed, for example, that children are asking more sophisticated and elaborate questions, and are no longer asking such racist questions as we used to get when we visited schools. Today I see kids asking more critical and less racist questions.

The articulation that led us to work together at UFBA to organise the exhibition was important in breaking down our individualities and strengthening us as a group around common actions to promote anti-racist art. Although our works discuss particular themes related to each of our peoples, almost everything we do can be summarised around the territorial question: the murders, the struggles of leaders, the violence and changes our communities have to face – all of this is linked to the question of land. The territorial issue is at the centre of discussions about racism against Indigenous peoples, and this is what the exhibition *Hãhãw: Anti-Racist Indigenous Art* showed.

CARLA: FINAL REFLECTIONS

Miriam Álvarez, Lorena Cañuqueo and Alejandra Egido

While discussing among ourselves what we wanted to say in these final reflections, we came across a photograph (see Figure C.1) that resonated with us. We saw in it a possible hint of the relationships between the Mapuche population and the Afro-descendant population that existed

FIGURE C.1 Photo of Mapuche women and children by Cristián Enrique Valck (1826–1899); probable date 1870; probable location Valdivia, Chile (source: Carlotta database, Swedish Museums of World Culture).

at various historical moments, relationships that we reactivated in the collaborations and dramatic texts that we created for CARLA. The photo was taken in about 1870 by Cristián Enrique Valck (1826–1899), a German immigrant to Chile, who established a studio in the southern city of Valdivia. The image caught our attention due to the very dark skin of the child in the centre. What might explain it? History relates that in colonial times Valdivia had a substantial Afro-descendant presence, made up of Black prisoners and soldiers, brought from areas further north, including Peru, and forced to work as labourers constructing fortifications in the city. A 1749 census reveals the coexistence in Valdivia of Black and Mapuche people and, while the authorities paid Mapuche people to hand over captured Black escapees, it is quite possible that intimate relations existed as well.[4] We also know that research is being done on how Afro people escaped enslavement by fleeing to Indigenous and Mapuche communities (Carmona 2024; Edwards 2020). Although in the case of this photo, it is a speculative theory that needs investigation, it helps us to stay connected, thinking together. This image for us is a sign of those alliances and relationships and above all it allows us to reconstruct that past and activate other chosen relationships.

To put Black and Indigenous bodies on the stage in Argentine theatres, as we did during the CARLA project, is to propose the representation of a corporeality made invisible by the constructions of whiteness in this country. The widespread discourse that Argentinians 'descended from ships' (foregrounding only migrants from Europe) has been reproduced over many years by different presidents and personalities. A large part of society is convinced that Argentina has no Indigenous population. They also affirm that there are no Blacks in the country, because 'they all died of yellow fever', as Alejandra Egido, director of the Teatro en Sepia company, jokingly says. These statements, although ridiculous and lacking any basis in history, are not usually questioned and form part of recurrent stereotypes within the Argentine racist imaginary. In the present, this imaginary even forms part of the government's own agendas.

The CARLA Project, in which the members of the Mapuche Theatre Group El Katango and the Teatro en Sepia company participated between 2020 and 2022, was a framework that led to a novel encounter for both teams. Although we belong to racialised and strongly stigmatised groups, our work agendas had not come into contact until we were

[4] See Museo de Sitio Castillo de Niebla, 'Historia', www.museodeniebla.gob.cl/643/w3-propertyvalue-42964.html?_noredirect=1.

invited to come together by our colleague, Dr Ana Vivaldi, researcher of the CARLA team. Although the beginning of our relationship was marked by the COVID-19 pandemic that led to quarantines and lockdowns, this did not prevent us from communicating and even creating dramatic texts together, such as 'Como dos gotas de agua', about two women, one Mapuche, the other Black, both displaced from their homes, who encounter one another in transit; and *Fuego amigo*, which features a Mapuche woman and a Black woman working alongside each other as city employees.[5]

Sustained over many months by virtual means, these encounters led us, with jokes, stories and anecdotes, to reflect among the four of us – two Indigenous women from Río Negro province (Patagonia), an Afro-descendant woman who is also a migrant in the city of Buenos Aires, and a white Latina woman from Argentina who lives in Canada – on racism, anti-racism and possible ways of dealing with it poetically in the theatre. We were full of similar stories that spoke of dispossession, forced displacement, invisibilisation and the ways in which our peoples related to their territories, which we shared in conversations in each virtual meeting, and we all thought: why didn't we get together before?

Navigating between terror and tenderness, by telling our stories we conjured up our ancestors, some of them quite remote. Enquiring into these relationships and links allows us to bring them into the present. In this way, the past and the present blend together, or rather, they interrelate, because they are in permanent communication. In our narratives, the 'sad stories' that our own families repressed – the forced relocations, the loss of land, the silencing of our ceremonies and ancestral knowledge – appeared and still appear. This happened and continues to happen to us because we are Mapuche and Afro-descendants, justification enough in the coloniser's view. We would come to this conclusion and burst out laughing, because we could not find a better way to cope with the 'sad stories'. They are traces that remain in our souls and in our bodies, but which have also generated new ways of understanding ourselves and formulating our desires.

Alejandra explained to us about *palenques* and what the *quilombos* mean for Afro-descendants, and Miriam and Lorena told of the

---

[5] See Chapter 6. For *Como dos gotas de agua* (Like Two Peas in a Pod), see also www.digitalexhibitions.manchester.ac.uk/s/carla-en/page/the-katango; and for *Fuego amigo* (Friendly Fire), see www.digitalexhibitions.manchester.ac.uk/s/carla-en/page/teatro-en-sepia.

deportations of Mapuche people of all ages from Patagonia to Buenos Aires.[6] Each shared idea led us to enquire into the representations that organise common-sense understandings. For example, in Argentina, the notion of *quilombo* does not refer to those spaces built by the enslaved Blacks who fled to live in freedom and in an organised way. On the contrary, the word *quilombo* is used often in a derogatory way to refer to disorder and chaos. What would happen if we knew that they were actually socio-political spaces of freedom? Alejandra told Miriam and Lorena that 'the first escaped slaves must have been owners of territories here in Argentina'. Miriam and Lorena shared stories of journeys of thousands of kilometres on foot and massive deportations of Indigenous people who were taken from their territory and forced to serve those who now hold the economic power in this country. And we also talked about how absurd it is that every time we claim rights, people say: 'the Mapuche are Chileans'. As if, before this time, borders had existed and as if this historical aberration could erase the violence committed against the Mapuche people. The conversation came to an end when Alejandra said: 'This is going to need another cup of coffee.' And yes, we could go on for hours and hours over coffee or *yerba mate*, because this long history of family and community relations runs through us, but it also allows us to generate a 'we' today, in the present. It is a way of generating a sense of belonging in this country that marks us from time to time as not being part of it, despite the fact that, in the case of Miriam and Lorena, we were born in this territory. It is like living in diaspora within one's own territory. As Alejandra put it in her script for *Fuego amigo*: 'I don't know how I can be moved by the anthem of a country that doesn't recognise me. How ridiculous, please!'

We reflected together on the political conjunctures that affected us before and during our journey in the project. Far from abating, there were acts of intense violence against our collectives, some of them promoted by the state itself, which reactivated a long memory of wounds, but also of struggles. But we also critically analysed our spaces of activism. We saw that our peoples, or the Indigenous and Afro-descendant organisations and political movements that fight for our rights within the institutions of the Argentine state, were each moving along their own path, without any alliance or link that we were aware of. Until our participation in the CARLA project, we had not had the opportunity to reflect on an anti-racist agenda linking Mapuche and Afro-descendants

---

[6] For discussions of *palenques* and *quilombos*, see Chapters 1, 4 and 7.

in Argentina. Each of us, Alejandra, Lorena and Miriam, participated in these political activisms. However, always being attentive to the problems of our own collectives had prevented us from observing the realities of other people who are also racialised.

We believe that this is the great contribution that the CARLA project has given us by allowing us to meet, to dialogue, to bring to light our pain and share the possibility of reversing it through laughter and creativity; and to propose approaches, albeit incipient, within our spaces that can mobilise projects to denaturalise and challenge racism in our country.

SOME THOUGHTS ON ART, ANTI-RACISM AND CARLA

Wilson Borja

Something that has stayed with me ever since I read his work is what the African-American artist Romare Bearden called the dilemma of the Black artist.[7] He asks whether, if we are in fact artists, do we have to be talking all the time about problems of race and discrimination? It was always a disjuncture for him. But in the end he says: If not us, then who? I think that's always echoing in my head and, in fact, I think this also emerged in the CARLA project. And the reason is that these issues actually traverse our bodies. So the main way of manifesting this as artists is simply through what we do. I think that the conversations we had in CARLA always revolved around these themes – or at least I saw them from this point of view – because racism penetrates us, it mistreats us, it murders us. We have to talk about these things, yes, but what would happen if we didn't? If it wasn't us, who would do it? This is precisely what the painter Romare Bearden talks about, having been part of the civil rights movement in the United States: If not us, then who? Who has the power, who has the right, who has the will to talk about these things?

These things are deeply uncomfortable and painful, but at the same time, extremely important and relevant, if we think about the current global context, where fascism, which has never ceased to exist, is now rampant and brazen across the planet. I believe that work that tackles anti-racism through art is more important than ever, and that it will always be there, unleashing the forces of struggle. Whether we like it or not, consciously or not, we artists decide how to show racism up and confront it. It is a form of struggle, it is a way of fighting for the fundamental

---

[7] On Bearden, see National Gallery of Art (2003).

rights of many people on the planet. I don't know if an image or an artistic project will change things, but it does mean that there is resistance, a way to fight against this structure that eats people alive.

In terms of the relationship between art and anti-racism and the project that we have been developing with the Aguaturbia Collective – the IRA Archive – I think that CARLA's project generates via its portal, its web page, its archive, a way of being able to record and effectively share this information with all the people who didn't know or don't know and don't understand.[8] They think racism is just a local thing and I guess this is the same in different countries. From the conversations we were able to have and the meetings we had with the rest of the people in the project, it's about being able to visualise a problem that crosses borders or rather that is not defined by borders. In fact, this colonial phenomenon crosses all of our lives, it crosses the entire globe. When one can effectively materialise, condense, archive or put in one place the various projects that address these issues, it is a very important tool. It has been very useful for me precisely in my role as an educator, because then it is not just me telling a story, me talking about a problem, and instead I can provide a tool, so that anyone who is interested in understanding a little more about these issues has some grounding.

I suppose surely this would have been considered when the project was designed, but it would have been very interesting to be able to hear voices from Ecuador, from Peru, from different countries in Latin America, Central America, and hear how the nuances of these issues effectively transgress borders. But I think that one of CARLA's important contributions is precisely to have condensed and generated a platform where people can learn about different experiences, which together give much more strength to what could be thought of as an anti-racist movement from the point of view of artistic practices.

Another aspect of the relationship between art and anti-racism that is very clear to me is that, if we look at the practices of artists who occupy racialised bodies, we are always effectively questioning and challenging oppressive structures. From our practices, we find tools that effectively allow us to engage in such conversations. During the process of working on the CARLA project, the conversations I have had with different people have been enriched by the fact that I can talk not only about my experience, the local experience, what happened to me, the anecdotes,

---

[8] On Aguaturbia and IRA (Imaginación Radical Afro), see Chapter 1. See also www.digitalexhibitions.manchester.ac.uk/s/carla-en/page/agua-turbia.

the trauma, the problems of growing up with these structures, but also by the fact that I can show them that this is a reality that crosses the borders of different countries. I think that one of the most relevant contributions of the project has been precisely this: for us, or for me in particular, to be able to weave these networks that started out being very local, understanding that in other places there are other kinds of struggles. Being able to see them, talk about them, discuss them first hand with the people who are actually doing them was very interesting and very important. I think it was a driving force, it was something that gave fuel to what we were already doing, to what we were doing in the Aguaturbia Collective, and in conversations with Liliana [Angulo Cortés] and in various projects. It effectively adds other dimensions to everything I'm doing.

In conversations with Liliana and with other artists in the Aguaturbia Collective – with Paola [Lucumi], with Natalia [Mosquera Valencia], with Loretta [Moreno] – the question often arises that if we didn't have to talk about the problems of racism on the planet, what would we actually be doing in our practices? Because we are not only elaborating or working on anti-racist projects. But in a way, it has become an effective and reliable tool that allows us, on the basis of our practices, to question and challenge the structures of racism, to generate conversations, to present the issues to people who had no idea that these things even exist. In my case, I have tried to do this using images. But I think that the CARLA project adds to those projects that were already in development by giving them a boost, like a push, a more solid base, precisely by thinking about the meeting of people from different countries, different places. It shows that racism is a global problem and not an anecdote that happens to one person, who suffers, but ends up talking about the problem in isolation. I think that weaving these networks and these dialogues strengthens what we do and allows us to continue working, and to continue generating these discussions.

Bibliography

Acevedo Latorre, Eduardo, Charles Saffray and Edouard Francois André, eds. 1968. *Geografía pintoresca de Colombia: la Nueva Granada vista por los viajeros franceses del siglo XIX*. Bogotá: Litografía Arco.
Adamovsky, Ezequiel. 2012. El color de la nación argentina. Conflictos y negociaciones por la definición de un *ethnos* nacional, de la crisis al Bicentenario. *Jahrbuch für Geschichte Lateinamerikas* 49(1): 343–364.
Adamovsky, Ezequiel. 2016. Race and class through the visual culture of Peronism. In *Rethinking Race in Modern Argentina*, edited by Paulina Alberto and Eduardo Elena, 155–183. Cambridge: Cambridge University Press.
Adamovsky, Ezequiel. 2017. Ethnic nicknaming: 'Negro' as a term of endearment and vicarious blackness in Argentina. *Latin American and Caribbean Ethnic Studies* 12(3): 273–289.
Adamovsky, Ezequiel. 2019. *El gaucho indómito: de Martín Fierro a Perón, el emblema imposible de una nación desgarrada*. Buenos Aires: Siglo Veintiuno.
Adamovsky, Ezequiel. 2020. *Historia de la Argentina: biografía de un país. Desde la conquista española hasta nuestros días*. Buenos Aires: Crítica.
Adamovsky, Ezequiel. 2022. Comparsas de (o con) afrodescendientes en el carnaval de Buenos Aires, 1869–1926: Relevamiento, descripción y aproximación al problema de las interraciales. *Revista de Historia Americana y Argentina* 57(1): 37–69.
Adi, Hakin. 2018. *Pan-Africanism: A History*. London: Bloomsbury Publishing.
Agudelo, Carlos. 2005. *Multiculturalismo en Colombia. Política, inclusión y exclusión de poblaciones negras*. Bogotá: Colección la Carreta Social.
Aguiló, Ignacio. 2018. *The Darkening Nation: Race, Neoliberalism and Crisis in Argentina*. Cardiff: University of Wales Press.
Aguiló, Ignacio and Ana Vivaldi. 2023. Race and the shantytown in a raceless country: Negros villeros, whiteness and urban space in Argentina. *Latin American and Caribbean Ethnic Studies* 18(4): 551–573.
Ahmed, Sara. 2004. Affective economies. *Social Text* 22(2): 117–139.
Ahmed, Sara. 2005. The politics of bad feeling. *Australian Journal of Critical Race and Whiteness Studies* 1(1): 72–85.

Ahmed, Sara. 2015. *The Cultural Politics of Emotion*. 2nd ed. London: Routledge.
Alberto, Paulina L. 2022. *Black Legend: The Many Lives of Raúl Grigera and the Power of Racial Storytelling in Argentina*. Cambridge: Cambridge University Press.
Alberto, Paulina L. and Eduardo Elena, eds. 2016. *Rethinking Race in Modern Argentina*. Cambridge: Cambridge University Press.
Alencar, José Martiniano de. 1883. *O Guarani*. Rio de Janeiro: Garnier.
Alencar, José Martiniano de. 1979. *Iracema*. Edited by M. Cavalcanti Proença. São Paulo: EDUSP.
Álvarez, Miriam. 2021. Prácticas escénicas mapuche contemporáneas: Poéticas de aboriginalidad en disputa. PhD thesis, Universidad Nacional de Rio Negro, Rio Negro.
Álvarez, Miriam and Laura Kropff Causa. 2021. Prácticas escénicas mapuche contemporáneas: un diálogo entre la antropología, el teatro y el activismo. In *XII Congreso Argentino de Antropología Social (CAAS)*: 1–18. https://sedici.unlp.edu.ar/handle/10915/134407
Álvarez, Miriam and Laura Kropff Causa. 2022. La diáspora puelche en la obra de teatro Tayiñ Kuify Kvpan. *Cadernos de Arte e Antropologia* 11(1): 48–65.
Álvarez, Miriam and Lorena Cañuqueo. 2018. Prácticas escénicas mapuche contemporáneas o cómo pensar las propuestas políticas del arte en contextos de violencia estatal. *Revista Transas: Letras y Arte de América Latina*. https://revistatransas.unsam.edu.ar/practicas-escenicas-mapuches-contemporaneas/
Anderson, Ben. 2009. Affective atmospheres. *Emotion, Space and Society* 2(2): 77–81.
Anderson, Judith M. 2018. The impossible Black Argentine political subject. In *Comparative Racial Politics in Latin America*, edited by Kwame Dixon and Ollie A. Johnson III, 211–228. London: Routledge.
Andrada, Damián. 2016. *Hacia un periodismo indígena*. Buenos Aires: Ediciones Universidad de El Salvador.
Andrade, Mário de. 1996. *Macunaíma. O Herói Sem Nenhum Caráter*. Edited by Telê Ancona Lopez. São Paulo: Archivos; Edusp.
Andrews, George Reid. 1980. *The Afro-Argentines of Buenos Aires, 1800–1900*. Madison: University of Wisconsin Press.
Andrews, Kehinde. 2018. *Back to Black: Retelling Black Radicalism for the 21st Century*. London: Zed Books.
Anzaldúa, Gloria. 1987. *Borderlands/La Frontera: The New Mestiza*. San Francisco: Aunt Lute Books.
Appelbaum, Nancy P. 2016. *Mapping the Country of Regions: The Chorographic Commission of Nineteenth-Century Colombia*. Chapel Hill: University of North Carolina Press.
Appelbaum, Nancy P., Anne S. Macpherson and Karin A. Rosemblatt, eds. 2003. *Race and Nation in Modern Latin America*. Chapel Hill: University of North Carolina Press.
Arboleda Quiñónez, Santiago. 2011. Le han florecido nuevas estrellas al cielo: suficiencias íntimas y clandestinización del pensamiento afrocolombiano. PhD thesis, Área de Estudios Sociales y Globales, Universidad Andina Simón Bolívar, Quito.

Ariza Aguilar, Margarita. 2015. *Blanco porcelana*. Barranquilla: Alcaldia de Barranquilla. https://issuu.com/margaritaarizaa/docs/bp-censurado-jun4
Austin, John L. 1990. *Cómo hacer cosas con palabras*. Barcelona: Paidós.
Ávila Domínguez, Freddy. 2019. Las representaciones de Cartagena de Indias y Palenque de San Basilio (Colombia) en el discurso turístico, 2005–2018. PhD thesis, University of Salamanca.
Badiane, Mamadou. 2010. *The Changing Face of Afro-Caribbean Cultural Identity: Negrismo and Négritude*. Lanham, MD: Lexington Books.
Baker, Gabriel, Sara Kindon and Emily Beausoleil. 2022. Danced movement in human geographic research: A methodological discussion. *Geography Compass* 16(8): e12653.
Baniwa, Denilson. 2018. Talk as part of workshop on Indigenous contemporary art (with Jaider Esbell), at Casa do Povo, São Paulo. November 2018.
Baniwa, Denilson. 2021. Talk (online) at the workshop 'Metamorfosis y perspectivismo en la narrativa latinoamericana'. 12 November 2021, University of Zurich. www.pim.uzh.ch/apps/cms/pageframes/events_files.php?f=70.pdf
Barber, Benjamin. 2011. Patriotism, autonomy and subversion: The role of the arts in democratic change. *Salmagundi* 170/171: 109–130.
Baudemann, Kristina. 2016. Indigenous futurisms in North American Indigenous art: The transforming visions of Ryan Singer, Daniel McCoy, Topaz Jones, Marla Allison and Debra Yepa-Pappan. *Extrapolation* 57(1–2): 117–150.
Beasley-Murray, Jon. 2010. *Posthegemony: Political Theory and Latin America*. Minneapolis: University of Minnesota Press.
Beliso-De Jesús, Aisha M. 2015. *Electric Santería: Racial and Sexual Assemblages of Transnational Religion*. New York: Columbia University Press.
Bell, Morgan F. 2011. Some thoughts on 'taking' pictures. Imaging 'Indians' and the counter-narratives of visual sovereignty. *Great Plains Quarterly* 31(2): 85–104.
Benites, Sandra. 2021. Curando com a arte indígena contemporânea. Online discussion. Pinacoteca de São Paulo and CARLA. https://youtube.com/live/GWIbftdAAlc
Benveniste, Émile. 1971. *Problems in General Linguistics*. Coral Gables, FL: University of Miami Press.
Berg, Ulla D. and Ana Y. Ramos-Zayas. 2015. Racializing affect: A theoretical proposition. *Current Anthropology* 56(5): 654–677.
Besserer Alatorre, Federico. 2014. Regímenes de sentimientos y la subversión del orden sentimental: hacia una economía política de los afectos. *Nueva Antropología* 27(81): 55–76.
Birenbaum Quintero, Michael. 2006: La 'música pacífica' al Pacífico violento: música, multiculturalismo y marginalización en el Pacífico negro colombiano. *Revista Transcultural de Música*, 10. www.redalyc.org/articulo.oa?id=82201002
Birenbaum Quintero, Michael. 2019. *Rites, Rights and Rhythms: A Genealogy of Musical Meaning in Colombia's Black Pacific*. New York: Oxford University Press.
Boas, Franz. 1930. *The Religion of the Kwakiutl Indians*. Part I: Texts. Vancouver: British Columbia University Press.
Boros, Diana. 2012. *Creative Rebellion for the Twenty-First Century: The Importance of Public and Interactive Art to Political Life in America*. New York: Palgrave Macmillan US.

Bourdieu, Pierre. 1977. *Outline of a Theory of Practice*. Cambridge: Cambridge University Press.
Braz Bomfim de Souza, Arissana and Felipe Milanez. 2023. Ecologias antirracistas na Bahia: retratos da luta Pataxó contra o ecocídio e o genocídio. *Tellus* 23(50): 163–190.
Brennan, Teresa. 2004. *The Transmission of Affect*. Ithaca, NY: Cornell University Press.
Briones, Claudia. 1998. *(Meta) cultura del estado-nación y estado de la (meta) cultura*. Brasília: Departamento de Antropologia Universidade de Brasília.
Briones, Claudia. 2002. Viviendo a la sombra de naciones sin sombra: poéticas y políticas de (auto) marcación de 'lo indígena' en las disputas contemporáneas por el derecho a una educación intercultural. In *Interculturalidad y política: desafíos y posibilidades*, edited by Norma Fuller, 381–417. Lima: Red para el Desarrollo de las Ciencias Sociales en el Perú.
Briones, Claudia. 2003. Mestizaje y blanqueamiento como coordenadas de aboriginalidad y nación en Argentina. *Runa* XXIII: 61–88.
Briones, Claudia, ed. 2005. *Cartografías argentinas: políticas indigenistas y formaciones provinciales de alteridad*. Buenos Aires: Antropofagia.
Briones, Claudia, Lorena Cañuqueo, Laura Kropff and Miguel Leuman. 2007. A perspective from the South of the South (Patagonia, Argentina). *Latin American and Caribbean Ethnic Studies* 2(1): 69–91.
Brizuela, Natalia. 2019. Global? Contemporary? Latin American? Time matters in/and art today. *Revista Hispánica Moderna* 72(2): 135–147.
Brown, Jonathan C. 2011. *A Brief History of Argentina*. 2nd ed. New York: Checkmark Books.
Bryan, T. Avril. 1988. García-Márquez' perception of the Black as seen in *Love in the Time of Cholera*. *Afro-Hispanic Review* 7(1/2/3): 5–9.
Buck-Morss, Susan. 1992. Aesthetics and anaesthetics: Walter Benjamin's artwork essay reconsidered. *October* 62: 3–41.
Bushnell, David. 1993. *The Making of Modern Colombia: A Nation in Spite of Itself*. Berkeley: University of California Press.
Butler, Judith. 1993. *Bodies That Matter: On the Discursive Limits of Sex*. New York: Routledge.
Butler, Judith. 2002. *Cuerpos que importan: Sobre los límites materiales y discursivos del sexo*. Buenos Aires: Paidos.
Caboco, Gustavo. 2020. O ser humano se reconhece como ser humano? In *Véxoa: Nós Sabemos*, edited by Naine Terena, 151–160. São Paulo: Pinacoteca do Estado.
Caggiano, Sergio. 2012. *El sentido común visual: Disputas en torno a género, raza, y clase en imágenes de circulación pública*. Buenos Aires: Miño y Dávila.
Caminha, Pero Vaz de. 1974. *Carta a El-Rei Dom Manuel Sobre o Achamento do Brasil: 10 de Maio de 1500*. Lisboa: Imprensa Nacional; Casa da Moeda.
Cañuqueo, Lorena. 2010. Pewma: la memoria de gira por su territorio. In *Teatro mapuche: sueños, memoria y política*, edited by Laura Kropff, 52–72. Buenos Aires: Ediciones Artes Escénicas.
Cañuqueo, Lorena. 2015. El territorio relevado, el territorio disputado: Apuntes sobre la implementación de Ley nacional 26.160 en Río Negro, Argentina. *Revista de Geografía Norte Grande* 62: 11–28.

Cañuqueo, Lorena and Laura Kropff. 2002. Campaña de Autoafirmación Mapuche Wefkvletuyiñ – Estamos Resurgiendo. *Cuadernos del Hemispheric Institute of Performance and Politics*. New York University. https://hemisphericinstitute.org/en/enco7-home/enco7-performances2/item/963-enco7-mapuche-theater-project.html

Cañuqueo, Lorena, Laura Kropff, Pilar Pérez and Julieta Wallace, eds. 2019. *La tierra de los otros*. Río Negro: Editorial UNRN.

Cárdenas, Roosbelinda. 2012. Multicultural politics for Afro-Colombians: An articulation 'without guarantees'. In *Black Social Movements in Latin America: From Monocultural Mestizaje to Multiculturalism*, edited by Jean Muteba Rahier, 113–134. New York: Palgrave Macmillan.

Cárdenas, Roosbelinda. 2024. *Raising Two Fists: Struggles for Black Citizenship in Multicultural Colombia*. Stanford, CA: Stanford University Press.

Carlos Fregoso, Gisela. 2024. Anti-racist alliances and solidarities: Typologies, cases and experiences. *Ethnic and Racial Studies* 47(11): 2433–2455.

Carmona Jiménez, Javiera. 2024. Pensar el patrimonio afrodiaspórico en los museos chilenos. Perspectivas sobre la puesta en orden y la puesta en escena de objetos y cuerpos decolonizados. *Revista de Humanidades* 49: 29–55.

Carrasco, Morita. 2000. *Los derechos de los pueblos indígenas en Argentina*. Copenhagen: IWGIA.

Caze, Marguerite and Henry Martyn Lloyd. 2011. Editors' introduction: Philosophy and the 'affective turn'. *Parrhesia* 13: 1–13.

Chacón Bernal, Carolina. 2021. Museos, etnoeducación y antirracismos. La exposición *La consentida es: La familia negra*. *Intervención* 12(23): 114–134.

Chamosa, Oscar. 2010. *The Argentine Folklore Movement: Sugar Elites, Criollo Workers, and the Politics of Cultural Nationalism, 1900–1955*. Tucson: University of Arizona Press.

Chernoff, John M. 1979. *African Rhythm and African Sensibility: Aesthetics and Social Action in African Musical Idioms*. Chicago: University of Chicago Press.

Citro, Silvia. 2017. Cuando «los descendientes de los barcos» comenzaron a mutar. Corporalidades y sonoridades multiculturales en el bicentenario argentino. *Revista de Antropología Iberoamericana* 12(1): 53–75.

Citro, Silvia and Soledad Torres Agüero. 2015. Multiculturalidad e imaginarios identitarios en la música y la danza. *Alteridades* 25(50): 117–128.

Clifford, James and George E. Marcus. 2010. *Writing Culture: The Poetics and Politics of Ethnography*. Berkeley: University of California Press.

CODHES. 2013. La crisis humanitaria en Colombia persiste: El Pacífico en disputa. Informe de desplazamiento forzado en 2012. *Documentos CODHES 26*. Bogotá: Consultoría para los Derechos Humanos y el Desplazamiento.

Colectivo GUIAS. 2010. *Antropología del genocidio. Identificación y restitución: 'colecciones' de restos humanos en el Museo de La Plata*. La Plata: Ediciones de la Campana.

Córdoba, Amalia. 2011. Estéticas enraizadas: aproximaciones al video indígena en América Latina. *Revista Comunicación y Medios* 24: 81–107.

Cornelio, José Marcellino and Robin Wright. 1999. *Waferinaipe ianheke. A Sabedoria dos Nossos Antepassados: Histórias dos Hohodene e dos Walipere-Dakenai do Rio Aiari*. São Gabriel da Cachoeira, Amazonas, Brasil: ACIRA/FOIRN.

Correa Angulo, Carlos. 2024. La enunciación antirracista en las practicas artísticas en Colombia: diálogos e in-comprensiones en la investigación colaborativa. *Boletín de Antropología, Universidad de Antioquia* 39(67): 59–89.

Correa Angulo, Carlos and Rossana Alarcón Velásquez. 2024. Subversión, irrupción e interpelación de las audiencias: los efectos de la práctica artística antirracista en Colombia. *Cuadernos de Música, Artes Visuales y Artes Escénicas* 19(1): 202–221.

Corrêa, Edgar Nunes (Edgar Kanaykõ). 2019. Etnovisão: O Olhar Indígena que Atravessa a Lente. MA thesis in Anthropology, Universidade Federal de Minas Gerais, Belo Horizonte.

Coscia, Jorge. 2011. *La encrucijada del Bicentenario: apuntes para comprender y profundizar el proyecto nacional y popular*. Buenos Aires: Peña Lillo; Ediciones Continente.

Cox, Rupert, Andrew Irving and Christopher Wright, eds. 2016. *Beyond Text? Critical Practices and Sensory Anthropology*. Manchester: Manchester Univerity Press.

Cragnolini, Alejandra. 2006. Articulaciones entre violencia social, significante sonoro y subjetividad: la cumbia 'villera' en Buenos Aires. *Revista Transcultural de Música, Transcultural Musical Review* 10. www.sibetrans.com/trans/articulo/147/articulaciones-entre-violencia-social-significante-sonoro-y-subjetividad-la-cumbia-villera-en-buenos-aires

Crenshaw, Kimberlé. 1991. Mapping the margins: Intersectionality, identity politics, and violence against women of color. *Stanford Law Review* 43(6): 1241–1299.

Cristancho Alvarez, Raúl and Mercedes Angola. 2006. *Viaje sin mapa: representaciones afro en el arte contemporáneo colombiano*. Bogotá: Banco de la República.

Cruz, Felipe Sotto Maior. 2019. Povos indígenas, radicalização e políticas afirmativas no ensino superior. In *Tecendo Redes Antirracistas. Áfricas, Brasis, Portugal*, edited by Anderson Ribeiro Oliva, Marjorie Nogueira Chaves, Renísia Cristina Garcia Filice and Wanderson Flor do Nascimento, 147–161. Belo Horizonte, São Paulo: Autêntica.

Cunha, Manuela Carneiro da. 2018. Índios na Constituição. *Novos Estudos CEBRAP* 37: 429–443.

Cunin, Elisabeth. 2003. *Identidades a flor de piel. Lo 'negro' entre apariencias y pertenencias: categorías raciales y mestizaje en Cartagena (Colombia)*. Bogotá: Instituto Colombiano de Antropología e Historia, Universidad de los Andes, Instituto Francés de Estudios Andinos, Observatorio del Caribe Colombiano.

Cunin, Elisabeth. 2007. De Kinshasa a Cartagena, pasando por París: itinerarios de una 'música negra', la champeta. *Aguaita* 15–16: 176–192.

Da Silva Ferreira, Denise. 2007. *Toward a Global Idea of Race*. Minneapolis: University of Minnesota Press.

Da Silva Ferreira, Denise. 2022. *Unpayable Debt*. Cambridge, MA: MIT Press.

Danto, Arthur. 2007. *Unnatural Wonders: Essays from the Gap between Art and Life*. New York: Columbia University Press.

Davis, Angela and Gina Dent. 2020. *Visualizing Abolition with Angela Y. Davis and Gina Dent*. UC Santa Cruz: Institute of the Arts and Sciences. www.youtube.com/watch?v=gjc9_Erax7I

de la Fuente, Alejandro. 2008. The new Afro-Cuban cultural movement and the debate on race in contemporary Cuba. *Journal of Latin American Studies* 40(4): 697–720.

de la Fuente, Alejandro. 2018. Afro-Latin American art. In *Afro-Latin American Studies: An Introduction*, edited by Alejandro de la Fuente and George Reid Andrews, 348–405. Cambridge: Cambridge University Press.

Deans-Smith, Susan. 2009. 'Dishonor in the hands of Indians, Spaniards, and Blacks': Painters and the (racial) politics of painting in early modern Mexico. In *Race and Classification: The Case of Mexican America*, edited by Ilona Katzew and Susan Deans-Smith, 43–72. Stanford: Stanford University Press.

Deleuze, Gilles and Félix Guattari. 1983. *Anti-Oedipus: Capitalism and Schizophrenia*. Minneapolis: University of Minnesota Press.

Delrio, Walter. 2005. *Memorias de expropiación. Sometimiento e incorporación indígena en la Patagonia (1872–1943)*. Bernal: Editorial de la Universidad Nacional de Quilmes.

Delrio, Walter. 2010. Del no evento al genocidio. Pueblos originarios y políticas de Estado en Argentina. *Eadem Utraque Europa* 6(10–11): 219–254.

Dennis, Christopher. 2014. Locating hip hop's place within Latin American cultural studies. *Alter/nativas, Latin American Cultural Studies Journal* 2: 1–20. https://alternativas.osu.edu/en/issues/spring-2014/essays1/dennis.html

Di Matteo, Angela. 2019. Teatro mapuche en Argentina: la memoria onírica del genocidio en *Pewma* de Miriam Álvarez. *Confluenze* 11(2): 339–354.

Dillon, Grace L. 2012. Imagining Indigenous futurisms. In *Walking the Clouds: An Anthology of Indigenous Science Fiction*, edited by Grace L. Dillon, 1–15. Tucson: University of Arizona Press.

Douglas, Gilbert, Adrienne Sichel, Adedayo M. Liadi, Ketty Noël, Reggie Danster, Augusto Cuvilas and Faustin Linyekula. 2006. Under fire: Defining a contemporary African dance aesthetic – can it be done? *Critical Arts* 20(2): 102–115.

Dubatti, Jorge. 2016. Teatro-matriz y teatro liminal: la liminalidad constitutiva del acontecimiento teatral. *Cena* 19. https://doi.org/10.22456/2236-3254.65486

Eagleton, Terry. 1990. *The Ideology of the Aesthetic*. Oxford: Blackwell.

Eddo-Lodge, Reni. 2021. *Por qué no hablo con blancos sobre racismo*. Barcelona: Ediciones Península.

Edwards, Erika D. 2018. The making of a White nation: The disappearance of the Black population in Argentina. *History Compass* 16(7): e12456.

Edwards, Erika D. 2020. *Hiding in Plain Sight: Black Women, the Law, and the Making of a White Argentine Republic*. Tuscaloosa: University Alabama Press.

Erber, Laura. 2021. Percorrer a imagem-limiar de Jaider Esbell (com algumas coisas de Marie-José Mondzain). ItaúCultural. www.itaucultural.org.br/secoes/colunistas/revelacao-percorrer-imagem-limiar-jaider-esbell

Esbell, Jaider. 2016. Índios: identidades, artes, mídias e conjunturas. *Em Tese* 22(2): 11–19.

Esbell, Jaider. 2018a. Além da visualidade: entrevista com Jaider Esbell. *Revista Usina*. https://revistausina.com/2018/03/16/alem-da-visualidade-entrevista-com-jaider-esbell/
Esbell, Jaider. 2018b. *Jaider Esbell (Coleção Tembetá)*. Rio de Janeiro: Azougue.
Esbell, Jaider. 2018c. Arte indígena contemporânea e o grande mundo. *Revista Select*, São Paulo 7(39). https://select.art.br/arte-indigena-contemporanea-e-o-grande-mundo/
Esbell, Jaider. 2020. A Arte Indígena Contemporânea como armadilha para armadilhas. Jaider Esbell. 9 July 2020. www.jaideresbell.com.br/site/2020/07/09/a-arte-indigena-contemporanea-como-armadilha-para-armadilhas/
Escobar, Arturo. 2010. *Territories of Difference: Place, Movements, Life, Redes*. Durham: Duke University Press.
Escolar, Diego y Leticia Saldi. 2018. Castas invisibles de la nueva nación. Los prisioneros indígenas de la Campaña del Desierto en el registro parroquial de Mendoza. In *En el país de nomeacuerdo. Archivos y memorias del genocidio del Estado argentino sobre los pueblos originarios, 1870–1950*, edited by Walter Delrio, Diego Escolar, Diana Lenton and Marisa Malvestitti, 99–136. Viedma: Editorial UNRN.
Espinosa Miñoso, Yuderkys. 2020. Interseccionalidad y feminismo descolonial. Volviendo sobre el tema. *Pikara Magazine*. www.pikaramagazine.com/2020/12/interseccionalidad-y-feminismo-descolonial-volviendo-sobre-el-tema/
Fanon, Frantz. 1986 [1952]. *Black Skin, White Masks*. London: Pluto Press.
Farris Thompson, Robert. 2005. *Tango: The Art History of Love*. New York: Pantheon Books.
Feldman, Heidi Carolyn. 2006. *Black Rhythms of Peru: Reviving African Musical Heritage in the Black Pacific*. Middletown, CT: Wesleyan University Press.
Fernandes, Sujatha. 2011. *Close to the Edge: In Search of the Global Hip Hop Generation*. London: Verso.
Fernández de Kirchner, Cristina. 2019. *Sinceramente*. Buenos Aires: Sudamericana.
Fernández de Lara Harada, Jessica A. 2021. Unstable identities in search of home: Introduction. ASAP/Review, Association for the Study of the Arts of the Present. https://asapjournal.com/unstable-identities-in-search-of-home-introduction-jessica-a-fernandez-de-lara-harada/
Ferrari, Matías. 2023. El 'odio racial' como hilo conductor de los casos de gatillo fácil. Eleditor.com.ar. www.eleditor.com.ar/nota-el-odio-racial-como-hilo-conductor-de-los-casos-de-gatillo-facil--2016
Fleetwood, Nicole R. 2011. *Troubling Vision: Performance, Visuality, and Blackness*. Chicago: University of Chicago Press.
Flórez Bolívar, Francisco. 2015. Un diálogo diaspórico: el lugar del Harlem Renaissance en el pensamiento racial e intelectual afrocolombiano (1920–1948). *Historia Crítica* 55: 101–124.
Flynn, Alex and Jonas Tinius, eds. 2015. *Anthropology, Theatre and Development: The Transformative Potential of Performance*. Basingstoke: Palgrave Macmillan.
Foucault, Michel. 1978. *The History of Sexuality. Volume 1: An Introduction*. New York: Pantheon Books.
Fraser, Nancy and Axel Honneth. 2003. *Redistribution or Recognition? A Political-Philosophical Exchange*. London: Verso.

Frigerio, Alejandro. 2006. 'Negros' y 'blancos' en Buenos Aires: repensando nuestras categorías raciales. *Temas de Patrimonio Cultural* 16: 77–98.
Frigerio, Alejandro. 2008. De la "desaparición" de los negros a la "reaparición" de los afrodescendientes: comprendiendo la política de las identidades negras, las clasificaciones raciales y de su estudio en la Argentina. In *Los estudios afroamericanos y africanos en América Latina: herencia, presencia y visiones del otro*, edited by Gladys Lechini, 117–144. Buenos Aires: CLACSO.
Frigerio, Alejandro. 2013. 'Sin otro delito que el color de su piel': imágenes del 'negro' en la revista *Caras y Caretas* (1900–1910). In *Cartografías afrolatinoamericanas: perspectivas situadas para análisis transfronterizos*, edited by Florencia Guzmán and Lea Geler, 151–172. Buenos Aires: Editorial Biblos.
Frigerio, Alejandro, Eva Lamborghini and Marta de Maffia. 2011. *Afrodescendientes y africanos en Argentina*. Buenos Aires: PNUD.
Gama, Basílio da. 1976. *O Uruguai*. Rio: Agir.
Garguin, Enrique. 2007. 'Los argentinos descendemos de los barcos': The racial articulation of middle class identity in Argentina (1920–1960). *Latin American and Caribbean Ethnic Studies* 2(2): 161–184.
Garín Martínez, Inma. 2018. Artes vivas: definición, polémicas y ejemplos. *Estudis Escènics. Quaderns de l'Institut del Teatre* 43: 1–25 https://raco.cat/index.php/EstudisEscenics/article/view/354454
Garner, Steve. 2007. *Whiteness: An Introduction*. London: Routledge.
Gates, Henry Louis, Elio Rodríguez Valdés and Alejandro de la Fuente. 2012. Race and racism in contemporary Cuban Art: A conversation with *Queloides* curators Alejandro de la Fuente and Elio Rodríguez Valdés. *Transition* 108: 33–51.
Geler, Lea. 2010. *Andares negros, caminos blancos. Afroporteños, estado y nación: Argentina a fines del siglo XIX*. Rosario: Prohistoria Ediciones.
Geler, Lea. 2012. Afrolatinoamericanas... una experiencia de subversión estereotípica en el museo de la mujer de Buenos Aires. *Horizontes Antropológicos* 18(38): 343–372.
Geler, Lea. 2016. Categorías raciales en Buenos Aires. Negritud, blanquitud, afrodescendencia y mestizaje en la blanca ciudad capital. *Runa: Archivos para las Ciencias del Hombre* 37(1): 71–87.
Geler, Lea, Alejandra Egido, Rosario Recalt and Carmen Yannone. 2018. Mujeres afroargentinas y el proyecto Certificar nuestra existencia. Una experiencia de trabajo multidisciplinar en Ciudad Evita (Gran Buenos Aires). *Población y Sociedad* 25(2): 28–54.
Geler, Lea, Carmen Yannone and Alejandra Egido. 2020. Afroargentinos de Buenos Aires en el siglo XX. El proceso de suburbanización. *Quinto Sol* 24(3): 90–116.
Gell, Alfred. 1998. *Art and Agency: An Anthropological Theory*. Oxford: Clarendon.
Giddens, Anthony. 1984. *The Constitution of Society: Outline of a Theory of Structuration*. Cambridge: Polity Press.
Gilard, Jacques. 1986. Surgimiento y recuperación de una contra-cultura en la Colombia contemporánea. *Huellas* 18: 41–46.
Gilroy, Paul. 1993. *The Black Atlantic: Modernity and Double Consciousness*. London: Verso.

Gilroy, Paul. 2000. *Between Camps: Nations, Cultures and the Allure of Race*. London: Penguin Books.
Giraldo Escobar, Sol Astrid. 2014. *Retratos en blanco y negro: Liliana Angulo*. Bogotá: Ministerio de Cultura.
Giraudo, Laura. 2017. ¿Qué/quién hay detrás de un nombre? Indigenismo e indigenistas. eldiario.es. www.eldiario.es/andalucia/la-cuadratura-del-circulo/quequien-detras-nombre_132_3587074.html
Giraudo, Laura and Stephen E. Lewis. 2012. Pan-American indigenismo (1940–1970): New approaches to an ongoing debate. *Latin American Perspectives* 39(5): 3–11.
Goldberg, David Theo. 2008. *The Threat of Race: Reflections on Racial Neoliberalism*. Malden, MA: Wiley-Blackwell.
Goldberg, David Theo. 2015. *Are We All Postracial Yet?* New York: John Wiley.
Golluscio, Lucía. 2006. *El Pueblo Mapuche: poéticas de pertenencia y devenir*. Buenos Aires: Biblos.
Gómez, Juan Carlos. 2013. En los muros del Palacio: Pedro Nel Gómez en el imaginario social en Medellín, 1930–1950. *HiSTOReLo. Revista de Historia Regional y Local* 5(10): 55–90.
Gómez-Barris, Macarena. 2017. *The Extractive Zone: Social Ecologies and Decolonial Perspectives*. Durham, NC: Duke University Press.
González, Beatriz. 2003. Las imágenes del negro en las colecciones de las instituciones oficiales. In *150 años de la abolición de la esclavización en Colombia. Desde la marginalidad a la construcción de la nación*, edited by Museo Nacional de Colombia, 458–473. Bogotá: Aguilar.
Gordillo, Gastón. 2016. The savage outside of white Argentina. In *Rethinking Race in Modern Argentina*, edited by Paulina Alberto and Eduardo Elena, 241–267. New York: Cambridge University Press.
Gordillo, Gastón. 2020. Se viene el malón. Las geografías afectivas del racismo argentino. *Cuadernos de Antropología Social* 52: 7–35.
Gordillo, Gastón and Silvia Hirsch, eds. 2010. *Movilizaciones indígenas e identidades en disputa en la Argentina*. Buenos Aires: La Crujía.
Gotkowitz, Laura, ed. 2011. *Histories of Race and Racism: The Andes and Mesoamerica From Colonial Times to the Present*. Durham, NC: Duke University Press.
Gregory, Derek and John Urry, eds. 1985. *Social Relations and Spatial Structures*. London: Macmillan.
Grimson, Alejandro. 2017. Raza y clase en los orígenes del peronismo: Argentina, 1945. *Desacatos. Revista de Ciencias Sociales* 55: 110–127.
Guajajara, Sonia. 2018. Interview with Alexandre Pankararu and Graciela Guarani, 30 October 2018. http://projects.alc.manchester.ac.uk/racism-Indigenous-brazil/outputs
Gutiérrez de Alba, José María. 2012. *Diario ilustrado de viajes por Colombia 1871–1873*. Bogotá: Villegas Editores.
Guzmán, Florencia. 2009. Representaciones familiares de las mujeres negras en el Tucumán colonial. Un análisis en torno al mundo doméstico subalterno. In *Poblaciones históricas. Fuentes, métodos y líneas de investigación*, edited by Dora Celton, Mónica Ghirardi and Adrián Carbonetti, 403–425. Río de Janeiro: Asociación Latinoamericana de Población.

Hale, Charles R. 2002. Does multiculturalism menace? Governance, cultural rights and the politics of identity in Guatemala. *Journal of Latin American Studies* 34(3): 485–524.
Hale, Charles R. 2004. Rethinking indigenous politics in the era of the '*indio permitido*'. *NACLA Report on the Americas* 38(2): 16–22.
Hale, Charles R. 2005. Neoliberal multiculturalism: The remaking of cultural rights and racial dominance in Central America. *Political and Legal Anthropology Review* 28(1): 10–28.
Hale, Charles R. 2014. Entre lo decolonial y la formación racial: luchas afro-indígenas por el territorio y por (¿o en contra de?) un nuevo lenguaje contencioso. *Cuadernos de Antropología Social* 40: 9–37.
Hancock, Ange-Marie. 2007. Intersectionality as a normative and empirical paradigm. *Politics & Gender* 3(2): 248–254.
Hanna, Judith Lyanne. 1988. Dance and ritual. *Journal of Physical Education, Recreation & Dance* 59(9): 40–43.
Haraway, Donna. 1991. *Simians, Cyborgs and Women: The Re-invention of Nature*. London: Free Association Books.
Hartigan, John, ed. 2013. *Anthropology of Race: Genes, Biology and Culture*. Santa Fe, NM: School for Advanced Research Press.
Hartman, Saidiya V. 2019. *Wayward Lives, Beautiful Experiments: Intimate Histories of Riotous Black Girls, Troublesome Women, and Queer Radicals*. New York: W. W. Norton & Company.
Hemmings, Clare. 2005. Invoking affect: Cultural theory and the ontological turn. *Cultural Studies* 19(5): 548–567.
Henao, Dario. 2010. Los hijos de Changó, la epopeya de la negritud en América (prólogo). In *Changó, el gran putas*, by Manuel Zapata Olivella, 11–29. Bogotá: Ministerio de Cultura.
Hinton, Perry R. 2000. *Stereotypes, Cognition and Culture*. Hove: Psychology Press.
Hoffmann, Odile and María Teresa Rodríguez. 2007. *Los retos de la diferencia: Los actores de la multiculturalidad entre México y Colombia*. México, DF: Centro de Estudios Mexicanos y Centroamericanos; Centro de Investigación y Estudios Superiores en Antropología Social; Institut de Recherche pour le Développement; Instituto Colombiano de Antropología e Historia; Publicaciones de la Casa Chata.
Holbraad, Martin and Morten Axel Pedersen. 2017. *The Ontological Turn: An Anthropological Exposition*. Cambridge: Cambridge University Press.
Hooker, Juliet, ed. 2020. *Black and Indigenous Resistance in the Americas from Multiculturalism to Racist Backlash*. Lanham: Lexington Books.
Hordge-Freeman, Elizabeth. 2015. *The Color of Love: Racial Features, Stigma, and Socialization in Black Brazilian Families*. Austin: University of Texas Press.
Hughes-Freeland, Felicia. 2008. *Embodied Communities: Dance Traditions and Change in Java*. Oxford: Berghahn Books.
Humboldt, Alexander Von. 1810. *Vues des Cordillères et monumens des peuples indigènes de l'Amérique*. Paris: F. Schoell.
Hurley, Erin and Sara Warner. 2012. Affect/performance/politics. *Journal of Dramatic Theory and Criticism* 26(2): 99–107.

Identidad Marrón. 2021. *Marrones escriben. Perspectivas antirracistas desde el Sur Global*. Buenos Aires: Identidad Marrón; Universidad Nacional de San Martín; CARLA.

Jackson, Richard L. 1975. Black phobia and the white aesthetic in Spanish American literature. *Hispania* 58(3): 467–480.

Jackson, Richard L. 1988. *Black Literature and Humanism in Latin America*. Athens: University of Georgia Press.

James, Wendy. 2000. Reforming the circle: Fragments of the social history of a vernacular African dance form. *Journal of African Cultural Studies* 13(1): 140–152.

Jáuregui, Carlos A. 1999. Candelario Obeso: entre la espada del romanticismo y la pared del proyecto nacional. *Revista Iberoamericana* 65: 567–590.

Jeronimo, Josie. 2020. Entrevista: Ailton Krenak fala com exclusividade à OPAN. *Revista Da Opan* 1: 4–10. https://amazonianativa.org.br/wp-content/uploads/2022/09/Amazona-Nativa-1-1.pdf

Juruna, Mário, Antonio Hohlfeldt and Assis Hoffmann. 1982. *O Gravador do Juruna*. Porto Alegre: Mercado Aberto Editora e Propaganda Ltda.

Kaeppler, Adrianne L. 1991. American approaches to the study of dance. *Yearbook for Traditional Music* 23: 11–21.

Kaeppler, Adrianne L. 2000. Dance ethnology and the anthropology of dance. *Dance Research Journal* 32(1): 116–125.

Karush, Matthew B. 2016. Black in Buenos Aires: The transnational career of Oscar Alemán. In *Rethinking Race in Modern Argentina*, edited by Paulina Alberto and Eduardo Elena, 73–98. Cambridge: Cambridge University Press.

Keane, Webb. 2018. Perspectives on affordances, or the anthropologically real: The 2018 Daryll Forde Lecture. *HAU: Journal of Ethnographic Theory* 8(1–2): 27–38.

King, Tiffany Lethabo. 2019. *The Black Shoals: Offshore Formations of Black and Native Studies*. Durham: Duke University Press.

King, Tiffany Lethabo, Jenell Navarro and Andrea Smith, eds. 2020. *Otherwise Worlds: Against Settler Colonialism and Anti-Blackness*. Durham: Duke University Press.

Knowles, Caroline. 2003. *Race and Social Analysis*. London: SAGE Publications.

Knudsen, Britta T. and Carsten Stage. 2015. *Affective Methodologies: Developing Cultural Research Strategies for the Study of Affect*. Basingstoke: Palgrave Macmillan.

Ko, Chisu Teresa. 2013. From whiteness to diversity: Crossing the racial threshold in bicentennial Argentina. *Ethnic and Racial Studies* 37(14): 2529–2546.

Kopenawa, Davi and Bruce Albert. 2013. *The Falling Sky: Words of a Yonamami Shaman*, translated by Nicholas Elliot and Alison Dundy. Cambridge: Harvard University Press. (First published as *La chute du ciel: Paroles d'un chaman yanomami*. 2013. Paris: PLON.)

Krenak, Ailton. 2020a. *A Vida Não é Útil*. São Paulo: Companhia das Letras.

Krenak, Ailton. 2020b. *Ideas to Postpone the End of the World*. Toronto: House of Anansi.

Kringelbach, Hélene Neveu and Jonathan Skinner. 2014. Introduction: The movement of dancing cultures. In *Dancing Cultures*, edited by Hélene Neveu Kringelbach and Jonathan Skinner, 1–26. Oxford: Berghahn Books.
Kropff, Laura. 2004. 'Mapurbe': jóvenes mapuche urbanos. *Kairos: Revista de Temas Sociales* 14: 1–12.
Kropff, Laura, ed. 2010. *Teatro mapuche: sueños, memoria y política*. Buenos Aires: Artes Escénicas.
Kropff, Laura. 2011. Los jóvenes mapuche en Argentina: entre el circuito punk y las recuperaciones de tierras. *Alteridades* 21(42): 77–89.
Lamborghini, Eva, Lea Geler and Florencia Guzmán. 2017. Los estudios afrodescendientes en Argentina: nuevas perspectivas y desafíos en un país 'sin razas'. *Tabula Rasa* 27: 67–101.
Laó-Montes, Agustín. 2009. Cartografías del campo político afrodescendiente en América Latina. *Universitas Humanística* 68: 207–245.
Laó-Montes, Agustín. 2010. Cartografías del campo político afrodescendiente en América Latina. In *Debates sobre ciudadanía y políticas raciales en las Américas Negras*, edited by Claudia Rosero-Labbé, Agustín Laó-Montes y César Rodríguez, 281–328. Bogotá: Universidad Nacional de Colombia.
Lasso, Marixa. 2007. *Myths of Harmony: Race and Republicanism during the Age of Revolution, Colombia 1795–1831*. Pittsburgh: University of Pittsburgh Press.
Leal, Claudia and Carl Langebaek. 2010. *Historias de raza y nación en América Latina*. Bogotá: Universidad de los Andes.
Lefebvre, Henri. 1991. *The Production of Space*. Trans. Donald Nicholson-Smith. Oxford: Blackwell.
Lehmann, David. 2018. *The Prism of Race: The Politics and Ideology of Affirmative Action in Brazil*. Ann Arbor: University of Michigan Press.
Lehmann, David. 2022. *After the Decolonial: Ethnicity, Gender and Social Justice in Latin America*. Cambridge: Polity Press.
Lentin, Alana. 2011. What happens to anti-racism when we are post race? *Feminist Legal Studies* 19(2): 159–168.
Lentin, Alana. 2014. Post-race, post politics: The paradoxical rise of culture after multiculturalism. *Ethnic and Racial Studies* 37(8): 1268–1285.
Lentin, Alana. 2016. Racism in public or public racism: Doing anti-racism in 'post-racial' times. *Ethnic and Racial Studies* 39(1): 33–48.
Lenton, Diana. 2010. The *Malón de la Paz* of 1946: Indigenous *descamisados* at the dawn of Peronism. Translated by Beatrice D. Gurwitz. In *The New Cultural History of Peronism: Power and Identity in Mid-Twentieth-Century Argentina*, edited by Matthew Karush and Oscar Chamosa, 85–112. Durham: Duke University Press.
Lenton, Diana, Walter Delrio, Pilar Pérez, Alexis Papazian, Mariano Nagy and Marcelo Musante [Red de Investigadores sobre Genocidio y Política Indígena]. 2015. Huellas de un genocidio silenciado: los indígenas en Argentina. *Conceptos* 90(493): 119–142.
Lewis, Marvin A. 1996. *Afro-Argentine Discourse: Another Dimension of the Black Diaspora*. Columbia: University of Missouri Press.

Leys, Ruth. 2011. The turn to affect: A critique. *Critical Inquiry* 37(3): 434–472.
Lipsitz, George. 2007. The racialization of space and the spatialization of race: Theorizing the hidden architecture of landscape. *Landscape Journal* 26(1): 10–23.
Lomax, Alan, ed. 2017. *Folk Song Style and Culture*. London: Routledge.
López Bayona, Álvaro Iván. 2016. El uribismo y su carácter populista. Una reconstrucción de sus condiciones de posibilidad. *Revista de Antropología y Sociología: Virajes* 18(1): 87–107.
Lorde, Audre. 1984. *Sister Outsider: Essays and Speeches*. Berkeley: Crossing Press.
Lugones, María. 2010. Toward a decolonial feminism. *Hypatia* 25(4): 742–759.
M'charek, Amade. 2014. Race, time and folded objects: The HeLa error. *Theory, Culture & Society* 31(6): 29–56.
M'charek, Amade, Katharina Schramm and David Skinner. 2014a. Technologies of belonging: the absent presence of race in Europe. *Science, Technology & Human Values* 39(4): 459–467.
M'charek, Amade, Katharina Schramm and David Skinner. 2014b. Topologies of race: Doing territory, population and identity in Europe. *Science, Technology & Human Values* 39(4): 468–487.
Maglia, Graciela, Miguel Rocha Vivas and Juan Duchesne Winter. 2015. Literaturas afrolatinoamericanas e indígenas. *Cuadernos de Literatura* 20(38): 45–57.
Malagón-Kurka, María Margarita. 2010. *Arte como presencia indéxica. La obra de tres artistas colombianos en tiempo de violencia: Beatriz González, Óscar Muñoz, y Doris Salcedo en la década de los noventa*. Bogotá: Universidad de los Andes.
Malagón-Kurka, María Margarita. 2015. Arte en y más allá de la violencia en Colombia. Cuestiones antropológicas y existenciales en obras de Clemencia Echeverri y Óscar Muñoz. *Karpa. Journal of Theatricalities and Visual Culture* 8. www.calstatela.edu/sites/default/files/malagonpdf.pdf
Malosetti Costa, Laura. 2022. *Los primeros modernos: arte y sociedad en Buenos Aires a fines del siglo XIX*. Buenos Aires: Fondo de Cultura Económica Argentina.
Martín, Eloísa. 2008. La cumbia villera y el fin de la cultura del trabajo en la Argentina de los 90. *Trans: Revista Transcultural de Música* 12. www.sibetrans.com/trans/articulo/90/la-cumbia-villera-y-el-fin-de-la-cultura-del-trabajo-en-la-argentina-de-los-90
Martínez Novo, Carmen and Pavel Shlossberg. 2018. Introduction: Lasting and resurgent racism after recognition in Latin America. *Cultural Studies* 32(3): 349–363.
Marx, Anthony. 1998. *Making Race and Nation: A Comparison of South Africa, the United States and Brazil*. Cambridge: Cambridge University Press.
Mases, Enrique Hugo. 2002. *Estado y cuestión indígena. El destino final de los indios sometidos en el sur del territorio (1878–1910)*. Buenos Aires: Prometeo Libros.
Massey, Doreen. 2005. *For Space*. London: SAGE Publications.
Massumi, Brian. 1995. The autonomy of affect. *Cultural Critique* 31: 83–109.
Mauss, Marcel. 1973. Techniques of the body. *Economy and Society* 2(1): 70–88.

Maxwell, Adeline. 2015. Introducción a lecturas emergentes sobre danza contemporánea. In *Lecturas emergentes sobre danza contemporánea*, edited by Adeline Maxwell, 19–32. Santiago de Chile: Universidad Academia del Humanismo Cristiano.
Maya, Restrepo, Luz Adriana, and Raúl Cristancho. 2015. *¡Mandinga sea! África en Antioquia: catálogo*. Bogotá: Ediciones Uniandes.
Mbembe, Achille. 2003. Necropolitics. *Public Culture* 15(1): 11–40.
McAleer, Paul Robert. 2018. The multiple functions of *criollo*, *gaucho* and Indigenous symbols in *La historieta Patoruzú*, 1936–50: The conflicts of Peronism, nationalism and migration. *Journal of Latin American Cultural Studies* 27(2): 253–270.
McCormack, Derek P. 2008. Geographies for moving bodies: Thinking, dancing, spaces. *Geography Compass* 2(6): 1822–1836.
McKittrick, Katherine. 2006. *Demonic Grounds: Black Women and the Cartographies of Struggle*. Minneapolis: University of Minnesota Press.
McKittrick, Katherine. 2011. On plantations, prisons, and a black sense of place. *Social & Cultural Geography* 12(8): 947–963.
McKittrick, Katherine and Clyde Adrian Woods, eds. 2007. *Black Geographies and the Politics of Place*. Toronto: Between the Lines.
Medina, Alvaro. 2000. *El arte del Caribe Colombiano*. Cartagena: Gobernación del Departamento de Bolívar, Secretaria de Educación y Cultura.
Mendoza, Zoila S. 2000. *Shaping Society through Dance: Mestizo Ritual Performance in the Peruvian Andes*. Chicago: University of Chicago Press.
Mendoza, Plinio Apuleyo, Ignacio Gómez Pulido and Olga Lucía Jordán. 1989. *Nuestros pintores en París*. Bogotá: Ediciones Gamma.
Mercer, Kobena. 1994. *Welcome to the Jungle: New Positions in Black Cultural Studies*. New York: Routledge.
Merino, Ann. 2015. Fake nostalgia for the Indian: the Argentinean fiction of national identity in the comics of Patoruzú. In *No Laughing Matter: Visual Humor in Ideas of Race, Nationality, and Ethnicity*, edited by Angela Rosenthal, David Bindman and Adrian W. B. Randolph, 149–175. Hanover, NH: University Press of New England.
Mignolo, Walter D. 2012. *Local Histories/Global Designs: Coloniality, Subaltern Knowledges, and Border Thinking*. Princeton: Princeton University Press.
Mignolo, Walter D. and Catherine E. Walsh. 2018. *On Decoloniality: Concepts, Analytics, Praxis*. Durham: Duke University Press.
Milanesio, Natalia. 2010. Peronists and *cabecitas*: Stereotypes and anxieties at the peak of social change. In *The New Cultural History of Peronism: Power and Identity in Mid-Twentieth-Century Argentina*, edited by Matthew Karush and Oscar Chamosa, 53–84. Durham: Duke University Press.
Milanez Pereira, Felipe and Jurema Machado de A. Souza. 2022. Insurgências estéticas e epistêmicas no Antropoceno: povos indígenas e a retomada da Mata Atlântica no sul da Bahia. *Liinc em Revista* 18(1): e5937–e5937.
Miles, Robert. 1989. *Racism*. London: Routledge.
Montero-Diaz, Fiorella. 2019. White cholos? Discourses around race, whiteness and Lima's fusion music. In *Cultures of Anti-Racism in Latin America and the Caribbean*, edited by Peter Wade, James Scorer and Ignacio Aguiló, 167–190. London: University of London Press.

Montoya Alzate, Juan D. 2019. Champeta's heritage: Diasporic music and racial struggle in the Colombian Caribbean. *Transposition* (8). https://doi.org/10.4000/transposition.3254

Moore, Henrietta L. 2007. *The Subject of Anthropology: Gender, Symbolism and Psychoanalysis*. Cambridge: Polity.

Morales, Orlando G. 2014. Representaciones de alteridades 'negras', africanas y afrodescendientes, en la sociedad nacional en argentina. PhD tesis, Universidad Nacional de La Plata, La Plata.

Moreno Figueroa, Mónica G. 2008. Historically-rooted transnationalism: Slightedness and the experience of racism in Mexican families. *Journal of Intercultural Studies* 29(3): 283–297.

Moreno Figueroa, Mónica G. 2010. Distributed intensities: Whiteness, mestizaje and the logics of Mexican racism. *Ethnicities* 10(3): 387–401.

Moreno Figueroa, Mónica. 2024. On Blackness, images and anti-racist work. *Ethnic and Racial Studies* 47(11): 2326–2346.

Moreno Figueroa, Mónica G. and Peter Wade, eds. 2022. *Against Racism: Organizing for Social Change in Latin America*. Pittsburgh: University of Pittsburgh Press.

Mosse, George L. 1985. *Toward the Final Solution: A History of European Racism*. Madison: University of Wisconsin Press.

Moya, Paula M. L. 2016. *The Social Imperative: Race, Close Reading and Contemporary Literary Criticism*. Stanford, CA: Stanford University Press.

Muldoon, Aaron. 2020. The fine line between subverting stereotypes and perpetuating them. Sleek.mag. www.sleek-mag.com/article/subverting-stereotypes-and-perpetuating-them-rotimi-fani-kayode/

Munduruku, Daniel. 2017. *Mundurucando 2: Sobre Vivências, Piolhos, e Afeto. Roda de Conversa com Educadores*. São Paulo: UK'A.

Munduruku, Daniel. 2020. Literatura Indígena. Abril Indígena Live 2021. Rádio Yandê. www.facebook.com/radioyande/videos/224121365565367/ (site inactive on 27 January 2025).

Múnera, Alfonso. 1998. *El fracaso de la nación. Región, clase y raza en el caribe colombiano: 1717–1810*. Bogotá: Banco de la República, El Ancora Editores.

Muñoz Arbelaez, Santiago. 2010. Las imágenes de viajeros en el siglo XIX. El caso de los grabados de Charles Saffray sobre Colombia. *Historia y Grafía* 34: 169–204.

Muñoz-Rojas, Catalina. 2022. *A Fervent Crusade for the National Soul: Cultural Politics in Colombia, 1930–1946*. Lanham, MD: Rowman and Littlefield.

Nagel, Joane. 2003. *Race, Ethnicity, and Sexuality: Intimate Intersections, Forbidden Frontiers*. Oxford: Oxford University Press.

Nagy, Mariano and Alexis Papazian. 2011. El campo de concentración de Martín García. Entre el control estatal dentro de la isla y las prácticas de distribución de indígenas (1871–1886). *Corpus* 1(2): 1–35. http://journals.openedition.org/corpusarchivos/1176

Nardone, Mariana. 2010. Arte comunitario: Criterios para su definición. *Miríada: Investigación en Ciencias Sociales* 3(6): 47–91.

Nascimento, Abdias. 1980. *O Quilombismo*. Petrópolis: Editora Vozes.
National Gallery of Art. 2003. *The Art of Romare Bearden*. Washington, DC: National Gallery of Art.
Navarro Hartmann, Herminia. 2015. El estudio del discurso desde la etnolingüística: un abordaje del cancionero mapuche. Paper given at the XXVII Congreso Nacional y I Internacional de Lingüística, Literatura y Semiótica, 9–12 October 2012, Universidad Pedagógica y Tecnológica de Colombia, Tunja. http://repositorio.uptc.edu.co/handle/001/7658
Neary, Janet. 2015. Cotton babies, mama's maybe: Invention, matter, and mythology in Kara Walker's *8 Possible Beginnings*. *J19* 3(1): 156–163.
Neely, Brooke and Michelle Samura. 2011. Social geographies of race: Connecting race and space. *Ethnic and Racial Studies* 34(11): 1933–1952.
Nelson, Alondra. 2002. Introduction: Future texts. *Social Text* 20(2): 1–15.
Obando Hernández, Luis Gabriel. 2018. Aportes de la Institución Universitaria Bellas Artes y Ciencias de Bolívar (UNIBAC) a la identidad visual Caribe en la ciudad de Cartagena de Indias. MA thesis, Universidad Nacional de Colombia, Sede Caribe, Cartagena.
Obeso, Candelario. 1977 [1877]. *Cantos populares de mi tierra*. Bogotá: Fondo de Publicaciones de la Fundación Colombiana de Investigaciones Folclóricas. Original edition, Bogotá: Imprenta de Borda.
Ochoa Gautier, Ana María. 2003. *Entre los deseos y los derechos: Un ensayo crítico sobre políticas culturales*. Bogotá: Instituto Colombiano de Antropología e Historia.
Omi, Michael and Howard Winant. 1994. *Racial Formation in the United States: From the 1960s to the 1990s*. New York: Routledge.
Oquist, Paul H. 1978. *Violencia, conflicto y política en Colombia*. Bogotá: Instituto de Estudios Colombianos.
Ortega Domínguez, Abeyamí and Sarah Abel. 2023. Public art and the grammars of antiracism. In *The New Public Art: Collectivity and Activism in Mexico since the 1980s*, edited by Mara Polgovsky Ezcurra, 165–186. Austin: University of Texas Press.
Ortiz, Lucía, ed. 2007. *'Chambacú, la historia la escribes tú'. Ensayos sobre la cultura afrocolombiana*. Madrid, Frankfurt: Iberoamericana, Vervuert.
Pace, Richard, ed. 2018. *From Filmmaker Warriors to Flash Drive Shamans: Indigenous Media Production and Engagement in Latin America*. Nashville: Vanderbilt University Press.
Pacheco de Oliveira, João. 2016. *O Nascimento do Brasil e Outros Ensaios: 'Pacificação', Regime Tutelar e Formação de Alteridades*. Rio de Janeiro: Contra Capa.
Palacios, Arnoldo. 2010 [1949]. *Las estrellas son negras*. Bogotá: Ministry of Culture.
Palacios Garrido, Alfredo. 2009. El arte comunitario: origen y evolución de las prácticas artísticas colaborativas. *Arteterapia. Papeles de Arteterapia y Educación Artística Para la Inclusión Social* 4: 197–211.
Palacios Palacios, George. 2010. El motivo de los 'bogas' en la imaginación literaria de Jorge Isaacs y Candelario Obeso. *Escritos* 18(40): 156–184.

Palacios Valencia, Yennesit and Sergio Mondragón. 2021. Precariedad laboral en población afrodescendiente e indígena agravada por el conflicto armado en Colombia. *Revista de Ciencias Sociales* 27(2): 338–351.

Paschel, Tianna S. 2016. *Becoming Black Political Subjects: Movements and Ethno-Racial Rights in Colombia and Brazil*. Princeton: Princeton University Press.

Pauwels, Matthias. 2021. Anti-racist critique through racial stereotype humour: What could go wrong? *Theoria* 68(4): 85–113.

PBS. 2000. Culture shock: You decide: The art of Kara Walker: The critics. PBS. org. www.pbs.org/wgbh/cultureshock/provocations/kara/3.html

Pedwell, Carolyn and Anne Whitehead. 2012. Affecting feminism: Questions of feeling in feminist theory. *Feminist Theory* 13(2): 115–129.

Penhos, Marta. 1999. Nativos en el Salón. Artes plásticas e identidad en la primera mitad del siglo XX. In *Tras los pasos de la norma. Salones Nacionales de Bellas Artes (1911–1989)*, edited by Marta Penhos and Diana Wechsler, 111–162. Buenos Aires: Ediciones del Jilguero.

Pérez, Pilar. 2016. *Archivos del silencio: Estado, indígenas y violencia en Patagonia Central, 1878–1941*. Buenos Aires: Prometeo.

Pérez Bugallo, Rubén. 1992–1993. El carnaval de los 'indios': una advertencia sobre el conflicto social. *Cuadernos del Instituto Nacional de Antropología y Pensamiento Latinoamericano* 14: 93–120.

Pérez Vejo, Tomás and Pablo Yankelevich, eds. 2017. *Raza y política en Hispanoamérica*. Mexico: El Colegio de México, Bonilla y Artigas Editores.

Pinheiro Dias, Jamille. 2021. Artistas indígenas reativam a vida em meio aos escombros da modernidade colonial. Pernambuco Revista. www.pernambucorevista.com.br/acervo/artigos/2646-reativar-a-vida-pela-arte.html

Pinheiro Dias, Jamille. 2022. Environmental thinking and Indigenous arts in Brazil today. *Journal of Latin American Cultural Studies* 31(1): 141–157.

Pinheiro Dias, Jamille. 2023. Indigeneity. In *Handbook of Latin American Environmental Aesthetics*, edited by Andermann Jens, Giorgi Gabriel and Saramago Victoria, 215–228. Berlin, Boston: De Gruyter.

Pisano, Pietro. 2012. *Liderazgo político 'negro' en Colombia, 1943–1964*. Bogotá: Universidad Nacional de Colombia.

Pita, Federico. 2021. *Afrodescendientes y equidad racial: Informe sobre política pública*. Buenos Aires: Comisión para el Reconocimiento Histórico de la Afroargentinidad, Instituto Nacional Contra la Discriminación.

Pitta, Fernanda Mendonça. 2021. A 'breve história da arte' e a arte indígena: a gênese de uma noção e sua problemática hoje. *MODOS: Revista de História da Arte* 5(3): 223–257.

Podgorny, Irina. 1999. De la antigüedad del hombre en el Plata a la distribución de las antigüedades en el mapa: los criterios de organización de las colecciones antropológicas del Museo de La Plata entre 1897 y 1930. *História, Ciências, Saúde-Manguinhos* 6: 81–101.

Potiguara, Eliane. 2018. *Metade Cara, Metade Máscara*. São Paulo: UK'A.

Pratt, Mary Louise. 1997. *Ojos imperiales*. Buenos Aires: Universidad Nacional de Quilmes.

Prescott, Laurence E. 1985. *Candelario Obeso y la iniciación de la poesía negra en Colombia*. Bogotá: Instituto Caro y Cuervo.
Prescott, Laurence E. 1996. Perfil histórico del autor afrocolombiano: problemas y perspectivas. *América Negra* 12: 104–125.
Prescott, Laurence E. 2000. *Without Hatreds or Fears: Jorge Artel and the Struggle for Black Literary Expression in Colombia*. Detroit: Wayne State University Press.
Prescott, Laurence E. 2007. Voces del litoral recóndito: tres poetas de la costa pacífica de Colombia (Helcías Martán Góngora; Hugo Salazar Valdés; Lino A. Sevillano). In *'Chambacú, la historia la escribes tú'. Ensayos sobre cultura afrocolombiana*, edited by Lucía Ortiz, 133–154. Frankfurt am Main, Madrid: Vervuert Verlagsgesellschaft.
Price, Sally. 2001. *Primitive Art in Civilized Places*. 2nd ed. Chicago: University of Chicago Press.
Pridgeon, Stephanie M. 2020. *Revolutionary Visions: Jewish Life and Politics in Latin American Film*. Toronto: University of Toronto Press.
Pyke, Karen D. 2010. What is internalized racial oppression and why don't we study it? Acknowledging racism's hidden injuries. *Sociological Perspectives* 53(4): 551–572.
Quijada, Mónica. 2000. Introducción. In *Homogeneidad y nación con un estudio de caso: Argentina, siglos XIX y XX*, edited by Mónica Quijada, Carmen Bernand Quijada and Arnd Schneider, 7–15. Madrid: Consejo Superior de Investigaciones Científicas.
Quijano, Aníbal. 1999. ¡Qué tal raza! *Revista Ecuador Debate: Etnicidades e Identificaciones* 48: 141–152.
Quijano, Aníbal. 2007. Coloniality and modernity/rationality. *Cultural Studies* 21(2–3): 168–178.
Quintero, Ángel G. 2020. *La danza de la insurrección. Para una sociología de la música latinoamericana: textos reunidos*. Buenos Aires: Clacso.
Radano, Ronald and Philip V. Bohlman, eds. 2000. *Music and the Racial Imagination*. Chicago: University of Chicago Press.
Rahier, Jean Muteba. 2014. *Blackness in the Andes: Ethnographic Vignettes of Cultural Politics in the Time of Multiculturalism*. New York: Palgrave Macmillan.
Rahier, Jean Muteba. 2020. Multiculturalism, Afro-descendant activism, and ethnoracial law and policy in Latin America. *Latin American Research Review* 55(3): 605–612.
Ramírez Botero, Isabel C. 2010. Arte en Cartagena a través de la colección del Banco de la República. Issuu.com. https://issuu.com/fundaciondivulgar/docs/arte_en_cartagena
Ramos, Alcida. 1998. *Indigenism: Ethnic Politics in Brazil*. Madison: University of Wisconsin Press.
Rancière, Jacques. 2000. Política, identificación y subjetivación. In *El reverso de la diferencia. Identidad y política*, edited by Benajamin Arditi, 145–152. Caracas: Nueva Sociedad.
Rancière, Jacques. 2005. *Sobre políticas estéticas*. Barcelona: Universitat Autónoma de Barcelona.

Rancière, Jacques. 2013. *The Politics of Aesthetics: The Distribution of the Sensible*. Translated by Gabriel Rockhill. London: Bloomsbury.
Ratier, Hugo. 1971. *Villeros y villas miseria*. Buenos Aires: Centro Editor de América Latina.
Ratier, Hugo. 2022. *El cabecita negra*. La Plata: Editorial de la Universidad Nacional de La Plata.
Ravindran, Tathagatan. 2020. What undecidability does: Enduring racism in the context of indigenous resurgence in Bolivia. *Ethnic and Racial Studies* 43(6): 976–994.
Ravindran, Tathagatan. 2021. The power of phenotype: Toward an ethnography of pigmentocracy in Andean Bolivia. *Journal of Latin American and Caribbean Anthropology* 26(2): 219–236.
Reed, Susan A. 1998. The politics and poetics of dance. *Annual Review of Anthropology*, 27: 503–532.
Reiter, Bernd. 2009. Fighting exclusion with culture and art: Examples from Brazil. *International Social Work* 52(2): 155–166.
Reiter, Bernd and Gladys Mitchell. 2008. Embracing hip hop as their own: Hip hop and Black racial identity in Brazil. *Studies in Latin American Popular Culture* 27: 1–15.
Restrepo, Eduardo. 2021. ¿Negro o afrodescendiente? Debates en torno a las políticas del nombrar en Colombia. *Perspectivas Afro* 1(1): 5–32.
Restrepo, Olga. 1999. Un imaginario de la nación. Lectura de láminas y descripciones de la Comisión Corográfica. *Anuario Colombiano de Historia Social y de la Cultura* 26: 30–58.
Ribeiro, Darcy. 1970. *Os Índios e a Civilização*. Rio: Civilização Brasileira.
Ribeiro, Darcy. 1989. *Maíra*. Rio: Record.
Rivas Pérez, Jorge F. 2021. Painters of African descent in colonial Spanish America. Denver Art Museum. www.denverartmuseum.org/en/blog/painters-african-descent-colonial-spanish-america
Robb, John Donald. 1961. The Matachines dance: A ritual folk dance. *Western Folklore* 20(2): 87–101.
Roberts, Elizabeth F. S. 2012. *God's Laboratory: Assisted Reproduction in the Andes*. Berkeley: University of California Press.
Rolnik, Suely. 2019. *Esferas de la insurrección: Apuntes para descolonizar el inconsciente*. Buenos Aires: Tinta Limón.
Romero, Sílvio. 1882. *Introducção à História da Litteratura Brazileira*. Rio de Janeiro: Typographia Nacional.
Rubiano, Elkin. 2015. El arte en el contexto de la violencia contemporánea en Colombia. *Karpa. Revista de Teatralidades e Cultura Visual* 8. www.calstatela.edu/sites/default/files/rubianopdf.pdf
Ruette-Orihuela, Krisna. 2022. Bodily anti-racism: What bodies can 'do' to contest racism in public spaces. In *Against Racism: Organizing for Social Change in Latin America*, edited by Mónica G. Moreno Figueroa and Peter Wade, 73–99. Pittsburg: Pittsburgh University Press.
Ruette-Orihuela, Krisna, Mara Viveros Vigoya, Danny Ramírez-Torres, Emilia Eneyda Valencia-Murraín and Lina Lucumí-Mosquera. 2024. Anti-racist beauty micro-enterprises: Black women's subversive entrepreneurship in Cali, Colombia. *Ethnic and Racial Studies* 47(11): 2411–2432.

Sá, Lúcia. 2004. *Rainforest Literatures: Amazonian Texts and Latin American Culture*. Minneapolis: University of Minnesota Press.
Sá, Lúcia and Felipe Milanez Pereira. 2020. Painting racism: Protest art by contemporary indigenous artists. In *Living (Il)Legalities in Brazil: Practices, Narratives and Institutions in a Country on the Edge*, edited by Sara Brandellero, Derek Pardue and Georg Wink, 160–178. London: Routledge.
Safa, Helen. 2005. Challenging mestizaje: A gender perspective on indigenous and Afrodescendant movements in Latin America. *Critique of Anthropology* 25(3): 307–330.
Saffray, Charles. 1948. *Viaje a Nueva Granada*. Bogotá: Ministerio de Educación Nacional.
Saldanha, Arun. 2004. *Psychedelic White: Goa Trance and the Viscosity of Race*. Minneapolis: University of Minnesota Press.
Samuel, Gerard M. 2011. Shampoo dancing and scars–(dis)embodiment in Afrocontemporary choreography in South Africa. *Dance Research Journal* 43(1): 40–47.
Santos, Milton. 2021. *The Nature of Space*. Durham: Duke University Press.
Schiwy, Freya. 2009. *Indianizing Film: Decolonization, the Andes, and the Question of Technology*. Piscataway: Rutgers University Press.
Schneider, Arnd. 1996. The transcontinental construction of European identities: A view from Argentina. *Anthropological Journal on European Cultures* 5(1): 95–105.
Schollaert, Jeannette. 2014. Silhouetted stereotypes in the art of Kara Walker. *New Errands* 1(2): 26–30.
Segalen, Víctor. 2017. *Ensayo sobre el exotismo: una estética de lo diverso*. Madrid: La Línea del Horizonte Ediciones.
Segato, Rita L. 1998. Identidades políticas / alteridades históricas: una crítica a las certezas del pluralismo global. *Runa* 23(1): 239–275.
Segato, Rita L. 2010. Los cauces profundos de la raza latinoamericana: una relectura del mestizaje. *Crítica y Emancipación* 2(3): 11–44.
Seidl, Monika. 2009. Racial stereotypes and the art of Kara Walker. *Revue LISA* 7(1): 24–39.
Semán, Pablo and Pablo Vila, eds. 2011. *Cumbia: raza, nación, etnia y género en Latinoamérica*. Buenos Aires: Editorial Gorla.
Semán, Pablo and Pablo Vila, eds. 2012. *Youth Identities and Argentine Popular Music Beyond Tango*. New York: Palgrave Macmillan.
Serafini, Paula. 2022. *Creating Worlds Otherwise: Art, Collective Action and (Post)Extractivism*. Nashville, TN: Vanderbilt University Press.
Sexton, Jared. 2016. The vel of slavery: Tracking the figure of the unsovereign. *Critical Sociology* 42(4–5): 583–597.
Sharma, Devika and Frederick Tygstrup. 2015. *Structures of Feeling: Affectivity and the Study of Culture*. Berlin: De Gruyter.
Shaw, Gwendolyn DuBois. 2004. *Seeing the Unspeakable: The Art of Kara Walker*. Durham, NC: Duke University Press.
Shepperson, George. 1962. Pan-Africanism and «Pan-Africanism»: Some historical notes. *Phylon* 23(4): 346–358.
Shouse, Eric. 2005. Feeling, emotion, affect. *M/C Journal* 8(6). https://journal.media-culture.org.au/index.php/mcjournal/article/view/2443

Siegmund, Gerard. 2003. El problema de la identidad en la danza contemporánea: del arte de la imitación al arte de la acción. In *Cuerpos sobre blanco*, edited by Jaime Conde-Salazar and José Antonio Sánchez Martínez, 51–62. Ciudad Real: Ediciones de la Universidad de Castilla–La Mancha.

Sierra Díaz, Diana C. 2016. El Muntu: la diáspora del pensamiento filosófico africano en *Changó, el gran putas* de Manuel Zapata Olivella. *La Palabra* 29: 23–44.

Simpson, Leanne Betasamosake. 2017. *As We Have Always Done: Indigenous Freedom through Radical Resistance*. Minneapolis: University of Minnesota Press.

Sirimarco, Mariana and Ana Spivak L'Hoste (eds.). 2018. Teorizar lo emotivo: antropología y emoción. Special issue, *Etnografías Contemporáneas: Revista del Centro de Estudios en Antropología* 7.

Smith, Christen A. 2016a. *Afro-Paradise: Blackness, Violence, and Performance in Brazil*. Urbana: University of Illinois Press.

Smith, Christen A. 2016b. Towards a Black feminist model of Black Atlantic liberation: Remembering Beatriz Nascimento. *Meridians* 14(2): 71–87.

Smith, T. Lynn. 1966. The racial composition of Colombia. *Journal of Inter-American Studies* 8: 213–235.

Solano D., Sergio Paolo and Roicer Flórez Bolívar. 2012. 'Artilleros pardos y morenos artistas': artesanos, raza, milicias y reconocimiento social en el Nuevo Reino de Granada, 1770–1812. *Historia Crítica* 48: 11–37.

Solano Roa, Juanita. 2013. The Mexican assimilation: Colombia in the 1930s – the case of Ignacio Gómez Jaramillo. *Revista Historia y Memoria* 7: 79–111.

Soler, Carolina. 2017. Enfocar nuestra trinchera. El surgimiento del cine indígena en la provincia del Chaco (Argentina). *Folia Histórica del Nordeste* 28: 71–97.

Sommer, Doris. 2006a. Introduction: Wiggle room. In *Cultural Agency in the Americas*, edited by Doris Sommer, 1–28. Durham, NC: Duke University Press.

Sommer, Doris, ed. 2006b. *Cultural Agency in the Americas*. Durham, NC: Duke University Press.

Sommer, Doris. 2014. *The Work of Art in the World: Civic Agency and Public Humanities*. Durham, NC: Duke University Press.

Sommer, Doris. 2018. Literary liberties: The authority of Afrodescendant authors. In *Afro-Latin American Studies: An Introduction*, edited by Alejandro de la Fuente and George Reid Andrews, 319–347. Cambridge: Cambridge University Press.

Spinoza, Baruch. 1996. *Ethics*. New York: Penguin.

Steinitz, Matti. 2025. *Afro-Latin Soul Music and the Rise of Black Power Cosmopolitanism*. Berlin, Boston: De Gruyter.

Stengers, Isabelle. 2010. *Cosmopolitics I*. Minneapolis: University of Minnesota Press.

Stengers, Isabelle. 2011. *Cosmopolitics II*. Minneapolis: University of Minnesota Press.

Stepan, Nancy Leys. 1982. *The Idea of Race in Science: Great Britain, 1800–1960*. London: Macmillan in association with St Antony's College, Oxford.

Stepan, Nancy Leys. 1991. 'The Hour of Eugenics': Race, Gender and Nation in Latin America. Ithaca, NY: Cornell University Press.
Stephen, Lynn and Charles R. Hale, eds. 2013. *Otros Saberes: Collaborative Research on Indigenous and Afro-Descendent Cultural Politics*. Santa Fe, NM: SAR Press.
Stolcke, Verena. 1995. Talking culture: New boundaries, new rhetorics of exclusion in Europe. *Current Anthropology* 36(1): 1–23.
Stoler, Ann Laura. 2004. Affective states. In *A Companion to the Anthropology of Politics*, edited by David Nugent and Joan Vincent, 4–29. Oxford: Blackwell.
Stoler, Ann Laura, ed. 2006. *Haunted by Empire: Geographies of Intimacy in North American History*. Durham, NC: Duke University Press.
Stoler, Ann Laura. 2016. *Duress: Imperial Durabilities in Our Times*. Durham, NC: Duke University Press.
Streicker, Joel. 1995. Policing boundaries: Race, class and gender in Cartagena, Colombia. *American Ethnologist* 22(1): 54–74.
Svampa, Maristella. 2019. *The Frontiers of Neo-Extractivism in Latin America*. Bielefeld: Bielefeld University Press.
Swanson, Amy. 2019. Codifying African dance: The Germaine Acogny technique and antinomies of postcolonial cultural production. *Critical African Studies* 11(1): 48–62.
Taussig, Michael. 1993. *Mimesis and Alterity: A Particular History of the Senses*. London: Routledge.
Taylor, Diana. 2002. Translating performance. *Profession* 2002: 44–50.
Taylor, Diana. 2020. *¡Presente! The Politics of Presence*. Durham: Duke University Press.
Telles, Edward E. 2004. *Race in Another America: The Significance of Skin Color in Brazil*. Princeton: Princeton University Press.
Telles, Edward E. and Project on Ethnicity and Race in Latin America. 2014. *Pigmentocracies: Ethnicity, Race and Color in Latin America*. Chapel Hill: University of North Carolina Press.
Terena, Naine. 2019. Lentes ativistas e a arte indígena. *Revista Zum*, 3 December. https://revistazum.com.br/radar/arte-indigena/
Terena, Naine, ed. 2020. *Véxoa: Nós Sabemos*. São Paulo: Pinacoteca do Estado de São Paulo.
Terena, Naine and Fernanda Pitta. 2022. Retomando narrativas: a Mostra do Redescobrimento e o protagonismo indígena. In *Bienal de São Paulo Desde 1951*, edited by Paulo Miyada, 267–276. São Paulo: Bienal.
Terena, Naine, Gabriela de Carvalho Freire and Laura Pérez Gil. 2022. Véxoa: nós sabemos e a cura indígena da arte brasileira – Entrevista com Naine Terena. *Campos-Revista de Antropologia* 23(2): 171–186.
Thompson, James. 2014. *Humanitarian Performance: From Disaster Tragedies to Spectacles of War*. Calcutta: Seagull Books.
Thrift, Nigel. 1997. The still point: Resistance, expressive embodiment and dance. In *Geographies of Resistance*, edited by Michael Keith and Steven Pile, 124–151. London: Routledge.
Thrift, Nigel. 2004. Intensities of feeling: Towards a spatial politics of affect. *Geografiska Annaler. Series B, Human Geography* 86(1): 57–78.

Torres Agüero, Soledad. 2013. Na lavill'llaGa'c qataq nalquii na qarhuo: apuntes sobre una experiencia de video participativo con jóvenes indígenas toba en Formosa, Argentina. *Revista Chilena de Antropología Visual* 22: 68–90.

Torres Perdigón, Andrea. 2021. Hacia un concepto de narratividad: cruces (posibles) entre su dimensión literaria, antropológica y cognitiva. *Acta Poética* 42(2): 79–105.

Treece, David. 2022. Música Popular Black and anti-racist struggles: Musical cosmopolitanism and the soul aesthetic in Brazil (1963–1978). *Brasiliana: Journal for Brazilian Studies* 10(2): 407–441.

Trinchero, Héctor Hugo. 2005. Estigmas del genocidio indígena en el cuerpo del estado-nación. *Espacios de Crítica y Producción* 32: 33–38.

Troyan, Brett. 2008. Re-imagining the 'Indian' and the state: indigenismo in Colombia, 1926–1947. *Canadian Journal of Latin American and Caribbean Studies / Revue canadienne des études latino-américaines et caraïbes* 33(65): 81–106.

Truque, Carlos Arturo. 1993. *Vivan los compañeros: cuentos completos*. Bogotá: Colcultura.

Tuck, Eve and K. Wayne Yang. 2012. Decolonization is not a metaphor. *Decolonization: Indigeneity, Education & Society* 1(1): 1–40.

Tupinambá, Glicéria. 2020. Manto Tupinambá. https://umoutroceu.ufba.br/exposicao/manto-tupinamba/

Tupinambá, Glicéria. 2021. A visão do manto. *Revista Zum* 21, 7 December 2021. https://revistazum.com.br/revista-zum-21/a-visao-do-manto/

Tupinambá, Olinda. 2023. A existência do indígena no futuro. Online talk, organised by MASP Professores, 16 September 2023. www.youtube.com/watch?v=g-q3mv6yZVA&t=2991s

Turner, Terence. 1992. Defiant images: The Kayapo appropriation of video. *Anthropology Today* 8(6): 5–16.

UFMG (Universidade Federal de Minas Gerais). 2020. A arte construiu a história do mundo, diz Denilson Baniwa. Universidade Federal de Minas Gerais, https://ufmg.br/comunicacao/noticias/a-arte-construiu-a-historia-do-mundo-diz-denilson-baniwa

Ulloa, Astrid. 2005. *The Ecological Native: Indigenous Peoples' Movements and Eco-Governmentality in Colombia*. London: Routledge.

Universidad Nacional de Colombia, ed. 1984. *El nacionalismo en el arte: textos*. Bogotá: Universidad Nacional de Colombia.

Uribe Celis, Carlos. 1992. *La mentalidad del colombiano: cultura y sociedad en el siglo XX*. Bogotá: Ediciones Alborada, Editorial Nueva América.

Valderrama, Carlos. 2013. Folclore, raza y racismo en la política cultural e intelectual de Delia Zapata Olivella. El campo político-intelectual Afrocolombiano. *Revista CS* 12: 259–296.

Valderrama, Carlos. 2018. The Negritude Movements in Colombia. PhD thesis, University of Massachusetts, Amherst.

Valero, Silvia. 2020. '*Los negros se toman la palabra'. Primer Congreso de la Cultura Negra de las Américas: debates al interior de las comisiones y plenarias*. Bogotá: Editorial Pontificia Universidad Javeriana.

Valoyes Villa, Sandra. 2018. Liliana Angulo Cortés y la redefinición del ser afro desde el arte. mujeresconfiar.com. https://mujeresconfiar.com/liliana-angulo-cortes-y-la-redefinicion-del-ser-afro-desde-el-arte/

Van Alphen, Ernst. 2008. Affective operations of art and literature. *RES: Anthropology and Aesthetics* 53(1): 20–30.

Van Dijk, Teun A. 2019. *El discurso como interacción social*. Barcelona: Editorial Gedisa.

Vanín, Alfredo and Álvaro Pedrosa. 1994. *La vertiente afropacífico de la tradición oral*. Cali: Universidad del Valle.

Vergara-Figueroa, Aurora. 2017. *Afrodescendant Resistance to Deracination in Colombia: Massacre at Bellavista-Bojayá-Chocó*. Cham: Springer.

Vergès, Françoise. 2019. Capitalocene, waste, race, and gender. *e-flux journal* 100(1): 1–11.

Vergès, Françoise. 2021. *A Decolonial Feminism*. London: Pluto Press.

Vivaldi, Ana. 2016. Traversing the City: The Making of Indigenous Spatialities Within and Beyond Buenos Aires. PhD thesis, University of British Columbia, Vancouver.

Vivaldi, Ana. 2019. Indigeneidades urbanas: formaciones espacializadas de raza y experiencia Toba (Qom) en Buenos Aires. *Quid* 16(11): 151–174.

Vivaldi, Ana and Pablo Cossio. 2021. *Malonear los museos: un estudio de público en el Palais de Glace sobre la exhibición '¿Qué necesitan aprender los museos?', curada por Identidad Marron y Poetas Villeres*. Manchester: University of Manchester.

Viveros Vigoya, Mara. 2002. Dionysian blacks: Sexuality, body, and racial order in Colombia. *Latin American Perspectives* 29(2): 60–77.

Viveros Vigoya, Mara. 2013. Manuel Zapata Olivella (1920–2004). In *Pensamiento colombiano en el siglo XX*, edited by Carmen Millán de Benavides, Santiago Castro-Gómez and Guillermo Hoyos Vásquez, 465–500. Bogotá: Universidad Javeriana.

Viveros Vigoya, Mara. 2016. La interseccionalidad: una aproximación situada a la dominación. *Debate Feminista* 52: 1–17.

Viveros Vigoya, Mara. 2021. *El oxímoron de las clases medias negras. Movilidad social e interseccionalidad en Colombia*. Guadalajara: Editorial Universidad de Guadalajara y Centro Maria Sibylla Merian de Estudios Latinoamericanos Avanzados en Humanidades y Ciencias Sociales.

Volli, Ugo. 1988. Técnicas de cuerpo. In *Anatomía del actor. Diccionario de antropología teatral*, edited by Eugenio Barba and Nicola Saverese, 195–208. Mexico City: Grupo Editorial Gaceta.

Wabgou, Maguemati, Jaime Arocha Rodríguez, Aiden José Salgado Cassiani, and Juan Alberto Carabalí Ospina. 2012. *Movimiento social afrocolombiano, negro, raizal y palanquero: el largo camino hacia la construcción de espacios comunes y alianzas estratégicas para la incidencia política en Colombia*. Bogotá: Universidad Nacional de Colombia; Facultad de Derecho, Ciencias Políticas y Sociales; Instituto Unidad de Investigaciones Jurídico-Sociales Gerardo Molina.

Wade, Peter. 1993. *Blackness and Race Mixture: The Dynamics of Racial Identity in Colombia*. Baltimore: Johns Hopkins University Press.

Wade, Peter. 1997. *Gente negra, nación mestiza: las dinámicas de las identidades raciales en Colombia*. Translated by Ana Cristina Mejía. Bogota: Ediciones Uniandes, Ediciones de la Universidad de Antioquia, Siglo del Hombre Editores, Instituto Colombiano de Antropología.
Wade, Peter. 2000. *Music, Race and Nation: Tropical Music in Colombia*. Chicago: University of Chicago Press.
Wade, Peter. 2002. *Race, Nature and Culture: An Anthropological Perspective*. London: Pluto Press.
Wade, Peter. 2009a. Defining blackness in Colombia. *Journal de la Société des Américanistes* 95(1): 165–184.
Wade, Peter. 2009b. *Race and Sex in Latin America*. London: Pluto Press.
Wade, Peter. 2010a. The presence and absence of race. *Patterns of Prejudice* 44(1): 43–60.
Wade, Peter. 2010b. *Race and Ethnicity in Latin America*. 2nd ed. London: Pluto Press.
Wade, Peter. 2011. Multiculturalismo y racismo. *Revista Colombiana de Antropología* 47(2): 15–35.
Wade, Peter. 2013. Definiendo la negridad en Colombia. In *Estudios afrocolombianos hoy: aportes a un campo transdisciplinario*, edited by Eduardo Restrepo, 21–42. Popayán: Editorial Universidad del Cauca.
Wade, Peter. 2015. *Race: An Introduction*. Cambridge: Cambridge University Press.
Wade, Peter. 2016. Mestizaje, multiculturalism, liberalism and violence. *Latin American and Caribbean Ethnic Studies* 11(3): 323–343.
Wade, Peter. 2017. *Degrees of Mixture, Degrees of Freedom: Genomics, Multiculturalism and Race in Latin America*. Durham, NC: Duke University Press.
Wade, Peter. 2018. Afro-indigenous interactions, relations and comparisons. In *Afro-Latin American Studies: An Introduction*, edited by George Reid Andrews and Alejandro de la Fuente, 92–129. Cambridge: Cambridge University Press.
Wade, Peter. 2020. Espacio, región y racialización en Colombia. *Revista de Geografía Norte Grande* 79: 31–49.
Wade, Peter. 2022a. Anti-racism in mestizo societies. In *Against Racism: Organizing for Social Change in Latin America*, edited by Mónica G. Moreno Figueroa and Peter Wade, 167–188. Pittsburgh: University of Pittsburgh Press.
Wade, Peter. 2022b. Territory and anti-racism. In *Against Racism: Organizing for Social Change in Latin America*, edited by Mónica G. Moreno Figueroa and Peter Wade, 100–122. University of Pittsburgh Press.
Wade, Peter. 2023. The ambivalence of Blackness in early twentieth-century Argentinian comics: 'Página del Dólar'. *Ethnic and Racial Studies* 47 (10): 2153–2173.
Wade, Peter and Mónica Moreno Figueroa. 2021. Alternative grammars of anti-racism in Latin America. *Interface: A Journal for and about Social Movements* 13(2): 20–50.
Wade, Peter, James Scorer and Ignacio Aguiló. 2019. Introduction: Latin American and Caribbean racisms in global and conceptual context. In *Cultures of Anti-Racism in Latin America and the Caribbean*, edited by Peter Wade, James Scorer and Ignacio Aguiló, 1–23. London: University of London Press.

Wade, Peter, Vivette García Deister, Michael Kent, María Fernanda Olarte Sierra and Adriana Díaz del Castillo Hernández. 2014. Nation and the absent presence of race in Latin American genomics. *Current Anthropology* 55(4): 497–522.

Warren, Jonathan W. 2001. *Racial Revolutions: Antiracism and Indian Resurgence in Brazil*. Durham: Duke University Press.

Weaver, Simon. 2010. The 'other' laughs back: Humour and resistance in anti-racist comedy. *Sociology* 44(1): 31–48.

Wetherell, Margaret. 2013. Feeling rules, atmospheres and affective practice: Some reflections on the analysis of emotional episodes. In *Privilege, Agency and Affect: Understanding the Production and Effects of Action*, edited by Claire Maxwell and Peter Aggleton, 221–239. London: Palgrave Macmillan UK.

Wiener, Charles, Jules Crévaux, Désiré Charnay, et al. 1884. *América pintoresca: descripción de viajes al nuevo continente por los más modernos exploradores*. Barcelona: Montaner y Simón.

Zapata Olivella, Manuel. 1967 [1963]. *Chambacú, corral de negros*. Medellín: Editorial Bedout.

Zapata Olivella, Manuel. 1983. La tradición oral, una historia que no envejece. In *El negro en la historia de Colombia: fuentes escritas y orales. Primer Simposio sobre Bibliografía del Negro en Colombia, October 12–15*, edited by Fundación Colombiana de Investigaciónes Folclóricas. Bogotá: Fondo Interamericano de Publicaciones de la Cultura Negra de las Américas; Unesco.

Zapata Olivella, Manuel. 2010. *Changó, el gran putas*. Bogotá: Ministerio de Cultura.

Index

Acogny, Germaine, 149
activism and art, 57–59, 65, 69
Acuña Tapias, Luis Alberto (1904–1993), 44
affect, 177–178, 206, 241
 affective atmospheres and, 139
 affordances of, 243
 anti-racist emotionality and, 139, 184, 238
 audience response and, 69, 121, 155
 body and, 60, 151, 213–214
 definition of, 17
 distributed agency and, 261–262
Afrolatinoamericanas: De voces, susurros, gritos y silencios play, 218
Afro-referentiality, 138, 141, 159
Ahmed, Sara, 177, 242
Alarcón, Rossana, xxi, 25
Albert, Bruce, 81, 193
Alejandra Egido. *See* Teatro en Sepia
Alencar, José de, 74
Álvares Cabral, Pedro, 73, 269
Álvarez, Miriam, 127, 205, 209
Andrade, Mário de, 75, 179
Angulo Cortés, Liliana, 29, 54, 58, 66, 252, 276
 use of stereotypes, 257
anti-racism
 alternative grammars of, 5, 102, 197
 for Brazilian Indigenous artists, 5
 inclusive forms of, 4, 196
 and interpellating publics, 67
 irruptive, 64

 mestizo people in, 5
 subversive, 60, 62
 as tiring, 31
 turn to, in Latin America, 4
 use of language of, 11
Arboleda, Santiago, 50–51
archives, 33
Argentina
 1994 constitution of, 208
 Afro-Argentine histories in, 213
 Afro-Argentines in, 111, 118, 120, 133, 207, 212
 afroporteños in, 104
 cabecitas negras in, 110, 114
 civilisation and barbarism in, 104, 207
 comics in, 107
 gaucho in, 101, 105–106, 109
 Kirchnerism in, 120
 military regimes in, 113, 116
 in nineteenth century, 103
 racial formation of, 19, 98, 103, 106, 117, 120, 207, 271
 subaltern resistance in, 99, 208
Arissana Pataxó, 92–94, 127
Ariza, Margarita, 5, 23, 61–62
art objects, agency of, 241, 261
art practices
 affective traction of, 17
 affordances of, 247
 ambivalent effects of, 241
 anti-racist modalities of, 13, 234, 240
 anti-racist potential of, 2, 13, 16, 275
 crafts and, 170, 184

305

art practices (cont.)
  Indigenous concepts of, 14, 187, 191
  racial capitalism and, 242
art world
  racism in, 31
  working with institutions of, 32–33, 165, 173
Artel, Jorge (1909–1994), 47
Ashanti Dinah, 65, 127
audiences, 69, 155, 210, 214, 222, 230, 247
audiovisual art, in Colombia, 56, 59
authenticity
  criollo and, 105
  Indigeneity and, 73, 109, 120, 185, 227
  national identity and, 7, 45, 114

Baartman, Sarah, 219
Bachué group, 44
bandeirantes, 128
Baniwa, Denilson. *See* Denilson Baniwa
Bariloche (Argentina), 128, 210
Barrientos, Rodrigo, 33, 67, 257
Bayunu, Ekua, 29
Berni, Antonio, 107
Black intellectuals, in Colombia, 46, 49
Black Lives Matter, xxi, 34
Black poetry
  in Argentina, 104
  in Caribbean, 43
  in Colombia, 43, 47, 64
Black Power, 38, 51
Black Rio, 1
Black women, 31, 55
  in Argentina, 129, 133, 218, 221
  in dance, 237
  invisibility of, 223
  labour segregation and, 123
  plays about, 212, 218
  sexualisation of, 47, 67, 224, 247
  writers, 128
Blackness
  Afro category and, 147
  assertion of, in public spaces, 260
  as everyday, 261
  Indigeneity and, 23, 41, 72, 174, 205, 226–228
  phenotype and, 214
Boal, Augusto, 1
bodies. *See* embodiment

Bogotá
  Black people in, 236
  Black territory in, 237
Bolsonaro, Jair, 19, 77, 173, 183, 190
Borja, Wilson, 59, 65, 236
Botanical Expedition. *See* Expedición Botánica (1783–1816)
Brazil. *See also marco temporal* (time frame)
  1988 Constitution of, 77, 91
  anti-Indigenous violence in, 19
  contemporary Indigenous visual arts in, 82
  Indigenous literature in, 79
  racial formation of, 18, 72
Brô MC's, 198
Buenaventura (Colombia), 30, 51, 61, 68
Buenos Aires, 97, 129
  afroporteños in, 104
  artistic elite of, 130
  centrality of, in Argentina, 103
  middle classes of, 114
  migrations to, 99, 110
  seen as white, 232

Caboco, Gustavo. *See* Gustavo Caboco
Cali (Colombia), 48, 50, 52, 68, 237
Cañuqueo, Lorena, xxi, 25, 205, 233
capoeira, 1, 236
CARABANTÚ (Afro-Colombian Corporation for Social and Cultural Development), 56, 67
CARLA (Cultures of Anti-Racism in Latin America), xx
  academic hierarchies in, 24
  context for, in Latin America, 4
  design of, xx, 23
  Festival of Anti-Racist Art, xxii, 24, 268
  horizontal and collaborative relations in, 24
  impact of COVID-19 on, xxi
  online exhibition of, 24, 164
  project members, xx, xxi
  YouTube channel, xxi, 24
carnival
  in Argentina, 105, 121
  in Brazil, 1
Carpani, Ricardo, 115–116
Carta a el-rei Dom Manuel (Letter to King Manuel), 73
Célia Tupinambá. *See* Glicéria (Célia) Tupinambá

Index

Changó, el gran putas, 141–146, 153, 155–156, 237
Chorographic Commission. *See* Comisión Corográfica
cimarrones, 53. *See also palenques*; *quilombos*
cinema
  in Argentina, 115, 117
  in Colombia, 57, 67
  ethno-educational, 56
  made by young people, in Colombia, 68
class. *See also* race, class and
  anti-racism and, 12, 169
  racism and, 4, 11
Cogollo, Heriberto, 53
Colectivo Aguaturbia, 59, 234–235, 275
collaborative practices, xxii, 23–26, 205
Colombia
  from 2005, 57
  after Independence, 39
  Caribbean region of, 128, 140
  civic protests in, 68
  colonial period in, 38
  late twentieth century in, 50
  mid-twentieth century in, 43
  Pacific region of, 140
  racial formation of, 21, 38
Comisión Corográfica, 39, 41
communities, working with, 241, 258
Conquista del Desierto (Conquest of the Desert), 132, 165, 207, 210, 217, 230
contemporary Indigenous Art, in Brazil, 87, 91, 178
Corrêa, Edgar Nunes. *See* Edgar Kanaykõ
cosmopolitics, 82
Cossio, Pablo, xxi
costumbrismo, 39, 41, 48
COVID-19 pandemic, xxi, xxii, 139, 173, 231, 237, 259, 266, 272
crafts. *See* art practices, crafts and
criollo
  in Argentina, 98, 105, 107, 111
  definition of, 20, 98
Cruz, Felipe, 72–73. *See also* Felipe Tuxá
Cultures of Anti-Racism in Latin America. *See* CARLA (Cultures of Anti-Racism in Latin America)
curation, 165–172, 267. *See also* museums
  healing and, 196

da Silva, Denise Ferreira, 206, 227
Daiara Tukano, 14, 29, 82, 192, 240
dance
  Afro-contemporary, 146
  as ambivalent space, 252
  anthropological approaches to, 138
  anti-racism in, 138, 235
  bullerengue, 254
  in Colombia, 60
  as community activity, 259
  as a coping resource, 256
  currulao, 152
  as healing, 238
  mapalé, 238
  as 'place of enunciation', 139
  in racial formations, 251
Daniel Munduruku, 80
Davis, Angela, 233
de-authorisation of Indigeneity, 72, 90, 96, 174, 183
  land and, 76
decolonisation/decoloniality, 10, 15, 32, 50, 127, 149, 179, 206, 233, 240
  ecological discourse and, 194
  in museums, 167, 173
  theatre and, 226, 230
Delia Zapata Olivella (1926–2001), 71
Denilson Baniwa, 4, 10, 25, 87–91, 127, 179, 188, 266
  paintings by, 248
Detrás del sur: Danzas para Manuel, 152–158
  documentary on making of, 158
diaspora, 52, 57, 147, 153
Dinah, Ashanti. *See* Ashanti Dinah
displacement
  in Argentina, 206, 209, 211, 215, 222
  in Colombia, 22, 45, 58
  of Indigenous peoples, 19, 198, 273
  shared histories of, 229, 272
drums, 260
  cununo, 152, 253
  llamador, 254
  tambor alegre, 254

Eagleton, Terry, 242
Edgar Kanaykõ, 193
Egido, Alejandra, 127, 205, 212. *See also* Teatro en Sepia
Eliane Potiguara, 80, 91
embodiment, 151, 169, 206, 215, 221–222, 227, 232, 235
  aesthetics and, 242
  dance and, 145–146

embodiment (cont.)
  decolonization and, 149
  memory and, 145, 213
  of race, 274
  spectacularisation and, 236
  of subalternity, 223
  techniques of the body and, 223
  as a vector for anti-racism, 256
emotions, 2. *See also* affect
  anti-Peronism and, 110
  anti-racist emotionality and, 139
  as anti-racist emotionality, 17
  awareness of, 144
  as different from affect, 17
  emotional toil and, 34
enslavement, 53, 67, 142, 145, 239, 256
  in Argentina, 213, 222, 229, 271
  of Black women, 220
  Indigenous, 74
  racism and, 8
eroticism. *See* sexualisation
Esbell, Jaider. *See* Jaider Esbell
ethno-education
  in Colombia, 67
  through film, 56, 67
exhibitions
  CARLA's online exhibition, xxii, 24
  A costura da memória, 181
  of Denilson Baniwa at Goethe Institut, 90
  Desobediências poéticas, 181
  Dja Guata Porã: Rio de Janeiro indígena, 182
  Hãhãw (Arte Indígena Antirracista), 14
  Indigenous Histories, 187
  ¡Mandinga sea!, 56
  Mira! – Artes visuais contemporâneas dos povos indígenas, 182
  Moquém_Surarî, 82
  ¿Qué necesitan aprender los museos?, 164
  ReAntropofagia, 182
  Territórios: Artistas afrodescendentes no acervo da Pinacoteca, 180
  Viaje sin mapa, 54, 59
exoticisation, 151, 212, 235–236, 238. *See also* primitivism
Expedición Botánica (1783–1816), 39, 67

Fani-Kayode, Rotimi, 252
fascism, 274
Felipe Tuxá, 268. *See also* Cruz, Felipe
feminism, 133, 224–225, 231
  anti-racist, 220
  white, 220, 226
festivals
  Bicentennial Parade, in Argentina, 121
  in Colombia, 51
  CURA street art festival, 86
  Festival of Anti-Racist and Decolonial Art, xxii
  Festival of Currulao, 51
  Festival of Decolonial and Anti-Racist Art, 24
  Green Moon Festival, 51–52
  Kunta Kinte Afro Film, 56, 68
  Petronio Álvarez, 52
First Congress of Black Culture of the Americas (Cali, 1977), 50
folklore
  in Argentina, 109, 115, 118, 229
  in Brazil, 194
  in Colombia, 43, 48–49, 130
  as political, in Colombia, 49

gaucho. *See* Argentina, gaucho in
Geler, Lea, 213, 219
Gell, Alfred, 241
gender, 221, 224. *See also* feminism
  bodily gestures and, 222
  racism and, 11, 67, 220, 223, 225
  violence and, 220
genocide, 32, 132, 209, 211, 217, 222
Glicéria (Célia) Tupinambá, 94–96, 266
Gómez, Pedro Nel (1899–1994), 45
Gómez Jaramillo, Ignacio (1910–1970), 45
Grau, Enrique (1920–2004), 46
Guajajara, Sonia, 78–79
Guarani
  language, 200
  people, 74, 202
  rap, 198
  territory, 186, 190, 202
Gustavo Caboco, 82, 89, 186, 266
Gutiérrez de Alba, José María (1822–1897), 40
Guzmán, Florencia, 220

Hãhãw (Arte Indígena Antirracista)
  exhibition, 14, 266
haunting, 241, 246, 249
hip-hop, 1, 198
  Qom group, 23

Identidad Marrón, 6, 12, 23, 97, 123, 164
Indigeneity
   Blackness and. *See* Blackness, Indigeneity and
   environmental activism and, 78
   futurism and, 249
   relegated to the past, 74, 90–91, 179, 245
indigenismo, 6
   in Brazil, 74
   in Colombia, 43
Indigenous women
   in Argentina, 215, 230, 268
   in Brazil, 80, 190, 193
   as research assistants, 24
indio
   figure of, 249, 251
   permitido, 249
   technology and, 250
intersectionality, 31, 195, 216, 220, 224, 228, 258, 262
invisibility
   of Black women, 223
   of Blackness, 6, 100
   hypervisibilisation and, 100
   of Indigenous people in Argentina, 210
   of Indigenous people in Brazil, 91, 173, 203
   of racial plurality, 123
   shared histories of, 272

jaguar
   Denilson Baniwa as jaguar-shaman, 90, 249
   sculptures of, 190
Jaider Esbell, 10, 82–87, 178, 192
Jara, Víctor, 1
Jekupé, Olivio. *See* Olivio Jekupé
Joênia Wapichana, 78
JOMBA! Contemporary Dance Experience festival, 148
Julio Romero, Pedro Blas, 64

Kanaykõ, Edgar. *See* Edgar Kanaykõ
Karapotó, Ziel. *See* Ziel Karapotó
Kopenawa, Davi, 80, 193
Krenak, Ailton, 77, 81, 176, 192
Kunumi MC, 198

land. *See also* territory
   in Argentina, 215
   in Brazil, 76, 175

Las Emperadoras de la Champeta, 11, 23, 67
Latin American racial formations
   in Argentina, Brazil and Colombia, 18
   specificity of, 4, 7, 12
limpieza de sangre, 9

malón (raid), 165
   Malón de la Paz (1946), 113
Manchester, 34
Manuel María Paz, 40–41
Mapplethorpe, Robert, 252
Mapuche
   displacement of, 215, 272
   encounters with Afro-Argentines, 228–229, 271
   genocide of, 211. *See also* genocide
   language, 209, 218, 222
   urban, 210, 225–226, 230
   ways of being, 209, 211
Mapuche Theatre Group El Katango, 123, 205, 209, 265, 268. *See also* Álvarez, Miriam
marco temporal (time frame), 76, 91, 183
marrón. *See* Identidad Marrón
marrón identity, 165, 167–171
Mato Grosso do Sul, 5, 198–199, 202
Medellín (Colombia), 32, 68, 140, 237
Meirelles, Victor, 74, 179
Mercer, Kobena, 252
mestiçagem, 3
mestizaje, 48
   in Argentina, 98
   in Colombia, 43
   national identity and, 3
Mexico, 1, 3, 6, 44
   Black women in, 247
Milei, Javier, 124
Miriam Álvarez. *See* Mapuche Theatre Group El Katango
Monumento às Bandeiras, 128
moreno, category of, 5
Moreno Figueroa, Mónica, 243
Mudra Afrique school of dance, 149
multiculturalism, 7, 22, 227
   in Argentina, 102, 118, 121, 208
   in Colombia, 52, 56
Munduruku, Daniel. *See* Daniel Munduruku
muntu, 153
   children of, 156, 161
   concept of, 142–143, 159–160
muralism, 44

museums, 33. *See also* curation
  decolonisation of, 164, 167
  Geological Museum, 266
  La Plata Museum, 105
  Museo de Antioquía, 67
  Museo de la Cárcova, 97
  Museo de la Mujer Argentina, 218, 224, 226
  Museum of Sacred Art, 266
  National Museum of Brazil, 189
  Palais de Glace, 165, 169
  Pinacoteca de São Paulo, 172. *See also* Pinacoteca de São Paulo
  ¿Qué necesitan aprender los museos? (exhibition), 164
  São Paulo Art Museum, 187
music. *See also* hip-hop
  Afro rhythms in Argentina, 109
  Afro-Colombian, 49
  Afro-urban rhythms, 141
  of Aimé Painé, 116
  as ambivalent space, 252
  in Argentina, 118
  in Brazil, 1
  bullerengue, 253
  champeta, 11, 53, 67
  chirimía, 253
  of Colombian Caribbean region, 47
  of Colombian Pacific region, 52
  cumbia, 46, 48, 119, 253
  currulao, 51
  dance and, 137
  folk, in Argentina, 109
  popular, in Argentina, 115
  in racial formations, 251
  tango, 105, 109

Naine Terena, 25, 82, 172, 266
Nascimento, Abdias do, 1
National Institute Against Discrimination, Xenophobia and Racism (INADI), 118, 208
negrismo, 6
  in Colombia, 43, 46
Négritude, 38, 43, 51
negro category
  in Argentina, 100, 119, 164
  in music, 252
  as *negro permitido*, 257, 263
non-whiteness
  acceptable forms of, 7
  in Argentine popular music, 115

authenticity and, 7
as backward, 41
denial of, 6
linked to gaucho, 107
in nation-building discourses, 20
vindication of, in Argentina, 125
working-class spaces and, 11

Obeso, Candelario (1849–1884), 41, 131
occupation. *See also retomada* (reclaiming, occupation)
  of museums, 266
Olinda Tupinambá, 187, 194, 266
Olivio Jekupé, 80
orisha, 142, 153, 159
Owerá. *See* Kunumi MC

Palacios, Arnoldo (1924–2015), 47
Palacios, Rafael, 25, 60, 62, 127
Palenque de San Basilio, 49, 51
palenques, 49, 272. *See also quilombos*
Pataxó, Arissana. *See* Arissana Pataxó
Paz, Manuel María, 39
Peronism, 100, 110
photography
  in Brazil, 193
  in Chile, 271
  in Colombia, 61
Pinacoteca de São Paulo, 172, 178, 190
Pitta, Fernanda, 180, 188
Poetas Villeres, writers' collective, 164, 170
post-raciality, 2–3
Potiguara, Eliane. *See* Eliane Potiguara
primitivism, 6
  in Brazil, 250–251
  in Colombia, 37, 46–47, 50

quilombos, 130, 257, 272. *See also palenques*
Quirós, Cesáreo Bernaldo de, 107
quotas
  fulfilling, 187
  in university admissions, 18, 79

race
  class and, 101, 111, 124, 169, 258
  embodiment of, 2
  scientific theories of, 3, 39
  as social construction, 2
  space and, 261
racial hierarchies, colonial roots of, 3
racial inequality

Index

increasing, 2
in Latin America, 3
Racionais MC's, 198
racism
  affective traction of, 2
  against Indigenous peoples, 23, 72, 204, 267
  biological, 9
  cultural, 9
  definition of, 8
  denial of, 3
  internalised, 258
  invisible, in Argentina, 164
  mestizo people and, 5
  social justice and, 196
  structural, 6, 196, 208, 212
Racism and Anti-Racism in Brazil: The Case of Indigenous Peoples (project), xix, 174
Rancière, Jacques, 16, 139, 243
religion
  African-influenced, 140, 143
  Christian, 5, 14, 64, 74, 76, 96, 218
  evangelical Christian, 86
  Indigenous, 194, 200, 217
  politics and, 175
retomada (reclaiming, occupation), 79, 91
Riascos, Yeison, 61–62
Rio de Janeiro, 129–130
Rivera Cusicanqui, Silvia, 249
Rizo Blanco, Salvador, 39
Rozenmacher, Germán, 114

Salazar Valdés, Hugo (1922–1997), 47
sankofa, concept of, 148
Sankofa Danzafro, 17, 60, 129, 251, 253, 258
São Paulo, 51, 75, 80, 91, 94, 128, 130, 190
  hip-hop in, 198
São Paulo Biennale, 86, 90, 181
schools
  racism in, 270
  representation of Indigenous peoples in, 269
sentipensamiento (feeling-thinking), 53
Serafini, Paula, 14, 245
sexism. *See* gender
sexualisation, 60, 149, 235, 238, 256. *See also* Black women
  of dance, 252
Silva, Lula da, 78

Smith, Christen, 246
social justice, racism and, 196
social movements, xvii, 20, 30
  Black and Indigenous as separate, 273
  in Colombia, 50, 69
  indigenist, in Argentina, 113
  Mapuche, 211
Sommer, Doris, 15, 243
space, race and, 261
stereotypes, 57
  challenging, 29, 154–158, 241, 244
  challenging, in visual art, 179
  challenging, through dance, 138, 151, 234, 238
  destabilising, 60
  as embodied, 151
  reinforcing, 241, 262
Stoler, Ann, 246
SuAndi, 29

Tamikuã Txihi, 190
Tayiñ kuify kvpan (Our Old-Ancient Ancestry) play, 215
Teatro en Sepia, 123, 205, 211, 265. *See also* Egido, Alejandra
Teatro Experimental do Negro, 1
Terena, Naine. *See* Naine Terena
Terena people, 202–203
Terra Fértil: Véxoa e a arte indígena, documentary, 175
Territórios: Artistas afrodescendentes no acervo da Pinacoteca exhibition, 180
territory. *See also* land
  in Brazil, 270
  in Colombia, 237
  in Colombian Pacific, 160
theatre
  Afro-Mapuche collaboration in, 229, 271
  anti-racism in, 215
tokenism, 33, 187, 262
Torres Méndez, Ramón (1809–1885), 40
Truque, Carlos Arturo (1927–1970), 47
Tukano, Daiara. *See* Daiara Tukano
Tumaco (Colombia), 51, 68, 152, 160, 237
Tupinambá, Glicéria (Célia). *See* Glicéria (Célia) Tupinambá
Tupinambá, Olinda. *See* Olinda Tupinambá
Tuxá, Felipe. *See* Cruz, Felipe; Felipe Tuxá
Tuxá, Yacunã. *See* Yacunã Tuxá
Txihi, Tamikuã. *See* Tamikuã Txihi

UFBA (Universidade Federal da Bahia), 266
United Kingdom, 29
United States
  civil rights movement in, 274
  comparisons with, 7, 49, 258
  influence of, 51
universities, 192
  as extractivist, 265
  Indigenous art in, 269
  quotas in, 18, 79
  racism in, 204

Valdivia (Chile), Black presence in, 271
van Alphen, Ernst, 177
violence
  anti-Black, in Colombia, 140, 159
  anti-Indigenous, in Argentina, 103, 211
  anti-Indigenous, in Brazil, 75, 77, 79, 83, 91, 95, 174, 182, 190, 198
  in Colombia, 52, 58, 61, 140, 160
  gendered, 220
  racist, in Argentina, 119, 206, 222, 273
visibilisation, strategies of, 6–7, 102, 155

Walker, Kara, 253
white people, as audience, 34
whiteness
  in Argentina, 271
  in Argentina under military, 116
  associated with *criollo*, 98
  celebrated by Javier Milei, 124
  civilisation and, 41, 104
  complexity of, in Argentina, 20
  in family context, 64
  limits of, in Argentina, 99
  Medellín associated with, 260
  mocked by Candelario Obeso, 131
  modernity and, 6, 39
  privileged in *mestizaje*, 3
  unattainable, 61
  in Western imaginary, 64
whitening, 3, 6
  in Argentina, 98–99
  of the Colombian nation, 48
  of colonial artists, 38
  discourses of, in Argentina, 100
  discourses of, undermined, 105
  of music, 46
Wi Da Monikongo, 56, 68
women. *See also* Black women; gender; Indigenous women
  ancestral wisdom of, 133
  anti-racist, in Argentina, 125
  enslaved, 220
  as musicians, 12, 67
  organisations of, 30
  working-class, 11

Yacunã Tuxá, 192, 266

Zapata Olivella, Delia (1926–2001), 48
Zapata Olivella, Manuel (1927–2008), 47, 71, 138, 141, 143, 145, 159. *See also* *Changó, el gran putas*
Ziel Karapotó, 14, 266

For EU product safety concerns, contact us at Calle de José Abascal, 56–1°,
28003 Madrid, Spain or eugpsr@cambridge.org.

www.ingramcontent.com/pod-product-compliance
Ingram Content Group UK Ltd.
Pitfield, Milton Keynes, MK11 3LW, UK
UKHW020113190126

467120UK00020B/703